HIDDEN®

Belize

HIDDEN®

Belize

Including Tikal and the Cayes

Richard Harris

FOURTH EDITION

Ulysses Press®
BERKELEY, CALIFORNIA

Published by:
ULYSSES PRESS
P.O. Box 3440
Berkeley, CA 94703
www.ulyssespress.com

ISSN 1524-5969
ISBN 1-56975-510-8

Printed in Canada by Transcontinental Printing

10 9 8 7 6

MANAGING EDITOR: Claire Chun
COPY EDITOR: Barbara Schultz
EDITORIAL ASSOCIATES: Kathryn Brooks, Lily Chou,
   Nicholas Denton-Brown, Sara Pflantzer
TYPESETTERS: Lisa Kester, Matt Orendorff
CARTOGRAPHY: Pease Press
HIDDEN BOOKS DESIGN: Sarah Levin
COVER DESIGN: Leslie Henriques
INDEXER: Sayre Van Young
COVER PHOTOGRAPHY: gettyimages.com (ocelot)
ILLUSTRATOR: Glenn Kim

Distributed by Publishers Group West

In memory of Judith Kahn, whom I deeply miss

What's Hidden?

At different points throughout this book, you'll find special listings marked with this symbol:

◀ HIDDEN

This means that you have come upon a place off the beaten tourist track, a spot that will carry you a step closer to the local people and natural environment of Belize.

The goal of this guide is to lead you beyond the realm of everyday tourist facilities. While we include traditional sightseeing listings and popular attractions, we also offer alternative sights and adventure activities. Instead of filling this guide with reviews of standard hotels and chain restaurants, we concentrate on one-of-a-kind places and locally owned establishments.

Our authors seek out locales that are popular with residents but usually overlooked by visitors. Some are more hidden than others (and are marked accordingly), but all the listings in this book are intended to help you discover the true nature of Belize and put you on the path of adventure.

Write to us!

If in your travels you discover a spot that captures the spirit of Belize, or if you live in the region and have a favorite place to share, or if you just feel like expressing your views, write to us and we'll pass your note along to the author.

We can't guarantee that the author will add your personal find to the next edition, but if the writer does use the suggestion, we'll acknowledge you in the credits and send you a free copy of the new edition.

ULYSSES PRESS
P.O. Box 3440
Berkeley, CA 94703
E-mail: readermail@ulyssespress.com

Contents

Maps

OUTDOOR ADVENTURE SYMBOLS

The following symbols accompany national and regional park listings, as well as beach descriptions throughout the text.

 Hiking

 Canoeing or Kayaking

Swimming

Boating

Snorkeling or Scuba Diving

Fishing

ONE

Exploring Belize

There are places in Belize where no human has ever laid foot, at least not in the last 1000 years, not since the time when the ancient Maya ruled these jungles from their lofty pyramids. Most regions that have been explored are still wild and rugged, possessed by beautiful beasts and birds, by silky green seas overflowing with life and palm-speckled shores reveling in seclusion, by mountains wrapped in colossal trees and forests carpeted with flamboyant flowers and emerald greenery, luxuriating, as it were, in nature's own hothouse.

How nature has reigned so long here, and how Belize has come to be so undiscovered, is due in part to its secret location. Indeed, the tiny country is but a blink on the map of Central America, wedged between formidable Guatemala and Mexico's vast Yucatán Peninsula, a mite-sized piece of jungle confronting two giants. Facing the Caribbean, Belize seems ready to break from land and fling itself out to sea.

But packed into this country the size of Massachusetts is an array of natural wonders, including the world's second-longest barrier reef (behind Australia's), where a thread of unspoiled isles are washed by the Caribbean Sea. Here also is the world's only jaguar preserve, the longest chain of caves in the Western Hemisphere, and the seventh-highest waterfall in the world.

Wild animals come in a splendorous array of shapes, sizes and names, from spiny anteaters, spider monkeys and red-eyed tree frogs to kinkajou bears, hawksbill turtles and bare-throated tiger herons. Fishing and scuba diving are so outstanding, their praises are whispered so as not to spoil their secrets.

Beyond the natural wonders is a lost manmade world slowly waking from its jungle slumber. Entire Maya cities, some only discovered in the last half century, are being resurrected by teams of archaeologists. Each day's excavations reveal marvels offering few explanations and many mysteries, beckoning outsiders to come ponder Belize's ancient treasures. Toothy pyramids loom on mountain ridges, and three-story-high masks stare out from jungle haunts. Elaborate networks of reservoirs, causeways and *sacbes*, or ancient roads, link age-old cities sprinkled down the length of this Adventure Coast.

▼ ▼ ▼ ▼ ▼ ▼ ▼ ▼ ▼
Where to Go

Here are five distinct regions—the Cayes, Belize City, northern Belize, western Belize and southern Belize. Of course, the **Cayes** actually extend off the coast, forming a thread of islands trimmed in coral rock and mangroves. Only about two dozen of the islands are inhabited and only two, Ambergris Caye and Caye Caulker, possess villages. Right on the coast, covering a finger of land, is **Belize City**. Belize's only real city, it is the country's center of business.

North of Belize City, **northern Belize** presents a lush, lonely landscape harboring the powerful ancient ceremonial center of Lamanai and the peaceful Altun Ha, where fantastic jade artifacts have been found. Here, too, are vast sanctuaries for birds, butterflies and baboons, the Belizean name for howler monkeys. **Western Belize** attracts chic adventurers who stay in charming jungle lodges and explore Maya medicine trails, the popular ruins at Xunantunich and the cool, shady depths of the Mountain Pine Ridge forest. The west is also home to the great Caracol, a Maya city swallowed in jungle, hours from civilization, and home to the tallest building in Belize.

Southern Belize is a far-flung outback where hard-core explorers go to see what few travelers have seen: primitive Maya and Garifuna villages and the profound ruins at Lubaantun and Nim Li Punit. Along the southern coast is an anomaly called Placencia, whose pure white beaches and sun-dappled waters are attracting a coterie of young travelers and fueling tourism and development. Inland, impermeable cloud forests cover much of the region, protecting an extraordinary web of life, including the world's densest population of jaguars, who reside at Cockscomb Basin Wildlife Sanctuary.

For those who would adventure beyond Belize's borders, thrilling **side trips** await to the north, west and south. To the north, Mexico's Chetumal offers intriguing Maya ruins and eco-tours to see manatees. Guatemala's Petén, North America's largest rainforest, sprawls across Belize's western border, thrilling travelers with the exquisite and daunting Maya city of Tikal. Southward from Belize is Guatemala's Río Dulce, the picturesque "Sweet River" that leads to relaxing, time-locked villages.

Throughout these regions, travelers will find few creature comforts. Instead, they will discover a land that still belongs to the rainforest and to the sea, not to the frills of tourism. For unlike the money-driven throngs of "developed" countries, the residents of Belize have chosen to stay undeveloped, preferring the old, natural ways to the new, glitzy ones, opting to build a simple thatched lodge instead of a seaside highrise, to make nature and culture, not some contrived theme park, the big attractions.

And therein lies the reason for Belize's decided allure, and for the traveler's compulsion to go back once she has returned home,

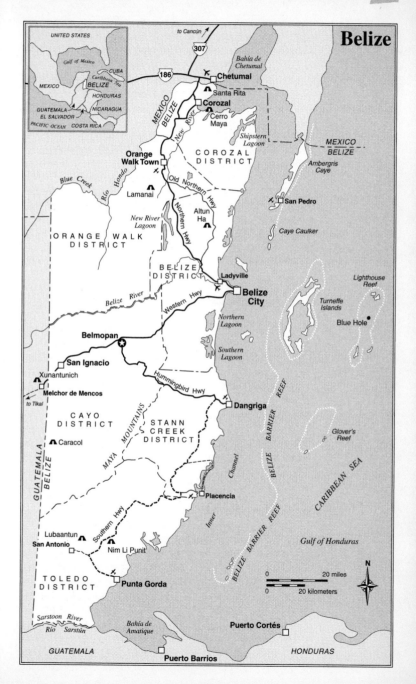

Belize

UNITED STATES

Gulf of Mexico

CUBA

MEXICO   Caribbean Sea

BELIZE

HONDURAS

GUATEMALA   NICARAGUA

EL SALVADOR

PACIFIC OCEAN   COSTA RICA

to Cancún

307

186

MEXICO
BELIZE

Bahía de
Chetumal

Chetumal

Santa Rita

Corozal

Cerro
Maya

Shipstern
Lagoon

MEXICO
BELIZE

COROZAL
DISTRICT

Ambergris
Caye

Orange
Walk Town

New River

Lamanai

Old Northern Hwy

San Pedro

Blue Creek

Río Hondo

New River
Lagoon

Altun
Ha

Northern Hwy

Caye Caulker

ORANGE WALK
DISTRICT

BELIZE
DISTRICT

Ladyville

Lighthouse
Reef

Belize River

Belize
City

Turneffe
Islands

Western Hwy

Northern
Lagoon

Blue Hole

Belmopan

Southern
Lagoon

San Ignacio

Hummingbird Hwy

Xunantunich

Melchor de Mencos

to Tikal

CAYO
DISTRICT

Dangriga

BELIZE BARRIER REEF

Glover's
Reef

MAYA MOUNTAINS

STANN
CREEK
DISTRICT

Caracol

GUATEMALA
BELIZE

Channel

CARIBBEAN SEA

Placencia

Inner

Lubaantun

San Antonio

Southern Hwy

Nim Li Punit

Gulf of Honduras

TOLEDO
DISTRICT

Punta Gorda

0   20 miles

N

0   20 kilometers

BELIZE BARRIER REEF

Sarstoon River

Río Sarstún

Bahía de
Amatique

Puerto Cortés

GUATEMALA

Puerto Barrios

HONDURAS

an affliction known as the "Belize Factor." Belize holds boundless opportunities for adventure, beckoning around every turn of a wornout jungle road, calling from every mountaintop washed in sun-dappled haze, waiting deep in a sea set with brilliant coral.

There is a certain innocence in Belize, a simple existence where the rigors of life have not yet slipped in. Events here often seem surreal: rabbits hop around a restaurant floor, a monkey joins you for breakfast and toucans fill the garden where you're having a jungle massage. Women wash their clothes in the rivers and cook iguanas on their wood-fired stoves. No one wears shoes on the islands, but why should they, since the streets are made of sand.

After awhile, when you begin thinking Belize might be a little too primitive, too far out there, something Belizean happens. Like a destitute farmer donating his land to save the animals. Or a Maya villager taking time to show a stranger how to grind corn. Or a wild dolphin taking you for a swim off an isolated island. And then you fall in love with Belize all over again.

Belize is just like that. In no time, it burrows deep into your consciousness. And before you know it, you find yourself humming a Garifuna tune, listening for the howl of a monkey, searching the horizon for the familiar site of a Maya village.

▼▼▼▼▼▼▼▼▼
When to Go

SEASONS

Located in a subtropical rainforest region, Belize has just two seasons: rainy and dry. Generally, rain falls and temperatures rise during summer and autumn months, from June through October. Daily rains can soak inland jungle roads, creating sludge trails that are impassable without four-wheel-drive vehicles.

Summer rains increase dramatically in Belize as you head from north to south. Northern Corozal, for instance, averages 50 inches of annual rain, while Punta Gorda, only 200 miles to the south, gets an incredible 170 inches a year. During the rainy season, afternoon showers give life to the forests and a welcome drop in temperatures for those who reside there. Temperatures along the coast and inland rainforests, however, often reach 95° by midday during summer months.

Late summer and early fall can also mean hurricane season, particularly along the Caribbean coast. It's not likely that you'll encounter one—they blow in every decade or so—but if you should, take it seriously: hurricanes are monsters that take lives and leave paths of destruction. In October, "northers" usually set in, bringing persistent winds from the north of 15 to 25 knots. Northers are the lower fringe of cold fronts that swirl down from North America.

During the dry season, from November through March, the thermometer registers in the comfortable low 80s. In the mountains of inland Belize, the mercury drops into the 50s at night during winter, with perfect daytime weather in the 70s. During winter, some lodges, particularly in the cayes, raise their prices as much as 30 percent in response to visitors arriving to enjoy the idyllic weather.

The months of April and May enjoy neither winter trade winds nor cooling afternoon rains, and can be intensely hot—in the 100s—and suffocatingly humid. May is when many Belizeans living inland head to the cayes for heat relief. This author, despite being a native Floridian accustomed to the tropics, finds an air-conditioned room a necessity in Belize during April and May.

> Springtime creates crystalline waters in the offshore cayes, with visibility reaching an amazing 100 feet in some dive spots.

All that said, visitors should know that those who follow Belize's weather say it is entirely unpredictable. For instance, during the "rainy" season, there may be many days with overcast skies but little rain. And in the dry season, there may be several days of drizzling or even torrential rains.

CALENDAR OF EVENTS

You may want to plan your Belize visit around a certain holiday or festival and join in the local spirit. Make your reservations at least three to four months in advance, because hotels fill up fast during special events.

During major holidays, rum and island music flow freely through towns and villages, and locals celebrate with street dances that can last until sunup. Remember that because of the festivities, everything else practically shuts down, including government agencies, businesses and professional offices. In other words, if there's a holiday, forget about business and join the party!

Here are the most important events in Belize:

January 1 New Year's Day is celebrated on January 1 as a national holiday, complete with parades and fireworks.

JANUARY

Late February Belizeans countrywide come out to participate in the Fiesta de Carnaval, held the week before Lent. Hopeful anglers ply the Caribbean for the largest catch of the International Billfish Tournament—its $50,000 grand prize.

FEBRUARY

March 9 Baron Bliss Day pays homage to the man who left his $2 million fortune to the tiny country. Belizeans remember him with a day of fishing and sailing, an apt memorial since the baron was devoted to both pursuits.

MARCH– APRIL

The week before Easter Holy Week rivals the Christmas season as the biggest holiday of the year. Businesses close for Good Friday, Holy Saturday, Easter Sunday and the following Monday so locals can celebrate at home.

MAY

May 1   Belizeans take a break from work every May 1, which is **Labour Day**. Kite contests, bicycling and horse races, and a harbor regatta are featured.

Late May   The people of Belize pay respects to the British Commonwealth on **Commonwealth Day**, May 24. Also in May, the residents of Crooked Tree Village in northern Belize celebrate the cashew harvest season; the **Crooked Tree Cashew Festival** features storytelling and Caribbean folklore performances, Belizean cuisine, nature walks, river trips and expeditions to local Maya ruins. In addition, Caye Caulker and Placencia both hold **Lobster Festivals** to celebrate the start of the lobster fishing season.

JUNE

June 29   June 29 is **Día de San Pedro**, the Feast Day of Saint Peter, patron saint of San Pedro, Ambergris Caye. Residents celebrate the 1848 founding of their village with merrymaking and a parade of fishing boats that are blessed in the town harbor.

AUGUST

Mid-August   Mexico, Guatemala, El Salvador and Honduras join Belize in the **International Costa Maya Festival**, held in San Pedro, Ambergris Caye. Showcasing myriads of ethnic dances and cuisines, costumes and crafts, the festival is a celebration of the countries' cooperation and work together on the Mundo Maya (Maya World) tourism project.

SEPTEMBER

September 10   September is a time of virtually nonstop celebrating in Belize. One of the biggest, most joyous national holidays, **St. George's Caye Day** remembers the September 10, 1798, victory of British buccaneers over a much larger Spanish naval force. Every town joins in with a week of parades, jumpup street dancing and community-wide feasting.

September 21   The British eventually gave Belize its independence on September 21, 1981, and Belizeans celebrate with **National Independence Day**. The whole country is like a carnival, and streets are filled with artisans, musicians, dancers, actors and delicious local food.

September 25   The Maya town of San Antonio stages a spectacular celebration of the **St. Louis Feast Day**.

OCTOBER

October 12   A double holiday can mean twice as much celebrating. October 12 brings **Columbus Day** and **Pan American Day**. Big events are horse races, boat racing and cross-country cycling competitions.

NOVEMBER

November 19   Pulsing drums and punta rock music signal the start of **Garifuna Settlement Day** in southern Belize. The November 19 festivities, centered in the Toledo District, mark the 1823 arrival of the Garifunas (African Indians).

Late December **Christmas** festivities begin on Christmas Eve, when Belizeans light the yule log and exchange presents. December 26 marks **Boxing Day**, a national holiday.

▼ ▼ ▼ ▼ ▼ ▼ ▼ ▼ ▼ ▼

The **Belize Tourism Board** provides the best travel information and has a toll-free number from the United States. ~ New Central Bank Building, Level 2, Gabourel Lane, P.O. Box 325, Belize City; 501-22-31913, 800-624-0686; www.travelbelize.org.

ONLINE RESOURCES   Belize has great websites. There are hundreds of hotels, tour companies, Maya sites, and fishing and diving outfitters online, many with beautiful photography. There's even a detailed walking tour of Ambergris Caye. Definitely take the time to browse around before your trip.

 Ambergris Caye ~ www.ambergriscaye.com; www.goamber griscaye.com

 Belize by Naturalight ~ www.belizenet.com
 Belize Chamber of Commerce ~ www.travelbelize.org
 Belize First ~ www.belizefirst.com
 Belize It ~ www.belizeit.com
 Belize Online ~ www.belize.com
 Belize Report ~ www.belizereport.com
 Belize Search Engine ~ www.belize.net
 Caye Caulker ~ www.gocayecaulker.com
 Placencia ~ www.placencia.com
 Unbelizeable ~ www.unbelizeable.com

Pack light! A camera plus whatever else you can fit in a large duffel bag and a backpack would be perfect. For a two-week trip, I carry a canvas French Army backpack and a sturdy, woven Guatemalan bag (available in Belize for about US$30–$35) packed light enough to tote on successive boat and commuter plane trips. There is nothing like lugging 75 pounds of suitcases around the jungle to make one feel absurdly materialistic.

 When choosing your clothing, remember that Belize is far from fashion conscious. In fact, both women and men dress in a practical, unpretentious manner. Flaunting a new pair of Nike Air Jordans around Belize City is not only in poor taste, it's an invitation to petty thieves. Keep your clothing modest and sensible, as befitting a country where wildlife and forests are held in higher regard than the latest styles.

 Bring along a minimum of sporty, summery clothing, T-shirts, shorts and a swimsuit, as well as a rain poncho and a pair of polarized sunglasses (essential for spotting fish). Cotton shirts breathe better and wick away perspiration. For treks to the Maya ruins and wildlife reserves, you'll need a sturdy but lightweight pair of hiking boots, a comfortable pair of slacks—I like loose-fitting cotton fatigues—and socks to protect your ankles from insects. A long-sleeve cotton shirt protects against bugs and brambly bush, while a light jacket will keep you warm on winter nights. Leave your blue jeans at home. Not only are they extremely hot, they get heavy when wet.

A walk in the jungle is like a walk in the dark, unless you take a good pair of binoculars. Binoculars help you find the hundreds of tiny critters that hide out in the dense foliage all around. The best binoculars are those with high magnification that let in plenty of light—all the better for seeing in the dim, shadowy forest. Many birdwatchers recommend Zeiss or Leitz 10x40 lenses.

A flashlight with extra batteries is a must for exploring caves and for those nights when hotel generators shut down early. I take a lighter and a couple of votive candles for reading at night. And don't forget to take a roll of toilet paper for the long forays into the jungle.

You should definitely pack a first-aid kit. Include a good insect repellent, aspirin, Band-aids, cold capsules, vitamins, motion sickness tablets, prescription drugs you use, iodine or alcohol for disinfecting wounds, antibiotic ointment, water purification tablets, sunscreen with at least a 15 SPF, lip balm and diarrhea medicine. For insect bites and jellyfish stings, carry a bottle of calamine lotion, a tube of Benadryl ointment or bottle of Benadryl spray, and a bottle of Benadryl pills. When you're covered with itchy red welts that keep you up all night, nothing gives relief like Benadryl.

Anyone with a medical condition should consider wearing a medic alert identification tag that identifies the problem and gives a phone number to call for more information. Contact **Medic Alert Foundation International**. ~ 2323 Turlock Avenue, Turlock, CA 95382; 888-633-4298; e-mail customer-service@medic alert.org.

Belize, filled as it is with quirky humanity, ancient crumbling cities and travel-poster islands, is a photographer's dream. At virtually every turn, you will find the makings of a great picture. But, be aware that the Adventure Coast can be tough on camera equipment, so unless you're competing in a photo contest, consider bringing something compact and inexpensive. Pocket-sized instamatic cameras hold up well, and are easy to tote around the jungle in a backpack. Disposable cameras are also practical because you don't have to worry about carrying rolls of film. I use an underwater camera that also takes decent above-water photos, and won't succumb to the Belize humidity.

The best way to protect your equipment is to keep it in a padded, zippered camera bag. Remember that if you tour on the mainland, you will be bouncing down rocky roads for hours on end.

Picture
Etiquette

While on the cayes and in larger towns, you can take pictures freely in almost any public place. Outlying villages are a different story. Many villagers, particularly the older Maya and Garifunas, don't want their picture taken—a taboo that we, as visitors, should respect. If you want to photograph village people, ask first.

You will no doubt be charmed by their colorful, elaborately handcrafted clothing and their exotic features with faces expressing everything from stoic nobility and ancient, mysterious wisdom to embarrassed amusement at the strange-looking tourist confronting them. With the coming of television to many villages, attitudes toward cameras are changing. Some people are more willing than in the past to pose for photographs. And if you converse with them for a while and let them get to know you, many people who would deeply resent having their likeness captured by a stranger are more than willing to offer it as a gift to a new friend.

You may want to reciprocate with a small gift, either a monetary tip or a souvenir. Village children love pens, hair barrettes, sunglasses—most anything a tourist has to offer.

Have your film developed back home. Belize's developing labs are not only expensive but few and far between. If you just can't wait to see your snapshots, take your film to **Spooner's One-Hour Photo Lab**, which offers fair prices and dependable service. ~ 89 North Front Street, Belize City; 22-31043; e-mail spooners@btl.net.

Belize's rains also wreak havoc on cameras, so keep a couple of ziplocked bags handy for sudden showers.

Definitely bring plenty of film: in Belize, film costs double or triple what it does in the U.S., and it's tough to find. Slide film is virtually unheard of. It's also wise to bring an extra camera battery and, if you're using a 35mm camera, a couple of clear lens filters. The jungle has a way of leaving its mark (scratches and dents) on camera lenses.

When it comes to toiletries, most towns in Belize carry everything you'll find in the United States, though usually at higher prices: toothpaste, deodorant, shampoo, soap, insect repellent, skin creams, shaving cream and batteries (buy the expensive ones; the cheapest kind often don't work). Imported items like tampons and suntan lotions are also widely available in larger towns, though they cost a lot more than in the United States.

Scuba divers should check with their lodge about available equipment. Few dive resorts carry enough for everyone, so plan to bring your own mask, snorkel, booties and fins, BCD (buoyancy control device), regulator, weights and, of course, your certification card. Tanks are normally provided. Always pack your dive gear in a suitcase; a dive bag checked alone is a prime target for thieves—in the U.S., not Belize. Make sure your dive knife is in your suitcase, checked with the rest of your gear. I know of a foolish diver who, attempting to carry his knife on the plane, had to surrender it at a Miami departure gate.

Likewise, anglers staying at fishing lodges will want to bring along their rods and tackle. Check with your individual lodge about what it has on hand.

Take along some good paperbacks (hard covers don't hold up well in the jungle). However, in English-speaking Belize, where the literacy rate is over 75 percent, you'll have no trouble finding good books on all subjects. Many innkeepers stock superb libraries on Belizean and Maya history and culture and are happy to loan books while you're a guest. In archaeological areas, you will find English-language books about the ancient Maya civilization that are not available in the United States. In areas of Belize where American expatriates congregate, such as San Ignacio and Placencia, English-language novels are recycled endlessly. There are used-book or trade-in racks full of paperback potboilers left over from decades past at bookstores, hotels and restaurants where foreign visitors gather. No matter where you plan to travel, don't forget to bring your copy of *Hidden Belize!*

PASSPORTS & VISAS   All visitors to Belize, except cruise ship passengers, must have valid passports. Besides clearing immigration, you will need to show your passport when renting a car, cashing traveler's checks or, in some cases, checking into a hotel.

Belize requires visas for visitors from 54 countries around the world, but not from the United States, Canada, the United Kingdom, Ireland, Australia, South Africa or other English-speaking countries. You can also enter Belize from neighboring Mexico and Guatemala without obtaining a visa in advance. Special security clearances from the Belizean Director of Immigration are required for visitors from Bangladesh, Bolivia, Columbia, the People's Republic of China, Cuba, the Czech Republic, Ecuador, Egypt, India, Iran, Iraq, Israel, Jordan, Lebanon, Libya, Myanmar, Nepal, Nigeria, Pakistan, Palestine, Peru, Sri Lanka, Syria and the United Arab Emirates. Travelers who plan to stay longer than 30 days in Belize, however, should obtain an extension from the Belize Immigration Office. Visa extensions cost US$25 for up to six months and $50 a month thereafter. ~ Belize Immigration and Nationality Department, Belmopan, Cayo District; 82-22423, fax 82-22662.

BELIZE CUSTOMS

Belize customs regulations are liberal to tourists. However, they are notoriously slow at the Belize City international airport. This is especially true on Monday mornings, when Belizeans returning from weekend shopping sprees in Miami must itemize their purchases and pay duties. Customs officials literally check every nook and cranny of every suitcase. Twice, I waited nearly two hours in the boiling heat to clear customs. If you find yourself in this waiting-forever situation, slow down and remember—this is the tropics!

Buyers beware! Vendors of items made from any part of an endangered species usually will not warn you that you can't take them home.

If you take your boat to Belize, the following documents must be presented to the customs officer who will board your vessel upon its arrival: (1) the boat's certificate of registration; (2) proof of clearance from your last port of call; (3) four copies of your crew and passenger list; (4) four copies of your stores list; and finally, (5) four copies of your cargo manifest, if you are transporting cargo.

For detailed information on Belizean customs, contact the Belize Comptroller of Customs, Customs House, Port Loyola, Belize City, 22-75031, fax 22-77091; e-mail comptrollr@btl.net.

Guatemala's customs regulations, as they apply to tourists, are minimal and somewhat vague. As a practical matter, instead of physically inspecting your luggage (except for arrivals at the international airport in Guatemala City), Guatemalan *Aduana* officials prefer to charge a small fee per bag for a tag certifying that they have inspected it.

U.S. CUSTOMS

Even if you live there, the United States can be harder to enter than Central American countries. When returning home, United States residents may bring in $800 worth of purchases duty-free for personal use or as gifts, not for resale. Anything over this amount is subject to a 10 percent tax on the next $1000 worth of items. Certain items, such as handicrafts, are tax-exempt. In case customs officials question the values you declare, save the receipts for goods you buy in retail stores and record your marketplace and street vendor purchases neatly in a notebook. Persons over 21 years of age are allowed one liter (or quart) of liquor duty-free, as well as 200 cigarettes or 100 cigars (not Cuban).

Fruits, vegetables and many other fresh foods are not allowed into the U.S. and will be confiscated. Fish, shrimp and any seafood that can be legally caught in Belize can be brought across the border. However, conservation-minded travelers will catch only what they can eat in Belize. There's nothing more embarrassing than an American tourist lugging a cooler full of lobsters from a country where many children don't get enough to eat.

All items made from any part of an endangered species—such as the sea turtle, crocodile, black coral or ocelot—are prohibited in the United States and will be confiscated.

Ancient relics, such as Maya artifacts or pre-Colombian art, cannot be taken from their country of origin and will be confiscated if found in your possession. All archaeological finds are considered national treasures and the property of the country in which they were found.

For more details, write **U.S. Customs**. ~ P.O. Box 7407, Washington, DC 20044; 202-927-6724; www.customs.ustreas.gov. Another government agency is the **U.S. Fish and Wildlife Service**. ~ Office of Management Authority, 4401 North Fairfax Drive, Arlington, VA 22203; 800-344-9453; www.fws.gov. The **World Wildlife Fund** is a helpful resource. ~ 1250 24th Street NW, Washington, DC 20090; 202-293-4800 or 800-225-5993, fax 202-293-9211; www.wwfus.org.

THE PRICE TO PAY

Sightseeing tours are expensive. This is partly because of the poor condition of some roads, which can destroy tour vehicles in a matter of months. What else makes them so expensive, I have not been able to ascertain. Expect to pay from US$100 to US$250, for one to four people, for a day trip to a Maya ruin or nature reserve. Travel agencies in Belize City and Ambergris Caye sometimes arrange less-expensive tours by organizing larger groups. In remote areas, however, your chances of joining a large group are slim. Single travelers will find tour prices exorbitant. Traveling alone, I have paid as much as US$200 for a six-hour tour to a ruin.

To avoid confiscation of prescribed drugs, label them carefully and bring along a doctor's certificate of prescription. As for contraband drugs, there's a war on. Smart travelers remain neutral.

Customs checks at the U.S. border can be stringent or swift, depending on how suspicious you look. To avoid any problems, dress neatly and declare your purchases.

SHOTS

No inoculations are required to enter Belize. Cases of hepatitis, malaria, typhoid, cholera, dengue fever and other tropical diseases do occur but seldom afflict travelers. If you are planning to visit remote areas, your doctor may recommend yellow fever, tetanus, typhoid, hepatitis A and gamma globulin shots and/or malaria pills.

MONEY MATTERS

Traveling Expenses   Travelers accustomed to low prices in Guatemala and Mexico may be surprised to find their next-door neighbor more expensive. Belize is in fact on par with Caribbean destinations such as Jamaica, St. Thomas and Grand Cayman when it comes to lodging, restaurant and tour prices. And in 1996, Belize implemented a Value Added Tax (VAT), which was raised to 19 percent in 2005, on most travel expenses, including meals, car rentals, sightseeing tours and gifts. The hotel tax remains at 7 percent, though a three-star hotel that's US$10 a night in Guatemala will probably be US$45 a night across the border in Belize. The best jungle lodges and beach hotels charge more than US$100 a night, and dinner at a "better" restaurant costs about US$30 a person.

If you're staying in remote areas, it will be necessary to have all of your meals at your lodge. Expect to pay from US$30 to US$60 per person per day for these meals. While I have found the meals at some of these "all-inclusive" lodges to be exceptional and well worth the price, others have been marginal and overpriced. Throughout this book, lodges are critiqued on the quality and value of their meals.

Groceries cost more (from 10 to 100 percent more) than they do in the United States, particularly convenience foods and toiletries. Bus transportation is inexpensive, costing about US 25 cents to travel around Belize City and only US$4 to travel from Belize City west all the way to the Guatemala border.

Stick to local beer and rum. A bottle of Belize beer, a mild, tasty brew called Belikin, sells for US$1 to US$2 and is consumed by locals and tourists alike. Cocktails made with Belize's Caribbean White Rum are about US$2.50. Imported brands will run you two to three times that price.

Currency   Belize currency, measured in Belize dollars (BZE$), is extremely stable. For the last few years, the exchange rate has stayed steady at BZE$2 to US$1. You'll have no trouble using U.S. dollars throughout Belize; in fact, many places now post their prices in U.S. currency to make them seem less expensive (which they rarely are). Foreigners, however, being respectful of where they are, should change their money and use Belize dollars. If you have any doubts about this issue, consider how you would like it if Belizeans insisted on using Belize dollars in the United States. Currencies other than Belizean and U.S. dollars are generally not accepted, though small amounts of Mexican pesos can often be spent in the northern Corozal District.

Keep in mind that most villages have no banks, and in these spots it's usually impossible to cash traveler's checks. On market days, there are often moneychangers around. At other times, only small-denomination local currency will work.

Because Belize is a tiny country with a limited currency supply, banks often run short of cash during the busy part of the tourist season. When this happens, stores and street vendors may be unable to make change, so you'll want to carry plenty of Belizean currency in small bills.

Changing Money   Be smart and protect your vacation by carrying traveler's checks. Even though you will get a slightly lower exchange rate, it's worth safeguarding your money. Well-known brands, especially American Express, are the easiest to cash. You will need your passport to cash them. Canadian and European traveler's checks and currency can pose problems; some banks will not cash them.

Most banks are open 8 a.m. to 1 p.m., Monday through Thursday. On Friday, hours are from 8 a.m. to 1 p.m. and 3 to 6 p.m. Banks often have specified hours for exchanging foreign money, which vary from bank to bank and day to day.

Personal checks drawn on banks outside Belize will be held for an eight-week waiting period before funds are disbursed.

Credit Cards   Credit cards are accepted at most lodges but only a few restaurants and shops, mainly those in Belize City. Many hotels add a surcharge if you pay by credit card. MasterCard, Visa and Discover are the most widely accepted cards; American Express cards are sometimes frowned upon because of their stiff fees to merchants.

If you need a financial transfusion while in Belize, most banks will provide a cash advance on your credit card. The transaction can take up to several hours, and there is usually a fee of three to five percent of the withdrawal amount. If you use an ATM (found mostly in Belize City) it will be treated as a credit card advance and will not result in a direct debit from your bank account. Money transfers can also be made via Western Union (*usually* taking one day) or via any big bank at home through one of its Belizean affiliates (which can take as long as three working days). Check before you leave home to see whether your bank offers this service. Western Union fees are high and must be paid in advance by the sender.

Tipping Belizeans are not as gratuity-oriented as Americans, but they do appreciate a tip for good service. In general, follow the same customs on tipping as you would back home. Tip taxi drivers and chambermaids 5 to 10 percent; restaurant waiters and waitresses, 15 percent; and airport porters, US$.50 per bag. Some hotels and restaurants include a service charge, so check your bill before tipping. Tour guides are some of the most knowledgeable, patient workers in Belize and deserve a generous tip when they do a good job.

Bribery & Bargaining While bribery for services is standard business in Mexico and other Central American countries, you'll rarely encounter it in Belize. Belizeans tend to take a practical, mild-tempered approach to life and don't subscribe to the system of *La Mordida* ("the bite"). The same philosophy applies to bickering over price. In fact, Belizeans take pride in fair pricing and prefer not to haggle. That's not to say you can't negotiate a custom-designed tour or private transportation from one place to another.

LODGING

After you have stayed awhile in Belize, you will become accustomed to (and endeared to) the country's funky style of accommodations. A Belize City guesthouse, for instance, may offer drapes made of seashells and battered furniture painted every primary color. Decor in your seaside motel may include a lava lamp, a vinyl '50s-era chair and a boat oar parked on the wall, but hey, the room's got character! Lodge owners often furnish rooms with the same care and Belizean quirkiness they use in their own houses. Before long, you'll feel right at home.

Be aware, though, that funky doesn't mean cheap. The clean, comfortable, low-priced lodging abundant throughout neighboring Mexico and Guatemala doesn't exist in Belize. Lodging prices here are more in line with those in the Caribbean, and in popular resort areas of the United States.

Every lodge is the unique creation of its owners, and its character is shaped by them. With the exception of a few places in Belize City, lodges and resorts rarely have as many units as a typical mom-and-pop motel in the United States. Most lodges are hand-built by the owners, who typically add a unit or two every year. Cabanas, made of stucco, wood or bamboo and crowned with palm thatching, are ubiquitous in Belize. They range from elegant bedrooms with glossy teakwood floors, mahogany furniture and canopy beds to basic round shelters with concrete floors and curtained closet doors. If you're staying in the jungle, make sure your room is properly protected from bugs by screens and other devices. During certain times of the year, insects migrate and can literally invade your room if it's not bug-proofed. I had this experience, and it is not one I wish to repeat.

During the November-to-April high season, and around major holidays like Christmas, Easter and National Independence Day, many hotels raise their rates and sell out weeks in advance. Reservations for these times of the year should be made at least two months ahead of time.

This book's lodging listings range from budget to very expensive, with an emphasis on unique or special midrange to upper midrange establishments. All price ranges are based on double occupancy, and *do not* include a 7 percent government tax. Lodging is rated as follows: *budget* facilities have rooms for less than US$50 a night for two people; *moderate* hotels are priced between US$50 and US$90; *deluxe* facilities offer rates from US$90 to US$120; and *ultra-deluxe* accommodations are priced above US$120.

Remember that, except for a few chain hotels in Belize City (such as the Radisson Fort George and Fiesta Inn Belize), most "deluxe" and "ultra-deluxe" lodges will be neither fancy nor elegant. Rather, they will assure comfort and charm, picturesque surroundings and excellent meals, and plenty of assistance with local excursions. Unless otherwise noted, all lodges listed in this book offer electricity, hot water and private baths.

Note that many Belizean hotels charge an additional 5 percent if you pay for your room with a credit card. Some resorts also add a service charge of 10 to 15 percent to their rates.

DINING   Belize is not known for its culinary achievements. In fact, its restaurants suffer a dismal reputation among travelers, a reputation that's not deserved. No matter where you travel in the country, you will have access to tasty, well-prepared food. The problem is, many eateries are inconsistent. The place that served a memorable meal one night may serve a forgettable one the next. Cooks hopscotch between restaurants, and high-quality ingredients are

THE PRICE OF A COOL BREEZE

Most towns and islands have at least one motel or lodge that offers electricity and, thus, air conditioning. However, you will pay a premium for cold air, often twice as much as a room without air conditioning—but it's worth it on suffocatingly hot days. Many lodges, particularly in the jungle, out islands and remote villages, receive their electricity from gasoline-powered generators. In some instances, electricity is rationed to a few hours after dusk. But their location makes the experience of staying there special enough to justify any mild inconveniences you might encounter. Indeed, I have found these jungle lodges to be some of the most memorable places in Belize.

not always available. But if you ask around town, locals will point you to the best spot.

In populated areas, such as Belize City and Ambergris Caye, you can choose from fresh seafood, Italian, Chinese and the ubiquitous Belizean soul food. In remote areas, you will rely on your lodge for meals—not a bad option, considering Belize lodges offer some of the country's best fare. Jungle lodges often grow their food organically and employ Maya or Creole cooks who know their way around a kitchen. And don't be surprised to learn that your delicious, filling entrée was prepared with low salt and low fat and without meat. Many innkeepers believe healthy, no-meat diets are in keeping with the principles of ecotourism. Of course, when it comes to dining, jungle lodges have a captive clientele, so meals tend to be expensive—often US$25 or more per person for dinner.

In this book, restaurants are separated into the following price categories: *budget* restaurants cost US$5 or less for dinner entrées; *moderate*-priced restaurants range between US$5 and US$12 at dinner and offer pleasant surroundings and a more varied menu; and *deluxe* establishments tab their entrées at US$12 and over, featuring cuisine that's more sophisticated, plus decor and more personalized service. A few hotel restaurants add a 15 percent service charge, and all restaurants add the 15 percent government VAT. Restaurants serve lunch and dinner unless otherwise noted.

Should you bring the kids to Belize? That depends. If you plan to spend a lot of time in the cayes and other resort areas, then by all means, take them along. As you move into remote jungle areas of Belize, you may want to consider taking only older children. The jungle does hold limitless fascination for older children; they adore hiking through mysterious forests and exploring on horseback and in canoes. In archaeological areas, ancient temples and pyramids are great for climbing and poking into secret passageways, and the mysteries of a vanished civilization can tantalize young minds for weeks on end. Belizeans love children and are very family oriented. Numerous lodges across the country are owned by families, and children often join the guests at mealtime. Many travelers find it easy to enjoy both worlds—parenting and adventuring.

Remember to get a tourist card for each child. Children traveling with only one parent must have notarized permission from the other parent (or, if applicable, divorce papers, guardianship document or death certificate). Minors traveling alone must have a notarized letter of permission signed by both parents or guardians.

Prepare a junior first-aid kit with baby aspirin, thermometer, vitamins, diarrhea medicine, sunblock, bug repellent, tissues and

TRAVELING WITH CHILDREN

cold medicine. Parents traveling with infants will want to pack cloth diapers, plastic bags for dirty diapers, and a wraparound or papoose-style baby carrier. Strollers aren't practical on Belize's crumbling city roads and island sand streets.

Disposable diapers, baby food and medicines are available in larger towns. Outside Belize City and Ambergris Caye, few lodges have cribs or childcare services. However, some lodge owners will help you find a local babysitter.

Belize restaurants are plenty casual for children, but the fare may not please picky eaters. You might want to bring some rolls, peanut butter and jelly, toaster pastries and other easy-to-pack munchies. In the meantime, encourage your child to try local foods. You'd be surprised how quickly they adapt to stewed chicken and beans and rice.

While you're at the Belize Zoo, pick up a copy of *Hoodwink the Owl*, a warm-hearted tale that introduces children to Belize's fascinating animals.

Go ahead and splurge on a rental car. Traveling with children, especially young ones, on public buses could be one stressor too many. If you tour by car with an infant, bring a portable car seat. For children of any age, be sure to pack toys, books and art supplies to drive away boredom during long trips.

Pace your trip so your child has time to adapt to changes. Don't plan exhausting whirlwind tours, and keep travel time to a minimum. Seek out beaches, parks, plazas and short excursions to amuse your child. The Belize Zoo is a wonderful place for children; thousands of local children visit each year.

WOMEN TRAVELING ALONE

Belize is quite liberated when it comes to women's issues. Women traveling here can expect at least the same freedom and respect they enjoy in the United States, if not more. Belize women are hard-working, independent individuals who are often the family breadwinners. It is not uncommon to hear a Belize man complaining that his girlfriend is "too busy with her career" to settle down. After traveling around Belize for three months, the only sexual harassment I experienced was from American men!

Traveling solo grants an independence and freedom different from that of traveling with a partner, but single travelers are more vulnerable to crime and must take additional precautions.

It's unwise to hitchhike and probably best to avoid inexpensive accommodations in towns such as Belize City and Orange Walk; the money saved does not outweigh the risk. In town, hotels and better-quality inns are your best bet; on the cayes and along the coast, opt for family-owned lodges over low-end motels. Out in the rainforest you'll feel right at home in most jungle lodges, which foster an environment ideal for bonding with fellow travelers.

While in Belize City and Orange Walk, keep all valuables well-hidden and clutch cameras and purses tightly. Better yet, wear a waist pack. Avoid late-night treks or strolls through undesirable parts of town, but if you find yourself in this situation, continue walking with a confident air until you reach a safe haven.

These hints should by no means deter you from seeking out adventure. Wherever you go, stay alert, use your common sense and trust your instincts. If you are hassled or threatened in some way, never be afraid to scream for assistance. It's a good idea to carry change or a phone card for a phone call and to know the number to call in case of emergency. For helpful hints, get a copy of *Safety and Security for Women Who Travel* (Travelers' Tales, 1998).

GAY & LESBIAN TRAVELERS

Perhaps because of its not-so-distant past as a British colony, Belize tends to take a conservative approach to the gay lifestyle. That's not to say you're likely to encounter hostility when traveling there, but you won't find a visible gay population—or a single gay nightspot. Most lodges cater to a mass spectrum of visitors, and "as long as gays are essentially closeted while there, they won't have a problem," says Jonathan Klein, owner of **Now Voyager**, a travel agency specializing in gay and lesbian tours worldwide. ~ 4406 18th Street, San Francisco, CA 94114; 415-626-1169, 800-255-6951, fax 415-626-8626; www.nowvoyager.com.

Klein says no place in Belize advertises as either gay-friendly or gay-unfriendly, and that none of their clients has ever reported a problem with discrimination. "Generally gay travelers to Belize are like any traveler—they're either divers looking to hit the reef or ecotourists heading to a jungle lodge."

Gay travelers looking for nightlife should head for Ambergris Caye, where sand-floored tiki bars come alive with reggae, roosters and young suntanned tourists. Inland, San Ignacio's bohemian jungle scene is perfect for gay people who want daytime adventure and nighttime camaraderie among expats and European backpackers. And over in Guatemala's Petén (see Chapter Nine), gay travelers will find Flores a convivial place at night.

For guided gay and lesbian group trips contact **Footprints Travel**, a Canadian outfitter combining the Belize rainforest and cayes with Guatemala's Petén on 13-day adventures. ~ 506 Church Street, Suite 200, Toronto, Canada M4Y 2C8; 416-962-8111, 888-962-6211, fax 416-962-6621; www.footprintstravel.com.

SENIOR TRAVELERS

Belize has much to offer seniors, including adventures tailored to individuals whose strength and endurance are no longer limitless. In other words, not every trek to the ruins has to last 12 hours. Older travelers will find companionship everywhere, from the fishing and jungle lodges to tiny beach motels. They will also discover that Belize seniors are often in astoundingly good shape; I met several Maya bushmen who looked (and acted) much younger than their years.

Some of the most rewarding senior excursions to Belize are the work programs offered by **Elderhostel**. Travelers can join a Maya ruin dig, track dolphins off an atoll or help collect data on howler monkeys in the northern rainforests. These are no luxury trips: accommodations are usually very basic, and there is hard work to be done. But the opportunities to experience a country from a local point of view and to contribute to the environment are un-matched. ~ 11 Avenue de Lafayette, Boston, MA 02111; 877-426-8056, fax 617-426-0701; www.elderhostel.org.

Be extra careful about health matters. Bring any medications you use, along with the prescriptions. Consider carrying a medical record with you—including your current medical status, your doctor's name, phone number and address. If possible, include a summary of your medical history. Check to see that your health insurance covers you while traveling in Belize.

DISABLED TRAVELERS

There are few sidewalks in Belize, and even the best roads tend to be narrow and bumpy. In the cayes, the streets are all sand. Most establishments and transportation systems do not provide special amenities, such as wheelchair access, for persons with disabil-ities. You may want to get help from a good travel agent to track down facilities to suit your situation.

Access-Able Travel Source has worldwide information online and operates **Travelin' Talk**, an international network of people and organizations dedicated to providing assistance to disabled travelers. ~ P.O. Box 1796, Wheat Ridge, CO 80034; 303-232-2979; www.access-able.com or www.travelintalk.net.

STUDENT TRAVELERS

While there are few organized student tours to Belize, the country is well-suited to young people traveling on a budget. Students can also choose from superb educational programs covering every-thing from breeding green iguanas to excavating Maya ruins. One of the best, **The Tropical Education Center** sits on 84 acres of pine savannah and has dormitories, a classroom and library. It's next to and part of the Belize Zoo, so naturally the focus is on wild an-imals. But there are also nature walks, canoe trips down the Sibun River, and lively discussions on the flora of Belize. ~ Mile Post 29, Western Highway; 22-08003, fax 22-08010; www.belizezoo.org/zoo/tec.html, e-mail tec@belizezoo.org.

Next door, the **Monkey Bay Wildlife Sanctuary** hosts training workshops on Belize's natural history and environment. You can stay in the bunkhouse, pitch a tent on a platform in the savannah prairie, or stay with a host family in a local village. ~ Mile Post 31, Western Highway, P.O. Box 187, Belmopan; 82-03032, fax 82-23361; www.monkeybaybelize.org, e-mail mbay@pobox.com.

Students at **Lamanai Field Research Centre**, on the New River Lagoon in northern Belize, join anthropologists from York

University and the Royal Ontario Museum in surveying, mapping and interpreting postclassical and early Spanish Colonial buildings at Lamanai—a fabulous experience. Accommodations are in private, thatch-roof cabañas at Lamanai Outpost Lodge. ~ Phone/fax 22-33578; www.lamanai. org, e-mail research@lamanai.org.

There is very little organized senior travel to Belize, mainly because modern tourism facilities, including transportation and roadways, are still developing. A good travel agent can recommend accommodations and sights to suit your needs.

Down on South Water Caye, Pelican Beach Resort's **Pelican University** is a rambling two-story house set among palm trees. Students study mangroves, the "spurs and grooves" outside the reef and the black clouds of frigate birds swarming nearby Man 'O War Caye. ~ P.O. Box 2, Dangriga; 52-22044, fax 52-22570; www.pelicanbeachbelize.com.

Numerous lodges across Belize are popular with students from the United States, Europe and Latin America, and the public bus system is extensive and inexpensive. And Belize's abundant outdoor experiences appeal to vigorous young travelers.

You'll find budget-priced rates and fellow students at the following lodges:

Ambergris Caye   **Lily's Caribbean Hotel** ~ Barrier Reef Drive, San Pedro; 20-62059; **Pedro's Backpackers Inn** ~ San Pedro; 22-63825; and **Camping on the Beach** ~ The Boat Yard, San Pedro; 22-63245.

Caye Caulker   **Trends Hotel** ~ 22-60094; and **Tina's Bakpak Youth Hostel** ~ 22-22351.

Belize City   **Seaside Guest House** ~ 3 Prince Street; 22-78339.

Western Belize   In addition to budget rates, **Macal Safari River Camp** has a Natural History Centre, Butterfly Farm and rainforest medicine trail. ~ At Chaa Creek on the Macal River, about eight miles outside San Ignacio; 82-22037. **Maya Mountain Lodge** offers educational programs on natural history, archaeology and social science. ~ Cristo Rey Road, near San Ignacio; 82-22164. You can also find excellent eco-programs and accommodations at **The Parrot's Nest**. ~ P.O. Box 108, San Ignacio; 82-23702. Other options are **Ian Anderson's Caves Branch Jungle Lodge** ~ Off the Hummingbird Highway, 14 miles south of Belmopan, phone/fax 82-22800; and **The Trek Stop** ~ Western Highway, six miles west of San Ignacio, 82-32265.

Southern Belize   **Serenade Guest House** ~ Placencia Village; 52-23163.

If you want to bring a pet into Belize, you must have an International Health Certificate for Dogs and Cats (Form 77-043) issued by a U.S. veterinarian within 48 hours before the animal enters the country, verifying that the animal is in good health, as well as a separate certification that it has been immunized against dis-

TRAVELING WITH PETS

temper and rabies within the last six months. If you adopt a pet while in Belize, before you can ship it home you need a health certificate from a Belizean vet, issued 30 days after the animal receives its vaccinations. Only TACA Airlines will carry animals to or from Belize during the summer months. For more information, contact the **Belize Humane Society and Animal Shelter**, Dr. Michael DeShield, 5 Landivar Street (at 1st Street), Belize City, 22-35963.

▼▼▼▼▼▼▼▼▼▼▼▼
Once You Arrive

VISITORS CENTERS

The best resource for travelers is in Belize City at the **Belize Tourism Board**. ~ New Central Bank Building, Level 2, Gabourel Lane, P.O. Box 325; 22-31913, 800-624-0686, fax 22-31943; www.travelbelize.org. For information on ecotourism in Belize, contact the **Belize Audubon Society**. ~ 12 Fort Street, Belize City, Belize; 22-35004, fax 22-34985; www.belizeaudubon.org. You can also try **Programme for Belize**, a private, non-profit conservation group that's one of the most effective and respected in Belize. (Among its high-profile supporters are the Nature Conservancy, Massachusetts Audubon Society and Coca-Cola Foods.) The Programme manages the 240,000-acre Rio Bravo Conservation and Management Area, including two fields stations where both scientists and travelers study forest particulars such as red-eyed tree frogs, leafcutter ants and cohune palms. ~ 1 Eyre Street, Belize City, Belize; 22-75616, fax 22-75635; www.pfbelize.org, e-mail pfbel@btl.net. Another excellent resource is the **Belize Zoo and Tropical Education Center**. ~ P.O. Box 1787, Belize City, Belize; 22-08004, fax 22-08010; www.belizezoo.org.

During a nighttime tour at The Tropical Education Center you get to hold a boa constrictor.

EMBASSIES & CONSULATES

Following is a list of foreign embassies and consulates in Belize:

BELGIUM Belgium Honorary Consul ~ 126 Freetown Road, Belize City; 22-30748, fax 22-30750.

CANADA Consulate of Canada/Consulat du Canada ~ 80 Princess Margaret Drive, P.O. Box 610, Belize City; 22-31060, fax 22-30060; e-mail cdncon,bze@btl.net.

CHILE Chilean Honorary Consul ~ 109 Hummingbird Highway, Belmopan; 82-22134, fax 82-23075.

COSTA RICA Embassy of Costa Rica ~ 10 Unity Boulevard, Belmopan; 82-1582, fax 82-21583; e-mail fborbon@btl.net.

CUBA Cuban Consul General ~ 6048 Manatee Drive, Belize City; 22-35345, fax 22-31105; e-mail embacuba@btl.net.

DENMARK Honorary Consul of Denmark ~ 35-A Regent Street, Belize City; 22-76629, fax 22-76072; e-mail eallp@btl.net.

EL SALVADOR Embassy of El Salvador ~ 49 Nache Street, Belmopan; 82-23404, fax 82-23569; e-mail embasalva@btl.net.

FRANCE French Honorary Consul ~ 109 New Road, Belize City; 22-32708, fax 22-32416.

GERMANY German Honorary Consul ~ Mile 3½ Western Highway, Belize City; 22-24371, fax 22-24375.

GUATEMALA Embassy of Guatemala ~ 8 "A" Street, Belize City; 22-33150, fax 22-35140.

HONDURAS Embassy of Honduras ~ 114 Bella Vista Street, Belize City; 22-45889, fax 22-30562.

ISRAEL Israel Honorary Consul ~ 4 Albert Street, Belize City; 22-73991, fax 22-30463.

ITALY Italian Consular Representative ~ 18 Albert Street, Belize City; 22-78449, fax 22-30385.

JAMAICA Jamaica Honorary Consul ~ 19/21 Ambergris Avenue, Belmopan; 82-22183, fax 82-23312.

MEXICO Mexican Embassy ~ 18 North Park Street, Belize City; 22-30194, fax 22-78742.

THE NETHERLANDS Netherlands Honorary Consul ~ 25 Regent Street, Belize City; 22-73227, fax 22-77037.

PANAMA Honorary Consul ~ Central American Boulevard at Mahogany Street, Belize City; 22-24551, fax 22-34863.

SWEDEN Swedish Honorary Consul General ~ 2 Daly Street, Belize City; 22-45176, fax 22-31843.

UNITED KINGDOM British High Commission ~ Embassy Square, Belmopan; 80-22146, fax 80-22761; e-mail brithicom@btl.net.

UNITED STATES United States Embassy, Consular Section ~ 29 Gabourel Lane, Belize City; 22-77161, fax 22-30802.

VENEZUELA Embassy of Venezuela ~ 19 Orchid Garden Road, Belmopan; 82-22384, fax 82-22022.

TIME

Belize is on Central Standard Time year-round. Daylight saving time is not observed here.

BUSINESS HOURS

Professional and government offices are open from 8 a.m. to noon and 1 to 4 p.m., Monday through Friday. Bank hours are from 8 a.m. to 1 p.m., Monday through Thursday. On Fridays, banks also open from 3 to 6 p.m. Retail businesses open from 8 a.m. to 5 p.m. weekdays, except for Wednesday afternoons, when they are closed. Some stores are open Friday nights from 7 to 9 p.m., and all day on Saturday.

WEIGHTS & MEASURES

Belize still uses the English system of weights and measures, the same as in the United States. Belizean units and their metric equivalents are as follows: 1 inch = 2.5 centimeters; 1 foot (12 inches) = 0.3 meter; 1 yard (3 feet) = 0.9 meter; 1 mile (5280 feet) = 1.6 kilometers; 1 ounce = 28 grams; 1 pound (16 ounces) = 0.45 kilograms; 1 quart (liquid) = 0.9 liter.

ELECTRIC VOLTAGE

You'll likely stay in places without electricity, but those that do have it carry current the same as in the United States—110 volt, 60 cycles. If you need to convert appliances from other countries, bring your own adapters.

PHONES

Belize has a good phone system. Calling into Belize is almost as easy as calling long-distance in the United States (though there's usually a bit of static). The country code for Belize is 501. Belize used to have a confusing phone system in which the number of digits in a phone number was different depending on not only what part of the country the phone customer was in but also what part you were calling from. In May 2003, the phone company switched to a new seven-digit system. A few signs, brochures and directory listings still contain the old five- or six-digit phone numbers, though. Here's how to convert from old phone numbers to new ones.

The first digit of the new phone number, the district code, works like a one-digit area code. The codes are:

Belize District (Belize City and the Cayes) ~ 2
Orange Walk District ~ 3
Corozal District ~ 4
Stann Creek District ~ 5
Cell phones ~ 6
Toledo District ~ 7
Cayo District ~ 8

IN THE WASH

After watching the local women scrub laundry every day in the rivers, the idea of having your clothes dry-cleaned seems extravagant. However, there is the **C A Coin Laundromat**. Outside the city, you can usually have your wash taken care of overnight at your lodge, though it's costly. I take a small bottle of laundry detergent, hand wash everything in the lodge sink, and hang it to dry in the trade winds. ~ 114 Barracks Road, Belize City; 20-33063.

The second digit is the type of phone service. It's usually a 2, indicating regular land-line service, but can be a 0 for prepaid service (either land-line or cellular) or 1 for regular mobile service.

The other five digits are the same as the last five digits of the old phone number. Well, usually. In some parts of the country, it seems that just about everybody has changed to a whole new phone number.

Confused? A new national phone directory was published in 2005, though it may not always be easy to find a copy—the paper in phone books is often used for other purposes. Travelers with internet access can check phone numbers at www.btl.net.

Many establishments in Belize have no phones because of the expense and, in many communities, because it literally takes years on a waiting list to get one installed. In many small towns and villages, there is no residential service and everyone shares a single public phone located at the main intersection.

All BTL (Belize Telecommunications Limited) public telephones require a prepaid phone card, available at gas stations, post offices, stores and BTL offices. You'll find public phones at BTL offices in all major towns. Calls to the U.S. cost about US$1.60 per minute.

For local or long-distance calls, your best bet is to get a phone card from your hotel or to ask your hotel manager for assistance in placing the call. You will pay any long-distance charges plus a small fee for the service.

AT&T and some other U.S.-based long-distance companies have special numbers you can dial in Belize that will connect you with an operator and let you charge international calls to your calling card, often at a lower cost than you would pay through the local phone company. Ask your long-distance carrier for a directory of international numbers.

For placing calls unassisted, here are some numbers to remember—long-distance operator: 91; international operator: 98; prefixes for dialing direct to the U.S., Canada and Europe: 95 (station to station) and 96 (person to person).

Internet cafés and e-mail offices have proliferated wherever there are phone lines. Even with computer-time charges of US$8 to US$10 per hour, e-mail is by far the most economical way to keep in touch with home. Virtually all hotels and guesthouses have internet connections (many receive 95 percent of their bookings via e-mail or the World Wide Web), and most will provide e-mail access to guests for a small charge.

So far, broadband and wireless Internet are virtually unknown in Belize.

A yellow-and-red-winged *Catonephele numilia*, a star-eyed hermit crab, a common lettuce slug—you never know what you'll find on Belize stamps. The beautiful butterflies and birds, beasts and blooms, sea life and even Maya ruins that adorn these little squares of paper are a celebration of the country's flora, fauna and history. Belize stamps are said to be some of most colorful and attractive in the world. Take a look and you'll surely agree. Besides decorating your postcards, stamps make unusual, inexpensive gifts. Stop by the **Belize City Post Office** (North Front Street, on the north side of the Swing Bridge; 22-72201) or at one of the many town offices across the country (some are run out of local homes). Postcard stamps to the United States are US$.15; stamps for letters are US$.30.

Unlike mail in other parts of Central America and in Mexico, Belize mail is highly reliable. From Belize to the U.S., mail takes one to two weeks; from the U.S. to Belize, about a week.

PRINT MEDIA

U.S. magazines, newspapers and paperback books can be found in Belize City and at some lodges throughout the country. All major Belize publications are in English. The country's biggest newspaper is the weekly *Amandala*, which is tabloid-size and full of quirky tidbits as well as breaking news. There's also the *Reporter*, which covers issues from screwworm eradication to the number of Guatemalan "aliens" who sneaked across the border that week. Pick up a copy—it's local color at its best.

The *San Pedro Sun* of Ambergris Caye is a great little island weekly with a visitors guide, the local magistrate's court news and an advice column by the anonymous Doctor Love, "the island's and possibly the world's greatest authority on just about everything, though the doctor seldom addresses matters involving the law or religion. . . ." If you're on Ambergris, don't miss Doctor Love.

HEALTH & SAFETY

Medical clinics and doctor's offices are available in towns and villages across Belize, but the level of care does not measure up to U.S. standards. The country's hospitals are typically sad-looking, overcrowded places that are not equipped to administer advanced health care. In fact, Belize City's public hospital was shut down in 2000 after three patients contracted the HIV virus from transfusions of contaminated blood. Improved blood-screening procedures are now in place, but the hospital was temporarily blocked from reopening because of building code problems that included collapsing ceilings.

A private Belize City Hospital has somewhat improved the situation. Belizeans who can afford it go to Miami or Houston for major surgery. For routine procedures and minor emergencies, **Belize Medical Associates Ltd.** is a private clinic recommended by some American expatriates. The facility employs seven physicians, including surgeons and specialists in internal medicine, pediatrics and obstetrics. A deposit in the amount of the estimated total cost of your medical treatment is required prior to admission. ~ Regent Street at Rectory Lane, Belize City; 22-70644, fax 22-33837; www.belizemedical.com.

Outside Belize City, lodges can usually recommend the best local physicians. Contact your health insurance carrier before you leave to find out the extent of your coverage while abroad.

For true medical emergencies, a San Diego–based service by the name of **Critical Air Medicine** provides air ambulance service to anywhere in Central America or Mexico—24 hours a day, every day of the year. ~ Call toll-free from Belize, 95-800-010-0268 or collect 858-571-0482.

Turista   The illness some people may encounter is diarrhea, euphemized as *turista*. Caused by food and drink carrying unfamiliar strains of bacteria, a bout can range from a 24-hour case of mild cramps to an all-out attack with several days of fever, chills and vomiting, followed by a lousy feeling that lingers on for weeks.

> Lime juice and jackass bitters are traditional preventives for stomach problems.

However, *turista* is much less common in Belize than in Mexico. This author, who consistently gets ill in Mexico (despite drastic precautions), has had no problems in Belize. No doubt it is because Belize, despite its developing country status, adheres closely to British standards of cleanliness and health. In Belize City, the British government has installed a modern purification system that seems to work just fine. In remote areas, motels and lodges usually provide bottled water in the rooms or will direct you to a grocery store that sells it. Always drink bottled liquids—mineral water, sodas, fruit drinks, soft drinks or beer—whenever possible.

Take it easy the first few days. If you sock your system with unfamiliar food and heavy liquor right away, your stomach may seek revenge. In other words, eating spicy stewed chicken followed by fried gibnut chased by Caribbean rum is asking for trouble.

Remember, those who stay healthy use the best defense: prevention. Eat with discretion. If you're in a jungle or island lodge frequented by tourists, the food is usually high quality and delicious. If you find yourself in a remote outpost, where the pickings are limited to a suspect Chinese hole-in-the-wall or a grocery store, opt for the grocer. Consume only thick-skinned fruits that you peel yourself, such as oranges and bananas, and vegetables that are cooked through. Nuts with shells, such as peanuts and coconuts, are pretty safe bets, too. Steer clear of raw seafood—*ceviche* is renowned for causing *turista*—as well as garden salads.

Be careful about street food, especially in small villages. Meat, seafood, peeled fruit used in drinks and candies on which flies have taken their naps are more risky. However, a lot of the food from stalls is delicious and very well prepared. I especially enjoy the street food in Belize City and in San Pedro, on Ambergris Caye. If the facilities look clean and the food is hot off the grill, it's probably okay. Be the judge and take your chances.

Many people believe in preventive medicine. Some take a slug of Pepto-Bismol before every meal; others, a shot of tequila, believing it will extinguish any threatening organisms. The antibiotic Doxycyclin is commonly prescribed as a preventive, although it causes sensitivity to the sun—a major inconvenience in the subtropics—and can disturb your digestive system. Belize bush doctors prescribe jackass bitters, an awful-tasting potion brewed with jungle plants, as both a preventive and remedy. One traveler from Texas, who contracted severe diarrhea, said jackass bitters cured him in several hours—though he could barely endure the taste. I also met several people, including former residents of Mexico, who swear by garlic pills as the best prevention.

If you take all the necessary precautions and still get hit with *turista*, try these remedies: Lomotil, the stopper-upper. Use sparingly. Not a cure, it's a morphine derivative that induces a kind of intestinal paralysis. Stop the dosage as soon as symptoms disappear. Paragoric, Kaopectate, Kaomycin, Imodium A.D. and Pepto-Bismol help keep the cramps down. For diarrhea with a fever, you can take Septra or Bactrium if you are not allergic to sulfa drugs. But remember that prolonged use of any antibiotic is not good for your immune system and can make you more susceptible to other tropical diseases.

Hot chamomile tea and peppermint tea soothe the stomach and often work wonders. Papaya restores the digestive tract. Light, easy-to-digest foods like toast and soup keep your strength up. Lots of nonalcoholic liquids—any kind—prevent dehydration. Carbonated water with juice of a lime is another popular stomach soother.

Rest and relaxation will help your body heal faster than if you run around sick and wear yourself down further. The symptoms should pass within 24 hours or so, and a case of *turista* seems to

GETTING THE ITCH OUT

For various bug bites, Benadryl ointment and pills take the itch out and reduce swelling. Caladryl (a blend of Benadryl and calamine lotion) also works well, as does lime juice. Sticking the affected part for a few minutes under water as hot as you can stand it has been recommended for mosquito bites. For sea thimble and sea lice bites, Belizeans splash on vinegar to reduce swelling and take the heat out. If you do get zapped with a rash of bites, avoid the sun for a few days. Direct sun causes even more swelling and inflammation, and slows healing.

have an immunizing effect—any subsequent bouts you may have will be less severe, and eventually your body will adjust to the foreign water's bacteria.

In rare cases, diarrhea may be a symptom of a more serious illness like amoebic dysentery or cholera. See a doctor if the diarrhea persists beyond three days or if you have a high fever.

Mosquitoes and Other Pests   Ask anyone who's spent a night in the jungle and they will tell you: The most ferocious animal is not a jaguar but a mosquito. Mosquitoes fiercely protect their territory in this region of the world, known aptly as "The Mosquito Coast." The little buzzers are thickest in rainforests, swamp areas and along coastal bush. The best defenses are long sleeves and pants, and plenty of good insect repellent.

What works for you may not work for someone else. People who wish to avoid DEET, the active chemical in most commercial mosquito repellents, may want to investigate some other methods. Herb shops and health food stores in the U.S. sell good-smelling potions that are more or less protective lotions made from oils and herbal essences. Some people swear by daily doses of Vitamin B$_6$ or garlic, others by tobacco smoke. The new electronic mosquito repellent devices, which emit a sound pitched at the high edge of human hearing, got high marks from a visitor to Guatemala's dense Petén jungle. Many Belizeans, following an ancient Maya custom, burn abandoned termite nests to chase away mosquitoes. After trying dozens of different brands, pills and treatments, I have found that only the strongest repellent (such as Deep Woods OFF!) keeps me bugless. For areas of moderate infestation, the pleasant-smelling Skintastic (also made by OFF!), sold either as a pump spray or lotion, does the trick.

Campers will find that mosquito netting is more important than a tent or a sleeping bag. Many jungle lodges drape mosquito nets over the beds and provide mosquito coils that will burn all night.

Sandflies, also called flying teeth or no-see-ums, are mite-sized bugs with a giant bite. Like mosquitoes, sandflies steal the best part of the day, emerging in droves at dawn and dusk. Unlike mosquitoes, they will prey on the tiny grooves and crevices of the human body—ears, nose, eyelids. Besides a powerful repellent, wear a hat and a pair of sunglasses.

Less well-known but no less of a pest, **bottlass**, or "bottle-ass," flies are minuscule rainforest dwellers that inflict angry, itching blisters. As the flies fill with blood, their stomachs puff up and give the appearance of tiny flying bottles—hence the nickname.

Bottlass flies should not be confused with **botflies**, which don't bite in the traditional sense, but whose larvae burrow under the flesh after being deposited by a mosquito or bottlass fly. It causes only minor itching the first few days, but as the larva grows

Text continued on page 32.

Custom
Adventures

To truly understand and appreciate Belize, it must be explored and then savored, like an exotic food one learns to enjoy. One way to experience the country's complex, multifaceted terrain and culture is to take a specialty tour. Specialty expeditions offer unusual insights into people, wildlife and places few travelers have seen, and encounters with a world virtually unchanged over centuries.

International Expeditions (One Environs Park, Helena, AL 35080; 205-428-1700, 800-633-4734; www.ietravel.com), widely regarded as one of the best stateside organizers of specialty tours to Belize, offers several unique expeditions:

• A nine-day **Rainforests of the Maya Heartland** trip offers exceptional opportunities for seeing peccaries, tapirs, scarlet macaws and much more wildlife. Naturalist walks, horseback rides through the rainforest, river rafting, a Garifuna cultural gathering and a side-trip to Tikal are other highlights of the trip.

• A 10-day **Naturalist's Quest** takes in more than a half-dozen reserves, parks and sanctuaries as well as the Maya sites of Lamanai, Xunantunich and the great ancient city of Tikal, Guatemala. The trip finishes with an exploration of the barrier reef off Ambergris Caye.

The Belize Adventure Week offered by **Slickrock Adventures** starts inland with mountain biking, Maya ruin treks and whitewater running on the Macal River, then moves out to Glover's Reef for kayaking, snorkeling and diving. You'll stay in screened cabins in the jungle, and sleep in beach tents on remote Long Caye. ~ P.O. Box 1400, Moab, UT 84532; 800-390-5715, fax 435-259-6996; www.slickrock.com, e-mail slickrock@slickrock.com.

You can explore cool mountain pine forest on horseback, float along a river through caves of dazzling limestone or stroll the jungle during the black of night (accompanied by a bush guide, of course) at **Mountain**

Equestrian Trails. Located in western Belize in the Slate Creek Preserve, "M.E.T." (as it's called locally) offers overnight accommodations in simple cabanas, and meals and drinks at its popular cantina. ~ Mile 8, Pine Ridge Road, Cayo; 82-04041, fax 82-23361; www.metbelize.com, e-mail aw2trav2bz@aol.com.

The educational field station at **Maya Mountain Lodge**, located near San Ignacio, is the starting point for **Archaeology and Natural History Tours** across western Belize. Two popular tours are the four-night **Ruta Maya Experience** and three-night **Maya Adventure**. ~ 82-22164, fax 82-42029; www.mayamountain.com/tour. Also near San Ignacio, **Chaa Creek Cottages** provides an array of nature and archaeological expeditions ranging from two to four days. ~ 82-42037, fax 82-42501; www.chaacreek.com, e-mail chaacreek@btl.net.

High-school and college students as well as educators can sign up for independent programs at **Language and Travel Study**. Professor Steve Tash runs the programs through the University of California at Santa Barbara and Seattle Central Community College. Students are eligible for college credit for traveling, working, volunteering, attending a language school or living with a family in Belize. Among the independent study courses offered: "Spanish-Language Enhancement and Social Science Research." ~ P.O. Box 16501, Irvine, CA 92623; 949-552-8332, fax 949-552-0740; e-mail travelstudy@yahoo.com.

Many tour companies specialize in environment-oriented expeditions across Belize. A few of the best include:

Belize Close Encounters, P.O. Box 1320, Detroit Lakes, MN 56502; 218-847-4441, 888-875-1822, fax 218-817-4442; www.belizeclose encounters.com, e-mail belizejg@tekstar.com.

International Zoological Expeditions (the oldest tour company operating in Belize, established in 1972); 210 Washington Street, Sherborn, MA 01770, 508-655-1461 or 800-548-5843, fax 508-655-4445; www.ize2belize.com, e-mail ize2belize@aol.com.

and feeds, its prickly body burns and pinches its victim. Botfly larvae breathe through a tiny hole in the victim's skin, so the way to kill them is to smother them by masking the hole (Belizeans use everything from Scotch tape and moistened tobacco leaves to petroleum jelly), then squeeze them out. If this sounds truly horrible, it isn't. Kids living and playing in the jungle get them all the time, and so do the animals. And chances are, unless you spend many days in the jungle during rainy season, you will probably never experience a botfly.

Before you head out to Belize's beautiful seas, you should become acquainted with **sea thimbles**, **sea lice** and **stingrays**. The first is a tiny brown, thimble-shaped jellyfish that scoots along the surface of the water. If you swim along the surface, it will scoot with you and inflict little bites that later turn into big red welts. Sea lice, the larvae of sea thimbles, also lurk on the surface and bestow measles-looking bite marks that itch for a week. Unfortunately, sea lice are invisible.

Even if you are with a group, the Swing Bridge is not safe at night. During the day, however, feel free to cross as often as you like.

You can usually avoid sea thimbles by not swimming where you see them. Occasionally, they are so small and pervasive, they look like underwater particles. Sea lice are impossible to avoid, but you can minimize the bites by rinsing your body in fresh water. Don't rinse until you've removed your swimsuit; fresh water trapped under your suit could cause the larvae to swell and sting you even worse.

Like sea lice, stingrays are tough to see. The flat slippery creatures camouflage themselves in the sand along shallow areas and can deliver a wicked puncture with their stingers. To avoid being stung, shuffle away. If you're stung, see a doctor at once.

Drugs   Drug problems have grown acute in some parts of Belize, which is on the Cocaine Trail from Colombia to the United States. Smugglers typically pay their local workers with cocaine, which is often converted into crack and sold to addicts. Tourist police generally do a good job of keeping crackheads from bothering visitors, but the majority of all prison inmates are serving time for cocaine-related crimes.

Marijuana farms abound in Belize. If you have any doubts, check a local map; the bigger fields are often clearly marked. Out in the bush, when locals want some "Belize breeze," they visit the village pot farmer. They *do not* help themselves to a local field; doing so could result in physical harm. If you should happen upon a marijuana field, resist any urges to go exploring. Many growers protect their crop as though it were their lives.

On the Cayes—especially Caye Caulker, whose past reputation as a druggie hangout still lingers—local breeze vendors will often sell bags of marijuana partly on credit. (This only seems to happen on the cayes, where it's easy to keep an eye on who leaves the island.) Visitors who buy marijuana on the pay-you-later plan are well advised to keep their word. If you forget to pay your debts, the dealer will report you to the police, who will search your hotel room. A typical fine for tourists is more than US$4000; the alternative would be up to five years in Belize's national prison at Hattieville.

(A peculiarity of the Belizean justice system is that anyone convicted of a crime other than rape or first-degree murder can pay a sizeable fine instead of serving prison time. The official attitude is, why spend money building prisons when you can make money from fines instead? Thus only the poor go to prison.)

Crime   Belize is sparsely populated and has very little big-city crime. Plus, most Belizeans are extremely proud, family-oriented and peace-loving. Traveling here is like traveling through a jungle version of the American midwest—lots of country roads and friendly people. I spent several weeks crisscrossing Belize in a four-wheel drive by myself and had not one problem. Even in Belize City, where everyone seems to have an "I-got-robbed" story, I felt quite at ease.

But Belize City is famous for petty thieves, just as certain U.S. cities have a well-deserved reputation for crime. When choosing a hotel, make sure it's in a safe part of town, preferably one that's frequented by travelers. All lodges recommended in this book are located in safe neighborhoods. After the stroke of dusk, stay away from the Swing Bridge, the infamous hangout of petty thieves.

The safest place to be in Belize City at night is at your hotel; the second safest is the Fort George neighborhood. Areas of downtown where there is a lot of activity after dark are safer than outlying neighborhoods. Don't tempt fate by wandering around dark back streets late at night. Stay away from drug deals. In short, exercise the same caution you would use at home. Observe these common-sense precautions, and feel fortunate that you are not in New York City, where—unlike in Belize City—the petty criminals carry guns.

Be aware that whenever you are in public, any thief who happens to be around will be checking you out. Foreign tourists are natural targets for theft because they stand out in a crowd and seem wealthy in a country where the average income amounts to US$10 a day. Use common sense. Watch out for pickpockets and purse-snatchers, especially in public markets and other crowded places. Carry your trip funds, passport and other important documents in a money pouch or hidden pocket inside your clothing. Keep cash in your side pocket, never a back pocket. Carry day-packs under one arm rather than on your back. Don't leave wallets or cameras lying on the beach while you go for a swim or sitting on a table while you go to the restroom. Always lock your hotel room and car. Park in a secured lot at night. Don't leave radios, gifts, cassettes or other temptations visible inside the car. Dress with humility; a thief will focus on the best-dressed, richest-looking tourist around, so make sure it's not you.

Once you leave Belize City, relax. Except for the town of Orange Walk, Belmopan and the island of Caye Caulker, which have their share of drug dealers, the rest of the country is rural and crime is rare. You should, of course, always exercise common sense. Never carry large amounts of cash or leave valuables unattended in public places. But don't be alarmed to find there aren't any locks on your lodge door—there are few thieves in the jungle!

Transportation

AIR

By far the best way to get to Belize is to fly. Commercial airlines fly daily between the United States and Canada and the international airport in Belize City. TACA and Continental offer daily service from major U.S. cities to Belize City. American Airlines offers daily service from Miami. US Airways offers service from Charlotte, North Carolina, five times a week.

Baggage allowances on international flights are generally the same as on U.S. domestic flights—two carry-on items that are small enough to fit under the seat or in an overhead rack, plus two pieces of checked luggage. In addition, some Latin American airlines have a weight limitation—typically 40 kilograms (88 pounds)—on checked luggage. All airlines allow considerably more baggage than you would want to carry around on this trip.

During special events, holidays and the November-to-April high season make flight reservations at least a month in advance. Air delays are common. So are flight cancellations—be sure to confirm your flight 72 hours before departure, and allow the same amount of time when confirming your return flight. Canceled flights seem to be a particular problem between Belize City and Flores (the airport for Guatemala's Tikal National Park), where the next flight out may not be for several days.

Visitors leaving Belize by air are required to pay a departure tax of US$35 (usually included in the price of international airline tickets) and a conservation fee of US$3.75.

When booking your international airline tickets, if you will be taking a connecting flight on your return trip be sure to allow plenty of time. At the hub airport where you first land in the United States—probably Miami, New Orleans or Houston—you will have to wait for and claim your baggage, clear U.S. Customs, and recheck your bags before boarding your onward flight. Allow one-and-a-half to two hours.

Local flights, usually aboard twin-engine puddle hoppers, leave from either the **Phillip S. W. Goldson International Airport** in Ladyville, nine miles north of Belize City, or from the **Belize City Municipal Airport**, on the north end of town. As with international flights, local flights must be confirmed by phone 72 hours before departure.

Tropic Air operates an hourly shuttle from Belize City to San Pedro (Ambergris Caye) and also flies to Caye Caulker, to Corozal in the north and to points in the south. Tropic Air also has flights twice daily to Flores, Guatemala, the gateway to Tikal. ~ 22-62012, 800-422-3435 in the U.S.; www.tropicair.com. **Maya Island Air** also has flights to Flores, to the Belize cayes and to points across Southern Belize. ~ 22-31140; www.mayaislandair.com.

For service to Belize's out islands, such as Lighthouse Reef, and to remote inland areas of Belize and Guatemala, call **Javier's Flying Service**. The charter company uses low-flying planes that offer enthralling views of the mountains and jungle as well as of the barrier reef running through iridescent blue waters. ~22-35360; www.javiersflying.com.

Getting to and from the Airport   Taxis charge about US$25 (BZ$50)—per trip, *not* per person—for the nine-mile trip from Phillip S. W. Goldson International Airport, in Ladyville, to Belize City. That's the maximum fare allowed by the government, so don't pay more. There is no bus service from the airport to Belize City.

BUS

There's only one class of bus in Belize, and it's closer to a school bus than a Greyhound bus. However, service is extensive and usually on time, and the fares are cheap. The express bus from Belize City to Corozal, near the Mexican border, is only US$5. To San Ignacio in the west, the fare is US$4. Be advised that if you're traveling during "rush" hour on a popular route, like the one between Belize City and Belmopan, get there early or you may not get a seat.

Current schedules and fares are available from the **Belize Tourism Board**. ~ New Central Bank Building, Level 2, Gabourel Lane, P.O. Box 325, Belize City; 22-31913, 800-624-0686 in the U.S.; www.travelbelize.org.

FASTEN YOUR SEATBELTS!

Within Belize, flying is still the quickest, least tiring way to get around, and is cheaper than hiring a taxi or renting a car. Most flights are aboard loud, twin-engine puddle hoppers that carry 10 to 20 passengers and feel like flying jalopies. The ride will either thrill or unnerve you, depending on your level of adventure, though you will no doubt find the scenery from above unsurpassed on the ground.

You can also find schedules and make reservations online at www.belizenet.com.

CAR

Traveling from the United States to Belize by car is a challenging and time-consuming adventure. Not that it's particularly dangerous—just demanding. The drive to Belize from Brownsville, Texas, through Mexico, is almost 1400 miles. It can be done in roughly 55 hours of actual driving time. To make the journey comfortably, without arriving in Belize exhausted, allow at least a week. Most Mexican highways are two-lane roads, not limited-access freeways, and driving takes longer than you would expect.

If you are driving to Belize from the U.S. border, plan well ahead for refueling and evening stops. Gas stations in Mexico are a government monopoly, and in much of the country they are few and far between. Never pass up an opportunity to fill your vehicle's tank. Driving after dark can be dangerous (the most common hazards are vehicles stopped in the traffic lane without lights and vehicles traveling without lights well after dusk—sometimes considered a display of Mexican machismo).

Unleaded fuel is sold by the gallon in Belize at about twice the price of gas in the United States. Most towns have gas stations that are open during the day. If you plan a long excursion into the rainforest, fill up beforehand. Otherwise, if you stick to the paved Western and Northern highways, you're never far from a gas station.

Motor Vehicle Requirements   For driving in Belize, your current driver's license is valid. If you're bringing your own car via Mexico, you'll need a Mexican car permit and Mexican auto insurance. To obtain a car permit (a special stamp on the owner's tourist card, issued for up to 180 days), you need proof of ownership—a current registration certificate and title. If the title shows a lien against the vehicle or if it is registered in another person's name or a company name, you need a notarized letter from the lienholder or owner authorizing you to take the vehicle

TAXI TIMES

Most taxi drivers are good public relations for Belize: they're friendly, knowledgeable and in a hurry when you need them to be. Otherwise, they'll admonish you to slow way down, reminding that you are, after all, in Belize. Indeed, some of the most memorable Belize experiences are in taxis. One American woman recalls how, in the middle of a trip, a driver asked for part of his fare in advance to buy his wife a chicken for dinner. After a brief stop at the market, the woman spent the rest of the trip in the back seat with a clucking, flapping chicken.

to Mexico for a specified time. The owner or driver who has the car permit stamp on his or her tourist card must be in the car whenever it is being driven.

Anyone bringing a motor vehicle into Mexico must show either a major credit card or a collision/comprehensive insurance policy valid for the duration of the stay. Otherwise, the owner can be required to post a cash bond guaranteeing that he or she will return with the vehicle to the United States. The Mexican government has promised to simplify procedures for temporarily importing vehicles; for current requirements, contact a Mexican consulate in the United States.

Auto insurance policies issued in the United States are not valid in Belize or Mexico. Purchase motor vehicle liability insurance (and, if you wish, collision/comprehensive) before crossing into Mexico. Insurance is sold by agencies on the U.S. side at all border crossings. Causing an auto accident is a crime under Mexican law, which presumes defendants guilty until proven innocent. This means that if you are involved in an accident that causes property damage, your vehicle will be impounded until you pay the damage and a fine. If any person is injured in the accident, you will go to jail.

The documentation you need to take your vehicle into Mexico is more than sufficient to bring it into Belize. However, Belize requires local liability insurance, which can be fairly expensive.

Driving in Belize   Nothing makes you feel more Belizean than bounding down a rocky, washed-out jungle road in a rented four-wheel drive, Maya beads swinging from the rear view mirror and punta rock music pounding from a radio that's ready to pop out of the dash. The scenery is priceless—barefoot village kids racing through banana groves, iguanas darting across the road, Maya women toting fresh-cut corn for their tortillas—but the pace is painfully slow. Except for five paved "highways," inland Belize is a tangle of dirt and rock roads. After a few days, you will learn that every dirt road is not created equal; they fall into three general categories:

Type 1: a wide, clay washboard surface that allows you to travel at a nice 35 mph clip

Type 2: narrow marl limestone road with scattered rocks the size of golf balls. Maximum speed: 25 mph

Type 3: a narrow, roller-coaster trail that looks like the scene of a bomb explosion. Rubble everywhere; rocks the size of baseballs. Maximum speed: 10 mph, with the windows clattering.

It is the Type 3 road that often leads to the best lodges, Maya ruins and nature reserves, and so must be reckoned with. After a while, your body becomes used to the jarring, and you learn to accept how long it takes to go a short distance. And perhaps for the first time in your life, you become overjoyed at the sight of asphalt.

Belize's five paved "highways" (actually two-lane roads with treacherous speed bumps) are in fairly good shape. The **Northern Highway** runs from Belize City north to the Mexico border; the **Old Northern Highway** parallels the Northern Highway for about 40 miles; and the **Western Highway**, which starts near Belize City, heads west to the Guatemala border. On the Western Highway, distances are measured in "mile posts," little white cement markers planted beside the road.

The **Hummingbird Highway** is a good paved road as far as Dangriga. All but nine miles of the **Southern Highway** south of Dangriga have recently been widened and paved, and the drive takes only four hours instead of ten as in the past. Financed by the Taiwanese government, which operates large-scale shrimp farms in the area, the highway is being paved for the benefit of agricultural trucking, not tourism; the road to Placencia remains as rough as ever—"painful driving," in local lingo. There are only a few gas stations along Belizean highways, located 40 miles apart. When in doubt, top off your tank.

I recommend driving a four-wheel-drive vehicle—preferably a small, easily maneuverable one, available from most car rental agencies. If you visit during the rainy season, check local road conditions before setting off through the jungle. Many roads flood and are impassable from June through September.

Belize is so undeveloped that though it's possible to get lost while driving, it's hard to stay that way for very long. Most towns have only a handful of roads (many without names), and getting around is as easy as driving around the block. When asking directions, don't be surprised if you get a reply like, "Head toward the ocean and take a right at the third palm tree." Only Belize City requires any real navigation, and even there the streets are laid out in an easy-to-get-around fashion. Pick up a free city and country map from the **Belize Tourism Board**. ~ New Central Bank Building, Level 2, Gabourel Lane, P.O. Box 325, Belize City; 22-31913, 800-624-0686 in the U.S.; www.travelbelize.org. Car-rental companies also provide good maps.

Renting a Car   Renting a car gives you the freedom to explore at leisure (and avoid the hot, tiny public buses). Reputable companies recommend four-wheel-drive vehicles—a necessity for navigating Belize's rocky roads. Be prepared to pay dearly; four-wheel drives run about US$100 per day, including unlimited miles and insurance. Beware of companies that offer lower rates for old, gas-guzzling American cars. After paying for gas (and possibly breaking down), you will have spent more than if you had rented a new four-wheel drive.

If you reserve a car through a company's toll-free U.S. office, be sure to reconfirm with the office in Belize City. The easiest, least expensive way is to send a fax. Anyone 25 years or older, with a passport, a driver's license and a major credit card, can rent a car in Belize. Take the optional extra insurance that lowers your deductible for damage to the vehicle. Rental cars in Belize lead hazardous existences, subjected as they are to the rocky, mountainous terrain and pothole-laced roads.

Though most car rental agencies won't let you take their vehicles out of the country, you can rent a car to drive to Tikal in Guatemala from **Crystal Auto Rental Ltd.**, Belize's longest-established car rental agency. ~ Belize International Airport; 22-31600, fax 22-31900, or 800-777-7777 in the U.S.; www.crystal-belize.com, e-mail crystal@btl.net. Otherwise, it's best to take a bus across the border.

TAXI

The Belize government sets maximum fares for regular taxi routes around the country. Reputable drivers will have the fare schedule posted in their cars. The prices are high by U.S. standards, but considering the condition of Belize roads and the price of gas, they are actually quite reasonable. One driver who frequently travels to southern Belize, the land of rugged roads, replaces his car every year.

Cars for Hire Almost all taxi drivers double as tour guides, and will customize an itinerary and negotiate a fair fee. Many specialize in certain Maya ruins and wildlife reserves, and will act as bush guides. If you enjoy your tour, a tip of 10 to 15 percent is in order. Ask your hotel about qualified drivers, or check with the **Belize Tourism Board**. ~ New Central Bank Building, Level 2, Gabourel Lane, P.O. Box 325, Belize City; 22-31913, 800-624-0686 in the U.S.; www.travelbelize.org.

HITCHING

Because bus service is widely available, there's really no need to hitchhike. Anyway, Belize is so small that if you do need a short ride, someone usually knows someone willing to give you a lift.

TWO

The Land and
Outdoor Adventures

 **GEOGRAPHY** Few regions as small as Belize are so physically diverse. Where else, in a space the size of Massachusetts, do you find cool pine forests and saunalike jungle, luscious green islands and parched brown savannah, majestic mountains and flat muddy swamps? There are hushed coastal lagoons and fizzing streams, thundering waterfalls and shadowy rivers cocooned in jungle. And then there is the emerald sea, which stretches to the horizon where it blends into sky. Everywhere there is wild landscape, but few people.

Offshore, many of the untamed and mostly uninhabited cayes are actually peaks of the Maya Mountain Range. These coral rock islets peek up from a shallow underwater valley, called the Inner Channel, that runs from the Belize coast out to a great barrier reef. The reef, in turn, stretches some 180 miles from the Gulf of Honduras to the Bay of Chetumal in southern Yucatán. Formed over thousands of years, and second in scope only to Australia's Great Barrier Reef, Belize's reef system is complex beyond imagination: millions of life forms interacting and interdepending, yet so fragile that humans could obliterate them in a few years.

If coral defines the reef, then limestone is the trademark of northern Belize. In fact, the northern region is the end of a great limestone shelf that reaches down from the Yucatán Peninsula. From the air, you can see the vast flat shelf poking out into the frothy green Caribbean Sea. A thin layer of soil covers much of the limestone and is fertile enough to support a healthy sugar business. In the winter, farmers burn underbrush from the cane fields, and dark smoke clings to the skies.

But most of northern Belize still belongs to the forests—mangrove along the coast, pine and palmetto along a central plain, and luxurious broadleaf rainforests in the west. Ponds, lagoons and swamps decorate the forests, as do abandoned logging camps—testaments to centuries when mowing down trees was the biggest business in Belize. Today, many camps lie within reserves where selective logging is practiced.

The land across central and western Belize is rippled with hills and valleys and terraced fields and with spidery rivers that nourish the fields. Out in the district

40

known as Cayo, broadleaf jungle is interspersed with great forests of slash pines, where the soil is a mix of sand and clay, and waterfalls and bubbling streams create vistas of stunning beauty. The limestone here is ancient, probably of the Cretaceous Age, and eons of percolating water have created vast sinkholes, caves and underground streams.

The Maya Mountains form a spine of granite down southern Belize. Most prominent of all Belize's natural features, they are marked by deep canyons and shallow valleys, snaking rivers and ebbing ridges that eventually rise to Victoria Peak, Belize's highest at 3675 feet. But mostly the area is solid jungle, with parts so dense and remote they have yet to be visited by modern-day humans. Southern Belize boasts true "cloud forests," tropical rainforests high enough to enjoy thick mists and rains most every day. Here there are double canopies of trees, with cohune palms that reach five stories high and deep webs of bromeliads and mosses that thrive in perpetual dampness.

Flora

Seeing the jungle for the first time is exhilarating, indeed overwhelming. Take just one tree. Soaring like an ancient column, its limbs drip with perfumed orchids and lacy mosses, its branches offer refuge to both a hawk's nest and a nest of yellow wasps, its trunk bears the scrapings of a jaguar along with the scars of a human machete. Vines and epiphytes—plants with aerial roots—creep and curl around the tree in orderly fashion and then slither away on the jungle floor. Wildly colored fungi cling to its wood and leaves and ferns blanket its feet. On this, a single tree, the intricate web of life is nearly beyond comprehension.

Yet this one tree is but a blink in the Belizean florascape. In fact, it would take volumes of books to do justice to the flora of Belize. Within this fabulously diverse region are more than 4000 species of flowering plants, including 250 different orchids and 700 types of trees. There are heart-shaped anthuriums and paddle-shaped heliconia, flaming bromeliads and purple passion flowers. And there is much beauty that does not bloom—water-gorged jungle plants and cathedrals of pine trees, island palms burdened with coconuts and grand old cedar and mahogany trees that somehow eluded the logger's axe. There are strangler figs that can fell a 100-foot oak tree, and vines that will wound with their thorns and then heal that wound with their leaves. And there are jungles so unimaginably dense they have buried whole cities for thousands of years.

Here, in Eden-like settings, bromeliads and orchids grow as big as tree trunks and trees grow as tall as skyscrapers. Guanacaste trees, which can reach 400 feet high, are decorated with flowering air plants—making them nature's own Christmas trees. The bookut also grows tall and wide, with a canopy spanning about

40 feet. Howler monkeys love to eat its seed pods, though the pods' musky smell gives the tree its nickname of "stinking toe."

The black oozing sap from the poisonwood tree inflicts angry blisters that last up to two weeks. The antidote, used since the time of the Maya, is to apply sap from the gumbo limbo. Near every poisonwood tree there's always a gumbo limbo tree.

The sap from the sapodilla tree fueled the country's largest industry during the first half of this century. Chicling, or the harvest of sapodilla sap, was accomplished by *chicleros*, rugged bushmen who would climb 40 to 60 feet up a sapodilla tree, then, working their way back down, use a machete to slash deep zigzags along the trunk. Chicle was used as a base for chewing gum (remember Chiclets?). Today, Belize forests are filled with sapodilla trees, though rare is the one that does not bear the scars of a *chiclero*.

But it is the cohune palm, with its thick trunk and elegant plumed fronds, that has come to symbolize Belize's jungles. Preferring to grow in deep, rich, well-drained soil, cohunes have been an integral part of local life since the time of the Maya. Virtually every part of this exquisite tree can be used—the sturdy fronds for making thatched roofs; the tender hearts, as a culinary delicacy; the tiny, coconutlike nuts, for making charcoal and oil. Today, Maya villagers boil the nuts to extract the oil, which is bottled in a glass jar, corked with a corn cob and sold at the markets. Surely no Belize sight is more mystical than that of cohune palms dripping in the foggy aftermath of a forest rain, looking like wispy giants of the jungle.

Riverbanks play host to dense webs of spiny bamboo, whose love of water makes it amenable to floods. The bamboo protects the banks from erosion, and protects itself with sharp barbs that can reach four inches long. Few trees can protect themselves from the strangler fig, which slowly and methodically kills its prey. The strangler wraps its roots around a tree trunk until, after a few years, the roots grow and fuse, choking the tree to death. The trunk falls and becomes hollow, providing shelter for a variety of animals. Bats particularly love the damp, dark space where they can escape the light of day.

The jungles are also thick with tropical fungi that bloom with brilliant color and take on exotic shapes. Ferns cool the forest with their double ceiling canopies and provide food for many animals. In less dense areas, ferns also form soft green carpets that make openings in the forest.

Out of the jungle and along the Caribbean coast, the flora resembles many people's idea of tropical paradise: shade-giving papaya, mango and breadfruit trees; rambling bougainvillea and hibiscus bursting with brilliant color; and wind-blown palms, heavy with coconuts. Exotic flowers, such as red ginger and birds of paradise, grow wild. Here, too, are the mangroves, propped along the shore, looking like bushes on stilts.

MEDICINAL PLANTS AND NATURAL HEALING   For thousands of years, Belize's rainforests have yielded plants, trees and shrubs prized for their medicinal value. These "healing" plants and their uses are carefully guarded secrets, passed down through generations of Maya bush doctors, though today many Maya villagers use the jungle as their backyard medicine cabinet. The leaves of the wild pineapple plant, for instance, can be heated and formed into a cast to set injured bones. The seeds from the custard apple are a sure cure for head lice and the sinewy, water-gorged grapevine supplies water so pure the Maya used it to cleanse newborn babies—a practice that continues today. The prickly "give and take" vine stabs with its spikes, then stops the blood flow with its leaves. And the gnarly bullhoof vine, when boiled and consumed as a liquid, will stop internal bleeding.

> During World War II, the U.S. Air Force used the husks of cohune palms to make charcoal filter masks for its pilots.

One tree, the negrito, is nicknamed the dysentery bark tree for its ability to cure that often-fatal disease. In the days of New World exploration, the tree's bark saved European sailors suffering from severe cases of dysentery and diarrhea. They promptly named it dysentery bark, and began shipping it to Europe, where it was worth its weight in gold for over 200 years.

For stomach problems experienced by many of today's travelers, there is jackass bitters, also known as *tres puntas*. The boiled leaves, turned into a tea or wine tincture, are a powerful antidote to parasites, amoebas, giardia and even malaria. The taste is so bitter, however, that some have trouble keeping it down.

Of course, there are hundreds, perhaps thousands, of other healing plants residing in the jungle. It is impossible to recognize them without some training. Several places around Belize offer jungle tours that explain basic medicinal plants. The best is the Rainforest Medicine Trail (formerly called the Panti Maya Medicine Trail) near San Ignacio, where Americans Rosita Arvigo and Gregory Shropshire are conducting research on natural cures for cancer, AIDS and other diseases. Grants from several U.S. organizations, including the National Cancer Research Institute and U.S. A.I.D., are funding their work.

Bottled herbal treatments, labeled Rainforest Remedies, and herb packets are available at the trail, or by mail by writing to Dr. Rosita Arvigo, Ix Chel Tropical Research Foundation, San Ignacio, Cayo, Belize, Central America. Among the potions are:

Belly Be Good, a mild sedative for indigestion, gastritis and constipation. Made with man vine.

Blood Tonic, for anemia, rheumatism, arthritis and fatigue. High in iron and minerals, and made with wild yam and China root.

Female Tonic, for menstrual cramps or irregularities. Made with man vine, contribo, guaco and copalchi.

Flu Away, for colds and flu. Made with garlic, cane, jackass bitters and alcohol.

Jackass Bitters Tea, a bitter-tasting brew for internal parasites, amoebas, malaria, ringworm and yeast infections.

Male Tonic, for impotence and kidney and bladder problems. Made with balsam bark, corn silk, man vine root and cane alcohol water.

Sunburn Ointment, made of beeswax, aloe, herbs and vegetable shortening.

Travelers Tonic, for that pesky *turista*. Made with guava leaf and jackass bitters.

Fauna

It is a feat of nature that a place as small as Belize should possess such a mindboggling array of exotic animals.

Here among the Maya mysteries live mysterious creatures like spiny anteaters and kinkajou bears, long-nosed bats and portly tapirs, scaly iguanas and gangly Jesus Christ lizards—who actually *can* walk on water.

These enchanting animals thrive in Belize's amazing range of environments—pine forest, dry savannah, moist jungle and rainforest, offshore islands, low coastal plains and swampland. However, as their homes quickly succumb to farming and development, many face extinction. During recent years, Belize has set aside protected sanctuaries where animals can flourish and people can view their worlds. With a little time and patience, one soon learns how easy it is to witness this wonderful wildlife.

MAMMALS

Jaguars "God decided to make man because the jaguar already existed," begins a Maya folktale, related in the book *Jaguar*. The jaguar was in fact a god to the ancient Maya, steeped in mystery and worshiped from a distance. Today's Maya still revere, and fear, this king of carnivores they call *balum*.

Jaguars are brooding creatures who prefer a solitary life and lots of room—a male will roam over a 100-square-mile area. They are massive, weighing as much as 300 pounds, and cloaked in downy soft coats with spots that are sometimes shaped like flowers and butterflies. Despite their reputation for aggression, jaguars rarely attack people unless provoked. A caged jaguar, however, will hypnotize you with his eyes; one flinch and he will charge his fence.

The jaguar is a night lover, using the cool blackness of the jungle underbrush to pursue its favorite meal—prickly, piglike peccaries. When a jaguar attacks, it is lightning-fast: one swipe to the neck with its massive paw, then a head-crushing blow with knifelike teeth. But a jaguar is not a picky eater, and will feast on whatever mammals come around: monkeys, deer, otters, birds, and even iguana and fish. During the day, it dozes on a bed of leaves or on fallen tree trunks.

Other Cats   The Belize jungles are also home to other exotic cats—pumas, ocelots, margays and jaguarundis—who, like the jaguar, are threatened by poaching. Pumas are in fact quite rare, having been nearly obliterated by hunters, and it is doubtful you will see one in the wild. Known also as cougars or mountain lions, they love the mountains as well as low forests and savannah. Pumas are slightly smaller than jaguars, weighing up to 200 pounds, and have wild, piercing eyes and fur the color of honey.

Mangroves are crucial to the environment, as they provide nurseries for birds and animals and protect the shore from erosion.

Ocelots are much smaller, less than 35 pounds, and margays are the size of big housecats. Both are slender and dainty, and exquisitely garbed in velvety coats with spots and stripes that run together like watercolors. Sadly, it is their gorgeous coats that make them more valuable dead than alive.

Jaguarundis do not look like cats as much as weasels, with long, barrel-shaped bodies, stumpy legs and snaking tails. Most common of all wild cats, with coats that are dark brown to black, they prefer to live in savannahs and scrub forests, foraging the ground for small prey.

Tapirs   Belize's national animal may also be its homeliest, growing as large as 650 pounds, sporting a long upper lip and splayed toes, covered with hairless ashen skin, and boasting characteristics of both the pig and cow. It is, in fact, a relative of the rhinoceros and the horse, though its nickname is mountain cow. Tapirs will live anywhere there are tasty plants and fruit, from dry savannah to swampy mangroves to dense rainforest, but they never pass up a chance to wallow in a mudhole. In fact, tapirs' primary defense mechanism is to submerge themselves in a pond with only their nostrils above the water's surface. Away from water, they are at the mercy of human and animal predators, though male tapirs often try to protect themselves by urinating on their enemies, which they can do with marksmanlike accuracy at a range of 20 feet or more.

Belize's most famous tapir, April, is one of several that live at the Belize Zoo. Every April, school children from around the country gather to celebrate her birthday and watch April gulp down a two-foot-tall cake of horse chow, bananas and carrots. Don't miss a chance to visit April; it will probably be your only encounter with a tapir. The bright animals are shy, having been hunted to near extinction in every Latin American country but Belize. Though they are not particularly good to eat, tapirs are thought to be cattle killers (which they're not), and local myths say they cast spells on people. Baby tapirs, which have spots and stripes, are especially feared. Unfortunately, some people shoot tapirs just for the sport of it, leaving them to die in the forest with bullet wounds.

Monkeys Two types of monkeys live in Belize: the spider monkey and the black howler. It takes a watchful eye to spy either species scrambling through the treetops, though if you spend even a few days in the Belize jungle, you will likely see many monkeys.

Spider monkeys range from southern Mexico south through Central America and into Columbia, Brazil and the Guyanas in South America; in Belize they were nearly wiped out by yellow fever in the 1950s. They have lanky arms and legs, and tails as long as their body. Their hands are thumbless—all the better for zipping gracefully from branch to branch.

Nearly twice as big as spider monkeys, weighing up to 22 pounds, black howlers (one of six species of howler monkeys, whose range includes much of tropical Central and South America) live only in Belize and parts of the Yucatán and Guatemala. Called baboons in Belize, they have faces that are hauntingly human, and a male and female will hold hands while resting. When they are ready to mate, the pair will lock eyes, then flick their tongues at each other and lick tails before the male approaches from behind, clinging with his tail to a tree limb for support.

Howlers howl to defend a troop's territory, or sometimes before a rain or if frightened. If you are ever awakened by the jackhammer scream of a howler at night, you may well think an angry jaguar is bearing down on your door.

Other Mammals Few jungle inhabitants seem so well equipped as the anteater, whose long slithery tongue is fitted with tiny prongs that keep the ants marching in the right direction—toward its stomach, where a special muscle crushes insect exoskeletons. An anteater spends its waking hours poking its uninvited nose into termite nests, where ants inhabit the outer compartments. Its front claws are curled and strong, useful for digging deep into nests. Anteaters are common, though their telltale signs—raided termite nests—are commoner still.

JAGUAR SMILE

Jaguars are rare throughout their range—Mexico to Argentina—though thanks to recent conservation efforts, Belize is thought to have the world's greatest concentration of the hulking spotted cats. The world's only jaguar preserve, the Cockscomb Basin Wildlife Sanctuary, lies in southern Belize, the very area where just ten years ago it was common for wealthy, rifle-toting Americans to hunt for "trophy jaguar." Poaching still occurs in Belize and perhaps will until people no longer feel compelled to display the animals' stuffed skulls and skins.

Like the anteater, a kinkajou makes its home in a hollow tree, preferring to snooze during the day. At night, it emerges to feed, flicking its long tongue in the honey pot of a bee's nest or the nectar pouch of a flower. Chestnut colored and rippled with soft fur, it is also called honey bear or nightwalker, although it is a relative of the raccoon. Kinkajous are so appealing they are frequently stolen from the jungle and turned into pets, though they make lousy ones, refusing to be housebroken and staying up all night wrecking one's house.

Coatimundis, also known as coatis or quash, look even more like their relative the raccoon, with their snouty masked face and tail of black rings. Found throughout the Belize forests, they have a wide diet, feasting on everything from lizards and snakes to mice and fruit. Tayras, or bushdogs, are lean and mean creatures a little smaller than coatimundis, but with the same culinary penchants. A member of the weasel family, the tayra isn't particularly dangerous but is extremely territorial and will snarl at anyone who encroaches on its homestead.

You will know a peccary is near even before you see him, because the odor that precedes him is not unlike that of a dairy farm. The smell radiates from musk glands on the animal's back and actually entices other peccaries, who will rub their head in it, though it would seem painful, since peccaries are covered with bristles.

Peccaries look a lot like wild pigs—in fact, that's what locals call them—and they are the favorite meal of jaguars and many other jungle predators, though humans do not find the taste appealing. There are two types in Belize: collared peccaries, who have bands of white hair around their necks; and white-lipped peccaries, with white whiskers. Both move in herds, and a herd of 100 or more white-lipped peccaries has been known to charge people who stumble upon them in the rainforest. Researcher John C. Kricher advises that "climbing a tree is the best escape route, though the peccaries may wait around beneath the tree for a while."

The agouti paca, known locally as a gibnut, is a handsome, intensely shy rodent the size of a long-legged rabbit. In less inhabited parts of the country, they are about as common as rabbits, too, and some jungle lodge proprietors grumble that they destroy gardens. The agouti paca normally leaves his hole only at night, but hunters chase the furry creatures from their holes and shoot them, for their white flesh is prized throughout Belize.

White-tailed deer and brocket deer have been hunted incessantly, though sightings in Belize are more frequent now that reserves provide some protection. White-tailed deer grow to 200 pounds, though they average about 60 pounds in Belize. They have an elegant, lustrous body sheathed in peppery brown to whitish brown fur, and a fluffy white tail that they hide when attempting to elude a predator. Brocket deer are diminutive, usually weighing less than 40 pounds, and have a silky auburn coat that blends nicely into the rainforest.

REPTILES &   **Frogs, Lizards and Turtles**   Belize has numerous frogs and also
AMPHIBIANS toads, but the most dazzling is the red-eyed tree frog, whose ruby gelatinous eyes are like night beacons of the jungle. As the frog perches on an emerald leaf, attached firmly by rubbery, neon-orange hands and feet, its eyes bulge out from its metallic green body, which is splashed with white dots and blue patches. All in all, it makes quite a spectacle.

Not nearly as resplendent as the tree frog but immensely entertaining, the basilisk lizard sprints on two hind legs right across the top of a river. Nicknamed the Jesus Christ lizard, he's a comical sight, really, a miniature dinosaur constantly on the run with nothing chasing him and nowhere in particular to go. The basilisk's lizard opposite is the iguana, who prefers to bask lethargically all day on a riverbank. Iguanas seem to be everywhere—including restaurant menus, where they're often listed as "bamboo chicken."

Hickatees have all but disappeared from the rivers, victims of relentless hunting and pollution and their inability to lay many eggs. Unlike sea turtles, who lay over 100 eggs at a time, these Central American river turtles may lay as few as a dozen eggs, depositing them under a canopy of floating vegetation or along a sheltered riverbank. If an egg is not snatched by a wood rail or otter, it will become a baby turtle hunted by crocodiles and raccoons. If it survives to adulthood, it will probably meet its fate at the end of an oar—the preferred weapon of human hunters, who whack the brownish green turtles as they float along the river's surface, snoozing the day away.

Amazingly, hickatee hunting is still legal in Belize, as is sea turtle hunting. Six species of sea turtles, however, including the green, the loggerhead and the hawksbill, are all endangered for countless reasons, including hunting, coastal development (which eliminates the turtles' eating and nesting grounds) and fishing nets that entangle and drown them. Hunting any of these six is, thankfully, banned by the Belize government.

Green turtles graze on sea grass, which turns their fat green and gives them their name. Unfortunately, as more seabeds are dredged, the turtles have fewer places to feed. Green turtles used to grow as large as four feet and weigh over 600 pounds, but thanks to humans, they no longer make it to such a ripe old age.

Loggerhead turtles have big heads, stocky necks and reddish shells shaped like hearts. The female returns each year to the same beach to lay her eggs, abandoning the safety of her sea home and swimming through dark waters toward a familiar shore, hauling her 300-pound body awkwardly across the sand and digging a giant pit, laboring for hours in the moonlight. Then, one by one, she painfully deposits her eggs—up to 100 of them—covers them with sand, and lumbers back to sea before dawn. For all her hard work, poachers will soon come and steal most of her eggs. The few they leave will hatch and wait for night, then scurry toward the surf, only to be picked off by birds, lizards and crabs. Today, fewer than five percent of baby loggerheads will grow to become adults, when they become eligible to be hunted—which is why tomorrow there may be no more loggerheads.

Paca is also known as gibnut and royal rat, the latter name being bestowed upon it several years ago when the queen of England ate stewed paca in Belize.

Hawksbill turtles have peculiar-looking, sharp-hooked beaks, but are also gloriously adorned with shells of golden brown and orange shingles. Their shells have been their doom, fetching big bucks in markets around the world for many years now.

Poisonous Snakes   When you walk in the jungle, your thoughts (and possibly fears) will eventually turn to poisonous snakes. Travelers worry more about snakes than they should, since the vast majority are neither aggressive nor poisonous. Those few that are venomous fall into two categories: rear-fanged and front-fanged. Venom from rear-fanged snakes is dangerous only to the snakes' small prey, such as lizards and toads, but is *not harmful to humans*.

Front-fanged snakes are a different story. The coral snake, also called a bead-and-coral snake, is a front-fanged snake whose venom attacks the nervous system, causing paralysis and sometimes death. Fortunately, the coral snake is rarely aggressive and an excellent coral snake antivenin is widely available.

The front-fanged snake Belizeans fear most is the fer-de-lance, a pit viper also known as a yellow-jawed tommygoff for the yellow jaws and throat that accentuate its brown body. The most poisonous snake in Central America and one of the most common, it has unusually long, spiked fangs that resemble inverted tusks. Mice are its main prey, so the fer-de-lance spends much of its time on the ground and around barns and wells and other places mice enjoy. It has a reputation for aggressiveness, but truth is it would rather flee than strike a human, if given the chance. Even when it does strike, the bite is not always fatal, since the snake rarely disgorges all its venom on something too large to eat.

If you encounter any snake, retreat as quietly as possible. If you are bitten by a poisonous snake, go immediately to a hospital or other emergency facility. Every public hospital and clinic in Belize stocks antivenin. Contrary to local bush practice, you should not cut the wound to make it bleed (you might cut a blood vessel or nerve, causing more harm than the snakebite) nor drink alcohol, which only speeds the flow of blood and therefore venom.

BIRDS

Belize's islands and coastal marshes are filled with beautiful and bizarre birds such as the red-footed booby, which has golden white feathers and outlandish red webbed feet. Its name comes from a lack of fear—sailors to the New World used to walk right up and strike it on the head. Much less friendly is the frigate bird, whose gaunt, black silhouette gives it an ominous appearance. Despite its penchant for fish, the frigate refuses to get wet, and so has become adept at swiping flying fish in midair from other birds. The cinnamon-colored jacana bird, which lives in marshes, ponds and rivers, is nicknamed the lily pad trotter—it gracefully hops across each pad with pencil-thin legs.

But the most famous of all Belize water birds is the jabiru stork. The largest flying bird in the Western Hemisphere, it reaches human proportions, growing as tall as five feet with an astounding wing span of up to ten feet. Unfortunately, it is greatly endangered, with fewer than 300 birds thought to still be alive.

Male curassows are extremely protective of females, and will risk their lives to keep others from getting near their mates.

Inland, birds are flamboyantly colorful. The tiny hummingbird shimmers in iridescent colors as it hovers motionless sucking out flower nectar. Its incredibly high metabolism forces it to feed from dawn to dusk. The turkey-like curassow, who mates for life, boasts lacy crests and lustrous black or crimson feathers.

The bird probably most associated with the Belize jungle is the keel-billed toucan, who sports a crayola-yellow bib and a fantastic, rainbow-hued bill fashioned like a capsized boat. It flies with the bill up and out, as if trying to keep up with the huge apparatus, though in fact the beak is quite light. The national bird of Belize, toucans are best seen in deep rainforest, far away from the people who want to trap them to sell as pets.

Woodpeckers are the jackhammers of the forest, spending hours drilling into tree trunks at unimaginable speeds. The hammering is so constant and tireless that one wonders how the bird's pointy little beak manages not to be mangled by day's end. There are many species of woodpeckers, ranging in color from black to red to green and richly embellished with stripes or streaks. All woodpeckers have tough-as-nails tails to prop them against trees while they do their jackhammering.

Woodpeckers will often drill nest holes only to have them stolen by woodcreepers. Though similar in appearance, woodpeckers and woodcreepers are not closely related, and woodcreepers do not drill their own holes—they probe holes made by others. The most intriguing woodcreeper is the scythebill, whose beak resembles a long, sharp upside-down scythe.

One reason birdwatchers come to Belize is for a glimpse of a blue-crowned motmot, distinguished by a tiara of shimmering blue feathers and a racquet-shaped, blue-green tail that's half as long as its body. There's no mistaking its call, either, a series of delicate *hoot-hoots* that echo through the forest. Montezuma oropendolas are also sought by bird lovers, though it is their nests, draped from trees like elaborate baskets, that are most fascinating. Montezuma oropendolas are blackish-brown and have the silhouette of a crow, their close relative.

INSECTS

Some of the jungle's most ingenious and industrious creatures are not much bigger than a pinhead. Take leaf cutter ants, who work all day and all night chopping leaves and shuttling them in perfect lines to piles that reach six feet high. Each leaf is lifted by a tiny ant who seems to have the strength of Hercules. Another ant pilots the leaf, sending codes to ants in the back of the parade to watch out for that stump, rock—or anteater.

The ants' leaf piles turn into deep, rich soil that trees love. In fact, it's not uncommon to see a cohune palm towering ten feet above surrounding cohune palms that were not lucky enough to grow in leaf cutter compost. What do the ants get out of it? They crave a fungus that grows on the cut leaves, kind of like ant caviar.

Termites are everywhere, as evidenced by their gray spun nests fastened to trees of all varieties. The nests, many larger than basketballs, are made of a papery glue formed by digested wood and termite feces. The obese queen, burdened by a yellow, pouchlike abdomen and hardly able to move, is hidden deep in the nest and is tended to (and impregnated) by zillions of worker termites. The workers are blind, making their way around the nest by sniffing chemical trails laid by other workers. Soldier termites defend the nest from invaders by discharging a sticky, musky liquid.

When termites eat wood, they expel chemical gases. Considering the size of a termite, this would seem inconsequential until you consider how many termites there are in the world. Some researchers believe the gases may contribute to global warming. John C. Kricher, quoting the studies of P. R. Zimmerman, suggests that the termites' "combined digestive abilities produce significant quantities of atmospheric methane, carbon dioxide and molecular hydrogen."

The forest-floor millipede spews its own chemicals, though they are harmless to humans and used strictly for self-defense. At the first hint of danger, the yellow-orange, many-legged creatures tuck themselves into a tight ball and squirt a liquid up to a foot away.

Above the forest floor, butterflies color the air with extraordinary poise and beauty. Most elusive and naturally most sought after by butterfly collectors is the blue morpho, or in Belize, the Belizean Blue. For several years, British naturalist Charles Wright has been living in the deep jungles of southern Belize studying blue morphos. About his subject, he writes that "this butterfly cruises the light and shadow pattern along a forest trail; electric flashes of turquoise blue accompany its passage. It is indeed something to remember."

Similarly fascinating, and cloaked in many Maya myths, is the lantern fly. Looking like a miniature crocodile with wings, it soars through the air toting a toothy, woody-brown snout, resembling some shrunken beast escaped from a Japanese horror movie. Actually, the tiny creatures are quite benign; indeed they spend most of their time eluding predators.

Outdoor Adventures

Belize *is* the outdoors. Here life revolves around the endless cycles of the rainforest and the sea. The complexities of the outdoors—the mysterious web of birth, death and dependency—overshadow everything else. Those who seek outdoor experiences and true adventures will find them everywhere—in the mangrove flats churning with fishing possibilities, in the primal forests riddled with hiking passages, and in the deliriously beautiful reefs offering incomparable scuba diving. You can explore 3000-year-old cities on horseback, canoe down rivers edged in jungle, bicycle to secret coves on hidden islands. You can even join a week-long climb up the treacherous, stony face of 3675-foot Victoria Peak—the ultimate Belize outdoor high.

PARKS, RESERVES & REFUGES

More of Belize lies inside the boundaries of a reserve than outside of one. Some 80 percent of the country's original rainforests have been preserved (a sharp contrast to neighboring El Salvador, which has saved only 2 percent), and most are protected by the government. More than 25 parks, refuges and archaeological preserves exist today. Some are so wild and impenetrable that they're impossible to visit. But most can been seen, indeed extensively explored, by outsiders.

Access to reserves varies widely. By far the easiest to reach are Guanacaste National Park and Blue Hole and St. Herman's Cave National Park (not to be confused with the Blue Hole in the sea), located a short stroll off main roads. At the other extreme is the lost Maya city of Caracol, which requires an arduous, hours-long journey on rocky, oft-flooded jungle roads.

The majority of reserves, however, fall somewhere in between. Prepare to spend at least an hour or two on rough roads (and don't lose your cool if the truck breaks down; Belize has a way of murdering vehicles). And plan to do some serious walking and/or hiking—five miles in one reserve is not uncommon. Neither are 12-hour days.

No matter where you visit, go with a guide. Unless you've had guerrilla training, you won't know your way around the jungle. There is no substitute for having someone along who knows the land, and who can point out all the life hiding in the forest.

Many Belize guides are Maya bushmen, earnest pioneers whose expertise ranges from baboon and jaguar calls to wild fern species and bizarre rituals performed by their ancient Maya ancestors. Some do not wear shoes, preferring to feel the jungle while they see and smell it. Their everyday conversations take on mystical proportions, with talk of Maya planet worship, universal energy and the healing secrets contained within the plants. When the day is done, they often retreat to the most comfortable home they know—the jungle.

Maya folktales say lantern flies glow in the dark, which they don't, and that if a girl is bitten by one, she must have sex with her boyfriend within 24 hours or she will perish. No doubt the tale was concocted by someone's frustrated boyfriend.

For recommendations on bush guides, check with your lodge. For general information on reserves and wildlife refuges, contact the **Belize Audubon Society**. ~ 12 Fort Street, Belize City; 22-35004; www.belizeaudubon.org. Or contact the **Programme for Belize**. ~ 1 Eyre Street, Belize City; 22-75616; www.pfbelize.org, e-mail pfbel@btl.net. For information on archaeological preserves, call the **National Institute of Culture and History, Institute of Archaeology**. ~ Belmopan; 82-22106, fax 82-23345; e-mail ia@nichbelize.org.

CAMPING

There is little organized camping in Belize. You will find makeshift shelters scattered throughout the reserves, but you have to bring your own equipment, food and water. Sometimes that means toting it through the jungle, *after* driving down a long bumpy dirt road. If you do camp in the forest, make sure it's the dry season. Summer rains can not only wash away your camp (and hatch zillions of mosquitoes), they can flood surrounding roads and strand you for days. The best bet for camping is on the cayes, where palmy, open seashores make way for tents, and trade winds cool you down at night. Cayes camping spots, along with other places and ways to pitch your tent, are mentioned throughout this book.

FISHING

Belize has many secrets, not the least of which is this: there are fish in Belize. Fish so big and so plentiful that even the most amateur angler can catch his limit in a few hours. Fish so anxious to impale themselves on a hook that they will rush toward a skiff, or toward a pair of human legs wading in the flats.

Belize owes its fishing phenomenon to a remarkably diverse underwater world—it boasts one of the hemisphere's most healthy reef systems—and to a lack of people. Whether you fish in one of the many inland rivers or on the mangrove flats, along the barrier reef or out in deep blue water, it is likely you will not see another angler *all day*. Of course, as more people "discover" these wonders, the solitude and diversity will diminish. In the meantime, if you love to fish, don't miss the chance to cast your line in Belize.

FLY-FISHING If you're into angling's hottest trend, saltwater fly-fishing, you'll find it in Belize, where bonefish, tarpon and permit churn up the flats everywhere. Belize's most renowned flats are those around the Turneffe Islands, where the bottom is a mix of hard-packed sand and sea grass, and the water is virtually always wadable. Turneffe's popularity means it is more crowded than other spots around Belize, though for those used to fishing in Florida or other "discovered" areas, it will no doubt seem secluded.

Also popular are the flats off Ambergris Caye, famed as one of the world's most lucrative tarpon spots. Year-round, you can count on at least a small tarpon (20 to 50 pounds), though 100-pounders also abound in these waters. Schools of scrappy lady-fish, jack crevalle, permit, bonefish and barracuda are plentiful here. The waters off Placencia are famous for permit, who thrive on the crystalline coral and mangrove "ocean flats" that emerge from deep water. The best time to try for them is at the end of an incoming tide, when tailing permit swarm the flats looking for food. Then even this most elusive of fish is inclined to strike your fly. Other superb places to cast your fly include the flats at St. George's Caye, Hickes Caye, Tobacco Reef, South Water Caye and Glover's Reef. If you're just learning to fly fish, most lodges offer instruction.

Peak fly-fishing seasons vary from place to place, but generally you'll find that tarpon are most plentiful from October to mid-December and in June and July; bonefishing is best from September through January; and permit fishing peaks from August through October and March through June. Be aware that March can be windy with scattered storm bursts, and July and August are usually rainy and buggy.

ANGLING AROUND

Belize has many first-rate fishing lodges offering week-long packages that include daily outings with an accomplished guide. Accommodations are rustic, but you can fish to your heart's content, assured that if you don't catch something, you are in the minority. Most locations include all meals. Tackle is not included, so bring your own. Fishing permits are not required in Belize. Details of the best fishing lodges are found throughout this book. Angler Adventures arranges stays at Belize fishing lodges. The company offers a wealth of fishing programs, and has a fine reputation in angling circles. You'll be informed about everything from weather conditions and the best tackle to what fish are running where. ~ P.O. Box 872, Old Lyme, CT 06371; 860-434-9624, 800-628-1447, fax 860-434-8605.

RIVER FISHING If it's too windy to fly fish, or if you feel more comfortable with a spinning rod, Belize's rivers offer snook, snapper, jack and tarpon fishing in an incomparable jungle setting. One of the most scenic and prolific inland waterways is the Belize River, which climbs in an easterly direction across western Belize to empty into the Caribbean near Ladyville. Here along placid waters, walls of bamboo and troops of monkeys decorate the shore and tarpon roll across the surface like a pack of piranhas thrashing at a hapless victim. Cast your lure into a pack of these tarpon and you can't help but catch one, though don't be surprised when he rears up out of the water—several times.

South of Placencia, the deep Monkey River is similarly striking, framed with massive vines and sugar cane and teeming with tarpon and snook. Southern Belize's inland backwater lagoons—pockets of shallow, muddy water between the Caribbean Sea and the Maya Mountains—are ideal for permit fishing since they are sheltered from wind.

Remember that during the rainy season, from June through October, rivers often flood and drive the fish (and fishermen) out to sea. The best time to river fish is from February through May, when the water is low and clear and the fish most plentiful.

REEF FISHING The ribbon of coral reef paralleling the Belize coast glints with healthy schools of big fish. Whether you're trolling or fishing the bottom, you're apt to catch big grouper, cobia, kingfish, wahoo, king mackerel, jack crevalles and prize snapper, including the ubiquitous yellowtail and the brawling cubera. The barrier reef is so warm year-round, and the food so abundant, that reef fish do not migrate. Hence, expect good fishing here at any time.

Belize is not known for its blue water fishing. In fact, few charter boats are available for deeper waters. However, during the spring and fall, sailfish and marlin are occasionally caught along the seaward side of the reef.

Ancient Maya treasures may lie deep in the Belize jungle, but offshore, glorious treasures await in the mysterious underwater world of the sea. Here, on the world's second-longest barrier reef, dive spots come in endless varieties, from bright shallow waters marbled with dazzling reefs to deep, dark holes dripping with underwater stalactites. In most places, visibility averages 100 feet, though on a clear spring day 150 feet is not uncommon. The scenery often resembles a silent, blossoming dream or a dazzling hallucination. To dive here is to enter another planet.

DIVING

The coral reefs, though they look like inanimate rock, are actually living colonies of polyps that absorb food from the nutrient-rich Gulf Stream and have slowly grown into a coral jungle as complex as the Amazon. Finger coral, elkhorn, mountainous star, brain coral, purple leaf and orange tube, precious black coral with sepia age rings, plus green stinging coral and red fire sponges (which burn when touched) are a few of the species that bloom to towering heights on the sea floor. Hewn into breathtaking landscapes, this coral world is dappled with vivid sea fans, treelike gorgonia, prickly sea urchins, sea whips and lush anemones.

Throughout this subterranean garden are brilliant schools of fish and myriad other sea creatures: candy bass, shortnose batfish, spiny puffers all bloated and prickly, polka-dotted rays, stoplight parrotfish whose scales look tie-dyed, tiny blond razorfish diving into the mottled sand, coral crabs skittering sideways like moving shards of reef, turquoise angelfish, flamefish and sea cucumbers, colossal sea turtles and guitar-shaped guitarfish—an astonishing visual symphony rippling by, beautiful beyond belief.

But Belize's most famous place to dive is not on the barrier reef. The Blue Hole, a monstrous sinkhole in the sea, lies within an atoll—a ring of coral isles surrounding a lagoon. It is a unique formation, famous for stalactites and stalagmites rather than teeming fish.

Like the Lighthouse Reef atoll, Belize's other two atolls—Glover's Reef and Turneffe Islands—are actually coral rock top hats of the Maya Mountains. The underwater ridges, valleys and ravines around the atolls make for sensational diving, and the varying terrain will please all levels of divers. And, because the atolls are circular in design, they always offer a leeward side where you can escape the wind and seas. Anyone who has dived in four- to six-foot swells—quite common on the barrier reef—knows the advantages of a leeward dive spot.

Glover's Reef possesses different forests, composed of luscious elkhorn coral that stretch up from depths of 100 feet. Best of all, much of the scenery lies inside the reef, where calm waters make for unparalleled diving.

Note: The fate of the resplendent atolls, and the rest of the Belize reef, lies with divers and others who visit it. Protecting the reef is as easy as not touching it. Even a slight brush from a fin is enough to damage a coral forever. No matter how tempted you may be, never take a piece of coral. That small souvenir will destroy in one second what it took nature thousands of years to build.

Always anchor your craft in the sand or grass flats, away from the reef. If you can't see where you're anchoring, send a diver down to check the sea bottom. Unfortunately, some Belize dive boats still anchor on the reef, lopping off huge pieces of coral and spreading disease. Perhaps if enough divers frown on the practice, dive operators will be more careful to preserve the future of their livelihood.

For your protection, avoid touching sea creatures. Inside crevices, where you should never poke a prying hand, live moray eels, whose saw-toothed fangs hold decayed food particles that can fatally poison an unsuspecting victim. Some anemones and sea urchins are poisonous, and their spines inflict painful, lasting wounds. An encounter with fire coral, a brownish, innocent-looking coral found everywhere, can leave you peppered with flaming welts that outlast your vacation.

Be a safe diver. Always dive with a buddy, preferably a Belizean buddy familiar with local waters and conditions. Stay well within the boundaries of the dive tables, and limit your dives at the beginning and end of your vacation. If you overdid the rum punches the night before, take the day off. A hangover can affect your judgment and even contribute to decompression sickness.

In case of decompression sickness, there is a **recompression chamber** next to the airstrip in San Pedro, Ambergris Caye. ~ 22-62851 or 22-62852. However, some Belize dive operators prefer to send their guests to U.S. medical facilities. For a US$29 annual fee, **Divers Alert Network** will provide air rescue from anywhere in the Americas for dive accidents or other medical emergencies. The international, non-profit organization also offers dive accident insurance. ~ Duke University Medical Center, Peter B. Bennett Center, #6 West Colony Place, Durham, NC 27705; emergencies: 919-684-8111, Latin American hotline 919-684-9111, non-emergencies: 919-684-2948 or 800-446-2671; www.diversalertnetwork.org.

> One of the most popular and challenging atoll dives is The Elbow, located in the Turneffe Islands, where the fish are big and the currents erratic.

Dive Lodges Whether you're a four-tank-a-day diver or one who enjoys the feel of a hammock as much as a BC, you will find your place in Belize. Half a dozen lodges specialize in diving, and another dozen offer some type of dive program. Most specialty lodges are located on secluded out islands and require minimum stays of four to seven nights. But they vary considerably when it comes to amenities (or lack of) and approach to diving. Some stress rigorous diving with little time for relaxation, while others strike a balance between diving and doing nothing. I stayed at one lodge that was so regimented, guests were either diving, eating or attending meetings about diving. This is dive dreamland for some people, but not for others. When making reservations at a lodge, ask about the facility's dive philosophy, the number of dives offered each day, and the experience of the divemasters. For critiques of individual dive lodges, see Chapter Six.

Dive Instruction If you've been thinking about getting certified to dive, why not do it in Belize? The pace is slow and the weather dependably warm, and there's not much to distract you from

Text continued on page 60.

Ecotourism
Awareness

It is hard to imagine that in just two centuries, more than 80 percent of Latin America's tropical forests have been erased from the planet. Population explosions, frenetic development, widespread logging and slash-and-burn farming—where forests are burned to grow crops and raise cattle—are mainly to blame. Much has been written about the destruction, but little has been done until recently, with the advent of a concept called ecotourism. The basic idea behind ecotourism is that visitors to a place can contribute to the environment and support the people who live in that environment. If villagers can make a living from tourism, it is reasoned, then there's no need to burn off the forest for food or hunt endangered animals for the price of their skins.

But ecotourism means much more than that. In fact, this catchword of the '90s has come to mean setting aside vast forests as sanctuaries and preserves and controlling tourism to those areas. It means fighting destruction of virgin lands planned for resorts and encouraging reforestation in decimated areas. It means giving someone tempted to loot a Maya ruin a job as a tour guide to those ruins. It means convincing a family who doesn't know where their next meal is coming from to preserve the forest that provides that meal. And for a traveler, it means safeguarding the areas you visit as if they were your own backyard. If you must leave something behind, let it be footprints.

Among Central American countries, Belize is a paradigm of ecotourism. Indeed, this tiny country, where the per capita income is only US$6500 a year, is waging an intense campaign to save its environment. More than 25 wildlife and archaeological preserves have been set aside, including the 100,000-acre Cockscomb Basin, the world's only jaguar sanctuary. Jaguars have been wiped out of other parts of Central America, where rainforests are ravaged every day. Belizeans point to this devastation, as well as to overdevelopment in Florida and the Caribbean, in the crusade to save their country. Bumper stickers proclaim Belizeans' love for wild animals, and local gossip is laced with the latest ecotourism news.

Every day, new ecotourism programs are being created. Numerous environmental organizations, as well as the Belize government, are working together to promote ecotourism. In 1992, Belize welcomed countries from around the world to an ecotourism "congress," which addressed the earth's environmental problems and needs. Environmentalists, government officials, developers, tour operators, hoteliers and others in the tourist industry met for intense discussions. The congress included field seminars where participants learned about such subjects as recycling and eco-sensitive diving and sportfishing.

Of course, ecotourism can only work if it is supported by tourists. To help visitors better enjoy and contribute to the environment of Belize, we've compiled a short environmental code of ethics:

1. **Do not disturb wildlife and natural habitats**. Stay on the trails and avoid using machetes and collecting plants or wildlife. Coral reefs are especially sensitive, and should never be touched. Even a slight brush with your fin can cause disease in the reef. Bird nests should be viewed from a safe distance with binoculars, and nesting sea turtles should be observed only with a trained guide. Do not feed monkeys or other wild animals, because it alters their diets and behaviors. Raccoons, who normally live alone, become pack animals when fed and spread diseases that kill them.

2. **Do not litter**. If you'll be in remote areas, take along a sack to carry out your garbage.

3. **Be conscious of helping local communities**. Use native tour guides—they *are* the best—and patronize locally owned inns and restaurants. Buy souvenirs from native crafts people; the Maya villagers make marvelous handicrafts.

4. **Be culturally sensitive**. Remember that you are a guest in a country. Make an effort to learn basic local customs and follow them. Don't judge Belize by your hometown. On one jungle tour, two travelers from Texas constantly compared everything to "how it is back home." Somehow, I couldn't imagine the Maya guide being interested in a four-hour litany on how things are done in Texas.

studying. More importantly, there are many experienced, first-rate dive instructors in Belize. Most dive lodges offer PADI or NAUI instruction, and most classes are so small (usually one to four people) you'll get special treatment. Allow at least four days for the course, which includes four open water dives divided between two days. Prices range from US$250 to US$400 a person, depending on the lodge and class size.

Many dive lodges also offer one-day resort courses for those who'd like a taste of diving, as well as advanced certification, refresher courses and specialty diving, such as rescue diving or night diving.

SWIMMING & SNORKEL-ING

Washed by stunning seas and crisscrossed with smooth-flowing rivers and jungle waterfalls, Belize offers many ways to get your body wet. Virtually anywhere inside the barrier reef, you'll find calm, shallow waters as clear as air, perfect for swimming and snorkeling. Unlike the Caribbean waters off the neighboring Yucatán, which are plagued by strong currents, the seas in Belize are sheltered by the barrier reef. Rip currents are rare, and the water is warm year-round—75 to 80° in winter, and up to 85° in summer.

Take your mask, snorkel and fins to Belize. Rentals are expensive, and sometimes unavailable on remote islands.

Inland, freshwater rivers are framed in lush jungle, where you can watch monkeys play while you swim. Incidentally, when monkeys swim across a river, they thrash about like they're drowning. If you see one, don't offer your assistance or you will have one angry monkey on your hands!

Here are some of the top swimming spots in Belize:

- Hol Chan Marine Reserve, off Ambergris Caye, is the place to snorkel
- Valley of the Rays, a sandbar off Ambergris Caye, where you can swim among gentle sting rays and nurse sharks
- The shallow, protected lagoons within the Turneffe, Lighthouse Reef and Glover's Reef atolls
- The Sibun River beaches within Monkey Bay Wildlife Sanctuary

BEACHLESS BELIZE

While Belize's barrier reef provides protection, it prevents the formation of beaches. Like the Florida Keys, which have their own barrier reef, Belize's cayes are ringed with mangroves and pebbly dirt, not sugar-white sand. Except at the atolls and a few resorts with imported sand, swimming beaches are scarce. Better to swim and snorkel from a boat.

- The Belize River, especially at Guanacaste National Park
- Río On Pools in western Belize, where clear water tumbles down rock terraces
- Along the Curassow Trail at Cockscomb Basin Wildlife Sanctuary
- Blue Creek, outside Punta Gorda

CANOEING, KAYAKING & TUBING

Few experiences are so truly Belizean as cruising down a silent, shimmering river draped in lavish jungle, fat iguanas sunning on tree limbs, monkeys skittering along the shore, parrots squawking in the air. Just 50 years ago, the rivers were the highways of Belize. Now that there are roads, the rivers are used by tourists as much as villagers, though they are hardly crowded.

You can pick your river transportation—canoeing, kayaking or (much easier) floating in an innertube. "Tubing" has in fact taken hold in recent years, and a few outfitters combine it with hiking and caving for an ambitious, all-day adventure. Some of the best tubing is along Caves Branch River in Western Belize and South Stann Creek River in Southern Belize's Cockscomb Basin Wildlife Sanctuary. There's great tubing and canoeing out west on the Macal and Mopan rivers and along Barton and Roaring creeks. Southern Belize is the place to kayak, whether you prefer the Monkey River, the Caribbean Sea or a combination of both.

BIRD-WATCHING

Birders love Belize. They love rising at 5 a.m., sneaking into the darkened web of jungle, and listening for the *hoot-hoot* call of a blue-crowned motmot. To see one of these exquisite birds in the sun-dappled dawn is a great event, especially since the birds are somewhat rare. Daybreak brings out other species of extraordinary beauty, including oropendolas, red-legged honeycreepers, white hawks, great curassows and slaty-tailed trogons. Toucans and macaws are fairly common here, and therefore are unexciting to birders, although the layperson rarely seems to grow accustomed to seeing these ravishing creatures color the sky.

Birdwatching in Belize has only come into vogue in the past few years. As new trails are carved through dense jungle and bird sanctuaries become more accessible, birders are discovering the thrills of this little country. Several areas offer wonderful birding. At Chan Chich Lodge in northwestern Belize, exotic birds actually nest near your jungle hut. When was the last time you walked out your front door to see a toucan feeding her young? Or an ocellated turkey preening for a mate?

Other prime birdwatching spots are Half Moon Caye Natural Monument, Crooked Tree Wildlife Sanctuary, the jungles around Caracol and Cockscomb Basin Wildlife Sanctuary.

In the United States, top organizers of birdwatching tours are scheduling more treks to view the beautiful birds of Belize. For dates and details of birding tours, contact the **Field Guides**. ~ 9433 Bee Cave Road, Building #1, Suite 150, Austin, TX 78733; 512-263-7295, 800-728-4953; www.fieldguides.com. The **Massachusetts Audubon Society** is another helpful resource. ~ 208 South Great Road, Lincoln, MA 01773; 781-259-9500, 800-289-9504; www.massaudubon.org. Or contact **Victor Emanuel Nature Tours**. ~ P.O. Box 33008, Austin, TX 78764; 512-328-5221, 800-328-8368; www.ventbird.com.

Within Belize itself, the **Belize Audubon Society** is an excellent source of information and tips on birdwatching. ~ 12 Fort Street, P.O. Box 1001, Belize City; 22-35004.

HIKING

You could hike forever in the Belize jungles. Some of the best trails are in the archaeological zones, where ancient Maya cities harbor a labyrinth of trails through cool, exhilarating forest with views of temples, pyramids and the green countryside. My favorite place to hike is at Chan Chich, a lodge built on a Maya plaza and enveloped by 275,000 acres of interminable jungle. Nine trails, offering a variety of lengths, difficulty and scenery, cover eight miles in the forest. The lodge publishes an excellent book, *Exploring the Rainforest*, that details 130 marked sites along the trails, including tombs, creeks and "nest condominiums" often inhabited by toucans, woodpeckers and red-lored Amazon parrots. If you're feeling unusually adventurous, take one of the lodge's night jungle hikes. There's nothing like shining a flashlight into a pitch-black thicket, only to discover a pair of jaguar eyes glowering back.

> One resort, the 18,000-acre Hidden Valley Inn, offers a trail system so vast it takes days to hike.

Elsewhere, the Community Baboon Sanctuary and Cockscomb Basin Wildlife Sanctuary offer splendid hiking through dense broadleaf rainforest. Both facilities sell inexpensive trail maps (about US$1), and the wardens can point you to the best spots. For hiking through cool, mountainous slash pine forest, head for the Mountain Pine Ridge. The terrain harbors vast caves, thundering waterfalls, scenic lookouts, racing rivers studded with black boulders, and marvelous views of wild animals. Maps of various trails are available from most lodges in the pine ridge.

HOW TO HELP

For information on environmental programs, contact one of these organizations:

Belize Audubon Society, 12 Fort Street, P.O. Box 1001, Belize City, Belize; 22-35004, fax 22-34985; www.belizeaudubon.org.

Belize Zoo & Tropical Education Center, P.O. Box 1787, Belize City, Belize; 22-08004, fax 22-08010; www.belizezoo.org.
Programme for Belize, 1 Eyre Street, Belize City, Belize; 22-75616, fax 22-75635; www.pfbelize.org.

The ancient Maya filled Belize's caves with delicate vessels and sculpture and painted messages on the slippery limestone walls. They held sacred ceremonies in the soupy blackness and treated the cascading stalagmites and stalagtites as an enthralling underworld. The caves have changed little in 2000 years, and if you prowl through the darkened passages and rooms with mountains of crystals you'll see ceremonial pots and hieroglyphs and other prominent reminders of the Maya World.

CAVING

THREE

History and Culture

Three thousand years ago, in the verdant, sun-drenched land that is now Belize, the Maya created a civilization that knew no equal. Appearing mysteriously like early-morning fog, they built magnificent cities, developed extensive trade routes and fashioned ceremonial centers that arched toward the heavens. Today, two of their temples remain the tallest buildings in Belize. For a traveler searching for historical truth, their lofty limestone summits are a haunting reminder of a civilization far grander than anything before or since in Belize history.

In fact, some legends tell that local human history began with the Maya. According to stories of the Quiché Maya, the great gods Tepeu and Gucumatz first made men from mud, but the rains came and washed them away. Then they honed them from trees, but the wooden men were mindless, so they made them of flesh and blood. These were the worst men, filled with cunning and wickedness, and had to be destroyed in a flood. Finally, Tepeu and Gucumatz pulled out some maize dough and molded the first "real men" of the world—Quiché Maya people.

Archaeologists' stories are just as vague and not nearly as entertaining, since there is little evidence of human life here before the Maya. Some speculate that primal hunters roamed the area from Mexico south through Central and South America about 13,000 years ago until the Pleistocene, or Ice Age, in 7500 B.C. Sometime during the next 3500 years, it is believed that Asians set out across the Bering Straits, perhaps even boatloads of Asians over several generations, all ending up on this part of the continent. In Belize, they probably subdued patches of swamp and jungle to grow rice, hunted the bounteous hot forests, caught plenty of fish in the rivers and seas, and laid the foundation for a society that would become the mighty Maya.

How the Maya became so mighty and so sophisticated over the next 2000 years, paralleling and even surpassing the other great thinkers of their time, is truly a mystery. What is known for sure is that it all started in the earliest, Preclassic days, from about 2000 B.C. to A.D. 250, when the Maya borrowed a calendar from neighboring Olmec tribes and learned how to calculate time. They planted fields of maize and tomatoes and cacao beans, and fashioned temples for the gods of sun and rain. And they spoke a language that became the root for all modern Maya dialects.

But it was the Classic Period, from A.D. 250 to 900, when Maya life skyrocketed into a golden age of exquisitely painted and or-namented temples and palaces and pyramids, fantastic works of art, astonishing achievements in math, science and astronomy, and a writing system more sophisticated than any other ever con-ceived in the Western Hemisphere. Colossal stelae, or carved stone monuments, were inscribed with fanciful text and dramatic stories of war and peace and everyday life. Belize's greatest cere-monial centers—Caracol, Xunantunich, Altun Ha, Lamanai—were built during the Classic Period, though Lamanai's architecture extends well before and after this time, amazingly spanning some 3000 years.

And though the Maya world stretched from Mexico's Yucatán Peninsula all the way south to El Salvador, recent findings point to Belize as the heart of that world, the crossroads of economic and cultural exchange, the "in" place to live. Part of it was Belize's coveted locale: a subtropical seacoast whose waters were speckled with lovely coral isles and whose interior was covered in flour-ishing rainforest, majestic mountains and fertile valleys.

Like the Morocco of the Western Hemisphere, Classic Period Belize overflowed with sophisticated trade and profound culture, mystical religions and mighty kingdoms. Great rulers and priests lived here, and so did artists, writers and aristocrats. There were peasants and farmers and also middle-class families, whose spa-cious thousand-year-old homes boasted big "king-size" bed slabs and ornate burial tombs, and a location convenient to reservoirs and "downtown" shopping areas. From the downtown, *sacbes*, or ancient limestone roads, ran out for miles around like spokes on a wheel, to Belize's first—and only—suburbs. (Today's sparsely populated Belize has no real suburbs, unless you count Hattieville, which grew from a temporary hurricane camp to a primitive vil-lage outside Belize City.) In fact, it is hard to imagine that one single ancient Maya city, the jungle-veiled Caracol, boasted nearly 190,000 residents—as many as live in all of Belize today. In A.D. 562, Caracol crushed its big neighbor, Tikal, Guatemala, and ruled the Maya world for more than 100 years.

And then something happened. Just as the Maya empire had mysteriously blossomed beyond belief, it mysteriously collapsed. The beginning of the end was around A.D. 900, when the Maya suddenly started abandoning their cities. This Postclassic Period of decline lasted over 600 years, during which time archaeologists theorize there may have been earthquakes, wars, famines, disease and massive peasant uprising. Any or all of these could have caused the Maya downfall, or perhaps the Maya simply evolved away from an elite society into a farming one. For the Maya are by no means gone; indeed, some four million Maya still thrive throughout Belize and the surrounding countries in an area known today as *La Ruta Maya*, or The Maya Route.

This 1500-mile-long Maya Route runs down the length of Mexico's Yucatán Peninsula, crosses the jungles and mountains of Guatemala, Honduras and El Salvador, and loops through lush Belize—a perfect place for today's travelers to begin a *Ruta Maya* odyssey. Along the way, there are hulking temples and steep pyramids that rise above the jungle canopies, thousands of stone dwellings and *sacbes*, intricate Maya sculptures and stelae and, greatest of all, a fascinating society of proud Maya people who live much as their Classic ancestors did. From thatched-hut villages stashed deep in the jungle, tucked along rushing rivers and parked atop hills, they grow their maize and beans and rice on *milpa* farms, in an ancient endless cycle inspired by gods of sun and rain and by the beasts of the jungle. In the heat of the day, Belize's Maya women squat for hours over wood set ablaze on their dirt floors, grilling corn tortillas on a *comal*, or griddle stone, for tortillas are the staple of modern Maya life, much as they were 2000 years ago.

The Maya were no doubt tending their corn fields when the Spanish arrived in the early 1500s. Explorers Vicente Yáñez Pinzón and Juan Díaz de Solís sailed up the coast from Honduras to Yucatán around 1506 and claimed everything they saw, including Belize, for the Spanish empire. Soon missionaries made their way down from Yucatán to Lamanai in northern Belize. The Maya at Lamanai were friendly to their uninvited guests until the guests built a church and told the Maya they had to attend. Angry, the Maya burned the church. Several years later, more missionaries fashioned a second, sturdier church at Lamanai, but the Maya burned it down, too.

Other than the Lamanai incidents, the Spanish strangely did little to bother the Maya in Belize. Instead, they concentrated their efforts in neighboring Guatemala and in Yucatán, where Hernando Cortez and a small army combed the land for slaves.

While on the outs with the Spanish government, Cortez and his 11 ships and 600 troops snuck away from Cuba to the Mexican shore in 1519 and over the next few years slaughtered thousands of Maya who refused to be enslaved. Cortez' tyranny laid the groundwork for nearly 400 years of Maya oppression in the Yucatán Peninsula, during which a stream of Maya and *Mestizo* (Spanish-Maya) refugees flowed into neighboring Belize. The most profound Yucatán war was the War of the Castes, from 1848 to 1858, when the Maya slaves rose against their Spanish masters.

It was a bloody decade, and those who could escaped south to Belize. Many settled on Ambergris Caye and Caye Caulker, just south of the Yucatán border, and today those islands are thriving *Mestizo* communities.

Just as refugees and former slaves helped give today's Belize its frontier veneer, so did the pirates and loggers who latched on to its shores in the early 1600s. The pirates found Belize's sheltered cayes a prime vantage point for raiding and plundering Spanish galleons gorged with gold and silver. Belize's treacherous barrier reef helped out, too, laying open the bowels of many a ship carrying treasure. The pirates particularly loved tiny St. George's Caye, where they would catch large sea turtles and smoke the meat over mangrove fires on large racks called "boucans"—hence the name buccaneers. They sold the meat to passing loggers, privateers and other pirates, and began what would become Belize's most lucrative fishing business through the late 1800s.

Discoveries in 1993 have revealed a rich mineral belt in southern Belize where the ancient Maya were likely mining hematite, pyrite, granite and other valuables crucial to their economy.

As for the loggers, many were driven south from Yucatán and north from Honduras by Spanish harassment, and they, too, settled on the Belize shores, building meager thatched huts on a muddy bank near the mouth of what is now the Belize River. By the mid-1600s, as logwood became prized in Europe for its black, blue and purple dyes, many pirates made a career change to logwood cutting. They soon became known as the Baymen, for they would haul the logs across the Bay of Honduras, though it was too romantic a name for such a disgraceful lot who regularly drank themselves to the bottom of rum bottles and tormented the Puritans who had migrated from Nicaragua and Honduras. One 1705 report to the British Trade Council called the Belize settlement a "River of Bullys." In fact it is said that ship's captains used to mark the spot on their maps with an "obelize" to signify a place of corruption, and then the word itself was eventually corrupted into "Belize." Others say Belize got its name from Scottish buccaneer Peter Wallace, who established a community at the river's mouth in 1638, and whose name was pronounced "Wal-EEZ." Still others claim the roots of the word go deeper in history, back to the ancient Maya word *belikin*, meaning "toward the east," as Belize faces east out to sea. No one can tell you the real truth, but most everyone in Belize can tell you that Belikin is the name of their good-tasting national beer.

By the 18th century, the logwood and mahogany business was flourishing and so was the lawless society of British Baymen, who hacked away at the forests and fought off frequent attacks by the Spanish. Spain still claimed the land, despite a 1763 agreement in which it gave England the "right" to cut logwood. Of course, it wasn't the English who did the actual cutting, but slaves who were imported by the Baymen. Most slaves were West Africans brought over via Jamaica and Bermuda, or Indian slaves from the Mosquito Tribes of Nicaragua. Many were women forced to care for the Baymen, primarily as sex slaves, though a number of Baymen did free their commonlaw wives—a custom that set the tone for a future ethnic-rich Belize. In fact, the beautiful, tan-skinned children of the Baymen and slaves would be the first of many generations of Creoles, who are today Belize's foremost ethnic group. The West African slaves also fused the growing settlement with their pulsing dances, drum-driven music—the first "goombay" sounds in Belize—and obeah black magic; the celebrations in the swamps outside their huts lasted all night, with the obeah man or woman appealing to dead ancestors to free them from the shackles of their white masters.

> The chicle business peaked at the height of World War II with Chiclets chewing gum.

It was not obeah but the British government that finally freed the slaves in 1807, though many Belizean landowners refused to give up their free labor. In 1812, slaves laid the cornerstone for Belize's first church, St. John's in Belize City, then spent 14 grueling years building the cathedral brick by brick. A few years after the church was finished, church fathers held a little ceremony for the slaves to celebrate their "emancipation."

While the 19th century heralded the beginnings of freedom for slaves, it also ended the pesky attacks by the Spanish. The attack that ended it all was in 1798, near St. George's Caye, then the capital of the colony. Recorded history recalls a great cannon battle between Spanish and British ships, though many say it was no more than a few Spanish galleons retreating after being threatened by a ragtag band of Baymen. Whatever the truth, the Battle of St. George's Caye officially ended Spanish claims and secured British dominion, though it was not until 1862 that the colony formally became British Honduras. Today, a national holiday commemorates St. George's Caye Day, though some political and cultural independents do not join the festivities, believing that the day commemorates British rule and not Belizean freedom.

Freedom was the reason thousands of new immigrants arrived during the 1800s. From the north came the Maya and *Mestizos* escaping Yucatán's Caste War; they settled in northern Belize and on outlying cayes. In northern areas, where the terrain had been stripped by logging, they planted sugar cane—and thus began the industry now number-one in Belize. They also flavored this northern area with Spanish-Maya culture, and travelers today who drive through the towns of Corozal, Santa Clara and Santa Elena Concepción will be met by pueblo and mission architecture.

The 1800s also saw a stream of new residents from Honduras in the south. The Garifuna, oddly enough, came to Belize to escape British oppression. Their story is one of great intrigue and mystery, as their history is woven with both true and questionable tales. What is certain is that in the 1600s, a ship carrying West African slaves ran aground on the Caribbean island of St. Vincent. The survivors either became slaves or citizens, or perhaps both, and eventually intermarried with the native Carib Indians and created the Garifuna. From these haphazard beginnings, they founded a culture on freedom—freedom to play their driving, soulful music now known as *punta rock*; freedom to farm their simple plots of earth; freedom to practice their obscure religion, which revolves around the *dugu* ceremony of calling to dead ancestors; and, most importantly, freedom of self-rule. But the British wouldn't allow it, and drove the Garifuna from St. Vincent. Most were banished to the deserted but paradisaic island of Roatan in the Bay of Honduras. From there, they made their way to mainland Honduras, Guatemala and Belize.

In southern Belize the Garifuna established outposts along the coast and began reviving their close-knit society. Over the years, the colonial government sought to suppress their religion and force the Garifuna into Catholicism, but the Garifuna simply pacified the British by adding a few Catholic practices to their own ceremonies. As late as the 1950s and 1960s, *dugus* were held in secret so as not to incite local magistrates. Today, however, Belize's 15,000 Garifuna worship freely and in recent years have even begun allowing outside observers. In the southern Belize town of Dangriga, artists' canvases dramatically re-create scenes from dugus and from the Garifunas' voyage from St. Vincent to Honduras and Belize.

While Belize broadened culturally during the 1800s, it struggled economically. The logging industry went boom and bust several times, and by the late 19th century large accessible forests were nearly wiped out. Sugar cane did reasonably well in northern Belize and bananas were planted in southern regions. By the turn of the 20th century, sapodilla trees were surrendering their precious sap for the chicle business.

But the 1900s brought many setbacks, not the least of which was a nameless 1931 hurricane that nearly blew away Belize City, killing 10 percent of the capital's 15,000 residents. In 1949, when colonial magistrates devalued local currency and raised the cost of living, British Hondurans formed a People's Committee to protest. A year later, the grassroots committee had strengthened and, changing its name to the People's United Party (or PUP, as it's called today), began rallying for Belize independence.

In 1950, Belizeans elected five party members to the Belize City Council to form a majority, and over the next decade worked toward national democracy. In 1965, Great Britain gave its blessing to the new nation but Belize stopped short of declaring independence because of Guatemala. Like Spanish conquerors of earlier centuries, big-neighbor Guatemala had long laid claim to the colony. And since Belizeans had been pushing for independence, Guatemala had begun pushing to take over Belize. So Belize waited 16 more years, until 1981, to officially become Belize. At the time, Belize struck a deal whereby British troops could train in the Belize jungles if they'd keep a show of force against Guatemala.

The soldiers stayed until 1994, when the majority were withdrawn, and today the British have only a token presence in Belize.

And while the British returned home, thousands of Guatemalans, Hondurans and El Salvadorans have streamed into Belize during recent years, searching, like so many immigrants of centuries past, for a better way of life.

In 1996, Belize implemented an Economic Citizenship Programme, which let immigrants obtain Belizean citizenship and a passport in just one month, and even change their identities, in exchange for a one-time US$25,000 payment to the government. Although the policy largely failed in its intended purpose of attracting U.S. and Canadian investment, it brought a flood of Chinese newcomers when Hong Kong became part of the People's Republic of China the following year. The citizenship program was repealed in 2002, but the influx has transformed Belize City and some other areas of the country, where most business signs are now bilingual—English and Chinese. During the six years the Economic Citizenship Programme was in effect, the country's population grew by nearly 30 percent, and its per-capita income more than doubled.

Culture

PEOPLE

Today, Belize's 230,000 residents are a truly diverse phenomenon, an improbable blend of Creoles and Maya, Mennonites and Chinese, East Indians and *Mestizos*, Germans and Garifuna, and of course, British. English is the country's official language, but Spanish is nearly as pervasive, and Maya, Garifuna and Creole comprise the other three major languages.

It is this kaleidoscope of humanity, of music and art and dress, of triumphs and defeats and expectations, all joined by a determination to exist free, that makes Belize so unusual. Born of Maya brilliance, baptized by raucous pirates and Spanish outlaws, ignited by African rhythms and only slightly refined by British gentility, Belize is branded with a tenacious pioneer mentality. That same mentality is what assures travelers of a great adventure on this tropical coast.

CUISINE

The Beans and Rice Syndrome   Except for Marie Sharp's Hot Sauce, nothing appears on more Belize tables than beans and rice.

Since the time of the Maya, this fiber-starch duo has sustained generations of people on a short but endless cycle: they'd eat beans and rice to get energy to work in the fields planting, growing and harvesting beans and rice, which they'd eat for energy to work in the fields, starting the cycle all over again. Today, some villagers carry on the cycle, but most people who eat the dish do not grow it.

Buy some Caribbean rum for your friends; a 750 ml bottle will only set you back about US$6.

As humble as the dish sounds, beans and rice come in a variety of preparations, from a fiery mélange of vegetables and ground meat or lobster stewed in coconut milk to a dry, bland combo cooked way too long. It's not hard to tell the difference. Good beans and rice look moist and colorful (the beans will be crimson red to bright purple and slightly cracked). Bad beans and rice look dry, and the beans will be cooked to little hard pieces. Most dishes are made with red kidney beans, though you will find concoctions prepared with black beans, turtle beans and even pink beans. Some of the tastiest beans and rice come from street vendors, who toss the brilliant mixture in drum-sized frying pans.

You may not become a beans and rice fan overnight, but you will quickly learn that the dish is remarkable human fuel. For climbing Maya ruins, hiking through the jungle or kayaking the seas, few foods keep you going like beans and rice.

By the way, you may run across a dish called "rice and beans," sometimes sharing the same menu with "beans and rice." The two are not quite the same. Beans and rice are mixed and cooked together, while rice and beans—spicy red kidney beans and coconut rice—are cooked separately and served side-by-side on the plate.

Gibnut, Bamboo Chicken and Cow's Foot Soup   One reason people come to Belize is for adventure. That's why you might want to try gibnut, bamboo chicken and cow's foot soup. When cooked right, it's Belizean soul food at its best, food that's crisp-fried tender or simmered all day until the meat falls off the bone.

Gibnut, or paca, is a large nocturnal rodent whose tender white flesh is considered tastier than steak. Sometimes it's breaded and fried; more often it's stewed in a big, dilapidated pot over a gas stove or open fire. In the late 1980s, Queen Elizabeth elevated the dish to "royal gibnut" after she ordered it (and purportedly cleaned her plate) at a Belize City hole-in-the-wall called Macy's. But before the queen's discovery, it was plain old gibnut.

Bamboo chicken is the nickname for iguana, which, when fried or grilled, does look and taste a lot like chicken. Cow's foot soup is also just like it sounds: a broth made hearty by slow cooking with a cow's foot (or, if company's coming, two cow's feet). Carrots, onions, garlic, cassava and other vegetables are simmered with the foot, and sometimes a pig's tail, oxtail or chicken foot is thrown in.

If you can get past the sight of feet in your soup, you will find the porridge is truly delicious.

Few hotel restaurants serve gibnut, bamboo chicken or cow's foot soup. Unless you're invited to a local home for dinner—an adventurer's dream—your best bet for soul food is a Belizean diner. These are typically tiny, meager establishments with fans teetering from the ceiling, a TV or transistor radio blaring, and a powerful-looking woman in the back hovering over numerous steaming pots.

The less adventurous will also find more familiar local cuisine. Fried chicken is ubiquitous, followed closely by "stew" chicken and "stew" fish, fried fish, fryjacks (sweet fried corn cakes) and johnnycakes (biscuits that are *not* fried). Street vendors sell spicy, flaky meat pies that are some of the best in the Caribbean. Tortillas and tamales are found in northern Belize, near the Mexican border, while lobster and conch prevail on the cayes. Order them only in season—July through October for lobster; October through June for conch. Chinese restaurants abound in certain small towns, with food of wildly varying quality. Some of the best Chinese food I ever had was in Belize, as was the worst. Ask around before you dine.

Alcohol   Belize's national beer, Belikin, must have the best beer label in the world: a Maya temple. It's the Temple of the Sun God, found at Altun Ha. If you don't get to see the temple in person, you'll see its likeness all over Belize, since Belikin is wildly popular. The mild, medium-amber beer costs about US$1 a bottle in groceries and local restaurants, and double that in tourist areas.

There are several different rums made in Belize, but by far the best and most pervasive is Caribbean rum. It comes in light or dark, and both are surprisingly good, considering no one's ever heard of Caribbean rum.

Other unusual alcoholic beverages made and sold in Belize include syrupy-sweet dessert wines made from ginger, cashews or hearts of palm. They sound better than they taste.

BROWSING BAMBOO BINS

For an introduction to Belize fruits and vegetables, visit the Belize City Market, where bamboo bins display dozens of colorful varieties. Opened in early 1993, it's a gleaming, indoor place where Belize women are more than happy to tell you about each produce item. ~ Regent Street, at the southeast corner of the Swing Bridge. Another excellent place to turn for information is to the Belize bush guides, who are infinitely versed in local fruits and vegetables. They'll tell you how the ancient Maya used the produce, and how you can prepare it today.

Fruits and Vegetables The Belizean landscape, so pristine and prolific, yields an extraordinary array of tropical fruits and vegetables. Many Belizean backyards are like mini produce markets, with selections ranging from papayas, mangoes and passion fruit to cacao beans, custard apples and habañero peppers. Banana plants and coconut palms abound, as do cohune palms, whose tiny white nuts taste like coconut and whose innermost cores, called hearts of palm, are considered a delicacy. You'll also find tamarinds, guavas, plantains and carambola, or star fruit, throughout Belize, and breadfruit on the cayes. Maize, or corn, is grown in *milpa* fields, and has been a diet staple of the Maya people for thousands of years. As for tubers, there are shaggy, white-fleshed malangas; the waxy, fibrous cassava, whose toxins are dispelled during cooking; and the knobby, rose-colored *boniatos*, the sweet potatoes of Central America.

Even if you don't forage the countryside for fresh produce, you'll find yourself enjoying it at virtually every meal. Belize lodges take advantage of the earth's bounty to supply their tables, and many have organic gardens. For breakfast, wedges of papaya and mango might be tucked around the eggs, and slushy watermelon juice served alongside steaming tea or coffee. At lunchtime, when the sun is hottest and humidity highest, locals cool off with fresh-squeezed lime juice, swirled with water and unrefined sugar. Dinner could bring malanga mashed with garlic or corn tortillas baked that very day. The finale might be banana cake, mango fool (a custardy dessert, made with brown sugar, cream and sweetened condensed milk) or perhaps papaya slices flambéed with Belizean rum over ice cream.

Here are a few tips on identifying and using some of Belize's best produce:

Breadfruit: Breadfruit trees are massive, towering above houses and other trees, while the fruit is the size of a cannonball. Plucked when still green, it ripens quickly, developing soft, brown patches much like a ripening avocado. It is typically sliced in rounds and fried, though sometimes the flesh is scooped out and baked in a variety of ways, including into breadfruit bread.

Cashew: The cashew tree is a dull tree, with plain round green leaves covering a plain round canopy that disappears amongst the more beautiful Belize trees. Its only distinguishing characteristic is its fruit, the cashew apple, which appears in the spring. The apple is pale red and fleshy, and its sweet meat is turned into mild jellies and strong wines. At the apple's crown is the curly cashew nut, whose kernel is roasted and then coveted by people around the world. The best time to experience Belize cashews is in May, at the Crooked Tree Cashew Festival, held in the village of Crooked Tree in northern Belize. In case you're tempted to pick your own,

Text continued on page 76.

A Taste
of Belize

Beans aren't always paired with rice in Belize. One of the best dishes I had in Belize was the spicy refried bean dip served at Chan Chich Lodge. When the dip is brought out every evening at sunset, guests literally mob the bowl.

CHAN CHICH'S SPICY REFRIED BEAN DIP
1/2 pound dried red or black beans
1 medium green pepper, chopped
1 small onion, diced
2 pickled jalapeño peppers, chopped, plus 1 teaspoon of their juice
2 cloves garlic
1/4 cup vegetable oil
salt and pepper to taste
tortilla chips, preferably blue corn chips

Rinse beans and place in a 2-quart pan. Cover beans with 2 inches of water, then cover with lid. Bring to a slow boil, reduce heat to medium-low, and simmer beans, partially covered, for 1 1/2 hours. Add more water during cooking if necessary.

Remove beans from heat and cool. In a blender, combine beans and their water, green pepper, jalapeños and their juice, and garlic. Blend until smooth. In a large skillet, heat the oil over medium heat. Add the onion and sauté until pale brown. Stir in the blended bean mixture and cook over medium-low heat until thick, about one hour, stirring occasionally.

Cool slightly and spoon dip into serving dish. Serve with tortilla chips. Recipe makes about 2 cups of dip.

Every Belizean has his or her own special recipe for rum punch. The one at Capricorn Resort on Ambergris Caye is a favorite of locals and travelers. It's a frosty swirl of just-picked tropical fruit and Belizean dark rum, with a dash of cherry juice, poured into a shapely hurricane glass and topped with a sweet, heady crown of banana liqueur. If you can't find fresh fruit, substitute frozen fruit or canned juice—but it won't be the same.

CAPRICORN RESORT'S RUM PUNCH

1 cup chopped tropical fruit (such as papaya, mango, banana, pineapple, orange and lime)
dash of cherry juice
dash of strawberry daiquiri mix (optional)
1 1/2 ounce dark Caribbean rum (or other dark rum)
crème de banana liqueur
fresh fruit for garnish

Blend fruit in blender. Add cherry juice and strawberry daiquiri mix to taste. Prepare a cocktail shaker with ice cubes. Pour fruit mixture over ice and add rum. Shake well. Pour into a tall hurricane glass and top with crème de banana liqueur. Garnish with wedges of fresh fruit, such as pineapple and orange.

Makes 1 tall rum punch.

be aware that the oily liquid inside the cashew shell is poisonous, and not only burns the skin but can kill you if ingested.

Cassava: A ruddy white tuber, and perhaps the humblest of Belize vegetables, cassava is a symbol of the Garifuna (African Carib) culture. In southern Belize villages, Garifuna women rise before the sun to dig hundreds of cassava roots from the hard clay ground. Then the roots are peeled, pressed through a grinder, and the juice wrung from it. The resulting mush is baked into a white waferlike bread. Other Belizeans use cassava widely, either mashing it like potatoes or slicing it into soups, stews and "boil ups," where it is boiled with whole fish, chicken or cow's feet.

Custard Apple: Like nature's own pudding cup, the custard apple has a creamy, rose-scented flesh designed to go straight from fruit to mouth with a spoon. About the size of an orange, with bumpy green skin that turns blackish-brown when ripe, the custard apple tastes best chilled. To eat, simply slice it in half and scoop out the black seeds.

Habañero Pepper: This is the hottest pepper on earth, registering 200,000 to 300,000 on the Scoville Chart, the Richter scale of chile peppers (jalapeños measure 5000), which sounds like enough to cause stomach meltdown. But the habañero can be eaten, indeed enjoyed, when tamed with shredded carrots and other vegetables and bottled as Marie Sharp's Hot Sauce. Marie Sharp's is consumed in mass quantities around Belize; the bottles sit on tables throughout the land. Many families have their own habañero bush. If you want to see fields of the lantern-shaped chilies, visit Melinda Farm in southern Belize, where Marie Sharp's is made (see Chapter Eight).

Hearts of Palm: It takes a great deal of strength and skill to hack into a palm tree and extract its heart. But once you have tasted the satiny core, encased in folds of delicate white flesh, you will understand why someone would go to all the trouble. After being wrenched from its tree, the heart is boiled until tender, then fanned across salads or served as a side dish, usually with a light sauce or a squeeze of lime juice.

Maize: Together with beans, maize has been the foundation of the Maya diet for thousands of years. Maya villagers today still rely on corn as a primary staple; the men harvest it and the women soak it overnight in lime juice. The next day, the women grind the corn into a powdery meal, mix it with water, and knead it on a cornmeal stone called a *metate*. Then they shape it into wafer-thin disks called tortillas, and grill the disks over an open fire on a *comal*, or griddle stone. The tortillas are kept warm until the meal, at which time a typical Maya man may consume up to 20. If you are lucky enough to visit a rural Maya village, you can watch the women squatting over the fires, making their daily tortillas.

Mango: There are more than 100 varieties of mango, which can weigh anywhere from a few ounces to a few pounds, with flesh that can be fragrant, lush and golden or stringy and tasteless. The best way to tell a good mango from a bad one is to sniff it. It if doesn't smell sweet, it's probably no good. A choice mango smells and tastes like a cross between a peach, a pineapple and a banana. To eat a mango "on the half shell," slice the fruit right next to its flat pit to get two fleshy "cheeks." With the skin-side down, score each cheek into small chunks, then slice the chunks away from the skin.

A word of caution: Mangoes are in the poison ivy family; the juice and peel may swell and blister the skin of some people. But even those who are allergic to it can usually eat the ripe fruit without any side effects.

Papaya: American food writer Elizabeth Schneider likens the papaya tree to "an Indian fertility goddess." No doubt it is because the branchless trunk dangles its lobes of luscious fruit beneath a sprawling, lacy canopy. Yellowish-green to pinkish-purple, papayas have slippery peach-colored flesh and glassy black seeds that are edible. Simply cut it in half lengthwise and scoop out the meat.

Passion Fruit: One would hope this fruit was named for the sensations it arouses when eaten. Alas, it was named by a most dispassionate group, European missionaries, who upon landing in South America thought its flower looked like a crown of thorns and other Crucifixion symbols. The fruit, for its part, bears a sweet-tart, gelatinous pulp that is indeed sensory-heightening. To eat, slice the purplish-yellow globe in half and scoop out the pulp and edible seeds.

Soursop: There is nothing like the taste of soursop, so spicy and perfumed and tropically addictive. There is nothing quite like the looks of it either—pimply, plump and evergreen. Inside, the fruit's pale custardlike flesh is the color of pale pink abalone. The flesh is rarely cooked, but rather strained, and the soursop juice used in ice creams and rum drinks.

While English is Belize's first language, don't expect everyone to speak your brand of English. Belizeans speak with a variety of accents, and may have just as much trouble understanding your English as you do theirs. In Belize City, Chinese is widely spoken, while in villages and areas near the Guatemala and Mexican borders, Spanish, Maya and other languages are common. If you know a little Spanish, or are good with body language, you'll have no problem communicating. Belizeans are gregarious people who enjoy making new friends.

LANGUAGE

FOUR

The Cayes

The Belize Cayes stretch eastward from the mainland, a sprinkling of coral rock and mangrove isles basking in the fabulous blues and greens of the Caribbean Sea. They range in size from tiny mangrove specks inhabited only by sea birds to substantial islands with thriving fishing villages. Their first inhabitants were the Maya, who established intricate island trading routes during the Classic Period, from A.D. 250 to 900. Seven hundred years later, British pirates used the isolated, scrubby isles to stash the treasure they had plundered from Spanish galleons. Today, little evidence exists of either the Spanish or the Maya, but the islands remain pristine and isolated.

The cayes (pronounced "keys") are why most visitors come to Belize, for here can be found some of the best diving and fishing in the world. Along this 200-mile-long barrier reef—the longest in the Western Hemisphere—is an underwater Eden of dazzling sea creatures, wildly colorful coral and see-through waters ribboned with sunlight. The marine life here, biologists say, is perhaps the most complex and diverse in all the Caribbean. Indeed, some claim Belize's reef sustains a greater variety of sea creatures per square foot than any other barrier reef in the world.

Beyond the barrier reef are secluded patch reefs with travel-poster islands, sandy flats superb for fly-fishing, and warm slurpy waters that beckon swimmers year-round. Then there are the atolls (pronounced "a-TOLS"), ringlike bands of coral isles surrounding lagoons. Belize's three atolls offer the ultimate in fishing and diving, for their circular shape ensures there is always a leeward side where you can escape wind and waves.

The pace of life is slow in the Cayes. There are no paved roads—only sand streets—and electricity is often provided by a generator, solar panels or even windmills. Getting to a caye usually means taking a small plane or boat, though hopefully the boat is not too small, as some voyages take as long as two to four hours. In fact, travel around the Cayes holds promise of adventure, considering the shaky dependability of boat motors and captains, the even less predictable weather, and the fact that Cayes' time is even slower than regular Belize time!

Though Belizeans don't particularly frown on nudity, there are no official nude beaches in Belize. However, there are dozens of deserted out islands with beaches perfect for sunbathing in the buff.

Surprisingly, beaches are scarce in the Belize Cayes, because, like the Florida Keys, they are formed of mangroves and coral rock. The choicest beaches are on the out islands, and so not within easy reach of the average visitor. On Ambergris Caye, the largest island, there is no official public beach, but good beaches can be found behind hotels on the north and south ends of the island.

Lodging on the Cayes ranges from charming seaside motels and thatched bungalows on the beach to fishing cabins on a secluded island. Most of the upscale accommodations are on Ambergris Caye, Belize's largest caye, and these are not ultra-luxurious. In fact, most cayes' hostelries are what you'll soon come to know as funky-Belizean: full of charm and personality but lacking in creature comforts. Only the few deluxe and ultra-deluxe lodges offer air conditioning, but sea breezes are adequate on all but the muggiest of summer days. To make sure you catch the breezes, ask for a room (preferably with lots of windows) on the windward side of the island. You'd be surprised what a difference a breeze will make—usually between a restful or a restless night.

Many cayes have only one or two lodges, offering that rare opportunity to stay at a castaway island. These out-island lodges are most popular with anglers and scuba divers who prefer nature over civilization. Some lodge owners take ecotourism quite seriously, even limiting the number of anglers allowed per week.

Lodge owners themselves can determine whether or not you love a place. When you're staying on a near-deserted island out in the middle of nowhere, the personalities running the show become quite crucial. (You should know that most lodge owners, like the guests, are North Americans.) I have had experiences where lodge owners were so intrusive, it was difficult for guests to relax and have a good time. Lodging reviews in this chapter reflect my impressions of each place. Before you book an out-island lodge, however, it's helpful to talk to someone who's stayed there recently.

Depending on how "out" the island is, you may be required to stay at least a week. Any less would be impractical, since getting there requires a lengthy boat trip or chartering a small plane. All out-island lodges will arrange your transportation. Most people find the journey not only an adventure but a marvelous window to the unspoiled Caribbean of Belize.

Like the lodges, Cayes' eateries possess those typical Belizean elements: eclectic decor, sand floors and fascinating characters hailing from all corners of the earth. Few restaurants keep "official" hours, but you'll always find something open to suit your needs. Besides the Belizean staple of rice and beans (which can be quite tasty), expect plenty of fresh seafood when dining on the islands. Here is a good place to try your first Belikin beer, Belize's ubiquitous national brew, which, by the way, happens to be very good beer.

On the out islands, you'll be dining at the lodge restaurant—the only one on the island—but most times you'll find the food quite good. A few resorts take advantage of their captive audience and charge ridiculously high prices for food. To avoid price gouging, buy a lodging package that includes meals. Most out island bars are run on the honor system—no problem if there are only 20 people on the whole island.

Ambergris Caye

Twenty-eight miles long and the country's biggest island, Ambergris Caye has the most and best resorts and the finest array of restaurants, shops and bars in all of Belize. Yet Ambergris is where people still go to get away, whether it be hippies escaping to a secluded campground or fishers and divers retreating to thatch-and-bamboo lodges. Ambergris also is still home to much wildlife, including many shore birds, nesting sea turtles and even ocelots, who find refuge in the swamps and mangrove forests unspoiled yet by people.

Situated northeast of Belize City, about a one-hour boat ride away, Ambergris is actually closer to Mexico than Belize. Only the skinny Boca Bacalar Chico Channel, dug by the ancient Maya, separates the north tip of the island from the Yucatán Peninsula. The caye gets its name from "ambergrease," the waxy secretion of sperm whales that was found on the beaches by 18th-century British explorers. Once a pricey substance used in making perfume, ambergrease can sometimes be seen today clouding sea waters in the area.

SIGHTS

Most of Ambergris' activity is concentrated near the island's south end, in the seaside village of **San Pedro**. Named for Saint Peter, patron saint of fishermen, the fishing village was founded in 1848 and was a refuge for *Mestizos* (persons of mixed Spanish and Indian blood) fleeing Yucatán's War of the Castes. Eleven years later, Englishman James Hume Blake bought San Pedro and the rest of Ambergris Caye for just $625 during a bankruptcy auction by the British government. Soon coconut plantations abounded on Blake's island, and San Pedro residents made their living husking and shredding the nuts. By the mid-1900s, the coconut business had gone bust and most plantations abandoned, and San Pedroans returned to fishing for a living.

Today, a boat is just as likely to be hauling tourists as fish. Tourism is the biggest business on Ambergris. During high season, visitors to San Pedro outnumber its 3400 residents. No matter when you visit, the village will seem a busy little place, with golf carts and bicycles buzzing up and down the sand streets and punta rock music drifting from outdoor bars. Wobbly docks loaded with boats are strung along the seafront, and old clapboard buildings huddle against new concrete condominiums. Unlike anywhere else in Belize, San Pedro has a definite feel of American influence, from the stark new buildings financed by American companies to the American-owned hotels, restaurants and bars.

Yet, for now at least, Ambergris Caye is still a place where visitors aren't subjected to the rigors of mass tourism. Locals frequent

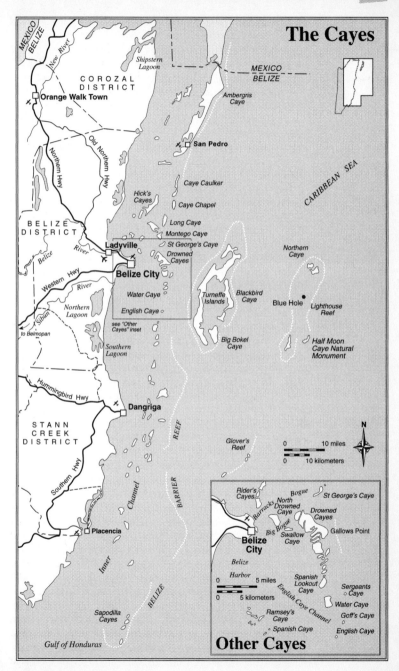

The Cayes

MEXICO / BELIZE

COROZAL DISTRICT

Shipstern Lagoon

New River

Orange Walk Town

Old Northern Hwy

Northern Hwy

MEXICO
BELIZE

Ambergris Caye

San Pedro

CARIBBEAN SEA

Caye Caulker

BELIZE DISTRICT

Hick's Cayes

Caye Chapel

Belize River

Long Caye

Montego Caye

Ladyville

St George's Caye

Belize City

Drowned Cayes

Northern Caye

Western Hwy

River

Water Caye

Sibun

Northern Lagoon

English Caye

Turneffe Islands

Blackbird Caye

Blue Hole

Lighthouse Reef

to Belmopan

see "Other Cayes" inset

Southern Lagoon

Big Bokel Caye

Half Moon Caye Natural Monument

Hummingbird Hwy

Dangriga

STANN CREEK DISTRICT

REEF

Glover's Reef

0   10 miles

0   10 kilometers

N

Southern Hwy

BARRIER

Channel

Inner

Placencia

REEF

Other Cayes

Rider's Cayes

Bogue

St George's Caye

Barracks

North Drowned Caye

Drowned Cayes

Big Bogue

Swallow Caye

Gallows Point

Belize City

Belize Harbor

0   5 miles

0   5 kilometers

English Caye Channel

Spanish Lookout Caye

Sergeants Caye

Water Caye

Goff's Caye

Ramsey's Caye

Spanish Caye

English Caye

Sapodilla Cayes

BELIZE

Gulf of Honduras

the same restaurants and shops as tourists, and everyone is treated with the usual brand of Belizean hospitality. And though most residents are of Mexican descent, they are bilingual, and are just as happy to converse with you in English as Spanish.

Only about seven blocks long and three blocks wide, San Pedro is easy to navigate. It will take you all of about one hour to stroll every sand street (not including tiki bar stops!). You'll soon learn that most everything happens along the slender, white-sand beach and on Barrier Reef Drive, also called Front Street, San Pedro's main drag and the street closest to the sea. Hotels and businesses are here, and so is the **San Pedro Town Hall**, a humble seaside building with peeling paint and a hand-painted sign imploring people to protect the Belize reefs. ~ 22-62198. There's also **Travel & Tour Belize**, an excellent source for island information and excursions. ~ Coconut Drive; 22-62031. Next to Central Park is the **Police Station**. ~ 22-62926.

Walking west from Barrier Reef Drive, you'll find Middle Street and Back Street. North are various unmarked and unnamed streets, and a couple of lanes called different local names just to keep things interesting. South is Coconut Drive, a sandy lane that boasts the latest developments, with new hotels and lodges lining the seafront. The scene starts around the 3000-foot **San Pedro Airstrip**, where visitors fly in and out every 20 minutes or so.

If you're lucky enough to be in San Pedro on a Saturday night, you'll see local families gather in the town square for their weekly get-together. It's a festive occasion, with folks cooking dinner on makeshift grills and kids playing basketball. Small children come all dressed up then promptly get dirty playing in the sand streets.

HIDDEN ▶ Located on the north end of Ambergris Caye, near Mexico, and accessible only by boat, **Bacalar Chico National Park** offers excellent snorkeling and diving opportunities. Onshore lie seven Maya sites, though only one, **Chac-balam**, has been excavated. A ranger station and visitors center are situated about a mile from the park border. For more information, see "Beaches & Parks" below. ~ 22-62247 in San Pedro.

LODGING Budget and moderate accommodations can be found in the town of San Pedro, while deluxe and ultra-deluxe resorts tend to be on the north and south ends of the island. Staying in town means you can walk to restaurants, stores and tiki bars, but town is also noisier and there are no real beaches. Outside of town, you'll pay more for solitude and for having a generous beach out your back door. However, lodging on the north end is accessible only by boat or by a four- to five-mile, potentially mucky bike ride—something to consider if you plan to spend a lot of time in San Pedro. Hotels there do provide ferry service to and from town, though schedules are infrequent. Water taxis are another option, though

Ambergris Escape

Day 1 • From Belize City, take a ferry ride or small plane to **San Pedro** (page 80) and check into **Changes in Latitudes B&B** (page 86). Or, if you prefer the ultimate escape (in other words, outside of town), check into the **Victoria House** (page 84).

• Rent a golf cart or bicycles and tool the dirt streets of San Pedro, stopping for lunch at **Elvi's Kitchen** (page 89) and shopping along **Barrier Reef Drive** (page 92).

• Head back to your lodge for a snooze beneath the palm tree before enjoying dinner at **Fido's Restaurant** (page 90).

Day 2 • Sign up for a snorkel or dive trip at **Hol Chan Marine Reserve** (page 87). If you're fonder of fishing, hire a guide to take you out on the flats or reef. Yet another possibility: a daytrip to Caye Caulker. Be back well before sunset so you can enjoy drinks and dinner at **Capricorn Resort** (page 92).

Day 3 • Check out of your lodge; if you're flying out of Ambergris, head to the airport to wait for your flight. Return to Belize City.

remember that they operate on island time and can get quite expensive (about US$10 per person, one way). If you stay on the south end of Ambergris, you'll need a bicycle or golf cart (available from most hotels) to get to town.

One of the southernmost hostelries is also one of the most engaging. Nestled on a sublime stretch of beach, the **Victoria House** boasts 29 rooms spread among a pretty Victorian plantation house, several row houses and Mexican-style *casitas*. Most desirable are the *casitas*, wrapped by spacious porches and warmly adorned with Mexican tile floors, hardwood furnishings, high-beamed ceilings and Belizean paintings. Rooms in the houses, though slightly smaller, are attractively appointed with white wicker. All rooms have small refrigerators. Complimentary bicycles, as well as van service to town throughout the day, are included in the rate. ~ Located about two miles south of San Pedro; 22-62067, fax 22-62429, or 800-247-5159 in the U.S.; www.victoria-house.com, e-mail victoria@btl.net. ULTRA-DELUXE.

Some of San Pedro's most comfortable and appealing accommodations are at **Caribbean Villas**. The white-stucco buildings, resting right on the beach, offer standard rooms and spacious two-room suites with kitchens (including blenders, handy for frozen drinks), ceiling fans and air conditioning. Rooms are arranged with guests' comfort in mind—plenty of space and storage and constant views of the beach and sea. Two outdoor hot tubs are prime for stargazing. A 35-foot "People Perch" invites splendid opportunities for birding, and an artificial reef just off the dock has great snorkeling. Upon arrival guests are treated to a golf cart tour of San Pedro by Wil Lala, who points out places to eat, drink, shop and just hang out. ~ Coconut Drive, three-quarters mile south of San Pedro; phone/fax 22-62715; www.caribbeanvillashotel.com, e-mail info@caribbeanvillashotel.com. DELUXE TO ULTRA-DELUXE.

Seafront **Coconuts Caribbean Hotel** is where you can unpack for a while. (One guest, in fact, booked a few days but stayed several weeks.) Hosts David and Karina make guests feel right at home, offering breakfasts of fresh-baked breads, just-squeezed juice and hearty coffee, and loaning bicycles for daytime use. The 12 pleasant rooms have white tile floors and sleeper sofas piled with downy pillows, ceiling fans and air conditioning. (There is an extra charge if you use your air conditioning.) ~ Coconut Drive, San Pedro; 22-63500, fax 22-63501, or 877-583-2687 in the U.S.; coconutshotel.com, e-mail coconuts@btl.net. DELUXE TO ULTRA-DELUXE.

If you enjoy cooking, consider **Corona del Mar**. The four suites have fully stocked kitchens and white wicker dining tables, ceiling fans and air conditioning, as well as two double beds and a hide-a-bed. A few steps out the back door is Woody's Wharf, a dock where boats will take you snorkeling, diving or fishing. ~

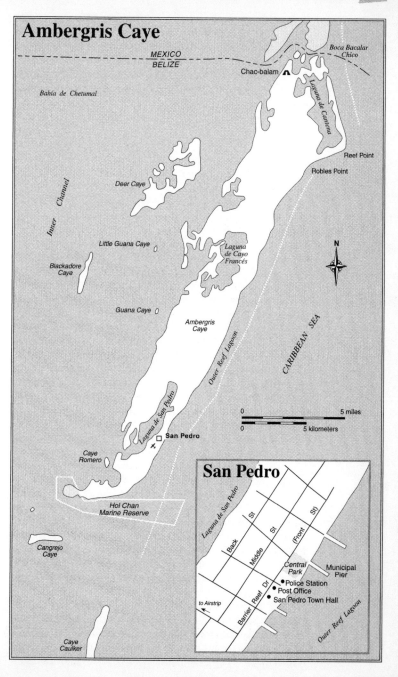

Ambergris Caye

MEXICO
BELIZE

Boca Bacalar
Chico

Chac-balam

Bahía de Chetumal

Laguna de Cantena

Reef Point

Robles Point

Inner Channel

Deer Caye

Little Guana Caye

Laguna
de Cayo
Francés

N

Blackadore
Caye

Guana Caye

Ambergris
Caye

CARIBBEAN SEA

Outer Reef Lagoon

Laguna de San Pedro

San Pedro

0   5 miles

0   5 kilometers

Caye
Romero

Hol Chan
Marine Reserve

San Pedro

Cangrejo
Caye

Laguna de San Pedro

St

St

(Front) St

Back St

Middle St

Central
Park

Municipal
Pier

Barrier Reef Dr

● Police Station
● Post Office
● San Pedro Town Hall

to Airstrip

Outer Reef Lagoon

Caye
Caulker

Coconut Drive, San Pedro; 22-62055, fax 22-62461; e-mail cor
ona@btl.net. MODERATE TO DELUXE.

The stylish, spacious **Belizean Beach Suites** is great for families or anyone else who wants to spread out among one-, two- or
three-bedroom digs. The three-story crisp white buildings have
arched porticoes and terraces and a white picket fence that wraps
around the seafront grounds. Inside there's rattan and tropically
patterned cushions, glass-topped tables and cool tile floors, ceiling fans, air conditioning, and red ginger residing in vases. The
sugary-white beach out back is tiny and perfect. ~ White Sands
Beach, San Pedro; phone/fax 22-62582, or 800-887-2054 in the
U.S.; belizebeachsuites.com, e-mail howard@belizebeachsuites.
com. DELUXE TO ULTRA-DELUXE.

San Pedro's upscale address is **Belize Yacht Club Hotel**—where
else can you sip espresso at the bar and then take a dip in a pool?
Fashioned in Mediterranean style, this complex of white stucco
and red Spanish tile harbors 44 suites with kitchenettes, Mexican
tile floors, front porches, ceiling fans, air conditioning, phones
and TVs—very nice, all in all. Most rooms have sea views. ~ Coconut Drive, San Pedro; 22-62777, fax 22-62768, or 800-688-0402
in the U.S.; www.belizeyachtclub.com, e-mail frontdesk@belize
yachtclub.com. ULTRA-DELUXE.

Set just off the sea, the two-story A-frame **Changes in Latitudes B&B** has just six rooms, all small but light and stylish, and
each with a private bath, ceiling fans and air conditioning. Over
breakfast (included in the rate) the congenial Canadian owner
will help organize your day. Guests have use of the Belize Yacht
Club pier next door. ~ Coconut Drive, San Pedro; phone/fax 22-
62986; www.ambergriscaye.com/latitudes, e-mail latitudesbelize@
yahoo.com. MODERATE

Situated along a curving, palmy beach, **Ramon's Village** enjoys the liveliest atmosphere of any island hotel. The sands are
alive with volleyball games, the freshwater pool is always filled
with people, and the outdoor bar stays busy from morning till late
night. Every Tuesday and Friday there is a beach barbecue with
live music. Accommodations are in 61 *palapa*-style cabanas,
squeezed together along the sand, with louvered windows, wood
or tile floors, comfortable furnishings and phones; rooms have
air conditioning. The price buys atmosphere, not cushy rooms. ~
Located just south of San Pedro; 22-62071, fax 22-62214, or 800-
624-4215 in the U.S.; www.ramons.com, e-mail info@ramons.
com. ULTRA-DELUXE.

With its white-stucco arches, spindle rails and Mexican tile
floors, the **SunBreeze Beach Hotel** recalls the architecture of San
Pedro's native Yucatecans. The low-slung hotel enjoys a splendid
location on a generous beach, right at the end of town. Everyone
eventually shows up here and stays for a while, and that's why

the place is always abuzz. Decor in most of the 42 recently renovated guest rooms is warm pink, and there's air conditioning, cable TV and phones. Best here are the five spacious rooms that feature modern decor as well as jacuzzi tubs. ~ Located on the seafront, south end of San Pedro; 22-62191, fax 22-62346, or 800-688-0191 in the U.S.; www.sunbreeze.net, e-mail sunbreeze hotel@sunbreeze.net. ULTRA-DELUXE.

Popular with divers, the seaside **Coral Beach Hotel** is better known for its topnotch scuba program than its accommodations. Though unspectacular, the 19 rooms are clean and decorated with wallpaper, and have ceiling fans and air conditioning. Many offer views of the sea. There's no beach, but there is the uproarious Tackle Box Bar, which sits at the end of a pier. If you want to spend the night on the water, venture out on the live-aboard boat that makes an overnight trip to the Blue Hole. ~ Barrier Reef Drive, near the middle of San Pedro; 22-62013, fax 22-62864; www.coralbeachhotel.com, e-mail forman@btl.net. BUDGET TO MODERATE.

Location is the best feature of **Lily's Caribbean Hotel**. Centrally located on San Pedro's beachfront, Lily's is a congenial, tumbledown sort of place, with myriad levels and cluttered rooftops. Bare white walls, floral bedspreads and vinyl floors are standard decor in the ten plain but clean rooms with ceiling fans and air conditioning. By far the best rooms are the three that face the sea. The owners, longtime residents of San Pedro, also offer delicious home cooking in a newly renovated restaurant. ~ Barrier Reef Drive, San Pedro; 20-62059, fax 22-62623; www.ambergriscaye.com/lilys; e-mail lilies@btl.net. MODERATE.

If you prefer comfort to character, visit the newer, American-style **Mayan Princess**. The coral-coated building boasts 23 stylish suites with white ceramic floors, whitewashed wicker furnishings,

AUTHOR FAVORITE

I love watching the moray eels at **Hol Chan Marine Reserve**, an underwater park accessible only by boat. Hol Chan is Maya for "little channel," and it was the Maya who first discovered the plethora of sea life in the narrow passage through the barrier reef here. Overfishing in the early 1980s nearly destroyed the area's fragile reef system and drove most of the life away. In 1987, the Belizean government made it a three-square-mile national reserve, and installed buoys for boats to tie to, thereby avoiding anchoring on the reef. Today, the reef is thriving again, and snorkelers and divers can admire the vibrant corals and colorful tropical fish. For more information, see page 93.

air conditioning and French doors that open onto a private veranda. The well-stocked kitchens in every room are especially helpful for families. Every room faces the sea. ~ Located on the seafront, in the middle of San Pedro; 22-62778, fax 22-62784, or 800-850-4101 in the U.S.; www.mayanprincesshotel.com, e-mail mayanprin@yahoo.com. DELUXE TO ULTRA-DELUXE.

The bright yellow three-story **Banana Beach Resort** offers suites with full kitchens and living room areas with locally made rattan furniture, decorated with Yucatecan handicrafts. The suites range in size from one-bedroom to four-bedroom, four-bath—a bargain for groups traveling together. All are air-conditioned and have cable TV. The 21 economical one-bedroom units overlook the central swimming pool, while another 24 luxury suites overlook the sea. ~ Barrier Reef Drive, San Pedro; 22-63890, fax 22-63891; www.bananabeach.com, e-mail bananas@btl.net. DELUXE TO ULTRA-DELUXE.

HIDDEN ▶
A plain white 40-bed hostel on stilts half a mile from downtown and just two minutes' walk from the beach, the newly opened **Pedro's Inn** has the most affordable accommodations on Ambergris Caye—US$12.50 per person per night for a dorm bed only, or $20 per person per night including the nightly barbecue, one cold Belikin beer, and a half-hour on the internet. ~ San Pedro; 22-63825; backpackersbelize.com, e-mail pedroback2000@yahoo.com. BUDGET.

If you're yearning for the luxuries of home, **Blue Tang Inn** offers some of the most modern, spacious rooms in all of Belize. Facing the sea, with a tiny beach, the white Mediterranean building houses 14 apartments with comfortable beds, sofas, dinettes, kitchens, air conditioning and big windows wrapped in pretty drapes. ~ Lo-

AUTHOR FAVORITE

The ultimate Belize cayes splurge, **Cayo Espanto** opened in 2000 with five high-fashion villas, each with its own "personal splash pool" and alfresco shower. Just three miles from Ambergris Caye, the private island resort has a staff ratio of two to one (that's two staff per guest) and a personal butler for each villa. He'll deliver fresh papayas and tortillas in the morning, then prepare the sun beds on your wood deck for a day of waterfront snoozing. Late afternoon, consider a soak in your marble bath and a look inside the butler's pantry before a pre-dinner nap. Sound too sedate? Then sign up for a day of diving, snorkeling or fly-fishing. Just be back in time for dinner—the coconut husk–smoked chicken breast with melanasian noodle cake is wonderful. ~ For reservations, call 910-323-8355, fax 910-323-4272, 888-666-4282 in the U.S.; www.aprivateisland.com, e-mail info@aprivateisland.com. ULTRA-DELUXE.

cated just north of San Pedro; 22-62326, fax 22-62358; www. bluetanginn.com, e-mail bluetanginn@btl.net. DELUXE.

Serious anglers will point you to **El Pescador**, whose nearby flats are world-renowned for tarpon and whose remote seaside setting feels worlds away from the daily grind. The two-story, wood-frame lodge is set among coconut palms on a lovely stretch of sand, and harbors a freshwater pool and 13 tidy but plain rooms (with ceiling fans) typical of a homey fishing camp. There's also a two-bedroom suite. In addition to the daily rates the packages include flats and/or reef fishing, daily guide services, all meals and the flight from Belize City. ~ Located at the north end of Ambergris Caye; 22-62398, or 800-242-2017 in the U.S., fax 22-62977; www.elpescador.com, e-mail info@elpescador.com. ULTRA-DELUXE.

Most visitors come to **Capricorn Resort** for the superb food or the atmospheric bar, but there's no reason not to stay awhile, checking into one of three simple, spacious cabanas (which have ceiling fans) set right in the sand, or into the air-conditioned suite perched atop the main building and looking out to sea. Hardwood floors, beamed ceilings and primitive island art adorn the rooms, and hammocks are strung along the balconies. ~ Located three and a half miles north of San Pedro toward the north end of the caye; 22-62809, fax 22-05091; www.ambergriscaye.com/capricorn, e-mail capricorn@btl.net. DELUXE TO ULTRA-DELUXE.

◀ HIDDEN

Like some sanctuary for shipwrecked souls, **Captain Morgan's Retreat** is stashed on a deserted ribbon of beach, accessible only by boat. The 14 simple, thatched-roof *casitas* virtually disappear into the palm trees, and the bamboo restaurant and sand-floored bar look like they were built by Captain Morgan himself. Furnishings in the casitas are simple but tasteful, with louvered wood windows, plank floors, vaulted ceilings, ceiling fans and roomy porches facing the sea. This place is a favorite of honeymooners and others who really want to escape. ~ Located at the north end of Ambergris Caye; 22-62567, or 888-653-9090, fax 307-587-8914 in the U.S.; www.captainmorgans.com, e-mail captainmorgan@ btl.net. ULTRA-DELUXE.

In a lovely South Seas–style building that looks across the beach, **Jade Garden** invites with its polished wood floors, soaring wood ceilings and pink and white linens. The Chinese fare does not shine as much as the decor, but it is a welcome change of pace. Chop suey, chow mein, sweet and sour and foo yong dishes are available, as well as American specials such as ribeye steak and seafood kebabs. ~ Located a half mile south of the airstrip, San Pedro; 22-62506. MODERATE TO DELUXE.

DINING

Elvi's Kitchen has sand floors, long picnic tables, an enormous palapa roof and a tree growing up through the middle—the perfect venue for trading tall tales. Waiters in bow ties and starched

BOAT TOUR
A Day in the Cayes

Some visitors—especially scuba enthusiasts in search of a reef less crowded than the one at Cozumel, Mexico—may opt to spend their whole vacation on Ambergris Caye (page 80). But most of us can fully appreciate the major cayes by spending one to three days as part of a well-balanced surf-and-turf Belizean adventure. Though it's easy enough to catch a small plane to the cayes, here's a way that's cheaper and lots more fun.

WATER TAXI TERMINAL   Water taxis are fast, open motorboats (with canvas tops for bad weather) that carry two dozen or so passengers, tourists and locals alike, as well as a surprising amount of luggage and cargo. They leave from the terminal near the north end of Belize City's **Swing Bridge** (page 122). Start your trip first thing in the morning, bearing in mind that departures start early in the day and the last boats return around mid-afternoon. Plan to eat when you arrive on Ambergris Caye; it's easier to find a good breakfast there than in the city. Schedules are posted at the ticket window, and you can buy your ticket any time before the boat leaves. A roundtrip ticket saves money.

AT SEA   Feel the cool saltwater spray as the water taxi careens across smooth turquoise water with an occasional thrilling bump over another boat's wake. If a passenger is going there, or if you pay the pilot a little extra for a detour, you may get a close-up view of secluded **St. George's Caye** (page 102) or the improbable golf course on Caye Chapel. Water taxis stop at Caye Caulker coming and going from Ambergris Caye. I

white shirts serve lobster, burgers, fish sandwiches, and fish platters, as well as such Belizean favorites as conch soup and shrimp in watermelon sauce. Closed Sunday. ~ Pescador Drive, San Pedro; 22-62176. MODERATE TO DELUXE.

To savor Jamaica food so authentic it will bring tears to your eyes, head for the **Jam Bel Jerk Pit**, a tiny three-table eatery located behind Big Daddy's bar. The main fare is chicken rubbed with jerk seasoning (piquant and salty, made from habañero peppers, scallions, allspice and secret ingredients) and barbecued. ~ Barrier Reef Drive, San Pedro; 22-62594. BUDGET.

If you arrive at San Pedro by boat, you'll immediately spot Fido's Courtyard, home to **Fido's Restaurant**. Once a burger-and-chicken-wings joint, it's reincarnated as a civilized place where you can order such tantalizing fare as shrimp fajitas, conch fritters, coconut chicken and English-style fish-and-chips. Sunday

suggest visiting Ambergris first; it will likely enhance your appreciation of less-touristy Caye Caulker. The trip to San Pedro on Ambergris Caye takes about one and a quarter hours.

AMBERGRIS CAYE   First make sure you can identify the water taxi dock from among the similar piers that line the whole waterfront. Then take a stroll north along the beach past rows of scuba outfitters and palapa bars. Too early for a Belikin? Then it's probably time for breakfast. If a scuba or snorkeling adventure is in your plans, arrange it for tomorrow and check into a hotel; while dive trips go to the same places from both islands, San Pedro is much closer to the reef than Caye Caulker is. Ambergris has more in the way of water sports rentals such as sea kayaks, too.

CAYE CAULKER   The half-hour trip from San Pedro back to Caye Caulker takes you close to the nearly deserted northern half of the island before docking at the nameless fishing village on the southern half. Disembarking here puts you in the center of the village. Turn left and walk along the beach to find friendly little seafood restaurants and palapa bars, dive shops, sailboard rentals, funky fishermen's shacks and a picturesque old seaside cemetery, as well as good, affordable hotels and guesthouses should you opt to stay the night.

RETURN TO THE MAINLAND   When you complete the last leg of the water taxi trip and return to Belize City, you'll find cab drivers waiting in front of the terminal to take you back to your hotel for about US$5. Save your cash: except for the Princess, every lodging listed in this chapter is within a few minutes' walk of the Swing Bridge.

San Pedro has the best nightlife in Belize, with possibilities ranging from intimate seaside bars to over-the-water pubs and sand-floored discos.

---

brunch is accompanied by live music. ~ Barrier Reef Drive, San Pedro; 22-63176. MODERATE TO DELUXE.

Look for true-blue regional cooking at **Mangos**, a folksy restaurant north of the water taxi dock with a beachfront terrace shaded by a palm-thatch roof. Try the Creole blackened chicken, the Caribbean mango-lime chicken, or another tantalizing dish such as jambalaya or shrimp étouffée. ~ On the beach, next to the public library, San Pedro; 22-62859. BUDGET TO MODERATE.

Far removed from the relative hustle and bustle of the central beach zone, you'll find the **Sweet Basil Café and Cheese Shoppe**   ◀ HIDDEN at the river, about 15 minutes' walk north of the village. With great sea view from the upstairs deck of the bright pink-and-blue building and a menu that runs the gamut from corned beef sandwiches to pasta with shrimp, artichokes and feta, as well as a long list of dinner salads, this semi-vegetarian café is worth going out of your way for. Follow the hand-painted signs from Barrier Reef Drive. ~ Tres Cocos area; 22-63870. BUDGET.

Celi's on the Beach is located on the waterfront in front of the Holiday Hotel, San Pedro's very first hotel. If it's Wednesday, head to the beach for Celi's barbecue. Chicken, fish and pork chops are all served with Belizean beans, tortillas and cole slaw. Local musicians add to the tropical atmosphere. The rest of the week salads, fajitas, burgers, fish sandwiches and rice and beans are served for lunch. For dinner, there's all manner of fresh seafood—stone crabs, shrimp, fish and lobster—that's equally as sumptuous. The restaurant closes on Wednesday, when there's a barbecue on the beach. ~ At the Holiday Hotel, Barrier Reef Drive, San Pedro; 22-62014. MODERATE.

Lily's Treasure Chest Restaurant is widely known among locals for its hefty home-cooked portions. For breakfast, there's huevos rancheros and shrimp omelettes; for lunch or dinner, try the fried shrimp or fish simmered in Mexican barbecue sauce. The surroundings—battered rattan chairs, laminated wood clocks and turtle shells parked on the walls—are perfectly Belizean. ~ Barrier Reef Drive, San Pedro; 22-62059. MODERATE.

HIDDEN ►

On a breezy seafront veranda, beneath the slope of a deep blue canvas, you can dine well at **Capricorn Resort**. Chef Clarence Burdes' menu has elements of French, Italian, Californian and Belizean cuisine, and there are daily chalkboard specials. Start with the ceviche or mozzarella, fresh basil and tomatoes with baguette slices. Then order the seafood in a mushroom and sherry sauce piled high in a clamshell and baked; or the seafood or chicken crêpes. Finish with a creamy rum chocolate cake. There's intimate dining indoors and something more casual (with a limited menu) at the beach bar. Locals love this place, so call for a reservation (and a water taxi, if you're staying in San Pedro). Closed Wednesday. ~ Located at the northern end of Ambergris Caye; 22-62809. DELUXE.

SHOPPING

At Fido's Courtyard, **Belizean Arts** has been selling original paintings of Maya and island scenes, as well as folk-art furniture, for more than 20 years. Among the artists represented is Nicaraguan expatriate Walter Castillo, whose exuberant depictions of Belizean life have made him one of the most celebrated painters in Belize. Also watch for works by Orlando Garrido, who grew up among the Garifuna people of central Belize and carries on their artistic traditions. ~ Barrier Reef Drive, San Pedro; 22-63019; www.belizeanarts.com.

Among the studio galleries along Barrier Reef Drive is Eden Art, featuring exotic paintings and painted vases by Katrina Samuels (phone/fax 22-63149).

Big Daddy's is the last word on disco around these parts. **NIGHTLIFE**
Nothing fancy, the bamboo shanty on the beach rocks until the
wee hours of the morning. Bands play on Saturday nights. Cover.
~ Located on the seafront, toward the south end of San Pedro;
no phone.

Tarzan's is Big Daddy's rival disco, where punta rock and
dancehall reggae pulsate until 2 a.m. Cover. ~ Barrier Reef Drive,
across from Central Park, San Pedro; 22-64077.

The **Barefoot Iguana** features live rock and
reggae music so loud you can find your way there
from just about anywhere in town. ~ Coconut
Drive; 22-62927.

> San Pedro has the best
> nightlife in Belize, with
> possibilities ranging from
> intimate seaside bars
> to over-the-water
> pubs and sand-
> floored discos.

The obvious choice for a pub is **Sharks Bar**, perched
over the water at the end of a pier on the former site of
the Tackle Box, a perennial favorite divers' drinking establishment that was wiped out by Hurricane Mitch. The
aquarium tanks full of marine life from the waters below
bring you even closer to the sea. ~ Coral Beach Dive Shop, San
Pedro; 22-64313.

For a before- or after-dinner drink, nestle up to the long, padded
bar at **The Pier Lounge**. The Wednesday Chicken Drop betting
game (guess what the chicken drops) draws big crowds—for San
Pedro, that is. ~ Seafront, near the center of San Pedro; 22-62002.

If you're feeling lucky you may wish to stop in at the **Palace
Casino**. It ain't Vegas, but this aquamarine and purple hole-in-the-
wall is probably the tiniest gambling hall you'll ever encounter,
with a $20-limit blackjack table and 30 slot and video poker ma-
chines. ~ Caribena Street at Pescador Drive; 22-63570.

BOCA DEL RIO PARK Local families come to picnic and play   **BEACHES**
in this park at the mouth of San Pedro Lagoon. Few visitors   **& PARKS**
make it up this far; it's a long walk from the tourist zone, though
only a short trip by golf cart. There's good, shallow swimming
for the kids. ~ Located at the north end of San Pedro.

HOL CHAN MARINE RESERVE Hol Chan, ac-
cessible only by boat, is Belize's first national marine reserve.
This three-square-mile park encompasses an area that was close
to destruction from overfishing. Today, it teems with star coral,
ethereal sea fans, resplendent sponges, bright blue damselfish and
vibrantly colored parrotfish. Most fascinating, though, are the
green moray eels that inhabit the walls of the reserve's channel,
which is only 15 to 30 feet deep. You will likely see divemasters
feeding the eels (which they shouldn't), but don't try it yourself.
Morays become aggressive when fed, and can nip off a finger in
an instant. At a minimum, they can inflict a nasty poisonous sting.

Many dive boats also stop at **Mexico Rocks**, just outside the
barrier reef and the reserve. Slightly shallower, with depths of 8

to 15 feet, the water is clear and etched with constellations of elkhorn and staghorn coral, and churning with exotic fish.

Coral Gardens, south of Hol Chan, is an incredibly healthy reef (for now, at least) with an average depth of 12 feet. Snapper and barracuda prowl the finger and brain coral and sea fans here. Nearby is **Shark Ray Alley**, a sandbar where docile sting rays and nurse sharks gather. ~ The entire park is underwater and located about four miles south of Ambergris Caye.

HIDDEN ▶ **BACALAR CHICO NATIONAL PARK** 🏃 🛶 🚤 🛥 ⚓ Covering about 41 square miles across northern Ambergris, the park takes in sandy sea floors and canyons of coral; rock ledges and caves prowled by enormous grouper; lagoons and mudflats; and chunks of island where the scenery might be lush ridge forest or exposed limestone boulders, deep sinkholes or dry savanna. Offshore, snorkeling and diving are remarkable, and fishing is permitted in specific areas; check with park rangers before casting your line. Onshore lie seven Maya sites. Puma and jaguar prowl the forest and savanna, though you probably won't see one. There's a ranger station and visitors center about a mile from the park border. ~ Located on the north end of Ambergris Caye, near Mexico, and accessible only by boat; 22-62247 in San Pedro.

▼▼▼▼▼▼▼▼▼▼▼▼
Caye Caulker

Just 20 scenic minutes by boat from Ambergris Caye but decades away in spirit, Caye Caulker is a quintessential hidden destination in the Caribbean. Electricity arrived in the mid-1980s, and the first crude guesthouses and restaurants opened soon afterward. Today the side of the island that faces the Caribbean is lined with small lodgings, including several with such luxuries as private baths. There are two dozen restaurants in town, most of them serving the catch that locals bring in each day. The rhythms of a traditional fishing village endure. Life here feels like a slowmotion film, with dogs lazing everywhere and rows of battered clapboard homes tilting ever-so-slightly to the wind. Barefoot children tote tubs of bananas on their heads, and fishermen wrestle conch meat from their shells along crooked docks.

Spanning a five-square-mile area, Caye Caulker is half inhabited; the other half is swamp and mangroves. The village is only three streets wide (Front Street, Middle Street and Back Street) and ten streets long—all sand, of course. A handful of silent electric golf carts serve as taxis. There's not an automobile on the entire island.

The island itself is filled with flowers and trees of raging color—flaming red flamboyants and purple bougainvillea, canary mandavilla and ruby hibiscus. Coconut palms are so plentiful that their fruit litters every sandy street. Breadfruit trees grow so big they camouflage stilt houses, and their fleshy fruits dangle like green bowling balls.

Perhaps it is the swamplands, or the island's thin ties with reality, that give Caulker its mysterious edge. Listen to the perpetual breezes that blow across the island and you will hear small-town whispers of strange people and places. There is a woman storyteller, locals will say, who spins yarns late at night, but only when storms are brewing, and somewhere is a lagoon filled with crocodiles, a disco that is haunted, and a mangrove forest where Maya cults worship. Who knows, they shrug, maybe it's the same place where the ancient Maya worshiped long ago.

Some 2000 years ago, the Maya were Caye Caulker's original islanders. They followed the buccaneers, who didn't stay very long but whose English accents gave the island its current nickname, Caye Corker. But many of Caulker's present-day residents are descendants of the Meztizos, who fled here in 1855 during Yucatan's War of the Castes, the Maya revolt in which warriors massacred most Mexicans living on the peninsula to the north. In 1870, a Meztizo named Luciano Reyes bought the island for US$150 when he lost the bid for Ambergris Caye. Reyes' descendants still live on the island and are some of its most prominent residents. A roughly equal number of residents are Creole families who have settled here over the years to fish the sheltered waters on the west side of the island. Together, they form a microcosm of Caribbean culture.

Caye Caulker is still very much a fishing village; every afternoon along the seafront, crayon-colored sloops arrive laden with snapper, grouper and, in season, pearly conch and bright pink lobsters. Some sloops suggest they may be loaded with something else; notice the boats named Suspect, Miss Conduct and Bong tied to the village docks. Right next to the docks is the tiny island cemetery, overgrown with weeds. Through the years, Caulker

---

THIS WAY TO TOWN

Caye Caulker's 700 residents are protective of their little paradise, keeping its development as a travel destination cautious and deliberate. When local officials announced plans to open an airstrip, residents rallied against it, saying it would bring too much tourism. In 1991, the airstrip did open, and now as many as seven planes a day land here en route to Ambergris Caye. If you arrive in one of them, you'll be deposited in a place that looks like the mangrove boonies, with only one house in sight. Not to worry, just pick up your bags and start walking north (toward that house), and you'll soon find yourself in town. If you arrive by water taxi, a 45-minute trip from Belize City, you'll disembark right in the middle of the village; consult the map at the dock to locate your lodging up or down the beach.

has existed in the shadow of Ambergris, which is larger and more sophisticated than its tiny neighbor. Here sophistication comes on a more basic level.

Not long ago Caulker was known as a druggie's hangout. Now a new hand-painted billboard in front of the police department notifies visitors that drugs are illegal everywhere in Belize, including Caye Caulker, yes, even on the beach, no matter what anybody tells you. Breeze is readily available, of course, but if you choose to buy, the dreadlocked hustler who provides it will warn you that it is only to be smoked in your room, never on the beach, mon! The island's unspoken policy is that the occasional mainstream tourist who comes here should see nothing that makes him or her uncomfortable.

The fact is that even for Belize, Caye Caulker is an especially safe place. As this book goes to press, the island has had only one violent crime (a bar fight between two drunken tourists) in the past two years.

In the morning, village women pluck the fruit from breadfruit trees and turn it into breadfruit bread; you can smell it baking through open windows. Kids with plastic baskets sell it along Front Street.

Caye Caulker's worst recent natural disaster came in October 2000, when Hurricane Keith stalled along the Belize coast, pounding the island with 100-mile-an-hour winds and waves that crashed all the way across to the other shore. When it was over, the mangroves and palms had been stripped bare, every telephone pole was snapped to the ground and the streets were so filled with debris that the only way to get from one part of the village to another was by boat. Yet by the time peak season came three months later, the vegetation had grown lush again and most of the hotels had been rebuilt sturdier than before. A disaster relief effort not only gave Caye Caulker an electricity and phone system far more reliable than the old one, but funded a $350,000 beach restoration project to create a 60-foot-wide crushed shell beach along the entire eastern shore. (The distant reef breaks the surf and so prevents beachbuilding from occurring naturally.)

SIGHTS Visitors can learn about the island, and Belize's fragile reef system, in slide shows offered at the BTIA Center near the airstrip. ~ 22-12079. Other than the slide show, nighttime activities are pretty much limited to dining on catch of the day, drinking rum at a tiki bar, and gazing at the stars.

For island information and tours to other cayes or the mainland, stop by the **Caye Caulker Tour Guide Association**. ~ Center of town; 22-60343. Nearby is the village message board with formal notices and odd bits of advertising ("Reflexology! Go to Little Blue House next door to Frenchies").

During the day, snorkeling, scuba diving and fishing are top pursuits. Several boats offer excursions, but by far the most popular trips are with **Chocolate,** the island's most famous boat captain. Chocolate lives in a thatched-roof house along the seashore with his partner, aptly named Annie Seashore. His manatee-watching trips, all-day excursions with a stop at Goff's Caye, are excellent and priced right: US$27.50 per person, including snorkel gear (but not lunch). ~ 22-60151.

If modest, back-to-nature accommodations are your style (and budget), you've come to the right place. Lodging on Caye Caulker means, for the most part, clean, nondescript rooms that have ceiling fans and hot water. The water on Caye Caulker is not purified, so use only bottled water for drinking and brushing your teeth.

LODGING

By far the best place to sleep on Caye Caulker is at **Chocolate.** There's only one room, a stylish and spacious second-floor perch staring at the sea, with a queen-size mahogany poster bed, vaulted mahogany ceilings, a ceiling fan, a table fan, a mini-refrigerator and pretty ceramic tile throughout. Chocolate's partner, Annie Seashore, runs the place, making sure there are freshly ground coffee beans in the coffeemaker every night. Call ahead for this room—it's a superb spot. ~ Seafront, north end of town; 22-60151; e-mail chocolate@btl.net. MODERATE.

Next door to the cemetery, the cheerful, yellow **Tropical Paradise Hotel** caps the south end of Front Street with a showy arched gateway. Owned by the Reyes family, descendants of Luciano Reyes, the hotel offers rooms in a main concrete building or along two rows of tiny, tin-roofed, plywood cabañas parked next to the beach. The cabanas, by far the best choice, feature vinyl floors, wood-paneled walls, newly remodeled bathrooms and ceiling fans. Some have TVs. Seven cabañas have wall-unit air conditioners. ~ Seafront on the south end of town; 22-60124, fax 22-60063; www.startoursbelize.com, e-mail startours@btl. net. BUDGET TO MODERATE.

Next door, the **Seabeezzz** really is a breeeezzzy place to stay. Constant trade winds cool three small clapboard buildings, where six tidy rooms provide clean, comfortable lodging. Best of all, the rooms open onto an immaculate courtyard brimming with tropical plants and exotic fruit trees. Closed mid-May to mid-November. ~ Seafront, south end of town; 22-60176, fax 22-60276; www. come.to/seabeezzz.com. MODERATE.

Located toward the south end of the beach, the European-run **Seaview Hotel** is a modern Mediterranean-style stucco villa with four ground-floor guest rooms and a beach cottage that can accommodate four people. Rooms have double beds, ceiling fans, tables and chairs, refrigerators and private baths with electric hot water. A veranda and a floating palapa at the end of the hotel dock offer cool, breezy relaxation. ~ P.O. Box 11, Caye Caulker; 22-60205; www.belizenet.com/seaview, e-mail seaview@btl.net. MODERATE.

HIDDEN ►

The road stops at Seabeezzz, so you'll have to walk along the beach to get to **Shirley's Guest House**. In a secluded, peaceful spot swept by sea breezes are ten rooms in a two-story building, as well as one duplex and one whitewashed cabin, all with Mennonite mahogany furnishings and fans. The rooms and duplex share baths (including three outdoor facilities), while the cabin has a private bath. ~ Seafront, south end of town; 22-60145; www.shirleysguest house.com, e-mail shirley@btl.net. MODERATE.

Vega Inn and Gardens has a handful of tidy rooms and two suites for rent (all with ceiling fans). The suites are rustic in appearance, with unfinished wood walls, mahogany plank floors and hammocks in the breezy front rooms, but feature such modern amenities as cable TV, coffeemakers, minibars and hairdryers. The grounds are expansive and beautifully landscaped with tropical flowering plants. The local family that owns the place treats the guests like family. They also manage several other rental properties around town. ~ Seafront near the middle of town; 22-60142, fax 22-60269; www.vega.com.bz, e-mail lifestyles@ vega.com.bz. BUDGET TO DELUXE.

De Real Macaw Guest House, a two-story wood structure 60 yards from the sea's edge, offers new, large guest rooms with air-conditioning, cable TV and private baths. Each of the seven sparely furnished units has a thatch-roofed porch with a hammock and lounging chairs. ~ Center of town; 22-60459, fax 22-60497; www.derealmacaw.com, e-mail derealmacaw@yahoo.com. MODERATE.

The owners of the Sand Box, the island's longtime local favorite restaurant, have opened two affordable hotels, both called Trends. **Trends Beachfront**, located near Caye Caulker's main pier, is a moderately priced divers' paradise with spacious, comfortable rooms—each with a queen-size bed and a double bed. There are ceiling fans but no air-conditioning, and each bath is shared by two guest units. Hammocks festoon the broad, breezy porches. Nearby, **Trends Hotel** has no-frills rooms with one or two double beds, ceiling fans, private baths and the lowest private room rates on the island. It's located near the center of town, five minutes from the beach. ~ 22-60094, fax 22-60097; www.trends bze.com, e-mail trendsbze@btl.net. BUDGET TO MODERATE.

HIDDEN ►

Tina's Bakpak Youth Hostel has dormitory bunk beds for US $7 a night and attracts fun groups of young adventurers. The proprietress, a Caye Caulker native, guided wildlife safaris in Africa and worked as a divemaster around the Caribbean islands before returning home to start this place. She also offers dive certification courses and organizes group ecotourism trips all over Belize. ~ 22-22351, fax 22-22078; e-mail t-travels@btl.net. BUDGET.

The prettiest pastel buildings on the waterfront can be found at the **Rainbow Hotel**. Inside the 17 rooms are attractive green tile floors, ceiling fans, battered dressers and mattresses that range from firm to lumpy. Eleven of the rooms have cable TV. Two apartments offer fully equipped kitchens. ~ North end of town; 22-60123, fax 22-60172. BUDGET TO MODERATE.

Classy Caye Caulker accommodations await on the leeward side of the island at the **Iguana Reef Inn**. This exclusive lodge offers 12 spacious, air-conditioned suites with furniture and artwork by local artisans. Most have two queen-size beds, bay windows and vaulted ceilings. The location, a few minutes' walk from the village but so far away in spirit that you could easily believe yourself on a deserted island, is ideal for fishing. Or you can simply kick back and while the day away on the wide verandas or sandy private beach. ~ P.O. Box 31, Caye Caulker; 22-60213, fax 22-60087; www.iguana reefinn.com, e-mail iguanareef@btl.net. DELUXE.

The cabanas at Tropical Paradise Hotel offer the only air-conditioned lodging on Caye Caulker.

Caye Caulker's only B&B, the **Lazy Iguana Bed and Breakfast** stands four stories tall, offering spectacular 360-degree views of the island and the sea, and has just four guest rooms. Each room is extra-large and individually decorated in a happy tropical color scheme. The complimentary breakfast highlights the native tropical fruits of Belize. ~ P.O. Box 59, Caye Caulker; 22-60350, fax 22-60320; www.lazyiguana.net, e-mail momiller77@aol.com. DELUXE.

DINING

Caye Caulker's eateries are offbeat, super casual (don't mind the cats or dogs) and full of weird possibilities. A hippie will serve you tonight, but tomorrow night's waiter may be a moonlighting preacher or even a kid from down the street. Chairs and tables never match—that would be boring—and hours are apt to change with boating conditions.

Considering the norm, then, the restaurant at the **Tropical Paradise Hotel** seems almost formal. Red and blue starched linens cover every table and the service is dependably good. The breakfast, lunch and dinner fare isn't spectacular, but most meals are under US$5. Fresh fish and shellfish, fried chicken, hamburgers and Creole dishes are available. ~ South end of town; 22-60124. BUDGET.

For fine dining, go to **Habaneros**, a new restaurant aimed at the resort crowd. It boasts internationally trained chefs and the best wine list in the Cayes. Choose from such house specialties as Brazilian pork charbroiled with cinnamon and allspice, Thai-style seafood coconut curry or breast of chicken stuffed with cheese and a julienne of garden vegetables, pan-fried and served with white wine dijon crème. ~ Beachfront; 22-60487. DELUXE.

The most happening place around is **Popeye's Bar**, where divers congregate at sundown to compare notes on the day's adventures. A television set blaring CNN news and a small bank of slot machines set the ambience. The fare includes American-style breakfasts and generous portions of shrimp, lobster and fish. Count on finding this place open when no place else is. ~ On the beach; 22-60032. MODERATE.

Rasta Pasta Rainforest Café, another very popular beachfront eatery, has a sand floor, Jamaican-motif decor, a *very* relaxed atmosphere and superfriendly waitstaff. The fare includes fresh breads and pastries baked on the premises, pizzas and an array of other choices including spicy vegetarian dishes. The huge burritos are locally legendary. The owners also package their own Genesis in the Jungle spice blends, which make ideal culinary souvenirs of Belize. ~ Beachfront; 22-60358. BUDGET TO MODERATE.

HIDDEN ▶ The place for lunch here is **Syd's**, a battered little house with mesh screens and Christmas lights strung across the ceiling. Syd is not in sight, but his wife will gladly throw a cheeseburger or grilled cheese on the griddle, or whip up some garnachos or burritos. Closed Sunday. ~ Avenida Langosto at Aventurera Street; 20-60294. BUDGET.

Among the best places on the island for traditional Belizean fare is **Marin's Restaurant and Bar**. The spotless, cheerful bamboo-paneled eatery serves lobster omelettes for breakfast, lobster ceviche for lunch and lobster pasta for dinner, as well as great rice and beans, pineapple shrimp and vegetarian choices. ~ Town center; 22-60104. BUDGET TO MODERATE.

Paper lanterns, Mennonite mahogany tables and sea views lure diners to the **Sand Box**. Once you're there, the talented chef and owner, a woman from southern Florida, treats you to fresh, inventive pasta and seafood dishes. Top choices are lobster lasagna, conch fritters, and snapper stuffed with spinach, shrimp and mushrooms. Easily the island's best food. ~ Facing the sea on the north end of town; 22-60200. BUDGET.

SHOPPING Shopping is a loose term here; it's more like whatever you happen to find that's open *and* has merchandise that day. Drop by **Celi's Gift Shop & Music Center**, owned by a local musician, for a wide selection of punta, soca, reggae and other Caribbean sounds, as well as handmade coconut jewelry. ~ Center of town; 22-60346.

Check out the striking jewelry handmade from Belizean materials including conch shells, tropical seeds, cow horns, rare hardwoods and amethyst by local artist **Hugo Rene Ba Aguilar** in his workshop adjoining Celi's. ~ Phone c/o Cyber Cafe Caye Caulker; 22-22402.

Near the north end of town is **Chocolate's**, where Annie Seashore, Chocolate's partner, sells good quality T-shirts, tropical wear and hammocks. ~ 22-60151.

Oceanside Restaurant & Bar, a bamboo hut with sand floors, dart boards and pool tables, gets crowded and a little raunchy. Live bands play on Friday and Saturday and on other nights recorded blues, punta and reggae entertain crowds who gladly heed the bar's sign that says "No Shoes, No Shirts, No Problem." ~ Seafront, on the north end of town; 22-60233.

NIGHTLIFE

North of the village where the populated part of the island ends at The Split, the **Lazy Lizard Bar & Grille** is a popular tiki bar, especially on weekend nights when beach parties tend to spill out of the bar and into the surrounding sand. ~ The Split; 22-22368.

THE SPLIT The Split was created in 1961, compliments of Hurricane Hattie. It's now the place to hang with locals, who cool off in the air-clear aquamarine channel (beware of strong currents) and warm up on little sun docks. The "public beach" is really a small patch of dirt with palm trees. There are a couple of marooned boats and a popular tiki bar. Despite treacherous currents, this is the most popular snorkeling spot on the island. ~ Located at the northern end of town.

BEACHES & PARKS

CAYE CAULKER FOREST RESERVE AND SIWA-BAN FOREST RESERVE The nearly uninhabited half of the island north of The Split has been set aside as a forest reserve with hiking trails. You can also get a taste of the mangrove, palm and gumbo-limbo jungle by walking the nature trail through the Siwa-Ban Forest Reserve just north of the airstrip. Simply walk to the end of the beach, keep going and you're on the trail. ~ South end of Caye Caulker.

CAYE CAULKER MARINE RESERVE This marine reserve runs between Caye Caulker and the barrier reef, taking in turtle grass lagoons and miles of transparent sea. There are the typical parrotfish and angelfish and crabs living here, but also some strange sea worms such as the Christmas tree worm with bristly branches, and the feather duster worm that looks just like

◄ HIDDEN

AUTHOR FAVORITE

The way I really get into a Caye Caulker mode is to walk upstairs into **I & I Reggae Bar** and have a drink. The outdoor terrace is as funky as can be, with haphazard tables, plants potted in plastic buckets, and reggae bands playing beneath the inky night sky. If you can't go late, go for sunset. ~ South end of town, a block from the Tropical Paradise; 22-22206.

a little feather duster. The snorkeling and diving are compelling, the fishing not bad. ~ Located along the east side of Caye Caulker.

St. George's Caye

The idyllic caye called St. George's is nearly two miles long and 800 feet wide at its broadest point, and is shaped like a wriggly crescent. From Belize City, it's just 20 minutes by boat across the clear sand flats, making it Belize's most accessible isle of escape. Little wonder that St. George's is a weekend haunt for wealthy Belizeans, whose charming stilt homes of painted clapboard are propped along the beach.

Given the island's eye-blink size and population (just 20 permanent residents), it is difficult to imagine that it was the capital of Belize from 1650 to 1784, or that for two centuries it was hotly fought over by the Spanish and British. By 1650, the island's residents were mainly English logwood and mahogany traders who grew numerous crops on the caye, despite the ban on crop growing that kept the colonies dependent on the Crown. The Spanish regularly raided the crops. As one islander tells it: "Every couple of years the Spanish Navy would sail in, burn all the crops, hoist up the Spanish flag, and sail away. By the time the crops were good and growing again, the Spanish were back. It was a frustrating cycle."

The Spanish called St. George's Caye Cayo Casino even after the British made it the capital of the Belizean colony in 1650.

The tug-of-war continued until 1798, when the Spanish lost the Battle of St. George's Caye. Belizeans commemorate the battle with a national holiday and much revelry. Some, however, claim it was not a battle at all, but simply some Spanish galleons retreating after being confronted by a ragtag band of Belizeans in boats. Official history, however, records the presence of a British schooner and the volleying of many cannon balls before the victory.

SIGHTS

Appropriately, a single cannon on the beach memorializes the battle today. Near the cannon are several graves, some occupied by early settlers and others by the recently deceased. A footpath wends past the graves to St. George's other inhabitants: three lodges, a few lobster fishers whose rickety traps are stacked higher than the palm trees, an aquarium builder (you can peek your head in, but there's not much to see), and the British Joint Forces "Adventurous Training Centre." The training, judging from the troops' activities, involves playing volleyball in the sand and drinking Belikin beer by the sea.

LODGING

St. George's Lodge is ideal for hard-core divers who prefer a rigorous schedule. Each day's agenda, organized and directed by owner Fred Good of Texas, calls for diving interspersed with dive instruction and discussion, with time for three meals but little time for relaxation. Which is too bad, considering the lodge enjoys a picturesque location on the sea. Guests can choose from six rustic cabanas perched on stilts over the water or ten bedrooms in a main house that are narrow and breezeless (some rooms have ceiling fans), quite monkish in design. Meals, dives and boat transfers from Belize City are included in the rates—among the highest lodging rates in all of Belize—and, in my opinion, not worth it. ~ For reservations, call 22-04444 in Belize City, or 800-849-2130 in the U.S.; www.gooddiving.com, e-mail aw2trav2 bz@aol.com. ULTRA-DELUXE.

At the opposite end of St. George's Caye is **Cottage Colony**, where six prim cottages are painted in sherbet colors, trimmed in gingerbread and framed by a white picket fence. Their interiors are airy and modern, with hardwood floors and white wicker furniture, and their porches face a shady courtyard next to the beach. About half have air conditioners—lifesavers on hot days! The official gathering place is the second-floor bar and restaurant overlooking the sea. Typical activities here are diving, fishing and beach bumming. Rates are by the week only and include all meals and boat transportation to the island. ~ 22-02020; e-mail fins@btl.net. DELUXE TO ULTRA-DELUXE.

◄ HIDDEN

DINING

Dining is restricted to the two island lodges, and non-guests (usually boaters at anchor) will need a reservation. **St. George's Lodge** serves healthy fare including homemade breads and soups, as well as special request meals. ~ Call 22-04444 in Belize City. ULTRA-DELUXE

Cottage Colony's restaurant specializes in Belizean fare such as fry chicken, grilled pork chops and T-bone steaks. If the fish are biting, they will be on the menu, too. ~ 22-02020. MODERATE TO DELUXE.

BEACHES & PARKS

St. George's is tiny, the patches of sand infinitesimal and unofficial. Almost everyone who comes here stays at **St. George's Lodge** or **Cottage Colony**, which have their own little beaches.

The Atolls

Farther out to sea lie three atolls, coral isles that form rings around lagoons. These dazzling island necklaces actually sit atop the Maya Mountains; over the eons, the coral blossomed on the mountains until it rose above the sea. The sea, in turn, pulverized their rocky shores into cushiony white sand that makes the atolls look like some exotic Pacific isles. Most of the world's atolls do in fact lie in the Pacific. Only four exist in the Western Hemisphere, and three of these are in Belize. The fourth atoll, Chinchorro, is in Mexico just across the Belize border.

From the air, the Belize atolls appear as stunning oddities, with the calm emerald waters of the lagoons seemingly corralled by the blustery blue waters of the sea. On land, the scenery is just as compelling. The faraway isles that make up Turneffe Islands, Lighthouse Reef and Glover's Reef atolls are the quintessence of tropical paradise: pearly beaches studded with swaying coconut palms and washed with warm, shallow waters. Bird life is prolific and bountiful, and giant sea turtles build their nests in virtual privacy. Northern promontories attract swarms of grouper and snapper, who spawn each year with little interruption from a hook and line.

Just offshore, the sea bottom plummets, then becomes wildly etched with spiked ridges, rolling canyons and lattice-like caverns. The ridges have brought down many a ship, laid them to rest in what is now a virtual nautical graveyard of the 18th and 19th centuries. These sunken ancients, together with the many sheer walls webbed with sea life, make the surrounding waters an extraordinary place to dive.

SIGHTS

Only a few years ago, Belize's atolls were considered the outer limits of Caribbean diving. But as word spread, they have become the "in" place to dive; their virtues are whispered on the diving grapevine and exalted in glossy dive magazines. Most divers hear about **Turneffe Islands** first. The largest and westernmost of Belize's atolls, Turneffe is located about two and a half hours from Belize City by boat. Here, one can dive the Black Beauty, where ebony coral blankets a reef, and The Elbow, where curtains of giant fish waft up and down a 150-foot wall of coral. There is an excellent dive lodge on Turneffe, as well as a fishing camp and an ecotourism retreat.

HIDDEN ▶

Besides its size and fantastic diving, what really sets Turneffe apart are its mangrove forests. Brilliant orchids drape from the mangrove limbs, and schools of fish seek protection in their roots. Mangrove lagoons provide safe haven for many manatees and dolphins, which are the main reason **Blackbird Caye Village** opened in 1991. This research center and ecotourist resort is the venture of Belizean Ray Lightburn and American Al Dugan, who have hired scientists to study marine life in the area. The 4000-acre island and its surrounding waters are still extremely pristine, and sea life is profuse. The village focal point is a dolphin research center, where scientists are studying the communication and other behaviors of these gregarious mammals. Lightburn and Dugan hope the village will make the Turneffe atoll a national park.

Within the Lighthouse Reef atoll are numerous natural wonders, most notably the **Blue Hole**, explored in the 1970s by Jacques Cousteau. Actually an ocean sinkhole, it measures a spectacular 1000 feet across and plunges 480 feet down from the atoll's ten-

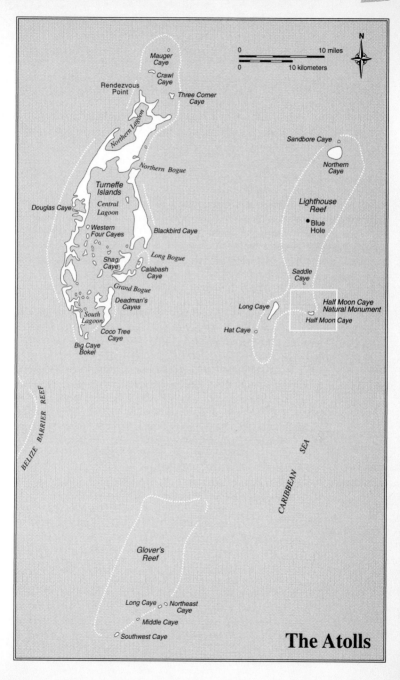

The Atolls

foot-deep lagoon. Riddled with stalactites and stalagmites and pitch-black caves, the Blue Hole is difficult to reach (on a calm day, it's three hours by boat from Belize City), but that only adds to its mystique. Several dive operators offer one-day trips, but dedicated scuba divers should consider staying at **Lighthouse Reef Resort,** which includes a trip to the Blue Hole in its one-week package. ~ 800-423-3114 in the U.S.

Located at the southeast corner of Lighthouse Reef atoll is **Half Moon Caye Natural Monument,** a haven for the rare red-footed booby. You may also spy loggerhead turtles, iguanas, ospreys and mangrove warblers. For more information, see "Beaches & Parks" below. ~ Belize Audubon Society; 22-35004 in Belize City; e-mail base@btl.net.

HIDDEN ▶

Because of its extreme remoteness, Belize's southernmost atoll is also its least visited. **Glover's Reef** is two-and-a-half to five hours (depending on the size and type of boat) from Belize City—not a pleasant trip on rough seas. But on calm days, it is a fantastic voyage, with mesmerizing vistas of sapphire waters that meet blue skies and the tiniest, most serene little islands.

The atoll is named for English buccaneer John Glover, who set up camp here during the 1700s, not knowing he was living on the hemisphere's most shapely atoll. Glover's coral outcroppings form a nearly unbroken oval whose vertical sides fall away to inky depths. If drained of their seas, they would look like a Pacific volcano.

Inside the coral lies an 80-square-mile lagoon of the most intensely beautiful water, riddled with hundreds of patch reefs and sea creatures of flamboyant colors and shapes. Outside its borders are the wrecks of five 18th-century English merchant ships, which met their doom on jagged coral. Glover's has but six cayes, all fringed with fabulous white sand and palm trees, and all located on the southeastern corner of the atoll.

LODGING

The most popular atoll resort is **Turneffe Island Lodge,** situated on a private 12-acre caye. A cluster of charming frame bungalows with ceiling fans, swallowed in palm trees, line the sandy shore and offer comfortable rooms with private baths and views of the sea; some have air conditioning. Guests spend most of their time in the sea, either diving the fabulous reef or fishing the flats. The waters around Turneffe are renowned for bonefish. To help keep them that way, the lodge limits the number of anglers to eight per week. The minimum stay is three nights; included are all meals and boat transportation from Belize City—about a two-and-a-half-hour trip. ~ Caye Bokel, Turneffe Islands atoll; for reservations, call 22-12011 in Belize City, or 713-236-7739 or, 800-874-0118, fax 713-236-7743 in the U.S.; www.turneffelodge.com, e-mail info@turneffelodge.com. ULTRA-DELUXE.

Kayaking, snorkeling, occupying a hammock—these are the primary pursuits of those fortunate enough to check into **Blackbird Caye Resort**. Set on a 166-acre jungle-covered island and surrounded by water that's deeply turquoise, the resort offers woodsy accommodations with air conditioning in ten thatched beach cabanas, a duplex and a triplex. Nature trails curl through the tropical brush, dolphins frequent the surrounding mangrove lagoons and three piers offer hook-and-line possibilities. Minimum stay is three nights. Meals and transfers from Belize City are included in the rate. ~ Turneffe Islands atoll; reservations, 888-271-3483, fax 206-463-4081 in the U.S.; www.blackbirdresort.com, e-mail dive@blackbirdresort.com. ULTRA-DELUXE.

◄ HIDDEN

For thousands of years, the site of **Turneffe Flats** has been a fishing camp, first for the Maya and now for visiting anglers who come armed with fly rods. Flats fishing is naturally the big draw, but guides are also available for reef and deep-sea fishing. The lodge can also arrange dive trips. Guests stay in one of sixteen comfortable wood-frame bungalows with porches on the beach. A 24-hour generator turns the ceiling fans in each room and provides the hot water for showers. There's a bar and family-style dining room, where Belizean entrées are the highlight. The minimum fishing or diving package is one week, which includes one night in Belize City at the Fiesta Inn, all meals, transportation and guides. Stays are for three, four or seven nights. ~ On Northern Bogue, on the northeast side of the Turneffe Islands atoll; for reser-

AUTHOR FAVORITE

Surrounded by coconut palms that light up like Christmas trees after dark, the **Portofino Beach Resort** on Ambergris Caye offers the kind of away-from-it-all seclusion that makes for an island daydream come true. Yet, it's less than half an hour by complimentary shuttle or commercial water taxi from the lively atmosphere of San Pedro. Located near the north end of the caye, and flanked by large private vacation homes, the resort has eight beach cabanas as well as three "treetop" suites built on stilts, all with tall palapa roofs and front decks that feature hammocks and unobstructed sea views. The white, sandy beach is one of the widest on the island, and the dock extends far out into the water to an enclosed saltwater swimming area. Nearby, herons, egrets and other wading birds scour shallow eelgrass flats and feast on tropical fish. The resort's Le Bistro restaurant, considered one of the finest on the island, serves Continental cuisine. ~ Six miles north of San Pedro, Ambergris Caye; 22-05096, fax 22-64272; www.portofinobelize.com, e-mail info@portofinobelize.com. ULTRA-DELUXE.

vations call 888-512-8812, fax 623-298-5008 in the U.S.;
www.tflats.com, e-mail vacation@tflats.com. ULTRA-DELUXE.

Two and a half hours by boat from the mainland, **Manta Resort**
is a seclusionist's paradise. It's nestled on its own 12-acre fantasy
island, with nothing but fluffy white sand, palm trees and sapphire
waters that plunge to inky black depths. The attention-getter is
a vast thatched cantina, stuck way out in the sea at the end of a
pier. Here, guests meet for eating, drinking and partaking of the
gorgeous sea views. The accommodations are nothing fancy: 12
cabanas (with ceiling fans) made of mahogany and featuring tiny
porches with hammocks over the sand. For those who want more
creature comforts, there's a modern two-bedroom family house
with air conditioning, kitchen, and even television and VCR (unheard of in the out islands!). Rates include all meals and boat
transfers from Belize City. Manta Resort is closed for renovation
until early 2004. ~ Glover's Reef atoll; for reservations, call 800-
326-1724, fax 206-463-4081 in the U.S.; www.mantaresortbe
lize.com, e-mail info@cayeresorts.com. ULTRA-DELUXE.

More modest accommodations are available at **Glover's Atoll
Resort**, on a nine-acre island set amid 700 coral patches with
good diving, swimming, snorkeling, windsurfing and kayaking
right from shore. Small dorm-style thatched cabins, available on
a first-come, first-served basis, are budget-priced US$149 per
person per week; there's also a beach cabana. Transportation is
available from Dangriga, leaving Sunday and returning Saturday,
so if you go, you'll be there for a full week. Bring your own food
and supplies. ~ P.O. Box 563, Belize City; 52-05216, fax 22-
35424; www.glovers.com.bz, e-mail tinfo@glovers.com.bz. BUDGET.

DINING   All out-island lodges include meals with their packages—there
simply is nowhere else to eat!

BEACHES   **HALF MOON CAYE NATURAL MONUMENT**
& PARKS   This 45-acre sanctuary, Belize's first national park, has sensational beaches and about 4000 red-footed booby birds, who
nest on the southern end of the caye and are very rare. Arrive
here at dusk and you may catch one of nature's intense shows:
aerial bird fights between the frigates and boobies. Among the

---

BEACH PATROL

There are few mangroves on the Lighthouse Reef atoll, but there are
ravishing beaches, whose promenades of luxuriant, crisp white sand are
sprinkled with palms and washed by pleated seas dyed green and blue
and, at sunset, blazing violet.

other fascinating creatures living here are mangrove warblers and frigate birds, wish-willy lizards, and loggerhead and hawksbill turtles, who lay their eggs on the eastern beaches. A raised platform provides bird's-eye views of all the animal action. For information, contact the Belize Audubon Society; 2-35004 in Belize City; e-mail base@btl.net. ~ Located at the southeast corner of Lighthouse Reef atoll.

BLUE HOLE NATIONAL MONUMENT ⌇ The legacy of the Blue Hole is more fascinating than the hole itself, as it's not a great place to see marine life. Explored and made famous by Jacques Cousteau, the sinkhole-in-the-sea is dim and lined with walls and narrow ledges inhabited by prehistoric-looking sharks. Your best bet for scenery is around the mouth of the hole, encased in exquisite coral, about ten feet deep and swimming pool clear, wriggling with fish, sponges and sea fans. ~ Located within Lighthouse Reef atoll, about eight miles north of Half Moon Caye.

Hundreds of other beautiful cayes are scattered off the Belize coast, including many that are uninhabited but can be visited by boat. Some have long been weekend haunts for Belize City residents, who motor out in their skiffs, unfold their chairs in the sand and take in the island seclusion. Others are fertile grounds for lobster fishers or research camps for marine scientists. And still others, such as South Water Caye, have some semblance of civilization—a lodge, a tiki bar, perhaps even a pool table

Other Cayes

SIGHTS

Spanish Lookout Caye, Sergeants Caye, Water Caye and **Goff's Caye,** about 45 minutes by boat from Belize City, are tiny sandy cayes. They're popular day destinations for Belizeans who love to picnic and snorkel. Also popular is nearby **English Caye,** which marks the entrance to the shipping channel and has a lighthouse, a lighthouse keeper and a few private houses.

South of Belize City, you can experience the life of a lobster fisher on the string of mangrove isles called the **Bluefield Range.**

Looking like a wedge of sand and palm trees set adrift, **South Water Caye** is encircled by the clearest, shallowest water, and beyond that, the resplendent coral reef, beckoning for exploration.

Next door, you'll notice a sandy jewel called **Carrie Bow Caye,** spanning all of one acre and acting as a field station for the Smithsonian Institute during the spring and summer. Smithsonian researchers, hunting for a good field station site, accidentally landed on the island in 1972 during a bad storm. They fell instantly in love and struck a deal with the Bowman family of Dangriga, who own the island, to use it for half the year. If you swim or motor over to Carrie Bow, the scientists will be happy to show you around. Research changes every season, of course, but past studies have included the mating habits of worms and jellyfish.

LODGING

HIDDEN ▶

Belizean Ricardo Castillo runs a commercial lobster camp on one of the islands in the Bluefield Range and also runs **Ricardo's Beach Huts**. He invites guests who stay in his four super-rustic stilt huts (no showers—the sea is your bathtub) to accompany him as he fishes for lobster. Or guests can do their own fishing and snorkeling in the surrounding crystalline waters. Meals (including much lobster, of course!), a day trip to surrounding cayes and boat transfers from Belize City are included in the rate. For the true adventurer who doesn't mind really roughing it, this is a memorable experience—even for Belize, where *everything* is an adventure. ~ For reservations, call 22-44970 in Belize City. MODERATE.

HIDDEN ▶

Unlike most of the "other cayes," South Water Caye has a few things going on, thanks to the **Blue Marlin Lodge**, which has lately become popular with anglers and divers. Here numerous buildings are sprinkled atop the sand, including several clapboard ones with casual, beachy rooms (with ceiling fans), and several concrete cabanas that offer air conditioning but smell musty—a hazard of island existence. The most coveted room is a spacious wooden bungalow that juts right out over the water and catches constant sea breezes. There's a glorious sand beach here and congenial thatched-roof restaurant and bar with a floating dock. Minimum stay is four nights. Rates include all meals and transportation from Belize City. ~ For reservations, call 52-22243, fax 52-22296, or 800-798-1558 in the U.S.; www.bluemarlinlodge. com, e-mail marlin@btl.net. ULTRA-DELUXE.

▼▼▼▼▼▼▼▼▼▼▼▼▼▼

Outdoor Adventures

FISHING

Fishing guides are abundant in Belize. In fact, some are former poachers who are now strict proponents of catch and release. Besides the famous tarpon you'll also find schools of scrappy ladyfish, permit, bonefish and barracuda on the flats. Out on the reef look for kingfish, grouper, snapper and jack crevalle. On Ambergris Caye, it's easy to secure guides for fly or spin tackle fishing. Check along the waterfront in San Pedro, check with your hotel, or try one of the following: **El Pescador** is a fisher's resort run by a brother-sister team. Those ready for a full fishing vacation will love it. ~ On the north end of Ambergris Caye; 22-62398, or 800-242-2017 in the U.S.; e-mail info@elpescador.com. **Captain Tom Thomas** is a relocated American who runs fishing excursions on his craft *Sea Boots*. ~ 22-62911. On Caye Caulker, **Chocolate** offers customized fishing trips around the cayes. ~ 22-60151. **Porfilio "Piggy" Guzman** provides similar services. ~ 22-60152.

On the atolls and other out islands, fishing trips can be arranged through your lodge.

Most Cayes visitors come to dive. Either the fantastically clear **DIVING**
and colorful coral reef—the world's second longest—or the dark,
strange Blue Hole. The hole was made famous by Jacques Cousteau
and PBS and is the most famous site in Belize. It is not your typical dive location. The hole does not glint with blinding color or
fantastic fish. It is dim and eerie, a pit of inky water streaked with
tiny tremors of light and looking like a scene from the Ice Age.
Deep in its jowls, great shafts of rock imitate giant icicles and
shelves of deep sand resemble snow banks. Prehistoric-looking
sharks peer out from narrow ledges, and caves tunnel back into
the walls. Caverns drip with stalactites formed by eons of percolating rain. Back near the surface, the mouth of the hole is encased in beautiful coral and the water is warm and shallow.

THE ATOLLS   Despite its fame, the **Blue Hole** doesn't attract
crowds of divers, primarily because it is three hours by boat from
the mainland. There is one nearby resort, **Lighthouse Reef Resort**,
accessible by plane from Belize City, which includes a trip to the
hole in its extensive daily dive program. My favorite dive lodge
in Belize, the resort offers a variety of dives around the gorgeous
Lighthouse Reef atoll with views of walls and wrecks and basket
sponges blossoming over a 15-foot span. ~ Northern Caye; 800-
423-3114 in the U.S.

At Belize's southernmost atoll, **Glover's Reef**, the coral stretches
up from depths of 100 feet. Dolphins, turtles and mantas are
abundant, and the waters are warm and clear as air year-round.
It's not surprise, then, that Glover's is reputed to have some of the
most extravagant underwater scenery in the Caribbean.

The **Turneffe Islands** atoll possesses one of the most challenging dives in Belize—the Elbow, where the fish are enormous and
the currents erratic. Turneffe is also famous for its miles of mangrove forests teeming with fish seeking shelter in the underwater
roots. Manatees love the warm waters created by mangroves,
and can sometimes be seen lumbering through the water.

AMBERGRIS CAYE   Because of its proximity and variety, **Hol
Chan Marine Reserve** is a popular destination from Ambergris

---

ISLAND HOPPING

For an all-around atoll adventure, try **Ecosummer Expeditions'** sailing trip
on the 48-foot *Excellence*. Built by a traditional Belizean shipwright, it's a
hardwood sloop that cruises the barrier reef and atolls on one-week
trips. Passengers sea kayak, snorkel, fish and camp. ~ P.O. Box 177,
Clearwater, BC, Canada V0E 1N0; 250-674-0102, 800-465-8884, fax
250-674-2197 or 866-465-8884 in the U.S.; www.ecosummer.com,
e-mail trips@ecosummer.com.

Caye. Divers also like to explore Palmetto Reef, which is rich with corals and sponges, and Sandy Point Reef and Caverns, which are remarkable sites for their living walls. Mexico Rocks has been a popular site as well but is suffering from overfishing. Once you've seen these sites, check with a dive operator about chartering a boat to a lesser-known site—the reef has too many treasures to list, and an operator may know where to find exactly what you're looking for.

Dive Shops More than 30 dive shops occupy the row of piers along the San Pedro waterfront. They usually have their tentacles in anything related to diving or the water—dive classes, trips, equipment rental. Some even arrange fishing or Maya site trips. **Amigos del Mar** takes divers on the *Krista* for half-day, two-dive excursions to the Blue Hole and other dive sites, and the shop is a full-service PADI outfit. They also offer snorkeling, fishing and more. ~ Seafront at Lily's hotel, San Pedro; 22-62706, fax 22-62706; www.amigosdive.com, e-mail amigosdive@btl.net. **Blue Hole Dive Center** is another PADI outfit. They can arrange any diving tour, class or charter imaginable, and they rent equipment, including such items as underwater cameras. ~ Barrier Reef Drive; 22-62982; www.bluedive.com, e-mail divebelize@yahoo.com. On Caye Caulker, **Belize Diving Services** has scuba excursions. It's owned by Frank Bouting, a very experienced diver with extensive local knowledge. ~ 22-22143. At **Frenchie's Diving Service**, Caye Caulker natives Frenchie and Gertraud Novelo will take you close by the marine reserve or out to the Blue Hole and beyond. ~ 22-60234, fax 22-60292; e-mail frenchies@btl.net.

> The waters at Hol Chun Marine Reserve maintain a year-round average of 81°F.

Also on Caye Caulker, **Big Fish Dive Center** offers trips and prices similar to the island's other dive operators. ~ Beachfront; 22-60450.

Second Nature Divers explores the little-dived terrain around Tobacco Caye, where a "spur and groove" network of coral buttresses houses big schools of tarpon, permit and jacks. They also offer dives to Glover's Reef, Turneffe, Sharks Cave or Grand Channel. ~ In Hopkins call 52-12033; e-mail divers@btl.net.

Live-aboard Dive Boats The way to get in the most diving around Belize's fantastic reefs is to stay on a boat. Several live-aboard dive boats ply the waters around the cayes, dropping anchor at the Blue Hole, Half Moon Caye, the walls of Turneffe and other famous dive spots. Boats range from 16-passenger skiffs with dorm-style camping to 40-passenger yachts with staterooms. Trips typically last from one to seven nights.

The 50-foot **Offshore Express** takes you on two- and three-day trips to Half Moon Caye Natural Monument, where you can see red-footed boobies, frigates and ospreys, and dive the Blue Hole.

~ 22-62817. The fancier 110-foot **Aggressor** has air-conditioned cabins that accommodate up to 18 people. ~ 800-348-2628 in the U.S. By far the most luxurious is the 120-foot **Wave Dancer**, whose air-conditioned staterooms are more than 90 square feet, twice the size of most live-aboard cabins. *Wave Dancer* offers a seven-night itinerary from Belize City, with a visit to the Turneffe Islands and Lighthouse Reef. ~ 800-932-6237 or 305-669-9391 in the U.S.

Ambergris Caye serves as an excellent base for snorkeling excursions. **Hol Chan** is one of Belize's top snorkeling spots. Numerous boats head there for half-day or shorter trips. You can arrange a tour from a listing below, or simply arrange a tour through your hotel or by going to the east-side San Pedro docks. You can also visit the Hol Chan Visitor Center on Caribena Street; they will offer advice on finding the finest captains and on how to best enjoy the reserve.

SNORKEL-ING

    At **Shark Ray Alley** you can swim among gentle sting rays and nurse sharks. Request this when you arrange a snorkeling tour.

    You can explore the reef from the San Pedro dock, but fast-moving boats have injured and killed snorkelers, so it's not a safe activity without a highly visible surface object (i.e., a boat with diver's flag or a diver's float with flag).

    St. George's Caye has excellent snorkeling. Inquire with the dive shops about excursions there, or simply hire a boat from the docks.

Snorkeling Trips   **Island Guides** runs twice-daily tours to Hol Chan and Shark Alley. ~ San Pedro Town; 22-62817.

    Blue Hole Dive Center also organizes snorkeling trips to Hol Chan, as well as glass-bottom boat excursions. Trip schedules vary in order to catch the incoming tide. ~ Barrier Reef Drive; 22-62982, 22-62394.

    The **Winnie Estelle** is one of the best-known snorkel-excursion crafts. Roberto Smith, the owner, runs a regular trip to Coral Gardens and Shark Alley with a lunch stop at Caye Caulker. The long craft is suited for long hauls; you can charter the boat all over the cayes, even up the Rio Dulce in Guatemala. ~ Blue Hole Dive Center, Barrier Reef Drive; 22-62394; e-mail winnie_estelle@yahoo.com.

    To rent snorkeling equipment on Caye Caulker, check toward the middle of town, across from the park, in a little building that says, "Snorkel Rental–Pastries."

If you like the idea of navigating your own vessel, fishing for your own dinner and sleeping under the stars on faraway islands, consider sea kayaking. On Ambergris Caye, contact **Travel & Tour Belize**. ~ Coconut Drive, San Pedro; 22-62031.

CANOEING & KAYAKING

Perhaps the most exhilarating way to explore Belize's hidden cayes is to kayak them. Utah-based **Slickrock Adventures** offers nine-night kayak tours to its private, eight-acre Long Caye at Glover's Reef. (Seven nights are spent on the island; the remaining two are in Belize City, where guests board a jet boat for a two-and-a-half-hour trip to Glover's Reef.) From Long Caye, kayakers can take day trips to nearby cayes and reefs for snorkeling, diving and sunning—or never leave the island. Cabanas provide basic but comfortable overnight accommodations, and meals are prepared in a fully staffed kitchen. There are daily activities, but don't think Club Med: things couldn't be more carefree on this castaway trip. ~ P.O. Box 1400, Moab, UT 84532; 435-259-4225, 800-390-5715, fax 435-259-6996; www.slickrock.com, e-mail slickrock@slickrock.com.

> Both Island Expeditions Co. and Slickrock Adventures offer week-long kayak trips to private islands within Glover's Reef. Most of the cayes are uninhabited islands ringed with palms and sugar-fine sand, surrounded by brilliantly clear waters.

Island Expeditions Co. also offers a week-long kayak tour to Glover's Reef, where travelers laze away the days on sand-fringed Southwest Caye. Schedule your trip between early December and the end of April and you can join a Garifuna gathering, usually held on Saturday or Sunday night, in the Sabal Community on mainland Dangriga. Garifuna culture is usually quite closed, and few travelers anywhere have the opportunity to experience the hard pulsing music and passionate dance of the punta. ~ 368–916 West Broadway, Vancouver, British Columbia, Canada V5Z 1K7; 604-452-3212, 800-667-1630, fax 604-452-3433; www.island expeditions.com, e-mail info@islandexpeditions.com.

Elsewhere around the cayes, you can rent kayaks by the hour or day. Check with your lodge.

GOLF

The only golf course in the entire country of Belize is on otherwise uninhabited Caye Chapel. It is part of an ongoing development project that also includes luxury villas and a clubhouse. The long, narrow 18-hole course is fraught with water hazards and sand bunkers on every hole. Stiff sea breezes add to the challenge. For non-guests, a round of golf here is not cheap—US$200 covers a day's unlimited play (no tee times or round limits) as well as club and cart rental, lunch, beverages and pool privileges. The course is bordered by the sea on both sides, and you're likely to be the only golfer on it. Day-use reservations are required. ~ 22-68250, 800-901-8938; www.belizegolf.cc, e-mail golf@caye chapel.com.

WIND-SURFING

On Ambergris Caye, **Sailsports Belize** offers windsurfing, kitesurfing and sailing. ~ 22-64488; www.sailsportsbelize.com, e-mail info@sailsportsbelize.com.

Stiff sea breezes and smooth waters are making windsurfing and kitesurfing increasingly popular on Caye Caulker, especially around The Split. You'll find sailboards and kiteboards for rent at **Michael's Windsurf & Water Sports**. ~ Beachfront, near The Split; 22-60457; www.windsurfbelize.com, e-mail windsurfbelize@btl.net.

BIKING

The most relaxing bicycling is on the hard-packed sand streets of Ambergris Caye and Caye Caulker. On Ambergris Caye, contact **Travel & Tour Belize** for information on bike rentals. ~ Barrier Reef Drive, San Pedro; 22-62031. You'll find bikes for rent at **Joe's Bike Rentals**. ~ South Barrier Reef Drive at Buccaneer Street. On Caye Caulker, bike rentals are available at the open-air **Caye Caulker Bicycle Rentals** next to the Caye Caulker Gift Shop. ~ Front Street; no phone.

▼▼▼▼▼▼▼▼▼▼
Transportation

AIR

If you're staying on Ambergris Caye, your lodge will arrange transportation from Belize City. If you're arriving on your own, Tropic Air and Maya Island Air have regular flights to the **San Pedro Airstrip** from Belize City. Tropic Air and Maya Island Air have as many as seven regularly scheduled flights to the San Pedro airstrip, stopping at Caye Caulker en route when there are passengers for that port of call.

BOAT

Water taxis to Caye Caulker take 45 minutes, and then it's another 30 minutes to Ambergris Caye. Boats leave from two Belize City locations: the **Belize Marine Terminal** on North Front Street and the **Court House Dock** across from the Bellevue Hotel. The one-way cost to Ambergris is about US$15 per person. To Caye Caulker, it's US$10.

All water taxis stop at Caye Caulker on the way to or from San Pedro. Any water taxi will stop at St. George's Caye on request; they also sometimes stop at Caye Chapel to drop off construction workers there.

From Ambergris Caye, shuttle boats leave from the **San Pedro docks** and charge approximately US$10 one-way to Caye Caulker.

Independent sightseers to St. George's Caye can usually hire a boat from the docks at the **Belize Marine Terminal**. Day trips to the outer cayes can be arranged through **S & L Travel**. ~ 91 North Front Street, Belize City; 22-77593, fax 22-77594.

Boat or air transportation to the atolls is arranged through your resort.

GOLF CARTS

There are no cars on Caye Caulker and very few in San Pedro. The only motorized way to get around the village streets is with a whisper-quiet electric golf cart. On Ambergris Caye, golf carts are for rent by the hour or day at **Cholo's**. ~ Beachfront next to Lily's; 22-62406. Another cart rental place is **Polo's**. ~ North end of Barrier Reef Drive; 22-63542. You'll find mopeds as well as golf carts for rent at **Moncho's Rentals**. ~ Four locations along Barrier Reef Drive, including one at the corner of Sea Star Street; 22-63262. Golf carts are rarer on Caye Caulker and serve mainly as taxis. If you want to rent one (though everywhere you can reach by road is within walking distance of everything else) arrangements can be made through your hotel or guesthouse.

▼ ▼

Addresses & Phone Numbers

San Pedro Tourist Information Center ~ 22-62903
Emergency Number for Police, Fire and Ambulance ~ 911
San Pedro Police Station ~ 22-62022
Caye Caulker Police Station ~ 22-22120
Divers' Recompression Chamber ~ next to San Pedro Airstrip; 22-62851 or 22-62073
Internet Place ~ San Pedro, next to El Patio; 22-63434
Cyber Cafe Caye Caulker ~ Across from Celi's Gift Shop; 22-22402

FIVE

Belize City

Although the Cayes are the most popular destination in Belize, Belize City is the place most travelers see first after arriving at the international airport. Unfortunately, it is not the best introduction. Sweltering hot all the time, the city is crowded with crumbling streets, tin-roofed shanties and British colonial buildings that have seen better days. Murky Haulover Creek slices through the center of the city, bubbling with sailboats and makeshift skiffs and fed by open sewage canals that line the streets. The 59,400 people who live and work here create a continuous grind of activity—quite unlike the rest of the country, where life is slow and the land virtually empty.

In the early 1700s, the city was conceived by a band of British Baymen, logwood cutters who were former pirates but who still clung to their buccaneer ways. From their stilt-shack settlement at the swampy mouth of the Belize River they would occasionally cut logwood and load it onto ships headed for England. Most of the time, however, "their chief Delight" was "in drinking," rum punch being their favorite, according to Captain Nathaniel Uring in 1720, who adds he "had a very unpleasant time living among these people." Little wonder that 18th-century mapmakers obelized, or marked the settlement with a symbol warning of a corrupt place, which, over time, was supposedly corrupted into the word "Belize."

More than a hundred years later, when Maya explorer John Lloyd Stephens sailed into the port city, conditions had changed considerably. Gleaming white colonial houses paraded up and down the waterfront and nearby streets, culminating in the elegant Government House, built in 1814 for the first governor of Belize. There was also an ornate Gothic church with a soaring spire and groves of coconut palms that, from the sea, reminded Stephens of the palm trees of Egypt and "gave the appearance of actual beauty."

Despite its new-found sophistication, vestiges of the unsavory Baymen remained deep in the city's foundation. As late as 1917, workers who dug down 60 feet found "mahogany chips mixed with rum bottles, with surprising regularity," according to one account in *The Baymen's Legacy, A Portrait of Belize City*.

It is a city that should not have been built, for its land is swampy and low-lying, confronted by water on three sides and forever vulnerable to rains, tides and hurricanes. The no-name hurricane of 1931 extinguished ten percent of the capital city's 15,000 residents, most of whom tragically believed the barrier reef would prove a natural force field. Thirty years later, Hurricane Hattie virtually picked up Belize City and flung it out to sea in a day of hell described by many as "an earthquake in a storm." It was Hattie that finally drove the country to move its capital inland, to a place called Belmopan.

Today, Belmopan is the official capital, but Belize City is the life pulse of Belize, the country's only genuine city. Despite its teetering existence, "it continues to swell and expand against all odds and without any plan," or so said the *Amandala*, Belize's biggest newspaper, in a 1986 editorial that became an infamous essay on Belize City. The editorial denounced the city as having a culture that "copies America too slavishly, and which has no stomach for sacrifice. But it is the culture that gives Belize City identity and makes it flashy and attractive, like a Saturday night hooker."

It is also that culture, that spicy slice of post-Colonial life by the sea that eventually tends to win visitors over. Of course, Belize (as locals call the city) does have its high points, not the least of which is its people. Like all Belizeans, city residents are gregarious, laidback and ever helpful to newcomers. Some are too helpful, though, as they hustle visitors to lend pocket change, buy drugs or join them in finding "some action." But visitors who stick to the better neighborhoods and avoid venturing out alone at night will find Belize City safer than big cities back home. At night, the infamous scene of petty crime is the Swing Bridge: avoid walking it from dusk to dawn, no matter how many people you're with.

If you're driving, the secret to finding your way around the maze of downtown streets is to remember which side of Haulover Creek you're on (there are only two vehicle bridges). You can't go far in one direction without running into the seashore, the creek bank, or the busy peripheral street that is called Princess Margaret Drive north of the creek and is called Central American Boulevard south of the creek. To find your way out of the city, take this street until you come to one of the two traffic roundabouts. The one north of the creek marks the start of the Northern Highway; the other, south of the creek, marks the start of the Western Highway.

SIGHTS   The very best neighborhood is the **Fort George neighborhood**. Here, along the waterfront Fort Street and Marine Parade, is **embassy row**, where a handful of embassies and consulates still occupy picturesque colonial-era buildings. One of the most appealing buildings in all of Belize, the **United States Embassy** is a distinguished whitewashed building that was actually constructed in New England and brought to Belize in the 1800s. Plans are under way to move the U.S. Embassy to Belmopan, though construction of the new facility there is proceeding slowly. ~ 29 Gabourel Lane; 22-77161.

At the tip of the peninsula stands the stately **Radisson Fort George Hotel**. Built in 1953 as a hotel, it once possessed the only swimming pool in Belize. (Times have changed, and now there are more than two dozen.) A block from the hotel is the **Baron Bliss Memorial** (Marine Parade), an unspectacular slab of stone commemorating a spectacular act of generosity. In 1926, Englishman Henry Edward Ernest Victor Bliss, known as Baron Bliss, sailed into the harbor at Belize City. Sick with food poisoning he'd contracted in Trinidad, he was unable to leave his boat. For the next few months Bliss lived onboard, fishing and trying to recover from his illness. He never recovered, but he did befriend many Belizeans, who brought him food and took care of him. When he died, he left his $2 million fortune to the people of Belize.

The baron's generosity made him a national hero and paid for numerous public buildings, including health clinics, schools and the Bliss Institute museum. And though he never walked on Belize in life, he is buried here in a tomb, where land meets the sea. The **Fort George Lighthouse** stands sentinel nearby.

Around the bend is the headquarters for information on Belize. The **Belize Audubon Society** will help plan excursions to the country's parks and preserves. Maps and books on Belize, as well as

Belize City

POINTS OF INTEREST

- **Ⓐ** Baron Bliss Memorial & Fort George Lighthouse
- **Ⓑ** Battlefield Park
- **Ⓒ** Belize Audubon Society
- **Ⓓ** Belize Commercial Center
- **Ⓔ** Belize Marine Terminal & Museum
- **Ⓕ** Belize Post Office
- **Ⓖ** Belize Tourism Board
- **Ⓗ** Bliss Institute
- **Ⓘ** Fort George Neighborhood & Embassy Row
- **Ⓙ** Government House
- **Ⓚ** Memorial Park
- **Ⓛ** St. John's Cathedral
- **Ⓜ** Supreme Court
- **Ⓝ** Swing Bridge

0   0.1 mile

0   0.1 kilometer

WALKING TOUR
Exploring Belize City

Travelers staying in the relatively chic Fort George neighborhood will find that a stroll around the neighborhood is self-explanatory, takes only a few minutes and doesn't reveal much about the daily rhythms of Belize's capital city. For a dose of a different reality, cross Haulover Creek into the boisterous, seedy, colorful kaleidoscope of everyday life in the urban tropics.

OVER THE SWING BRIDGE   Start at the **Swing Bridge** (page 122), the center for much of the city's activity. (Don't worry—it doesn't swing back and forth like a suspension bridge; it swings open like a gate twice daily to let boats with tall masts through, and only when there are no pedestrians on it.) On the south side of the bridge, you'll pass the public market, which is open at erratic hours. On the other side of the street, vendors tempt you with fruit salads and bags of cashews. A block up the street, you can recognize **Battlefield Park** (page 123) by the taxi drivers out front and the homeless people asleep on the benches. Walk through (or around) the park toward the colonial-looking **Supreme Court** building (page 123) with the clock tower on top.

SOUTHERN FORESHORE   Turn left at the first corner—Church Street, which swings south to become Southern Foreshore, though no sign marks either street. Continue south for six blocks past similarly unsigned streets known to locals as Bishop, King, Prince, Dean and South streets. Lined

volumes about birding, wildlife and ecotourism are for sale. ~ 12 Fort Street; 22-35004, fax 22-34985; www.belizeaudubon.com.

A short distance north of the Audubon Society headquarters, the new **Fort Street Tourist Village** was designed to accommodate the cruise ship passengers who arrive in the city by tender boat on an almost daily basis. It serves as a tour bus terminal and features the usual cruise-dock array of snack bars, T-shirt shops and jewelry stores. ~ 8 Fort Street; 22-37789; e-mail fstv@btl.net.

The **Belize Tourism Board** has helpful employees, as well as maps and guides. ~ New Central Bank Building, Level 2, Gabourel Lane, P.O. Box 325; 22-31913; www.travelbelize.com. Near the tourist board office stands the new **Museum of Belize**, opened in 2002 with financial support from the Republic of China (Taiwan). The building was originally built in 1857 as a colonial prison and housed convicts until 1993. Now it is the first national museum in Belize, though plans are under way to establish a second branch in Belmopan. On display are ancient Maya

by a concrete seawall, the Foreshore offers cool breezes and a fine view of the **Fort George Lighthouse** (page 119) across the water. When the foreshore ends at a locked gate, turn inland for one block to Regent Street; turn left and go two more blocks to the end of Regent, and then turn right and go one block to Albert Street, where you'll find yourself directly in front of **St. John's Cathedral** (page 123).

ALBERT STREET   Walking north along Albert Street, the city's main commercial street, will bring you back to the Swing Bridge in ten blocks. Along the way you'll meet lively throngs of locals and pass enough store windows to convince you that, unless you're in the market for cheap and truly tasteless clothing, there's not much to buy. The experience, of course, is fun and free. If you'd like to sample what the urban residential zone is like (though you can see it just as well taking a taxi to the bus terminal), turn left at any side street and walk north to the canal.

CANAL STREET   A long block west of Albert Street is the Southside Canal, with main streets East Canal Street and West Canal Street along its banks. Beyond West Canal Street is a labyrinthine neighborhood of ramshackle stilt houses with laundry hung out to dry on second-floor porches. It's best not to venture too far into this area on foot; tourists rarely do, so you will quickly attract the unwelcome attentions of every drunk, drug dealer and panhandler for blocks around—not necessarily dangerous, but annoying. Besides, temperatures run much hotter this far from the seafront. Turn right and continue north along the Canal to Regent Street West, which runs along the Haulover Creek Waterfront. Turn right again, and you'll soon find yourself back at the Swing Bridge.

pottery and artifacts from sites throughout the country, as well as historical photographs, memorabilia from the British colonial era and a preserved jail cell. ~ Gabourelle Street; 22-34524.

Over on Front Street, the **Belize Marine Terminal & Museum** is where you catch the ferry to San Pedro, Ambergris Caye, or wander among the little museum's coral reef models, maps and sealife exhibits. A third option is to order a Belikin and black beans from the takeout counter, have a seat along the riverfront and enjoy all the hubbub. Admission. ~ North Front Street; 22-31969.

Continue west a few paces and you'll notice the white clapboard **Paslow Building**, looking tired but dignified and housing numerous government offices, including the **Belize Post Office** (22-72201). On the west side of the building, hiding out in a teeny room, is the **Belize Philatelic Bureau**, showcasing the country's marvelous stamps. You can purchase souvenir sheets of various editions; my favorites: the dazzling Coral Reef series and the poignant, infinitely detailed Maya Monuments. ~ Front and Queen streets.

From here, you can spot the **Swing Bridge** and its constant hum of activity. The city's geographic frame of reference, the bridge crosses Haulover Creek and swings open at about 6 a.m. and 5:30 p.m. daily, causing instant gridlock. Built in Liverpool, England, and brought to Belize in 1923, it is thought to be the only manually operated swing bridge still being used in the world. If you watch the four skinny men straining with their long poles to open the bridge every morning and night, you will know why it is the only one.

South of the bridge lies the heart of the city, centered around Albert and Regent streets and the Southern Foreshore. Here buildings crowd shoulder to shoulder and street vendors hawk baskets of bread and tropical ices. Bicyclists, pedestrians with parasols, rickety old school buses and kamikaze taxis compete for the same narrow stretch of pavement. At high noon, the roadside park benches get so hot they burn right through your pants.

At the southeastern foot of the Swing Bridge, you'll be met by the sparkling modern yellow-with-black-trim **Belize Commercial Center**. Opened in 1993, it feels like a mini-convention center; the first floor is crowded with Creole and Latin American foods and the second and third floors are lined with vendor-style shops, businesses and eateries. The first-floor **market** features wobbly tables and baskets overflowing with all sorts of produce, from glassy red scotch bonnet peppers and shaggy boniato (a tuber) to silky red beans and juicy passion fruit. You'll also find catches of the day—anything from grouper and snapper to live iguana and sea turtles. The turtles are endangered, so don't support the industry. If you have questions about produce, the friendly Belizean women (anxious to make a sale) will happily answer them. *Remember:* Buy only what you can peel yourself, and wash everything in purified water.

Away from the bridge, and where everyone seems to be heading, is **Brodies Department Store**. It's Belize's official department

AUTHOR FAVORITE

The **Fort George neighborhood** is my favorite strolling ground in Belize City. Named for the fort built here in 1803 but since destroyed, it's also the city's best neighborhood. Back in the early 1800s, the area was a swampy island, but today it is draped across the tip of a peninsula on the northern side of Haulover Creek. The neighborhood's beauty lies in its big old whitewashed homes trimmed in filigree and framed by white picket fences and well-groomed lawns, and in the lavish traveler's palms and poinciana trees that decorate the yards and street corners.

store, but don't expect Macy's; it's more like a crowded Kmart with iffy air conditioning. ~ 255 Albert Street; 22-74472.

Near here, Belize's own **Battlefield Park** is bustling, small and strange, a sort of outdoor way station for street vendors, street people and salesmen of questionable character. ~ Bounded by Albert, Regent and Church streets. Banks and other businesses line the park, as does the white clapboard **Supreme Court**. The third Supreme Court to be built on the site (fires destroyed the first two), it's an attractive two-story building with neoclassic columns, a four-sided clock tower (pay no attention to the time—it's usually wrong) and a filigreed iron balcony, the prettiest in town. ~ Regent Street across from Battlefield Park.

A couple of blocks over, along the sea, you'll find the newly renovated **Bliss Institute**, a white concrete edifice that serves as the center of Belize culture. Inside are a few permanent exhibits, including limestone altars uncovered from the ancient Maya city of Caracol. Traveling exhibits, sponsored by the resident Belize Arts Council, feature bamboo crafts and paintings by Belizean and international artists. ~ 1 Bliss Promenade; 22-72110, fax 22-70726.

Near Regent Street's southern end, visiting dignitaries are often entertained at the graceful **Government House**, built around 1814. Across the street, you'll instantly recognize **St. John's Cathedral** by its manicured lawns and dignified red-brick facade. The oldest Anglican church in Central America, it was built from 1812 to 1826 by slaves, who were conveniently emancipated by the church in a formal ceremony in 1838. Despite many fires and hurricanes, St. John's still boasts its original sapodilla roof, mahogany beams and 1826 organ. ~ Regent and Albert streets.

For a slice of Belize City life, wander the side streets between Regent Street and Southern Foreshore. Under the canopies of shady poinciana trees, brilliant parrots squawk from cages and women scrub their wash in big tubs. Children tote heavy strings of fish, fresh from the wooden sloops bobbing in the nearby harbor.

West of the city center are neighborhoods not worth visiting but whose street names are worth mentioning: Armadillo, Iguana, Antelope, Gibnut and Pelican.

On the north end of Belize City, you can look over to **Moho Caye**, a half-mile offshore from the airstrip. Earlier this century, the mite-size island yielded more historical mementos than all of Belize City. Pottery shards, pottery rings used as fishing sinkers, spear heads and two burial grounds testify to its days as a Maya fishing outpost. Even more remarkable were the thousands of manatee bones washed on the northern shore. Today, manatees still seek the warmth of nearby waters, and the tiny island is owned by **Maya Landings**, a marina and dive/sail boat operation. ~ 22-35350, fax 22-35466.

◄ HIDDEN

You can also board a sailboat to Sergeants Caye or Goff's Caye for a day of snorkeling and fishing. **Discovery Expeditions** offers full-day trips, and has several locations around Belize City, including one at the Fiesta Inn Belize. ~ 6916 Monarchy Drive; 22-30748, fax 22-30750, or 888-535-8832 in the U.S.

LODGING   In 2001, the Belize government implemented new, higher standards for guesthouses, closing the shabbiest spots. Still, accommodations remain simple, with clean sheets, four walls, a bed and a ceiling fan as standard accoutrements. Occasionally you'll find air conditioning and even tropically inspired decor. If you're new to developing countries, I highly recommend a room in or near the Fort George neighborhood, which has the city's finest accommodations. But if you're looking for local color and something more bohemian and very friendly, stick to the lodges of the Southern Foreshore.

The Great House occupies one of the city's oldest buildings, a 1927 Grand Colonial whose sweeping balconies and staircases and whitewashed façade have been crisply restored. Upstairs you'll find 12 guest rooms with lemon-washed walls and pine floors, amenities like air conditioners, cable TV, hairdryers, mini-fridges and safes, and terraces where you can pluck mangoes from trees. Downstairs there's a gallery of boutiques and stores behind French doors (even a wine shop!) and a wonderful outdoor space called the Smoky Mermaid Restaurant and Bar. The Great House is also one of the few places in all of Belize where you'll find a wireless Internet hot spot. ~ 13 Cork Street; 22-33400, fax 22-33444; www.greathousebelize.com, e-mail greathouse@btl.net. DELUXE TO ULTRA-DELUXE.

The pink **Château Caribbean** is showing some wear, but it still imparts island charm. Overlooking the sea, with a large pool encased in palmy grounds, the colonial mansion has 20 pleasant rooms with private balconies, air conditioning and cable TV. ~ 6 Marine Parade; 22-30800, fax 22-30900; www.chateaucaribbean. com, e-mail chateaucar@btl.net. DELUXE.

The largest hotel in Belize, the **Princess Hotel & Casino** with its 181 rooms and suites is something of a white elephant in a land of small guesthouses and intimate jungle lodges, but if you stay here you may quickly forget you're in Belize. The six-story hotel sprawls like a cruise ship along the city's northern bayfront, a long walk or a slightly pricey taxi ride from downtown attractions, and its wealth of entertainment options invites guests to stay on the premises. Guest rooms are furnished in contemporary style with tropical pastel hues accented with bright floral prints; all are air-conditioned and have direct-dial phones, cable TV and bay views. Among the amenities are an Olympic-size swimming pool with a swim-up bar, a kids' gym and playground, a fitness center, massage facilities and a family picnic area amid gardens lush with 52 species of plants. There are also two restaurants, an eight-lane bowling alley, a video arcade and a duplex movie theater, as well as a marina and Belize's only large casino. (*Note:* If you're driving to this hotel on a Saturday or Sunday, watch very carefully for the only vehicle entrance, which is hard to spot. The road in front of it becomes one-way on weekends to allow parking for the many locals who congregate at the waterfront, and if you miss the hotel driveway, you'll drive a long way through a tangle of side streets before you find it again.) ~ Newton Barracks, King's Park; 22-32670, fax 22-32660, or 800-233-9784 in the U.S.; www.princessbelize.com, e-mail resprincess@btl.net. ULTRA-DELUXE.

Another decent area to stay, especially for budget-conscious travelers, is the Southern Foreshore, a mixed neighborhood of law offices (it's near the Supreme Court building) and residences festooned with flowers. Here you'll find the **Bellevue Hotel**, whose two-story brick facade with arched windows curves along the seafront. It's a comfortable, timeworn place with a little garden, a wedge-shaped swimming pool and a bar called the Maya Tavern. All 37 rooms are air conditioned, carpeted and decorated with seashell-patterned bedspreads and rattan tables and chairs in unexciting shades of brown and olive; cable TV is also included. A few have a view to the sea, but, unfortunately, it's through chain-link tacked over all the windows. ~ 5 Southern Foreshore; 22-77051, fax 22-73253; e-mail fins@btl.net. MODERATE.

Exotic orchids line the entrance walkway to the friendly, American-owned **Seaside Guest House**, around the corner from the Bellevue. A shaded veranda looks out across a dirt parking lot

AUTHOR FAVORITE

I'll never forget my first night in Belize at the **Radisson Fort George Hotel**. The lobby glowed with tropical hardwoods, the garden was thick with heliconia and red ginger, and my spacious room stared straight at the sea. The city's most distinguished establishment, the Fort George has 102 rooms that are among the plushest in Belize—and well worth the price. Favored by business travelers, its lush, walled grounds with brick lanai and pool seem worlds away from the bustling street life. Rooms in the main building offer commanding views of the sea, and have air conditioning and that Belize rarity, cable TV. Near the gardens, rooms take on a tropical flavor. A fine restaurant and lounge round out the amenities. ~ Marine Parade; 22-33333; www.radissonbelize.com, e-mail amin.dredge@ radisson.com. ULTRA-DELUXE.

to the seawall and, beyond that, to a view of the Fort George Lighthouse across the water, perfectly framed by palm trees. To catch the cool breeze, get one of the rooms with a window facing the sea. On steamy afternoons the fans in the plainly furnished rooms may lose the battle to keep things cool. Three private guest rooms and two four-bed dorm rooms open onto a central lounge stocked with travelers' resources. Inexpensive breakfasts, sandwiches and evening beverages are available. Security is tighter here than anyplace else in town. ~ 3 Prince Street; 22-78339; e-mail friends@ btl.net. BUDGET.

For decades, **Hotel Mopan** attracted a coterie of archaeologists, zoologists and other conservation devotees, who converged at the hotel bar for nights of impassioned discussion and didn't seem to mind that the hotel was entirely run-down. As this book goes to press, the hotel is undergoing a complete renovation. Because of the construction noise, rooms are for rent at bargain rates until the project is completed in 2004, when rates are scheduled to take a big jump. The 16 bedrooms are pleasant (apart from the aforementioned noise) and offer clean sheets, private baths, ceiling fans and jalousie windows. Several rooms have wall-unit air conditioners. ~ 55 Regent Street; 22-77351, fax 22-75383; e-mail hotelmopan@btl.net. BUDGET TO MODERATE.

DINING

Despite its reputation as a rice-and-beans country, Belize has much to offer in the way of skillfully prepared seafood dishes and gratifying home cooking. In Belize City, fine dining exists in hotel restaurants, while soulful fare can be found in seedy diners tucked here and there.

When the heat in the city becomes too much, cool down at **Scoops**, an old-fashioned ice cream parlor. The ice cream is creamy and the milkshakes will satisfy any sweet tooth. ~ 17 Eve Street; 22-44699. BUDGET.

The fresh, inventive cuisine at **St. George's** is not only delicious, it's reasonable. Situated along the sea, featuring pink starched linens and vases brimming with tropical flowers, the handsome dining room turns out dishes such as red snapper topped with shrimp and a tapenade of black and green olives; chicken breast deep fried in a black sesame-seed batter; and Jamaican jerk pork chops with papaya relish. For breakfast, there are thick slabs of french toast; for lunch, try the cobb salad, bacon cheeseburger or American-style pizza. ~ At the Radisson Fort George Hotel, Marine Parade; 22-33333. DELUXE. Also in the Radisson is the new **Stonegrill Restaurant**, where fajitas, shrimp and chicken satay are cooked tableside on a bed of hot volcanic rocks with no fat or oil. ~ MODERATE.

Belize's multi-ethnic population is reflected in the variety of restaurants in Belize City. Chinese cuisine is a favorite, even among non-Asians, and according to the tourist board, nine out of ten Belize City restaurants are owned and operated by Belizeans of Chinese descent. The best of the lot—in fact, some claim, the best restaurant in Belize—is **Chon Saan Palace**. Lustrous wood paneling, black lacquer furnishings and crisp white tablecloths set the stage for a selection of more than 200 dishes ranging from standards like chow mein and sweet-and-sour pork to such house specialties as shrimp with cashews and Chinese-style crab legs. A row of seafood tanks hold Australian lobsters farmed locally, giant white shrimp and the daily fish catch, kept alive in the water until dinnertime. Portions are huge. The restaurant also delivers anywhere in the city. ~ 1 Kelly Street; 22-33008. MODERATE.

Neria's Kitchen, a friendly little diner that's popular with the locals, is one of the best places in town to sample traditional Belizean dishes such as cowfoot soup and gibnut. The restaurant also serves tall glasses of seven different kinds of fruit juice squeezed fresh while you wait. ~ Queen Street at Daly Street; 22-34028. BUDGET.

◄ HIDDEN

Dit's Saloon is as Belizean as they come: friendly and uproarious, with plastic tables and local artwork. Choose from meat pies, "fry" chicken, *garnaches* (fried tortillas stuffed with tomatoes and onions), and rice and beans with stew chicken, beef or fish. ~ 50 King Street; 22-73330. BUDGET.

The funkiest diner in town, **Macy's** became famous in the late 1980s when England's Queen Elizabeth dined here on gibnut (a large rodent). The rodent has been elevated to "royal gibnut" on the menu. Right beside it is oxtail soup, and more traditional offerings like stew rice and beans and grouper. Sweet local fruit

AUTHOR FAVORITE

I smelled the **Smoky Mermaid** before I ever saw it—rich, juicy smells of lobster and chicken smoldering in the stone smokehouse among mango trees. One step into the gardeny courtyard with mermaid fountains, lime-green umbrellas and bar stools carved from tree trunks, and I knew I'd found the city's most atmospheric eatery. The food is splendid, from the lobster burgers and snapper caribe to the New Zealand lamb chops brushed with rosemary oil, grilled and served with sautéed creamed spinach and garlic mashed potatoes. There's a "smokehouse" oven sending out wonderful smells with the grilled meat and seafood, and a bar churning out tropically colored drinks for travelers and diplomats alike. ~ 13 Cork Street, at The Great House Inn; 22-34759. DELUXE.

juices, from pulpy papaya to slushy watermelon, come in tall cool glasses. It's all served in a little room with folding iron chairs, clanking screen doors and a TV playing American soap operas. ~ 18 Bishop Street; 20-73419. MODERATE.

There's a classic Las Vegas-style buffet just off the gaming floor in the **Princess Hotel & Casino**. The food may bring back memories of high school cafeteria fare, but at US$7.50 for all you can eat, the price is right. The only trouble is, when entering the casino you have to go through a security check so thorough it makes U.S. airport security seem like a snap by comparison. ~ Newton Barracks, Kings Park; 22-32670. MODERATE.

SHOPPING

For a wide selection of Belizean arts, go to the **National Handicraft Sales Center**, where the work of over 500 artisans is displayed, including carvings of ziricote, mahogany, redwood, jabillo, rosewood, granadillo and Santa Maria woods. The store also features ceramics, stone carvings, pottery, baskets and jewelry. ~ 2 South Park, right in front of Memorial Park; 22-33636.

Few people would think to go shopping at the **Belize Philatelic Bureau**, but the country's exquisitely designed stamps really do make great gifts. Souvenir stamp sheets include dozens of historical and environmental themes. ~ In the Paslow Building, corner of Front and Queen streets; 22-22201.

If you want to slum it for bargain prices, shop along **King Street** between Albert and Canal streets. The narrow stores here are jammed with electronics, sneakers, cosmetics, lingerie and T-shirts.

You'll find vintage greeting cards at **The Book Centre**, as well as Belizean literature, two-day-old copies of the *Miami Herald*, and references on local cuisine, history and art. ~ 4 Church Street; 22-77457.

The pleasant, colorful **Go Tees** designs, produces and purveys tropical clothing, wood jewelry and books on Belize. ~ 6238 Park Avenue; 22-34660.

NIGHTLIFE

Most local bars are seedy joints and not places for travelers. Stick to the hotel bars, such as the Radisson Fort George's **Baymen's Tavern**, where a big-screen TV shows the latest American sports. ~ Marine Parade; 22-33333.

The most pleasant place for a drink in Belize City is the courtyard at the **Smoky Mermaid**. Have a seat beneath the big mango tree, on a bar stool carved from tree trunks. The frozen drinks come in curvy glasses and electric colors. ~ 13 Cork Street, at The Great House inn; 22-34759.

The only movie house in the entire country is the nameless twin-screen theater in the **Princess Hotel & Casino**. The casino itself, Belize's only large gambling establishment, opened in 2000 and immediately became the hottest nightspot in town—especially among the local Chinese. More than 500 slot and video poker machines fill the vast hall, with live blackjack, roulette, craps and poker tables toward the back. Drinks are free while you're playing. Russian dancing girls perform a twice-nightly lounge show. ~ Newton Barracks, Kings Park; 22-32670; www.princessbelize.com, e-mail resprincess@btl.net.

Calypso, also at the Princess, is high-ceilinged, open to the sea and cooled by breezes. There's live music Thursday through Sunday ranging from calypso to reggae. ~ Newtown Barracks; 22-32670.

Indoors at the Princess' **Blue Hole Lounge** is not nearly as happening, but you can settle into a cane-back chair and watch the big screen. ~ 22-32670, The Belize Arts Council sponsors concerts and national and international theater and dance performances at the **Bliss Institute.** ~ 1 Bliss Promenade; 22-72110.

MEMORIAL PARK There are no truly pleasant parks in Belize City but the best open space is Memorial Park, a rambling grassy area facing the sea, with queues of concrete benches, a tin-roofed gazebo, amphitheater and obelisk honoring the 40 Belizean men who died in World War I. ~ Marine Parade.

BEACHES & PARKS

No one comes to Belize City for outdoor adventure. But there are city-based outfitters ready to take you out to sea while you're here.

Outdoor Adventures

If you'd like to schedule a day of fishing, check with **Zippy Zappy Boating Services.** ~ 36 St. Thomas Street; 20-34955. **Sea Sports Belize** also rents boats and provides fishing guide services. ~ 83 North Front Street; 22-35505.

FISHING

From a hut on the dock at Radisson Fort George Hotel, **Hugh Parkey's Belize Dive Connection** takes divers out to the reef or to the Turneffe or Lighthouse Reef atolls. ~ 71 North Front Street; phone/fax 22-34526, or 888-223-5403 in the U.S.; www.belizediving.com, e-mail hugh@belizediving.com.

DIVING & SNORKEL-ING

AUTHOR FAVORITE

I caught my first tarpon—a 35-pounder, small for these parts—on a guided trip arranged by the **Belize River Lodge**. Located near the international airport, it offers excellent Belize River and flats fishing trips. ~ Northern Highway, Ladyville; 22-52002, fax 22-52298, or 888-275-4843 in the U.S.; www.belizeriverlodge.com, e-mail info@belizeriverlodge.com.

Maya Travel Services, an affiliate of Maya Island Air, claims to have "hiked, paddled, galloped, driven and flown across much of Belize." In other words, they will custom-design virtually any tour, including snorkel and dive trips. There's even a nine-night "Beach/Bush/Beach" trip that sandwiches horseback riding and caving between snorkel outings. ~ 42 Cleghorn Street, Belize City; 22-31623, fax 22-30585; www.mayatravelservices.com, e-mail mayatravel@btl.net.

You can board a sailboat to Sergeants Caye or Goff's Caye for a day of snorkeling and fishing. **Discovery Expeditions** offers full-day trips, which include a box lunch, snorkel and fishing gear, and use of a dinghy and motor. Discovery has several locations around Belize City. ~ 5916 Manatee Drive; 22-30748, fax 22-30750.

Transportation

AIR

International flights land at **Phillip S. W. Goldson International Airport** in Ladyville, located nine miles from Belize City. Daily flights arrive on TACA and American Airlines from Miami.

CAR RENTALS

The company with the best reputation in Belize is **Budget Rent A Car**, which offers four-wheel-drives in top condition. Budget owner Alan Auil will brief you on the area and provide essential driving tips. ~ 771 Bella Vista Road, two and a half miles north of Belize City; 22-32435, fax 22-32368; e-mail jmagroup@btl.net.

Elsewhere, try **Avis Rent A Car** (Poinsetta Road, Ladyville; 22-52629, fax 22-53062), which can deliver to the Radisson Fort George Hotel; **Safari/Hertz Car Rental** (11-A Cork Street; 22-30886; e-mail safarihz@btl.net); and **Jabiru Auto Rental** (5576 Princess Margaret Drive; 22-44680; e-mail jabiru@btl.net.

TAXIS

The easiest way to get into Belize City is by taxi, which costs US$20 (the maximum fare per trip—*not* per person—allowed by the government, so don't pay more). Taxi drivers know the international flight schedules and will be awaiting your arrival.

Addresses & Phone Numbers

Emergency for Police, Fire and Ambulance ~ 911
Karl Heusner Memorial Hospital ~ Princess Margaret Drive; 22-31548
Belize City Central Police Office ~ #3 Raccoon Street; 22-72222
Belize Tourism Board ~ Central Bank Building, Level 2, Gabourel Lane; 22-31913
Rico's Cybernet ~ The Great House, 13 Cork Street; 22-33997

SIX

Northern Belize

Just three decades ago, northern Belize was a forbidding land choked by dense jungle and mired in swamps, and the only road was a potholed trail that rarely got you from here to there without some calamity. Today, the Northern Highway is fairly smooth and lined with small villages, fields of shaggy sugar cane and ponds populated by wood storks and egrets. Of course, the jungle retains its hold—thanks to conservation efforts by Belizeans—and "highway" traffic is just as likely to be a sprinting Jesus Christ lizard as a car.

From Belize City, the Northern Highway wends 100 miles to the Yucatán border, past several modern-day villages and two magnificent and mysterious ancient cities that are testaments to Maya greatness, Altun Ha and Lamanai, as well as endless remnants of stone houses and walls. Traveling this northern corridor, you are constantly reminded of the ancient Maya civilization, whether by the house mounds at your jungle lodge or the 1000-year-old well near a swimming hole.

▼ ▼ ▼ ▼ ▼ ▼ ▼ ▼ ▼ ▼ ▼ ▼ ▼

Ladyville and Crooked Tree Area

Ladyville is actually where you land when you think you're flying to Belize City. The international airport is located here (north of Belize City) and so is a community bubbling with activity. The Belize River winds through like a fat snake; you snatch little glimpses from the road every now and then, and can catch fish if you care to spend a day with a guide. North from Ladyville, the patchwork asphalt called the Northern Highway launches into wide-open savannah and low-lying mangrove forests, with occasional pit stops like the cinderblock Chillville Lodge, announcing "cool A/C and TV," but looking unlike like any place one would stop lest she were positively down on her luck or had imbibed an unconscionable amount of Belizean rum.

SIGHTS   The first town north of Belize City is neither ancient nor mysterious. Rather, **Ladyville** is best known as the site of Belize's **Phillip S. W. Goldson International Airport**. It's pint-sized, as international airports go, but locals love to hang out on the receiving deck and watch the 747s come booming in. Just south of the airport on the Northern Highway, and one of the first sites visitors see in Belize, stands a steel monument depicting five Belizeans, each representing one of the country's five major ethnic groups—Creole, Garifuna, *Mestizo*, Mopan Maya and Kekchi Maya. North of the airport is "downtown" Ladyville: a gas station, a tumbledown schoolhouse, several no-name bars and usually dozens of children playing along the street.

Several miles north of the airport comes the turnoff for the village of **Burrell Boom**, which will take you nine miles down a dusty, rocky trail into forests of pine-oak and cohune and swamp,
HIDDEN ▶ until you arrive in **Bermudian Landing**. The Landing and surrounding villages were originally settled by Maya, who left their calling cards in the form of house mounds, which still pepper the wooded landscape, and in the Maya people—many direct descendants—who live and farm here. The spot was formerly called Butchers Landing because local cattle were brought here to be slaughtered before heading downriver to Belize City markets. Several decades ago, it was renamed for the band of Bermudian buccaneers who settled on this high bank in the 1600s.

It was the logging industry that shaped the area, starting in 1650 and continuing for some three hundred years. Villages testify to those logging days with their whimsical names of "boom," "landing," "bank," "walk" and "pen." Loggers first settling an area called it a landing or bank (for riverbank); once established, they would stretch a boom, or heavy iron chain, across the river to trap floating logs. They might also plant fields of crops where you could "walk," or raise cattle in pens. Today, you'll find villages such as Flowers Bank (formerly Flowers Walk), Lime Walk, May Pen and Isabella Bank. There's also Scotland Half-Moon, named for its Scottish settlers, and Ben Bow Creek, the namesake of one pirate, Admiral Ben Bow, who supposedly spent several rum-crazed nights in these wilds.

Bermudian Landing may seem just as wild to visitors today. Few people own cars and fewer have telephones, but most any teenager can tell you the jungle cure for stomachache, and even small children know the difference between a good snake and a bad one. Absorbing exhibits on snakes and on endangered black howler
HIDDEN ▶ monkeys await in the museum at the **Community Baboon Sanctuary** (admission). Black howlers, which are also known as baboons, are one of six species of howler monkeys; the black howlers are found only in Belize, southern Mexico, the Yucatán and northern Guatemala, and are rarely spotted in great numbers.

Northern Belize

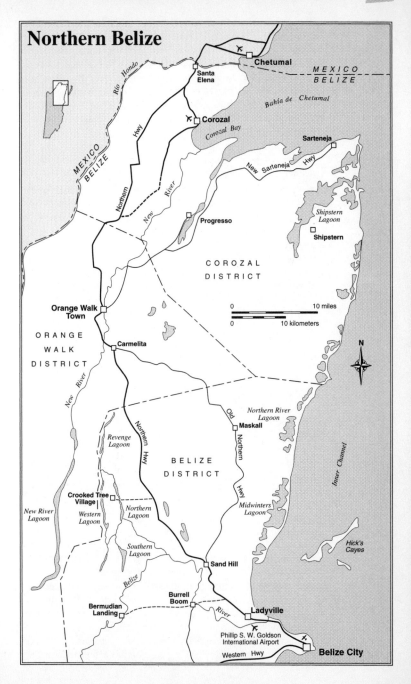

MEXICO
BELIZE

Chetumal

Santa Elena

Rio Hondo

Bahía de Chetumal

Corozal

Corozal Bay

MEXICO
BELIZE

Northern Hwy

New River

Sarteneja

New Sarteneja Hwy

Progresso

Shipstern Lagoon

Shipstern

COROZAL DISTRICT

Orange Walk Town

ORANGE WALK DISTRICT

Carmelita

New River

0   10 miles
0   10 kilometers

N

Old Northern Hwy

Northern River Lagoon

Maskall

Northern Hwy

Revenge Lagoon

Northern Hwy

BELIZE DISTRICT

Crooked Tree Village

Western Lagoon

Northern Lagoon

Midwinters Lagoon

Inner Channel

New River Lagoon

Southern Lagoon

Hick's Cayes

Belize River

Sand Hill

Burrell Boom

Bermudian Landing

River

Ladyville

Phillip S. W. Goldson International Airport

Western Hwy

Belize City

Little was known about the howlers in 1980 when Dr. Robert Horwich, a Wisconsin primatologist, watched a documentary titled *Amate—The Fig Tree*. It was made by well-known filmmaker Richard Foster, who lives in Belize and who had captured footage of an endearing troop of howlers living in a fig tree near Bermudian Landing. Horwich immediately flew to Belize and began research on the howlers. What he found was not only a healthy population of the monkeys, but a group of villagers willing to protect them.

In 1985, at a small gathering in a tiny clapboard house, the villagers of Bermudian Landing and surrounding areas formally opened their Community Baboon Sanctuary. The event not only secured the future of the howlers, it began what was perhaps the world's first grassroots sanctuary, where residents—not the government or some conservation organization—rallied to save the wildlife in their own jungle backyards.

Eleven villagers first signed a pledge to change their farming methods in a three-square-mile area. Their mission was to protect vegetation along the Belize River banks, various corridors of trees, and other areas where the howlers thrive. For the villagers—most of whom were surviving at poverty level—it meant using even less land to grow their crops; hence, less food for their families.

Over the years, the hardships have pulled the villagers together, and today 125 farmers and ranchers are members of the sanctuary, which, in turn, has blossomed to 20 square miles. Former howler and jaguar hunters now serve as sanctuary guides, and local families earn small fees by hosting visitors in their homes. Studies by sanctuary manager Camille Young show that about 90 percent of the villagers have kept their promise to protect the vegetation. Perhaps the most convincing evidence of success, however, is that while there were 500 howlers here in 1985, today there are more than 1400.

This means visitors to the Community Baboon Sanctuary will most certainly see a howler, even a whole family of howlers, who are instantly appealing with their cherublike faces, beseeching eyes and tiny hands and feet. Their narrow throats magnify their thunderous roars—often mistaken for jaguar screams—so they can be heard more than a mile away.

To find the howlers you will, of course, need a guide, and a museum attendant will be happy to fetch you one from "downtown" Bermudian Landing. Local guides are infinitely versed on the native flora, pointing out the spiny bamboo, red ginger, bromeliads and guanacaste trees that line the three and a half miles of trails and the Belize River, which flows through the sanctuary.

Spiny bamboo, one learns, protects the riverbanks from erosion, and red ginger is called "forest Visine" because its juice takes the red out of irritated eyes. The petals of the bromeliads can store up to two gallons of water and provide a home for 12 species of insects, while the trunk of the guanacaste tree was used by the Maya to make dugout canoes. The acidlike sap of the poisonwood tree is so poisonous it burns its own trunk. The stately kapok tree— the rainforest's tallest—towers more than 200 feet, but alas, all its limbs cling to its crown. Here, also, are many mapola trees, whose canopies are loved by howler monkeys. On most days, you'll spot families of monkeys scurrying through the treetops. The babies are not much bigger than your hand.

The monkeys are just some of the thousands of jungle residents you're apt to see. Foot-wide butterflies dance in and out of forest shadows and red-eyed tree frogs emit flashes of color. Iguanas sun on splintered logs poking out across the river, and leafcutter ants parade across the jungle floor, hoisting freshly cut leaves in their own antish, Herculean style. My guide and I even encountered a boa constrictor, all seven feet of him, stretched across the footpath.

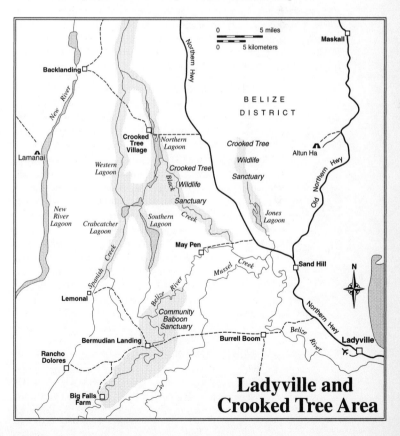

Ladyville and Crooked Tree Area

The Northern Highway

If you're exploring Belize by rental car, you'll find maximum adventure and diversity along the Northern Highway. This easy-to-drive paved route runs for 80 miles from Belize City to Corozal near the Mexican border. The roundtrip could be completed in a single day, but you'd miss most of the region's top sights. Instead, plan a three-day journey climaxed by a river trip to Lamanai, one of the Maya world's most important ancient sites.

COMMUNITY BABOON SANCTUARY   Leaving Belize City, follow the signs to the International Airport—or better yet, simplify navigation by taking a cab to the airport and renting your car there. Your first adventure starts just a few miles up the highway at the turnoff on your left to Burrell Boom and Bermudian Landing. Nine miles along this slow, bumpy unpaved road will bring you to the Community Baboon Sanctuary (page 132), a grassroots effort to rescue endangered black howlers. Listen and you may hear these small monkeys roar like jaguars.

ALTUN HA   Return the way you came to the main highway, turn left and continue north for about five miles to the village of Sand Hill, where the "Old Northern Highway" turns off to the right. Fourteen paved miles

If you'd rather explore the sanctuary on horseback or by canoe, guided excursions are available. Fishing guides are also available for those who'd like to try for tarpon, snapper or catfish in the Belize River—though it's strictly catch and release. ~ Bermudian Landing, nine miles west of the Northern Highway (take the Burrell Boom turnoff a few miles north of the airport).

Back on the Northern Highway, about 19 paved miles north and 4 miles west down a white marl road, lies a bird sanctuary. The centerpiece of the 3000-acre **Crooked Tree Wildlife Sanctuary** (admission) is the vast Northern Lagoon, whose shallow waters are perennially darkened by flocks of fantastic birds. Birdwatchers and birders (there is a difference, the former being a more casual observer) also flock to this place, setting up their telescopes and cameras along the shores, scouting out such unusual creatures as purple gallinules and ruddy crakes, social flycatchers and lesser yellowlegs, olive-throated parakeets and white-collared seedeaters. Most species have funny local names; the spot-breasted wren, for instance, has been creolized to "katy-yu-baby-di-cry," no doubt because a man claimed its song mimics the voice of a certain woman.

will bring you to Altun Ha (page 140). Though close to Belize, this famous Maya site can't be reached by bus.

ORANGE WALK   Return again to the Northern Highway, turn right and continue north. (You could continue on the old highway instead, but beyond Altun Ha the paved road is narrow and badly deteriorated.) Crossing a landscape of cane fields and scrub, you'll travel the 35 miles to Orange Walk (page 144) in less than an hour. There, you may want to book a boat tour to Lamanai for your return trip.

COROZAL   Share the highway with sugar cane trucks and an occasional Mennonite horse-drawn carriage as you cover the remaining 28 miles to the colorful seaside border town of Corozal (page 149), a good base for further explorations in the northern region. Start by climbing the Maya pyramid of Santa Rita for a great view of the town and bay. Possibilities for the following day include a boat trip to the hidden Maya site of Cerros, a guided tour to the Shipstern Nature Reserve with its clouds of butterflies, or a quick trip across the border to the Mexican city of Chetumal, where many Belizeans go to shop.

LAMANAI   On your return trip southward, take an all-day boat tour from Orange Walk up the New River to the huge Maya site of Lamanai, which has been inhabited almost continuously for 3500 years. Afterward, you'll be able to return to Belize City in time for dinner.

The unusual creature most people come to see is the jabiru stork. The Western Hemisphere's largest flying bird, it is formidable and fascinating, boasting a 12-foot wing span. Arrive during the dry season (October through February is the best time), when the storks and thousands of other birds, including peregrine falcons and boat-billed herons, create a flurry of activity. Once at the sanctuary, stop by the **visitors center** and pick up a map and list of birds.

It is usually easy to get close-up views of the birds from the paths that follow the Northern Lagoon, as well as from the Western Lagoon, located on the opposite side of Crooked Tree Village. Along the paths are many anhingas, who dive underwater to snag fish, then emerge to dry their water-gorged wings on a tree branch. Locals rent boats and offer guided boat trips, but they're deluxe (up to US$80), and the scenery is much the same. When the rainy season starts, the sanctuary floods and many birds leave. Before you visit, call the **Belize Audubon Society** (Belize City; 22-35004) to check current conditions. ~ Located four miles west of the Northern Highway (the turnoff is 19 miles north of the Bermudian Landing road).

The sanctuary warden at the visitors center can also provide other information or arrange for a local guide, and can tell you about **Crooked Tree Village,** home to 700 people and seemingly just as many pigs, chickens and skinny dogs. Half a dozen dirt roads wind through the village, past Jones Bar, Alice Store, the town telephone, and the town generator.

South of Crooked Tree Village lies **Chau Hiix,** the remains of an ancient Maya city. (*Chau hiix* is the Maya name for the jagarundi, a small jungle cat that is common in the area.) Local villagers first revealed the site's existence to archaeologists in 1990, and it is still being studied by field research teams from the University of Indiana. The central pyramid has been excavated and partially restored, and scientists have mapped about ten acres of the site, though the full extent of the former settlement remains unknown. It appears to have been occupied continuously from around 1200 B.C. until at least A.D. 1450. Artifacts are so abundant that workers attempting to dig outhouse trenches keep finding layers of relics. Surrounding the ruins area are enormous agricultural complexes irrigated by an impressive system of canals, dams and lagoons. Although archaeologists would prefer that the site remain closed to the general public while they are working there, they also acknowledge the reality that the modest but sustainable income ecotourism provides to the local people is the key factor that protects the site from looting and slash-and-burn farming. They cooperate with villagers who guide limited numbers of visitors through Chau Hiix on most days. Guided tours can be arranged through Chau Hiix Lodge near the perimeter of the site. A day or two notice may be required. ~ 800-654-4424, fax 407-322-6389 in the U.S.

LODGING   If you need a room near the international airport, the place to stay is the **Belize Biltmore Plaza.** Built in the early '90s, the low-slung, coral-washed buildings encase a lush courtyard of traveler's palms and oleanders, a swimming pool and pond. The lobby is done in British colonial style, with white-paned glass, white wicker and

CROOKED TREE CASHEWS

If you have some time, take one of the horse-and-buggy rides (ask at the visitors center) offered by several local farmers in Crooked Tree Village. Ask them to point out all the mango and cashew trees the village is known for. Every May, at the Crooked Tree Cashew Festival, locals go all out with nonstop parties, including Caribbean storytelling and outdoor theater. Attending visitors are invited on nature walks, river trips and tours of the nearby Maya ruins.

attendants in pith helmets. Each of the 75 air-conditioned rooms opens onto the courtyard and gives the feeling of a spacious motel with contemporary comforts such as bathtubs (unusual in Belize), air conditioning, cable television and telephones. This place is popular with business travelers, who enjoy the hotel's clubby bar and semiformal restaurant. ~ Mile 3, Northern Highway; 22-32302, fax 22-32301; www.belizebiltmore.com, e-mail biltmore@btl.net. DELUXE TO ULTRA-DELUXE.

Just around the corner from the airport but worlds away in ambience, the **Belize River Lodge** offers total escapism. Here, ◀ HIDDEN tucked along a flourishing riverbank, with stands of coconut palms and banana plants and carpets of green lawn running down to the river, are several clapboard cottages whose mahogany walls harbor decades of fish tales. The lodge is indeed renowned among anglers, who return each year to stalk the giant tarpon that seethe, piranha-like, in the river. For those who prefer flats or reef fishing, Belizean owners Marguerite Miles and Mike Heusner have an ample fleet of skiffs and topnotch guides to take you just about anywhere. They also offer six- and seven-night fishing "cruises" aboard their larger cruisers. Those who stay at the lodge will find cozy all-wood cottages with eclectic touches such as driftwood lamps, brown patchwork quilts and comfortingly worn books lining the shelves. Minimum stay is six nights, and includes family-style meals and a guide for five days, with only two anglers per guide—the best way to fish. ~ Northern Highway, Ladyville; 22-52002, fax 22-52298, or 888-275-4843 in the U.S.; www.belize riverlodge.com. ULTRA-DELUXE.

Birders know **Chau Hiix Lodge** as one of the choicest spots ◀ HIDDEN for catching a glimpse of Belize's unusual winged creatures. Of course, it doesn't hurt that the lodge is wonderfully remote, located downriver from the Crooked Tree Wildlife Sanctuary and upriver from the Community Baboon Sanctuary. Just getting to Chau Hiix usually involves animal encounters, as guests travel 45 minutes by boat down jungle-lined Spanish Creek from the outpost of Lemonal. Four rooms in two duplex cabañas aren't fancy, but they are comfortable enough, offering hot showers, ceiling fans and screened jalousie windows. Three cottages offer a little more privacy, with hot showers and air conditioning. The lodge rests on the widest point of Sapodilla Lagoon and is enveloped by more than 4000 acres of jungle and low pine ridge. More importantly, it borders the ancient Maya town of Chau Hiix, where archaeologists are still uncovering fascinating clues to the site's past, including structures dating all the way from 1500 B.C. to A.D. 1500. Tours of the ruins, as well as guided nature walks, guided boat excursions and use of canoes, meals and snacks and transportation from Belize City are included in the rate. Because getting there is so time consuming, a three-night stay is required.

Closed September and October. ~ South of Crooked Tree; for reservations, call 800-654-4424, fax 407-322-6389 in the U.S. ULTRA-DELUXE.

In the village of Crooked Tree, two rustic lodges open their doors to visitors. All are extremely basic, so expect to rough it. Along the northeastern rim of Crooked Tree Lagoon, facing a dirt beach and a wobbly pier, **Crooked Tree Resort** features seven round bamboo cabañas peaked with thatch roofs and shaded by bullet trees. Furnishings are simple but clean, with well-swept mahogany floors, pine walls and private baths with hot water. There's a small restaurant serving home cooking, and the village bar is spitting distance—not a good situation if there's a party going on; two birdwatchers I met stayed awake several nights, listening to the boom-boom-boom of a band that played until dawn. So before you book a room, ask if there are any special events scheduled at the bar. ~ Crooked Tree; 22-09896, fax 22-74007. MODERATE TO DELUXE.

On the opposite side of the village set along a picturesque shore of a lagoon, **Bird's Eye View Lodge** is a drab two-story cinder-block building whose rooms are surprisingly attractive and comfortable. There are ten private rooms with ceiling fans, as well as a hostel-style dormitory. Belizean tile covers the floors and hot water emanates from the private bath. The dining room is the fanciest in Crooked Tree. ~ Crooked Tree; 22-57027. MODERATE.

DINING

Rich maroon carpets, sheer lacy drapes and mahogany tables and chairs give the Biltmore Plaza's **Victorian Room** a slightly formal air. For many travelers, it's a welcome change from the wear-your-flip-flops funkiness of most Belize eateries. Grilled beef, pork or seafood is the name of the game, with such specialties as filet mignon and a sizable seafood platter for two. ~ Belize Biltmore Plaza, Mile 3, Northern Highway; 22-32302. DELUXE.

There aren't any formal restaurants in the Crooked Tree area, so plan on dining at your lodge.

NIGHTLIFE

In Ladyville, your best bet is an after-dinner drink at the American-style **Squire's Lounge**. ~ Belize Biltmore Plaza, Mile 3, Northern Highway; 22-32302. In other spots, you can order a cocktail at your fishing or jungle lodge bar, or spend some time outdoors staring at the moon and stars—an incomparable experience in this black-night wilderness.

Altun Ha

▼▼▼▼▼▼▼▼▼▼

Just south of Crooked Tree Village and the sanctuary is a fork where the Northern Highway meets the Old Northern Highway. Formerly *the* highway in northern Belize, this sliver of lonesome, well-worn pavement bumps and turns for 40 miles past cohune palms, thick bush and a scattering of clapboard houses. It is so narrow, a taxi driver points out, that when he meets a car, "we play chicken." The road is the reason Altun Ha was discovered.

In 1957, quarriers looking for stone to build the Old Northern Highway selected some 2000-year-old specimens at Altun Ha. As they dug, they uncovered more than just rock mounds at this Maya site. There were 13 structures surrounding two plazas, including one 60-foot temple now called **Temple of the Sun God**. Several years later, as archaeologists did their own digging at the temple, they made a thrilling find: the head of Kinich Ahau, the sun god, carved around A.D. 600 from a single piece of jade. The largest carved jade artifact ever discovered on the Maya Route, it weighs nearly ten pounds and is masterfully sculpted. (Unfortunately, you won't be able to look upon its hideous countenance—forked tongue, crossed eyes and cauliflower ears—as Kinich Ahau now resides in a Belize bank vault.)

SIGHTS

What made the jade head even more spectacular was that it was located next to the remains of a priest. The holy man had been laid atop a wooden platform, adorned with jaguar and puma skins and necklaces of oyster and jade, and buried in a small pyramid. Rarely did the Maya bury their dead in temples, so what was the significance? The excavation team, led by Canadian archaeologist David Pendergast, never reached a conclusion. What they did find,

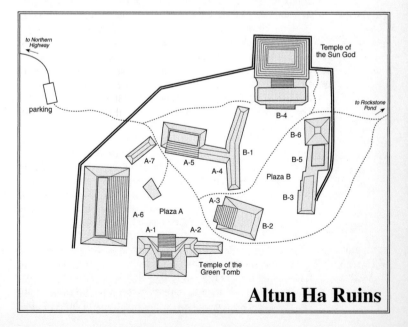

Altun Ha Ruins

however, were six more priests entombed in the temple—an exhilarating discovery in the first full-scale excavation in Belize. Several of the crypts had been defiled by fire, soil or broken roof slabs. The desecraters were not modern-day looters but early Maya—an indication, Pendergast wrote, that the society may have collapsed at the hands of revolting peasants.

A Classical city that reaches out for one and a half miles, Altun Ha was a link in the Caribbean trade route that ran north through the Yucatán. It was a town and minor ceremonial center, lacking any stelae, yet Pendergast found remnants of jade and copal tree resin obviously used in rituals—a practice rare among the Maya. Many of the fragments were found on the round altar atop the Sun God temple, now known as **building B-4** in **Plaza B**, including exquisitely carved pendants that had been shattered and cast into a blazing fire. Pendergast believes that this altar held some unique significance, noting that "the bits of jade, resin and charcoal were scattered over the floor around the altar and left as some sort of fossilized ceremony, to be discovered some 1300 years later."

Like many Maya structures, the Temple of the Sun God was constantly being improved on; Pendergast noted eight separate construction periods. And while it was obviously the premier building, Altun Ha boasts five additional temples, surrounding **Plaza A**. Four are dedicated to the forces of nature—the sun, rain, wind and moon—while the fifth, the **Temple of the Green Tomb**, held human remains and hundreds of pieces of jade jewelry, some quite elaborate.

Away from the plazas, a quarter-mile trail through the jungle leads to a misty, lime-colored reservoir. Called **Rockstone Pond**, the clay-lined, spring-fed basin was enlarged by the Maya, as evidenced by the sharp stone blocks—probably digging tools—found around the shoreline. At the south end, they built a dam of stone and clay to keep the water from seeping into surrounding swamps. The reservoir is surrounded by house mounds, the remains of waterfront residences.

Standing at the lip of the pond, watching the parrots skip through the trees, listening to the *hoot-hoot* call of blue-crowned motmots, spying the tail of a fleeing opossum, it is impossible not to wonder if the occupants of those houses saw and heard these same creatures, felt the same steamy haze before an afternoon rain, inhaled the skunky smell of the forest floor. After all, though more than 1000 years have passed the jungle has remained virtually unchanged.

And therein lies Altun Ha's added appeal. One of Belize's most popular Maya sites—it is close to Belize City and easy to find—Altun Ha still belongs to the rainforest. Except for the occasional mid-morning and mid-afternoon tour buses, there are no crowds—only mosquitoes, whose swarms will blacken your

Bats, Butterflies
and Bejeweled Skeletons

L a Milpa was once the exclusive domain of scientists and others researching the luscious, rarely touched northwestern jungles of Belize. But now travelers are welcomed to this field station in the 240,000-acre **Río Bravo Conservation and Management Area** run by the excellent Programme for Belize. Jungle trekking and birding are exceptional, and there are opportunities to visit remote Maya, Mestizo and Mennonite villages. There's an Education Center where researchers lead discussions on forest life, from bats, butterflies and red-eyed tree frogs to palm harvests and oil extraction. And just three miles away lies a royal tomb with a bejeweled male Maya skeleton discovered in 1996. It's almost always open from January to July, when archaeologists are excavating.

Families love it here, and usually stay two or three nights in one of the four comfortable palm-thatched mahogany cabañas. Each cabaña comes with solar- or gas-powered hot showers and two double beds covered in Guatemalan bedspreads and veiled in mosquito netting. There's also a loft with a twin bed. Single travelers and students usually opt for the 30-bed dormitory with solar power and composting toilets. Rates are the same either way and include three family-style meals. For dinner, that might mean pork chops, peas and rice, green salad and desserts like potato pudding and banana cakes. In the morning you'll find scrambled eggs, sliced cheese, johnny cakes and perhaps even exotic fruit such as atemoya or custard apple.

Plan to rise before dawn to watch the white-tailed deer, grey foxes and ocellated turkey roam the grounds looking for their own breakfasts. Call well in advance (several weeks, preferably) for reservations and directions. ~ Located an hour and a half southwest of Orange Walk, past Blue Creek Village. Transfers from Belize City and the international airport are available. For reservations, contact Programme for Belize: 22-75616, fax 22-75635 in Belize City; www.pfbelize.org. DELUXE.

skin and attack your body in the most troublesome places. Coat yourself in repellent, then sightsee at leisure, exploring the ceremonial structures and house mounds sprinkled around the lush jungle clearing. Admission. ~ Old Northern Highway, 31 miles north of Belize City.

Most visitors to Altun Ha stay at either Crooked Tree Village or in Corozal. For lodging and dining, see those listings in this chapter. You could also easily stay in Belize City, about an hour away by car. For lodging and dining there, see Chapter Five.

▼ ▼ ▼ ▼ ▼ ▼ ▼ ▼ ▼ ▼ ▼ ▼ ▼

Orange Walk Town and Lamanai

Orange Walk, the modern-day hub of Northern Belize, is second only to Belize City in size. Home to 11,000 people, Orange Walk was originally a logging outpost that became a refuge for *Mestizos* fleeing the Caste War in nearby Yucatán. Mexican influence is evident everywhere, from the tortilla bakeries and Wild West–style storefronts to the weathered mission churches. In recent decades, Orange Walk has attracted a rich ethnic mix that includes Chinese, Hindu Indians, Maya and Mennonites. The last, dressed in tattered straw hats and baggy overalls cinched with twine, ride into town in horse-drawn buggies to trade crops for sugar or supplies.

That's not to suggest Orange Walk possesses a great deal of visual beauty or charm. In fact it's not a place most travelers care to spend time—they tend to pass through on their way to the secluded Maya city of Lamanai. That two-square-mile site is secreted among profuse jungle along the wide, steamy New River and has a great ceremonial center dating back to 1500 B.C. Maya caretakers live in a thatched village; excavations and restorations are continuous, not only on ancient, hulking buildings but on those dating to the 19th century—making Lamanai one of the longest-occupied Maya sites.

SIGHTS   Driving along the Old Northern Highway, you'll know you're getting close to **Orange Walk Town** when you see the old trucks stuffed with cut sugar cane and notice a sweet molasses smell in the air. Sugar cane is the number-one business in this working town. The "downtown" consists mainly of tired cinderblock buildings, ice factories and a string of churches. Walking around isn't particularly pleasant—it's hot, loud and dusty. So do what other travelers do and get on your way to Lamanai.

HIDDEN ►   The Maya would no doubt be pleased with the present-day way to arrive at **Lamanai**: a two-hour backwater boat trip. After all, Lamanai means "submerged crocodile," a name befitting a city sprawled on the jowls of a gorged lagoon. The trip starts near Orange Walk, on the New River, which winds southward past an old rum factory, slash-and-burn farms and Mennonite villages.

Along the way, women wash their clothes in the clear warmth of the water and long-nose bats sleep in hollow tree trunks above the river. Long-legged jacana birds, flaunting fluorescent green wings and neon yellow beaks, trot across colossal lily pads, and fields of emerald sea grass wave beneath the water's surface. Shy boat-billed herons hide along the riverbanks and snail kites whisk through the sky.

It would be enough just to witness the surreality of the river, but what awaits afterward is even more riveting. Here, where the

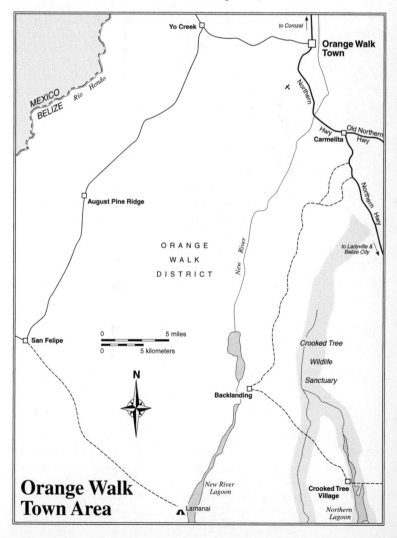

Orange Walk
Town Area

river yawns into a wide lagoon, several thatched buildings gather at the water's edge. At their flanks is a once-grand city that still presides over this part of the jungle—an ancient Manhattan, some 720 buildings spread across 950 acres, obscured in a mantle of massive trees and greedy vines. Leaf and rubble paths curl between Lamanai's buildings, many of which tower above the jungle canopy and form a mystical maze. The rattling purrs of unseen cicadas flood the forest, and the panicked squawk of a brown jay—the jungle siren—warns of potential danger.

The waterfront thatched buildings (including a mini-museum, gift shop and restrooms) are left over from the days of Canadian archaeologist David Pendergast, who excavated the area during the 1970s and 1980s. While Pendergast's teams resurrected buildings, they also sought clues to the lives of Lamanai's former inhabitants. They took samples of lagoon sediment, for instance, which revealed good levels of pollen and suggested the Maya were growing corn as early as 1500 B.C. And they combed the primeval rot of Lamanai's garbage dumps, only to find that these ancient Manhattanites fancied deer and turtle.

Pendergast also brought some modern-day gentility to the jungle setting, for when *Equinox* writer Ronald Wright dined with him in the late 1980s, he recalls that their meal "was followed by cookies and tea, and it would have been hard to imagine oneself in the heart of Belize were it not for the tarantula that one of the archaeology students discovered in the teapot."

In 1860, the British Honduras Company Ltd. showed up on Lamanai's shores with dreams of building a sugar factory. It did indeed construct a mill and import laborers from Jamaica, Barbados and China, but the workers were not trained in making sugar and the mill was too primitive for the task. In 1875, sugar making became history at Lamanai, though the brief attempt is remembered today in the ruins of the old mill, including a flywheel and boiler, located south of the city center.

Two hundred years earlier, the Spanish had come to Lamanai and, eager to force their religion on the Maya, built a Christian church. The Maya were not so eager to convert and destroyed most of the building. Missionaries soon arrived and put up a second, more stylish church, but the Maya were not impressed. This, too, they tried to demolish, though more of it survived. Remnants of both missions can be seen today north of Lamanai's center.

Far greater than those houses of worship are the Maya ceremonial structures. The one known as **Lag**, or **structure N10-43**, rises to 112 feet and was the tallest in the Maya civilization when it was created in 100 B.C. Today, it is the largest Preclassic building on the Maya Route. A sturdy flight of stairs runs up the front, depositing visitors on a platform that looks across the pastoral Maya lowlands and slow, snaking New River. It is on this platform that the Maya likely performed complex religious ceremonies. Among the more bizarre, men pierced their penises with stingray spines and women dragged strings of thorns across their tongues. Prisoners of war were typically beheaded, though noble ones received special treatment: their hearts were torn out while still alive.

Lag faces a good-sized **ball court**, where Maya athletes played *pok-ta-pok*, a basketball-style sport using a small rubber ball. In the center of the court Pendergast found a massive stone disc; under the disc, he made one of his most thrilling discoveries: a pool of liquid mercury, the first ever uncovered at a Maya site. The mercury was among several pottery vessels containing jade and shell objects that were no doubt part of a special offering.

The offerings made at **structure N10-7**, south of the ball court, seem to have included children. Here, behind a remarkably detailed stone stele of a Maya ruler, Pendergast found the bones of six children. Why the people of Lamanai would sacrifice their own children remains a mystery, since human sacrifice was not customary among the Maya.

Across the plaza stands the **Temple of the Jaguar Masks** (**structure N10-9**), built in the 6th century and embellished with stairs in the 8th and 13th centuries. Among the finds here have been a giant red and black bowl, a jade mask and a pair of Early Classic jade earrings.

North of here, the 60-foot-tall **Mask Temple**, or **structure N9-56**, rises hauntingly along the New River Lagoon. It is wildly adorned with stone masks, though the eye is instantly drawn to one particular visage—the 12-foot-tall face of a man, his nose fat and flattened, his eyes heavily lidded and slitted like a jaguar's, his features markedly Asian. The temple's architecture reveals four separate construction phases, beginning in 200 B.C. and ending, incredibly, some 1500 years later.

There are numerous other masks and stelae, and buildings containing flint and pottery, at Lamanai. In fact, it takes at least four hours to explore the city center—with a guide, of course. But don't count on finding any at Lamanai; it's best to hire a guide a day before you plan to visit.

A WAY TO THE RUINS

Boats leave from various points around Orange Walk Town for the four-hour roundtrip ride to the ruins. One of the more popular launch spots is **Jim's Cool Pool,** at the Northern Highway toll bridge south of Orange Walk. Brothers Joel and Anthony Armstrong, who live with their families and flea-bitten dogs in an old yellow school bus along the river, will usually take you to Lamanai in their motorboat.

LODGING   Near the south end of Orange Walk Town, 31-room **D*Victoria Hotel** offers basic rooms with private baths and hot water. You have your choice of air conditioning or a ceiling fan, but considering the reliably sweltering Orange Walk heat, I recommend the A/C. Better yet, take a dip in the swimming pool—definitely the motel's most welcome feature. The disco downstairs may be less welcome for those who prefer peace and quiet. ~ 40 Belize Corozal Road, Orange Walk Town; 32-22518, fax 32-22847; www.dvictoriahotel.com, e-mail dvictoria@btl.net. MODERATE.

My favorite thing about **Lamanai Outpost Lodge** is the nighttime crocodile cruise. That's not to suggest the 18 cabañas aren't completely comfortable; they are cooled by ceiling fans and attractively decorated. The lodge is set up high along the banks of the New River Lagoon, with views of the water and the lofty temples of Lamanai. You can walk to Lamanai from your cabaña to explore the ruins at leisure or take a canoe out for a lagoon ride. There's a dining room and bar, and plenty of daily excursions. Roundtrip transportation from Belize City is included in the rate. Spend the night here—you won't regret it. ~ Reservations: 22-33578, fax 22-09061 or 888-733-7864, fax 727-864-4062 in the U.S.; www.lamanai.com, e-mail mail@lamanai.com. ULTRA-DELUXE.

One of Belize's most unusual accommodations, **Maruba Resort Jungle Spa** goes all-out to offer a fantasy version of the jungle lodge experience. The huge palapa lobby area, guest-room fourplexes and other structures secluded in the slightly landscaped rainforest were built out of rock by the resort's owner, a champion weight lifter. Decor features rough-textured silver walls, fragmented tile floors and bright-colored local furniture and folk art collected from Africa, India and other ports of call. There are no phones in the rooms—and only one in the whole resort. Hibiscus flowers and palmilla fronds are strewn everywhere, from your bedspread to your dining table. Facilities include two swimming pools (one with a waterfall), tennis courts, stables, a meditation room and a separate TV hut hidden away down a jungle path. The spa offers seaweed wraps and "Mood

AUTHOR FAVORITE

Maruba Resort Jungle Spa claims to be the most luxurious lodging in Belize, and I suspect it's true. Certainly among the most unusual (and the priciest), it was the setting for the TV reality show "Temptation Island." This place was designed with romance in mind, with beds strewn with bright red flowers, secret hideaways along jungle trails, a glow-in-the-dark restaurant, and even a jungle wedding bower. See above for more information.

Mud" massages. The candlelit restaurant, with its glow-in-the-dark jaguar-spotted tablecloths, serves elegantly presented lobster, shrimp and conch, along with fresh fruits and vegetables from the resort's gardens. Beware the "viper rum," a concoction so potent you can light it on fire, distilled like moonshine in the nearby village of Maskall. (Environmentalists at the Belize Zoo claim that it is made using real snakes, which is in violation of Belizean law, but the charge remains unproven; a court case over it was recently dismissed.) ~ One and a half miles from Maskall on the old highway to Altun Ha; 22-55555, 800-627-8227, fax 22-55506; www.maruba-spa.com, e-mail maruba@ btl.net. ULTRA-DELUXE.

DINING

Of the many Chinese restaurants in Orange Walk, **Lee's** stands out. The interior is cool, clean and modern, if not utilitarian, and the portions generous and tasty. Besides the traditional sweet and sours, chop sueys and chow meins, there's baked fish and pork chops. ~ 11 San Antonio Road; 32-22174. BUDGET TO MODERATE.

◀ HIDDEN

If you're staying at **Lamanai Outpost Lodge** you'll get three solid, tasty meals a day in the dining room. Reasonable prices, too.

NIGHTLIFE

The best way to spend a night at Lamanai is looking for crocodiles. Start with a Belikin in the bar at Lamanai Outpost Lodge, then join the crocodile cruise (as in, you cruise in a boat scouting for crocodiles) around New River lagoon. Lodge guests can also go for nighttime jungle walks, shining flashlights around in the hopes of picking up a jaguar's eyes.

Corozal Area

Set in the curve of Corozal Bay, Corozal Town is a good base camp for northern Belize and southern Mexico. Many of the buildings are clapboard, built on stilts, architecture that sprung up after a 1955 hurricane tore through town. Corozal is now mostly a quiet place of less than 15,000 people, some of whom are descendants of the original founding Maya who fled a Spanish massacre. The town is also part of the old Santa Rita Maya territory. A mural in town hall portrays the struggle of the Maya, particularly in the Caste War.

SIGHTS

If you've been awed by the brilliant butterflies weaving around the Belize forests, don't miss the **Shipstern Nature Reserve** (about an hour's drive north from Orange Walk). More than 200 species reside within a mesh enclosure that resembles a mini-forest. Of course, many more creatures reside within this 22,000-acre reserve, which is unique in Belize because it takes in hardwood and mangrove and swamp, or bajo, forests. Wading birds find the miles of salt lagoons and mangrove marshes safe places to raise their young, and white-tailed deer, brocket deer and tapir take shelter in the vast hardwood forests. Botanical trails offer peeks at these animals; guides are available at the reserve's visitors center. For information, call the Belize Audubon Society at 2-35004.

North of the reserve, the last real town before the Mexico border is **Corozal**. Stretching along a pale blue, blustery sea, with a shore saturated in coconut palms, Corozal is scenic and peaceful, especially in the northern area of Cansejo Shores, where handsome, well-tended homes are sprinkled along the water. Wealthy Belizeans own vacation homes here, but it's the Americans and Europeans who fuel much of the real estate market. In downtown Corozal, local pride shines through in the picturesque **central park** with its pretty fountains and canopies of poinciana trees. Around town, you'll also notice the hand-written signs, tacked to electric poles, that read: "Don't Be Mean. Keep Corozal Clean." ~ 1st Street North, one block from the sea.

HIDDEN ▶

On the outskirts of Corozal, two minor Maya sites offer interesting side trips. It's best to take a boat to **Cerro Maya**, located south of Corozal, near where the New River empties into Corozal Bay. Cerro Maya (meaning "Maya Hill") is spread across more than 50 acres of forest, though the city center—resting on a gentle hill—is easily explored in an hour. Several plazas are surrounded by pyramids, including one that's 72 feet tall. Like these buildings, the ball courts and artifacts here date from 400 B.C. to A.D. 100. Boats leave from downtown Corozal; or, check at **Tony's Inn**. ~ South end of town; 42-22055.

HIDDEN ▶

Archaeologists believe **Santa Rita** was the Maya city of Chetumal, located about 35 miles south of today's Chetumal, Mexico. Situated on Corozal Bay, near the New River and Río Hondo, Santa Rita likely controlled the trade arteries that funneled cacao, honey and vanilla from Belize to the northern Yucatán. The city was discovered around the turn of the century by Thomas Gann, amateur archaeologist and Corozal's town doctor. Gann uncovered fantastic Mixtec-style frescoes, jade jewelry and pottery, though the frescoes have since been destroyed. Today's site will not impress visitors as it did Gann. Only one structure survives: a Classic building, riddled with doorways and connecting rooms, including a main room where burnt offerings were made. ~ Off the Northern Highway, just north of Corozal.

For the eight miles from Corozal to the Mexico border, the Northern Highway yields rural vistas of wide-open pastures, scrub forest, and fields swelled with corn, bananas and sugar cane. There are a few eye-blink towns, including the pueblo-like Santa Clara and Santa Elena Concepción, that look more like Mexico than Belize. Mexico officially starts at the bridge spanning the Río Hondo. When passing from Belize to Mexico (or vice versa), the border crossing is quick and simple on the Belize side, long and complicated on the Mexican side, especially if a public bus has

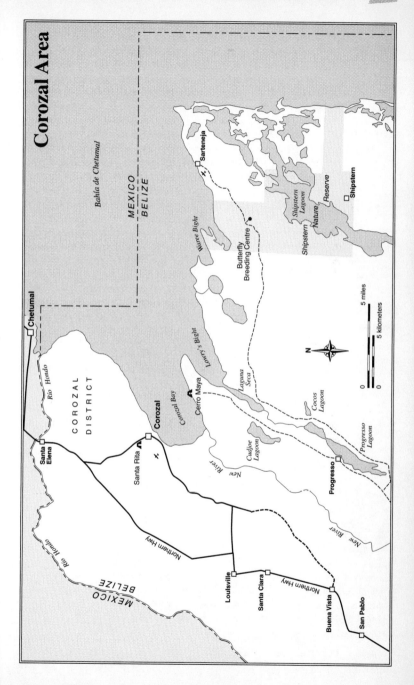

Corozal Area

Bahía de Chetumal

MEXICO
BELIZE

Chetumal

Río Hondo

COROZAL
DISTRICT

Santa Elena

Santa Rita

Corozal

Corozal Bay

Cerro Maya

Lowry's Bight

Wattee Bight

Sarteneja

Butterfly
Breeding Centre

Shipstern
Lagoon

Shipstern Nature Reserve

Shipstern

New River

Cudjoe Lagoon

Laguna Seca

Cocos Lagoon

Progresso Lagoon

Progresso

N

5 miles

5 kilometers

0

0

New River

Northern Hwy

Louisville

Santa Clara

Northern Hwy

Buena Vista

San Pablo

Río Hondo

MEXICO
BELIZE

just disgorged its riders. American citizens, who need a passport, will be issued a Mexican tourist card. The card will be reclaimed by the border officials upon re-entering Belize. Most people crossing into Mexico are taking a day trip to **Chetumal**, mainly to shop the crowded markets. Buses are the cheapest way to go, costing US$1.50 each way. Taxis are considerably more: one way is about US$20.

LODGING

By far the best choice for Corozal lodging is **Tony's Inn & Beach Resort**, which feels like an upscale motor court. The crisp white two-story buildings enjoy a breezy seaside locale, complete with outdoor palapa bar and precious patch of white beach. The rooms are big and modern, with tile floors and ceiling fans; some rooms have air conditioning, some have satellite TV. ~ South end of town; 42-22055, fax 42-22829; www.tonysinn.com. MODERATE TO DELUXE.

If you're short on cash, check out the **Hotel Maya**, across from the sea. The 20 rooms are very clean, but the dressers are beat-up and the draperies look like sheets. Some of the rooms have air conditioning, some have ceiling fans. The owners are a friendly local family. ~ South end of Corozal; 42-22082, fax 42-22827. BUDGET.

DINING

The fare is not spectacular, but **Tony's Inn & Beach Resort** easily wins as Corozal's top restaurant. Choose from a variety of seafood dishes, baked, broiled or fried, as well as pork chops, fried chicken, and rice and beans. Linens cover the tables, and jalousie windows funnel in sea breezes. Breakfast and lunch are also available. ~ South end of town; 42-22055. MODERATE TO DELUXE.

With only four tables, the **Hotel Maya** feels like someone's private dining room. In a way it is, since it belongs to a family that prepares homestyle meals for a loyal local following. The menu changes depending on what's fresh each day, but entrées might include fried chicken or T-bone steaks. Breakfast features omelettes and eggs with refried beans. ~ South end of town; 42-22082. MODERATE.

sights

AUTHOR FAVORITE

For me, standing in a cloud of brilliant butterflies was just as surreal as standing atop a mighty Maya pyramid. At **Shipstern Nature Reserve**, the butterflies are often so thick they appear a constant whirlwind of color (they hide in the foliage on cloudy days). In addition to more than 200 species of butterflies, Shipstern is home to an assortment of birds, reptiles and mammals. This is a wonderful sidetrip from Corozal on a sunny day. For more information see page 149.

Nightlife is scarce around Corozal. There are a couple of in-town **NIGHTLIFE**
bars, but things can get rough. I like sitting on the beach at **Tony's**
Inn, listening to the waves slap at the shore, watching the silent
leaps of lightning across the nighttime sky. ~ South end of town;
42-22055.

One of the very best Belize experiences is a
motor boat ride from Orange Walk to **Outdoor Adventures**
Lamanai. **Ruben Ramos Guide Service** does
excellent daytrips to Lamanai, complete with extensive narrative **BOAT TRIPS**
on birds and other wildlife, medicinal plants and archaeology. ~
44 San Antonio Road, Orange Walk Town; 32-23466.

Birdwatchers will find the ultimate canoe trip at Crooked Tree **CANOEING**
Wildlife Sanctuary. Rentals are available at the visitors center or
at nearby **Bird's Eye View Lodge** (20-32040) or **Paradise Inn** (20-
12084). Guests at **Lamanai Outpost Lodge** (22-33578) will definitely want to take a complimentary canoe out on the New River
lagoon and watch for hickatee turtles, bats, howler monkeys and
crocodiles. Sunset and sunrise are particularly atmospheric.

The ride from Corozal north to the Mexico border is nearly flat **BIKING**
and quite scenic. Pick up a bike in Corozal from **Stephan Moer-**
man. ~ 37 1st Avenue, on the seafront; 42-22833.

International flights land at the small and personal **Phil-**
lip S. W. Goldson International Airport, located in Lady- **Transportation**
ville. If you're headed to Corozal and prefer to fly,
Tropic Air and Maya Island Air both have daily flights from the **AIR**
international airport and from the municipal airport in Belize City.

If you've just arrived at Phillip S. W. Goldson International Air- **CAR**
port, it's easy to rent a car inside or near the terminal. From here
you simply head north on the only paved road—the Northern
Highway—"paved" being a relative word at times, as potholes
do tend to crop up. However, the driving's entirely pleasurable,
with little villages and open savannah on either side of the road,
and hardly ever another car. The "highway" runs for 100 miles to
the Mexican border and delivers you to Orange Walk and Corozal. For an adventurous sidetrip, veer off onto the Old Northern
Highway, which parallels the new Northern Highway for 40 miles.
The old road is similar to a wide sidewalk edged in dense brush
and tumbledown stilt homes.

If you plan on attempting a drive to Lamanai, do it in the dry
season (November through February). It's 36 miles from Orange
Walk, down a rocky, rutted path that looks a lot like a road. The
jarring trip takes about two hours.

Before you strike out on your own, check road conditions and get directions from a local hotel or travel agency. **Caribbean Holiday and Travel Service** is a good place to try. ~ Queen Victoria Avenue, Orange Walk Town; 32-22803, fax 32-20544.

BUS

Buses no longer run from the international airport so you'll have to take a taxi to Belize City, then catch a **Batty Brothers** (22-72025), **Urbina's** (32-22048) or **Venus** (22-77390) bus. All three travel the northern corridor and offer service to Chetumal.

Jex Bus Service (no phone) goes to Crooked Tree from their Pound Yard Bridge location in Belize City. **MacFadzean's Blue Bus** (no phone) travels between Bermudian Landing and the Belize City terminal at the corner of Mosel and Orange Streets. You might also try **Russell's Bus Service** (no phone); located on Cairo Street in Belize City, it has buses that go to Bermudian Landing and Maskall Village, off the Old Northern Road.

▼ ▼ ▼ ▼ ▼ ▼ ▼ ▼ ▼ ▼ ▼ ▼ ▼ ▼ ▼ ▼ ▼ ▼ ▼ ▼

Addresses & Phone Numbers

Emergency for Police, Fire and Ambulance ~ 911
Orange Walk Police Station ~ 32-22022
Corozal Police Station ~ 42-22022
Charlotte's Web Internet Cafe ~ 78 Fifth Avenue, Corozal; 42-20135

SEVEN

Western Belize

While the Belize cayes offer visitors a window to the world at sea, barely an hour away, western Belize opens onto a world of luscious jungle, forest-clad mountains and mighty temples shrouded in mystery. The gateway to this world is the Western Highway, which runs 82 paved miles from Belize City to the Guatemala border. Heading west from the city, the landscape is at once lonely and rugged, with scrub palmetto, mangrove swamps and a few clapboard homes on stilts. Then mountains are slowly etched on the horizon, jagged summits with intense green forest cascading down their slopes.

This western route is measured in mile posts; you'll begin noticing the concrete posts with white signs and black numbers as you leave Belize City. You'll also notice the weedy cemetery, whose sunbaked, bone-white, above-ground tombs bid goodbye as you head west.

Western Belize is a land of country cottages, ranches and jungle lodges that seem etched into the earth. Many lie more than an hour from the paved road, down winding, rocky trails that look down the sides of hills. Most have not progressed to electricity (kerosene lamps light up the night), but accommodations are usually quite comfortable. Best of all, the nature encounters and cultural experiences are unmatched.

Belize Zoo to Belmopan

The first 50 miles of Western Highway angle southwest through lonely landscape, flat scrub oak and reedy savannah and pine woods simmering beneath subtropical sun. Wood shacks, palmetto huts and semblances of villages are sprinkled throughout, and there is the occasional man on donkey-back, or a woman scrubbing clothes in a galvanized tub. There's also the Belize Zoo and Tropical Education Center, one of the country's premier sights and most important ecotourism organizations. Across the "highway" from the zoo, Monkey Bay is a private reserve devoted to educating students about the environment through field studies, though anyone passing by will want to take a picnic hike to the white-sand river beach.

Belmopan has no beaches, only clusters of concrete buildings that form the country's capital. The town secured that status in 1961, when Hurricane Hattie devastated Belize City, which had been the capital. Though the government was moved, residents were slow to follow, preferring to live in Belize City even though they worked in Belmopan. In fact, the town was so desolate at night it was called the "City of Sadness." But Belmopan is slowly attracting new residents. Today it is home to 7000 people and is said to be the smallest national capital on earth.

SIGHTS
The first village is not for 16 miles, and it wasn't even meant to be a village. After Hurricane Hattie nearly blew away Belize City in 1961, survivors fled inland and set up a temporary camp that was, naturally, called **Hattieville**. Belize City was eventually rebuilt, and the capital of Belmopan opened to the west, but many people preferred to stay in their new clapboard homes dotting the scrub palmetto. Today, the homes don't look so new, but the 1179 residents of Hattieville enjoy their status as suburbanites.

Around Mile Post 29, you'll see a small sign for the **Belize Zoo & Tropical Education Center**. A wonderful introduction to Belize's wildlife, the zoo is home to Rambo the toucan, Balboa the boa constrictor, Pete the jaguar, Sarge the crocodile, Boomer the jabiru stork and many other rare and colorful creatures.

Gravel paths wend through thick stands of slash pine trees dripping with moss and bromeliads, past a preening curassow, a fanged crocodile snoozing in the mud, a statue-still jaguar hunching beneath a palm frond, locking his eyes onto yours. His are not the beaten-down eyes of a zoo animal, but of a retired king come to rest in a comfortable home. Signs sprinkled among the enclosures plead for the animals' autonomy: "I'm a great black hawk, but guys who take shots at me are Great Big Turkeys," says the sign where a black hawk lives. And at the spider monkey home: "Listen! We make bad pets! We would much rather spend time with other monkeys than with human primates!"

The clever signs are the work of Sharon Matola, an American biologist who founded the zoo in 1983 after several animals were abandoned by a wildlife filmmaker. Since then, the zoo has gone from a funky little place with a few pens to one of Belize's shining ecotourism stars. In 1991, when a bigger and better Belize Zoo opened next to the old one, *National Geographic* filmed the animals moving into their new homes for a television special on animal caretakers. Included in the documentary were then accomplished zoo curator, Belizean Tony Garel, and a staff of more than 20 villagers, some of whom were former wildlife poachers. Admission. ~ 22-08004, fax 22-08010; www.belizezoo.org.

Four-Day Getaway

The Wild Belize West

Day 1
- From Belize City, rent a four-wheel-drive and head west. In less than an hour you'll see the sign for the **Belize Zoo & Tropical Education Center** (page 156). Take your time with the wild animals, then take time for lunch a mile down the road at **J.B.'s** (page 160).

- Keep pressing west until you reach the turnoff for **Chaa Creek Adventure Centre, Rainforest Reserve and Spa** (page 172). Check into your exotic jungle cottage and don't miss the sunset canoe trip down the Macal River.

Day 2
- After breakfast, explore Chaa Creek's **Natural History Centre** and **Blue Morpho Butterfly Breeding Centre**. (Oh, and ask the lodge to pack you a picnic for the day.) Then visit **Ix Chel Tropical Research Centre** and the **Rainforest Medicine Trail** (page 166) before heading to the ruins at **Xunantunich** (page 167).

- Enjoy lunch at the pyramids, then drive into **San Ignacio** (page 164) by late afternoon for dinner at the **Running W Steak House** (page 175) before returning to Chaa Creek for the night.

Day 3
- Rise early, have breakfast and order a picnic lunch from Chaa Creek's kitchen. Then check out and drive over to Mountain Pine Ridge. Have a look at **Hidden Valley Falls** (page 181), then stop at **Río On Pools** (page 181) and **Río Frio Cave** (page 181).

- By lunchtime, arrive at **Caracol** (page 182) for a picnic followed by—if it's springtime—a guided tour. Then check into **Blancaneaux Lodge** (page 187). Don't miss dinner at the lodge restaurant. Or, for something more friendly, rustic and Belizean, check into **Five Sisters Lodge** (page 188).

Day 4
- Drive from San Ignacio to Belize City, stopping at **Caesar's Place Gift Shop** (page 176) for lunch and shopping if time permits. Continue exploring Belize, or return home.

Many animals are born at the zoo, but those who aren't come from other zoos or from people who donate wild pets. Poachers are told to take their quarry elsewhere. Iguanas are among the animals being born at the zoo lately. The Green Iguana Breeding Project, started in 1995, hopefully will help replenish Belize's iguana population, fast diminishing because of overhunting (iguana, nicknamed "bamboo chicken," is a popular Belizean dish). Educating residents about iguanas, and teaching them to raise the reptiles much as they would raise chickens, is also part of the project.

In fact, public education is one of Matola's main goals. Back in the early zoo days, Matola constantly pestered schools to offer field trips. She would hop on her Kawasaki 650, with a boa constrictor and slide show in tow, and visit classrooms in rural areas. Today, the Tropical Education Center regularly hosts student groups who study native animals and the human threats to their survival. Belizean schoolchildren visit the zoo nearly every day, and though the youth of Belize may not know about Mickey Mouse, they are well acquainted with April, the tapir, which is Belize's national animal.

While Matola is known around Belize as an animal rights radical, she has also been elevated to folk hero, a Belizean version of Dian Fossey (portrayed in *Gorillas in the Mist*). The former Florida lion tamer, Mexican circus showgirl and Central American fungi specialist has received publicity from *Sports Illustrated*, *National Geographic* and numerous other magazines.

Today, Matola lives about a mile from the zoo in a thatched bungalow where, in the predawn hours of the jungle, she writes children's books. One of her titles, *I Live in an American Forest*, features an accompanying soundtrack of animal voices. During her early mornings, the former showgirl also pumps iron in a screened, thatched-roof gymnasium she built single-handedly. Working out keeps her in shape for the expeditions she leads across Belizean mountains and through the jungles. In the summer of 1992, she led the first all-woman expedition to the top of Victoria Peak, Belize's highest at 3675 feet. A few months earlier, she was the only woman on a grueling ten-day hike across the Maya Mountains divide. The expedition included British military troops who acquired jungle training and researchers who learned about Maya history at numerous ruins along the way.

Some of Matola's hiking terrain lies just two miles west at the 1070-acre **Monkey Bay Wildlife Sanctuary**. Here, in a privately owned reserve that welcomes visitors, slash pine, scrub palmetto and supine savanna stretch for miles against a hazy backdrop of jagged foothills. There are no monkeys (the park is named for its founders, Monkey Bay Wildlife Sanctuary Tokyo), but there are many species of birds to be found, as well as peccaries. An arboretum with labeled plants and trees introduces visitors to the vegetation. A picturesque beach on the Sibun (pronounced Si-BOON) River is ideal for daytrippers who don't mind hiking 40 minutes from the sanctuary entrance. There are more than two miles of solitary trails waiting for hikers; ask for directions at the wood stilt house near the entrance. The house is a loosely run place that is the sanctuary headquarters and home to various wayfarers getting to know Belize. It has an extensive library on native flora, and is also home to American Matt Miller, who runs Monkey Bay, organizing visits from numerous United States student groups each year. ~ Mile Post 31, Western Highway; 82-03032, fax 82-23361; www.monkeybaybelize.org, e-mail mbay@btl.net.

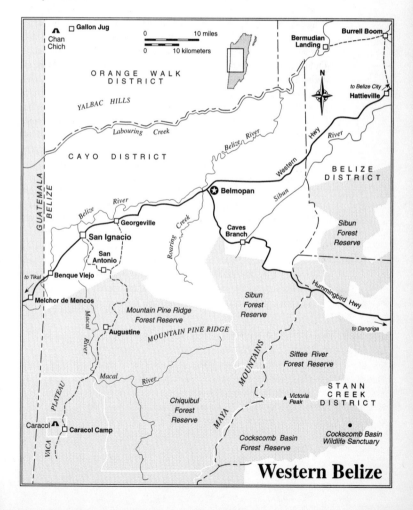

Western Belize

Within the next mile, looking like nothing much, is one of Belize's most famous stopovers, **J.B.'s**. J.B.'s was the stomping grounds of many a British soldier, Belizean politician and imported movie star (Harrison Ford hung out here during the filming of *Mosquito Coast*), having begun its illustrious career in the late 1970s at the hands of an American expatriate who everyone knew simply as J.B. Reputed around town as either a flamboyant, highly entertaining character or a hard-drinking rogue, depending on who you talk to, J.B. brought the bar to great fame with his sardonic stories, late-night rock and roll parties and endless supply of rum and ice cubes (the latter being a luxury around these parts). Alas, in 1991, J.B. picked up and left one day, but only after selling out to two teenage girls from Canada whose RV had broken down in his parking lot. The girls ran J.B.'s for four years, learned plenty about the bar and restaurant business, became young women and opened another bar up the road. J.B.'s changed hands several times before collapsing due to termites; in the mid-'90s the new South African owners demolished the building and built a larger one on the site. Now officially known as the Mountain View Restaurant, it continues to display the J.B.'s sign in front, and that's what locals still call it. ~ Mile 32, Western Highway; 82-02071; www.jb-belize.com.

About 20 miles down the highway comes the first hint of civilization, though unfortunately **Belmopan** is not the most pleasant example, being an organized but aseptic assembly of cinderblock buildings. It takes about five minutes to see the entire city, built in a contemporary Maya style and corralled by chainlink. There is no real reason to linger here as Belmopan has lately been plagued by petty thieves and other undesirables.

LODGING   If you'd literally like to sleep under the stars, bunk down at **Monkey Bay Wildlife Sanctuary**. A dozen or so thatched camping platforms are scattered among the scrub savanna, including some

AUTHOR FAVORITE

The **Belize Zoo & Tropical Education Center** discounted everything I knew about zoos. Instead of animals cooped up in cages amid miles of concrete, here was a forest with mesh enclosures so large that a beast could actually hide from visitors if it was so inclined. In fact it seems inaccurate to call it a zoo, since the more than 100 wildlife species do not occupy cages, and can retreat into *their* world if they so desire. Public education is a central tenet at the Belize Zoo, where dedicated staff include local villagers and former poachers. See page 156 for detailed information on this must-see destination.

with little thatched roofs (but no walls, so pray it doesn't rain) for those who didn't bring a tent. Bunk rooms (very basic), cold showers and meals are available at a main house run by sanctuary director Matt Miller, an American raising his family in Belize. Rates, as you might expect, are rock-bottom. ~ Mile Post 31, Western Highway; 82-03032, fax 82-23361; www.monkeybay belize.org, e-mail mbay@btl.com. BUDGET.

Few places come so strange and unexpected as **Jaguar Paw Jungle Resort**. For there, rising out of dense rainforest, is an imitation Maya temple, something very Disney in design, a towering block of concrete with faux Maya hieroglyphs attached to the outside walls. Inside is a voluminous space, a lobby and eatery and mirrored bar flooded with air conditioning and the blinking of a TV screen compliments of a satellite dish. Americans Cy and Donna Young designed the temple and its attendant 16 rooms in zinc-roofed cabañas. When they opened in 1996, they installed air conditioning in all the buildings and a swimming pool out back, and posted some of Belize's highest lodging rates. Every guest room is themed, quite contrived, from the Asian room with a black lacquer chest and a silk kimono on the wall to the American room with cranberry and hunter green walls and a mahogany four-poster bed. There's terrific river caving nearby, and you can cruise in a small boat or an inner tube through a honeycomb of caves. Or, join an all-day hike into numerous underground caverns. A full breakfast is included in the rate; lunch and dinner are served à la carte in the lodge restaurant. ~ Mile Post 37, Western Highway, then seven miles west; 82-02023, fax 82-02024, or 888-775-8645 in the U.S.; www. jaguarpaw.com, e-mail cyoung@jaguarpaw.com. ULTRA-DELUXE.

◀ HIDDEN

Despite its countrified name, the **Bull Frog Inn** is in the capital of Belmopan. The grounds are lush and filled with singing birds, but the rooms, though clean, carpeted and cooled by air conditioners, are rather featureless. On the positive side, the restaurant here is one of the best in town. ~ 25 Half Moon Avenue, Belmopan; 82-22111, fax 82-23155. MODERATE.

Considered the business traveler's choice, the **Belmopan Hotel** is a gracious hacienda-style hostelry with a swimming pool. But don't expect Holiday Inn–style rooms; these are funky, featuring bright orange carpet, orange-striped bedspreads and hand-me-down furniture (with fans, air conditioning and cable TV). Oh well, this *is* Belize! ~ Corner of Bliss Parade and Constitution Drive, Belmopan; 82-22130, fax 82-22682. MODERATE.

If you're looking for a Belizean ranch experience, I highly recommend **Warrie Head Ranch and Lodge**. Named for the spine-covered warrie, a type of wild boar that lives in surrounding forests, the ranch is draped across 639 pastoral acres, with grassy knolls, clear creeks and tropical fruit trees. Warrie Head Ranch offers ten cozy rooms decorated with Belizean tile floors, knotty pine walls, ceiling fans and jalousie windows. A library exudes real warmth with its wildlife photos, board games and books on Belize. While you are here, you will be very lucky to meet Lydia, the lodge's virtuoso host and cook, who rustles up giant meals of steak, chicken and fresh vegetables (for vegetarians). ~ Western Highway, six miles west of Belmopan; 22-77185, fax 22-72513 in Belize City. MODERATE TO DELUXE.

The road to **Banana Bank Lodge** dead-ends above the steep bank of the Belize River near Guanacaste National Park. After you cross the river by hand-drawn ferry and climb the far bank, the lodge grounds, with acres of green lawn and lush rainforest vegetation, come as a surprise. Guest accommodations include spacious wood cabañas and lodge rooms colorfully decorated in shades of pink, some with special touches such as four-poster queen-sized beds, solarium tubs, Maya pottery or stained glass. The lodge has one of the best equestrian centers in the country, with over 50 horses. "Horse whisperer" John Carr, who originally came here from Montana in 1973 to ranch cattle and now runs the lodge with his wife Carolyn, guides tours into the surrounding rainforest. Meals are served family-style in a central dining area, where Carr brings in a horse to demonstrate riding skills during breakfast. Though close to Belmopan and the planned new U.S. Embassy, Banana Bank feels so secluded that my imagination easily slips back into the 1800s, when a historic (and notoriously rowdy) logging camp occupied the site. ~ Box 48, Belmopan, Belize; 82-02020, fax 82-02026; www.banana bank.com, e-mail bbl@starbank.com. ULTRA-DELUXE.

DINING

Near the Belize Zoo and Monkey Bay Wildlife Sanctuary, **J.B.'s Watering Hole and Mountain View Restaurant** serves simple, tasty food that's easy on the wallet. Fare ranges from Belize basics such as stew chicken with rice and beans to T-bone steaks

AUTHOR FAVORITE

The trip across the river in a boat powered by hand and the setting surrounded by rainforest make **Banana Bank Lodge** feel like one of the most remote jungle lodges in Belize. The location, just a few miles from Belmopan and the junction of the Western Highway and the Hummingbird Highway, puts it within easy daytrip distance of most of the country's key sightseeing highlights. Yet it's the exceptionally friendly, knowledgeable owners that make Banana Bank one of my all-time favorite accommodations in Belize. See above for detailed information.

and English fish-and-chips. ~ Mile Post 32, Western Highway; 82-02071; www.jbbelize.com. BUDGET.

Checkered tablecloths, arched porticoes and fresh flowers lend real charm to the **Bull Frog Inn**. The most popular eatery in Belmopan, with politicians and visiting VIPs often gracing its tables, it has an open-air terrace that faces a tropical garden. Steaks, chicken, fish and hamburgers are standard here, and there's an attached cocktail bar. ~ 25 Half Moon Avenue, Belmopan; 82-22111. MODERATE.

Across from the Belmopan bus station, the air-conditioned **Caladium Restaurant** features a chalkboard menu of home-cooked fare. Fried fish or chicken, pork chops and T-bone steaks are local favorites. Daily specials might include curried mutton, Spanish meatloaf, fish or boil-ups and leg of lamb. ~ Market Square, Belmopan; 80-22754. BUDGET.

SHOPPING

The **Market Square** in downtown Belmopan is made up of stalls where vendors sell everything from copycat designer jewelry and radios to watermelons and chickens. Even if you don't buy, it's fun to watch. Open most days.

The **Carolyn Carr Galeria** exhibits Carr's strikingly realistic paintings of Belizean people and wildlife, along with works by other local artists including nationally renowned painter Pen Cayetano. ~ Near the turnoff to Belmopan from the Hummingbird Highway; for information, call Banana Bank Lodge at 82-02020.

BEACHES & PARKS

GUANACASTE NATIONAL PARK 🏊 Just outside Belmopan, Guanacaste offers a splendid walk in the forest. Packed into these 50 acres of cool, damp woods are colossal trees that make you feel like you're wandering past nature's own highrises. A guide from the visitors center will join you (don't explore unaccompanied, as muggings have been a problem) and describe the abundance of life that exists along the leafy trails. Among the more interesting: armadillo houses, termite nests and logs lined with bulldog bats, who feed on fish as well as lizards and small mammals. Birders will be happy to know that blue-crowned motmots, collared aracaris, green-breasted mangos and other extraordinary, elusive birds are permanent residents here. There's also the imposing 300-foot-tall guanacaste tree, which the park is named for, laden with over 35 species of air plants, many as big as normal trees. If you're lucky, the guide will pluck a pod from a cohune palm and break it open so you can taste the coconutty flavor. Bring your swimsuit for a dip in the clear, fast-flowing Belize River, which cuts right through the park. Admission. ~ At the intersection of the Western Highway and the Hummingbird Highway.

▼ ▼ ▼ ▼ ▼ ▼ ▼ ▼ ▼ ▼
Cayo Country

Cayo is as west as you can get in Belize, and at moments feels like the Wild West. Cattle and horse ranches, traced in tree trunk fence, climb the hilly sides of the Western Highway and stretch all the way to the rainforest and pine woods. Mennonite farmers ride in horse-drawn wagons to bring just-picked vegetables to the market in San Ignacio, ground zero for Cayo comings-and-goings. The town is draped along the banks of the Macal River, ringed with hills, and a bit noisy and rough around the edges—as any real western town ought to be. Restaurants, shops and businesses line the skinny streets, as do homes for the nearly 9000 people who keep the town bubbling along. West of San Ignacio to the Guatemala border, the Western Highway rises and falls through pine-clad mountain ridges and rocky pasturelands speckled with modest villages.

This region that was once rich with logging and chicle farming is now also a hub for ecotourists. Jungle lodges use solar power, nurture organic gardens and employ native Maya guides to lead travelers on rainforest treks. You can hike, bike, canoe and kayak through Cayo, and you can ride a horse along deeply shaded trails. You can birdwatch and climb through caves, and stroll trails thick with rainforest medicine plants. Or, you could simply spend the day in a hammock beneath a great guanacaste tree, watching butterflies and hummingbirds drift by.

SIGHTS

On the Western Highway, just west of Belmopan, take the turnoff for **Spanish Lookout** and you will soon feel as if you've left Belize. There, stretching to the edge of the horizon, is a scene right out of Pennsylvania's Dutch Country: folded green hills, windtickled fields of corn and straw-hatted Mennonite farmers in horsedrawn buggies. Blond, freckle-faced Mennonite children race down the dirt roads and through the corn fields, and windmills churn against a bright blue country sky.

The pulse of Cayo, as it's called around Belize, is **San Ignacio**, located 22 miles west of Belmopan. San Ignacio has long attracted a vast spectrum of humanity, from Maya and *Mestizos* to Guatemalan refugees, Lebanese entrepreneurs, Mennonite farmers, and adventure-seeking Americans and Europeans. Watching the various walks of life and listening to jungle tales told around town, one gets the distinct feeling that something exciting is about to happen.

After a stroll in San Ignacio, you may want to have a look at the minor ruins of **Cahal Pech**. Its name means "Place of the Ticks" and the first impression it conveys is not impressive, but if you wander the forested grounds you'll find the Preclassic city quite extensive. A guide will be happy to show you around the seven courtyards and 34 structures, including several temples, two ball courts and a sweathouse, sprinkled across two acres.

The largest ceremonial structure is 77 feet high, with sharply tiered steps running up its face. Sadly, several buildings have been layered with concrete to slow down erosion. Admission. ~ Buena Vista Road; take the trail leading away from Cahal Pech Disco.

San Ignacio is the headquarters for booking tours to surrounding Maya ruins and various sights, and for arranging horseback riding and hiking in the hills. It is also the place to arrange a canoe trip or taxi ride to **Ix Chel Tropical Research Centre** and the Rainforest Medicine Trail. On the crest of a hill, amid five cleared acres of high bush country, the farm is owned by Americans Rosita Arvigo and Gregory Shropshire. The couple call it Ix Chel, after the Maya goddess of healing and of rainbows. On many summer afternoons, after the rain-gorged clouds have unleashed their showers on the forest, rainbows arch across the hilltop farm. Admission. ~ Located eight miles north of San Ignacio next to Chaa Creek Adventure Centre.

For several years, Arvigo and Shropshire have been collecting and researching the jungle vegetation that lies at their back door. So far, the husband-and-wife team have collected more than 750 plant species, which are being catalogued by the New York Botanical Garden. The garden, along with the National Institute of Health, Metropolitan Life Insurance and other organizations, have provided grants for research at the farm. Already, the world's forests have produced treatments for dysentery (the bark and root from the negrito tree) and for arthritis (cocol mecca tree root). The cocol mecca also provides cortison, from which cortisone is synthesized. It is hoped that the forest also holds cures for cancers

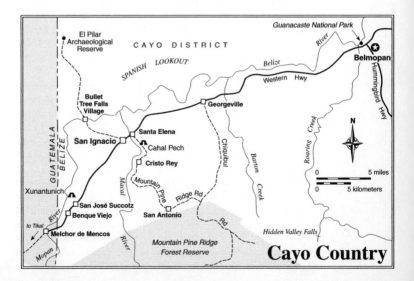

Cayo Country

and for AIDS. The couple's latest research is aimed at cultivating medicinal plants that can become cash crops for local farmers.

The **Rainforest Medicine Trail**, formerly called the Panti Maya Trail, which begins near the couple's house, helps visitors learn about their research here. You can take a self-guided tour from 7 a.m. to 5 p.m. Guided tours are available for groups by appointment only. With his descriptions of jungle healing secrets, a bush guide makes the trail come to life. Sunlight and dewy rain filter through the jungle ceiling as he reveals such cures as cowfoot, cocol mecca, negrita, grapevine and bullhoof vine—foliage that, to the untrained eye, seems no different from any other forest specimen. Bullhoof, he says, will stanch internal bleeding, and grapevine conceals a fountain of fresh water. For more than an hour he goes on like this, explaining mysteries and relating healing stories that make life here seem even more mysterious. ~ 82-43870. Arvigo and Shropshire were also the founders of the **Terra-Nova Medicinal Plant Reserve** (the world's first), a 6000-acre expanse in a remote area of the Cayo District, where healing plants are transplanted from jungle areas that are slated to be cleared for development. Later operated by other organizations, the reserve has had a spotty history and now serves as an environmental education camp for Belizean children.

If you have children, definitely stop at **The Trek Stop**. The kids will love the Butterfly House where they can walk through clouds of butterflies—red-splashed postmen and false-eyed owls, apricot sulphurs and gold-beaded monarchs. And the adjacent Nature Center has lots of great jungle animal displays, including an "unpetting" zoo with black velvet tarantulas, rhinoceros beetles, bark scorpions and a leaf-cutting ant colony swarming behind glass. Admission. ~ Western Highway, six miles west of San Ignacio; 82-32265; e-mail susa@btl.net.

HIDDEN ►   One of Belize's lesser-known Maya sites, **El Pilar Archaeological Reserve** lies twelve miles northwest of San Ignacio, much of it down washed-out, rocky roads with dim, humid jungle scenes. The ancient city is high in the hills, cocooned within dense bush and tree canopy, which anthropologists have only minimally cleared to reveal pieces of dozens of Preclassic to Classic pyramids and homes (the idea being to keep the site as lush and natural as possible). Sunlight barely trickles in as you ease into limestone chambers with etched openings along the wall—Maya cubbyholes for torches—and into plaster-roofed bedrooms with arching entries and original calabash wood beams. Pilar means "things that contain water" and there is much water here, in the limestone grottos and natural springs, in the waterfalls and the river that flows toward the Caribbean Sea. The

Half of El Pilar is in fact in Guatemala, though excavations have not yet begun.

water draws wildlife and so you should keep a lookout for deer, tapir, ocellated turkey and scarlet macaws as you wind along the Edenic natural trails. The trails go for miles and can easily eat up a whole day, so pack a picnic and enjoy it on the clove wood benches near H'Mena Pyramid. With an elevation of 1000 feet and a sweeping view across Guatemala, it's a fabulous spot. Before you start exploring, stop at the park entrance and pick up a trail map. If the park caretaker isn't busy he'll provide a tour of El Pilar, complete with florid discussion on medicinal plants and trees. Admission. ~ Off Bullet Tree Road, 12 miles northwest of San Ignacio and seven miles north of Bullet Tree Falls Village; 82-23612, fax 82-23002; e-mail elpilar@btl.net.

West of San Ignacio on the Western Highway, you'll find the village of San José Succotz, where you can board the hand-cranked car ferry across the gurgling Mopan River (notice the women washing their clothes). From here, a dirt road leads to **Xunantunich** (admission). One of the few Maya cities built atop a hill, Xunantunich (Shoo-NA-tu-NISH) is a stirring place looming along a limestone ridge in the Belize River Valley. Its name means "Stone Woman," a modern-day moniker alluding not only to this rocky plateau but to the erotic female images that could be conjured from the sleek, shapely temples. Additional structures are being resurrected under the guidance of Dr. Richard Leventhal of the Anthropology Department at Harvard.

Xunantunich flourished more than 1100 years ago, during the Classic Period. More than a century ago, amateur archaeologist Dr. Thomas Gann first explored the site, but did no excavations until he returned in 1924. At that time, he uncovered caches of burial items as well as hieroglyphs that were circling a main altar. He took them with him, and their whereabouts are a mystery today.

Over the years, excavations at Xunantunich have been piecemeal. In 1938, British archaeologist Eric S. Thompson unearthed a residential group, while in 1949, then–Archaeology Commissioner A. H. Anderson discovered the remnants of a stucco frieze. In 1952, an amateur British archaeologist named Michael Stewart discovered burials and offerings. Seven years later, a Cambridge University researcher named Euan Mackie uncovered evidence in one of the temples that Xunantunich had been wrenched by an earthquake in about A.D. 900. It was at least one possible explanation for why the city was abandoned at this same time.

During the 1970s, various teams worked to excavate and preserve Xunantunich's greatest structures. Today the site is small but immensely scenic, a one-mile oasis of emerald grasses speckled with cohune palms and limestone outcroppings. The city's buildings encase three plazas fashioned in north–south design and its outskirts are sprinkled with house mounds. The structures go from grand to comfortable to tiny, no doubt accommodating a spectrum of Maya classes.

Attention is naturally focused on where the elite spent their time. That would be **Group A**, where several temples gather around two grassy plazas. Dominating **Plazas A1** and **A2**—and all of Xunantunich—is 130-foot **El Castillo**, a terraced palace with a toothy contour and a skirt of velvety green grass. In Belize, it is second only in height to another great Maya palace, Caana, in the nearby city-state of Caracol. Climb the face of El Castillo and—when you've recovered from the overwhelming view of the countryside—notice the platform topped with two temples. The temples are famous for their elaborate bone-colored friezes, including an astronomical frieze and a frieze portraying a headless man. The palace's exposed blue-and-white limestone, glinting in the sunlight, takes on haunting shapes.

Like many Maya temples, Castillo is actually a series of buildings superimposed upon each other over the centuries. You can see evidence of earlier levels and layers everywhere; notice the wide terrace, about 35 feet up the north side, that at one point had buildings lining its edges. And if you look closely at the two upper temples, one resting upon the other, you'll see that the Maya originally covered the lower temple to make a foundation for the higher one. Only now, after archaeologists have cleared away debris and centuries of vegetation, is their construction so obvious.

Smaller temples congregate around Plaza A, one of the most interesting being **Structure A15**, which has a stone bench. Just off Plaza A is a small **ball court**, which now resembles a grassy alley. Nearby, the structures around **Group B** are thought to be upper- and middle-class homes, hinting that Xunantunich was once occupied by a cultured, elite society.

The ruins are an excellent place to have lunch, but bring your own. The closest refreshments are in San José Succotz, back across the Mopan River.

West from Xunantunich on the Western Highway, the last place before Guatemala is **Benque Viejo**. The small border town is a peaceful place with two-story clapboard homes painted in crayon colors, wash strung across the porches and chicken-wire fences (and chickens) running all over the place. There are no real sites here other than the friendly residents, *Mestizos* and Mopan Maya, who tip their hats to you as you stroll down the dusty streets.

After Benque Viejo, you can turn back into the familiar terrain of Belize or make the adventurer's choice and cross into Guatemala. What awaits beyond the border are some of Mesoamerica's most spectacular rainforests and truly its most sensational Maya city. The 2500-year-old kingdom of Tikal still rules the vast jungles of northern Guatemala, known as the Petén, drawing more than 100,000 visitors each year. Tikal is only about 40 miles from the Belize/Guatemala border, but it's one long hellacious ride down a body-battering dirt road, with possibilities (albeit slim) of bandits hiding in the roadside bush. The border crossing, however, is not so much a test of courage as of patience.

On the Belize side, you will surrender your tourist card, have your passport stamped and pass through with relative ease. On the Guatemala side, at Melchor de Mencos, you must show your passport and visa and, depending on the time of day and mood of the border officials, pay a small fee, or *propina*. Several officials may also have to "review" your documents before allowing you to pass.

Despite ongoing political conflicts within Guatemala and its tenuous relationship with Belize, it's unlikely you'll encounter problems at the border or while traveling in Guatemala, especially in the Petén, where the government is focusing its tourism efforts. For more on visiting Guatemala, see Chapter Nine.

LODGING

There's not a whole lot going on between Belmopan and San Ignacio, unless you detour off the Western Highway to **Pook's Hill**. Here, around a small Maya plaza of soft green lawns, is a sprinkling of stucco cabins crowned with palm thatching and simply decorated with Belizean hardwood and woven Guate-

◄ HIDDEN

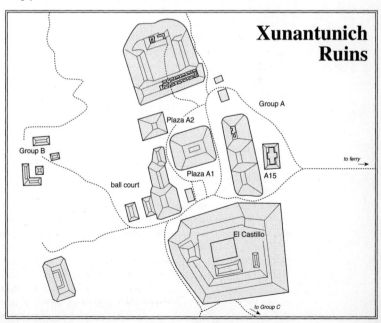

Xunantunich Ruins

Group A

Plaza A2

Group B

Plaza A1

ball court

A15

to ferry

El Castillo

to Group C

malan fabrics. The lodge sits within a 300-acre reserve in the foothills of the Maya Mountains and offers superior opportunities for hiking and birding, river tubing, mountain biking and horseback riding. Meals are extra. ~ From Mile Post 52 of the Western Highway, go five miles south on dirt roads; 82-02017, fax 82-23361; www.pookshillbelize.com, e-mail pookshill@btl. net. ULTRA-DELUXE.

Caesar's Guest House, a roadside scattering of buildings and bougainvillea, is a friendly place to stop for a cold Belikin, hot home cooking or a room for the night. Four large rooms feature cedar paneling, Mexican tile floors, ceiling fans and private baths with hot water. If you happen to be traveling by RV (unlikely, but possible!), Caesar's is one of the few places in Belize with full hookups. Out back, you can take a dip in Barton Creek. ~ Mile Post 64, Western Highway; 82-42341, fax 82-43449; e-mail blackrock@btl.net. MODERATE.

In Cayo, the **San Ignacio Resort Hotel** is as close as you get to a real hotel. Its hillside venue offers lovely vistas across Cayo and the Macal River, and there's a pretty swimming pool decorated with tropical planters and wrought-iron furniture where one could easily lose an afternoon sampling Belizean rum (the margaritas are also memorable). Rooms are spacious and contemporary, adorned with Honduran mahogany furniture and offering private balconies; rooms have either ceiling fans or air conditioning. ~ 18 Buena Vista Road, San Ignacio; 82-42034, fax 82-42134; www.sanignaciobelize.com, e-mail sanighot@btl.net. DELUXE.

Just uphill from the San Ignacio Hotel (though, strangely, sharing the same address), the **Piache Hotel** is the thrifty traveler's choice. The grounds, sprinkled with plants potted in an assortment of tin cans, tubs and tires, reflect the style of a friendly eccentric. That would be Godsman Ellis, a gregarious Garifuna who can tell you much about San Ignacio and about Belize, preferably at his thatched cabaña bar. Just off the bar, in a cinderblock building, are ten extremely basic but clean rooms, with rummage-sale furnishings, ceiling fans and curtained bathroom doors. Some rooms here have air conditioners that more or less work. ~ 18 Buena Vista Road, San Ignacio; 82-42032, fax 82-42685; e-mail piache. hot@btl.net. BUDGET.

At **Mida's Resort**, you can pitch a tent or string a hammock between the trees and sleep under the stars. Most people, however, prefer to stay in one of the duplex cabaña units, even if they are somewhat primitive with their cement walls, fans and open windows. The setting is homey and pure country, seven riverside acres of former pastureland owned by Englishman Mike Preston and his wife, Maria Preston, who was born in San Ignacio. Among their many ecotourism projects, the couple and their two sons are working to restore the land. ~ Branch Mouth Road, a quarter-mile north of San Ignacio; 82-43172, fax 82-43845; www.midasbelize.com, e-mail eva@btl.net. BUDGET.

Popular with backpackers, hikers and naturalists, **Maya Mountain Lodge** is an ecotourism retreat set along a verdant green hillside with tropical gardens and chirping cicadas. There are eight comfortable cottages, as well as six very basic rooms with vinyl floors, plywood walls and private curtained bathrooms (two have private baths down the hall; all units have fans). The real highlight is the lovely indoor-outdoor dining room, with a mango tree growing right through the middle. An extensive schedule of daytrips and cultural programs is offered here, including the ever-popular "Belize Night" held every Friday during the winter and featuring a presentation on local topics. ~ On Cristo Rey Road, three-quarters of a mile from the Western Highway, near San Ignacio; 82-42164, fax 82-42029; www.mayamountain.com, e-mail adventure@mayamountain.com. MODERATE.

Rubble from Maya ruins sprinkle the grounds at the remote **Clarissa Falls Resort**. Like glorified camping, the 11 basic cottages have concrete floors and bamboo walls. Three have a shared bath, but all have hot water. There's also a dorm-style room with hammocks and folding beds where you can sleep for cheap, or you can pitch a tent along the water. The lodge resides in a most coveted spot along a bubbling creek, where iguanas and bromeliads decorate the trees. Canoe and tube rentals are available; guests can take a tour to the ruins Xunantunich and then float back downriver to the lodge on giant inner tubes. A thatched-roof restaurant serves tasty Belizean food. ~ Off the Western Highway, about three miles from San Ignacio; phone/fax 82-43916; e-mail clarifalls@btl.net. BUDGET.

The granddaddy of Cayo jungle lodges, the **Parrot Nest** was accommodating adventurous travelers when Belize was still a British colonial outpost. Located three miles from San Ignacio, with a free daily shuttle that takes guests into San Ignacio at 8:30 in the morning and returns at 4:30, the lodge has two treehouses

◆◆

HORSE AND WAGON COUNTRY

The Mennonites, who trace their roots to 16th-century Switzerland and Germany, began immigrating to Belize in the 1800s. Since then, they have slowly turned the unforgiving limestone ground into fruitful soil, and are now considered Belize's most prolific farmers. The remote Spanish Lookout is one of their largest greenbelts, and is where you'll see farmers with their horses and wagons headed to market. If you drive there, take a truck. The road is very rutted and covered with rocks, and delivers a real beating to your vehicle.

overhead, each with a double bed. At ground level, cabañas nestle along the bank of the Mopan River amid lush, tropical gardens purring with wildlife. Shared baths come with hot and cold water, and breakfast and dinner are served in the central dining area. ~ P.O. Box 108, San Ignacio, Cayo; 82-04058; www.parrot-nest.com, e-mail parrot@btl.net. MODERATE.

Set on a grassy hilltop overlooking the Mopan River, the **Red Jaguar Inn** offers two large luxury apartments and first-class hospitality. Fine wine and cheese greet new arrivals, local rum and Cuban cigars await each guest apartment's minibar, and breakfast features locally grown coffee and pineapple. A profusion of white herons and other large wading birds frequent the river bank below, an ideal spot for swimming and canoeing. ~ San Ignacio; 82-32757; www.theredjaguar.com, e-mail museplan@btl.net. ULTRA-DELUXE.

Run by the bilingual (English/Spanish), native Belizean Martinez family, **Crystal Paradise Resort** has 20 guest units, including thatch-roofed cabañas with hammocks on porches and garden or river views, as well as lower-priced standard rooms, which have no porches but are near hammocks hung under palapas scattered around the lushly landscaped grounds. All rooms have private baths with hot showers, and all have ceiling fans but no air conditioning. A broad deck adjacent to the dining room is an ideal bird viewing spot, and binoculars and spotting scopes are available for guests' use. ~ Cristo Rey Village; phone/fax 82-42772; www.crystalparadise.com, e-mail cparadise@btl.net. MODERATE TO DELUXE.

If I could stay in just one place in Belize, it would be **Chaa Creek Adventure Centre, Rainforest Reserve and Spa**. Situated in an idyllic hillside setting above the Macal River, this elegant jungle lodge is unsurpassed for service and stylish surroundings. Chaa Creek gives the feeling of being pampered—in the jungle. Its adobe cabañas are warm and inviting, with chestnut-colored Mexican tile floors, mahogany beds, Guatemalan blankets and thatched roofs soaring above the trees. By far the most coveted room is "The Screamer," a voluminous 12-sided cabaña propped high atop a water tower and affording views of the mountains and jungle. None of the cabañas at Chaa Creek has window screens, but not to worry: there are few mosquitoes, only dazzling butterflies that float in one window and out the other. A Butterfly House, built for the scientist who started Chaa Creek's butterfly-breeding center, now accommodates guests with solar electricity and a kitchen. And then there's the **Macal Safari River Camp**, an elegant tent camp that's easily Belize's best budget accommodation. A 20-minute walk through cohune forest from the main

> One of the most popular accommodations at Chaa Creek is "The Screamer," a cabaña named after the sounds made by honeymooners and other couples who love it up here.

lodge, it's a scattering of wooden platforms on stilts set with green tents and yellow, peak-roofed tarpaulins. The tents are suspended on the riverbanks, encased in trees, and outfitted with twin cots, screens and kerosene lamps on front porches. A main bath house with three hot-water showers is immaculate. At night there are campfires and Maya meals—stew chicken and pork, mashed potatoes, rice and beans—served on pine picnic tables inside an airy screened enclosure. The meals are prepared by Frencelia and Docia Juarez, a resident Maya family who cook in a traditional limestone and wattle-and-daub kitchen and play host to visitors (their kids are especially happy to see other kids— just one reason the camp is so popular with families). Away from the lodge and camp, you can visit Chaa Creek's Natural History Centre, with exhibits on local culture and ecosystems and archaeology, then learn about the elusive, fabulously colored blue morpho butterfly, also called Belizean Blues, at the lodge's Blue Morpho Butterfly Breeding Centre. Other possible pursuits include: swimming and canoeing the Macal River, hiking the jungle and exploring caves, waterfalls and Maya ruins near and far. Around dinnertime, you'll be welcomed by the owners, a gregarious couple named Mick and Lucy Fleming (he's English, she's American), who are well-known around Belize. The indoor/outdoor dining room is a romantic affair offering tasty, locally grown cuisine. Before dinner, everyone gathers on the birdwatching deck, near the elegant wood bar, to trade "You wouldn't believe it . . ." stories of the day. ~ On the Macal River, about eight miles outside San Ignacio; 82-42037, fax 82-43912; www.chaacreek.com, e-mail reservations@chaacreek.com. BUDGET TO ULTRA-DELUXE.

Downriver from Chaa Creek is **duPlooy's**. Though not as fancy as its neighbor, duPlooy's offers the same feeling of rural peacefulness. Accommodations have ceiling fans and range from rooms with stone floors, private baths and screened porches to basic rooms with a shared bath in a pink guest lodge. Three pretty bungalows, opened in 1995, come with coffeemakers and mini-refrigerators. Co-owner Ken duPlooy, originally from Zimbabwe, is an avid birder who will point out the many species camouflaged in the foliage. Three-night minimum stay. ~ About ten miles outside San Ignacio; 82-43101, fax 82-43301; www.du plooys.com, e-mail duplooys@btl.net. BUDGET TO ULTRA-DELUXE.

There's no road to **Ek' Tun**. Guests reach this secluded rain-   ◀ HIDDEN
forest retreat by a half-hour four-wheel-drive trip to the launch point for a boat trip up the Macal River. Guests stay in Mayan-style cottages scattered over Ek' Tun's 200-acre grounds, where lavish tropical landscaping blends seamlessly into the primeval forest just a few yards from the doorstep. Though the thatch-roofed huts appear modest from the outside, inside they are bright and contemporary, with handmade mahogany and wicker

furnishings. Each has a private bath and is spacious enough to sleep up to five people. Miles of trails wind through the surrounding woods, teeming with howler monkeys and exotic birds. Guests can swim in the large, bright blue mineral pool or bask on sandy beaches along the river. Oil lamps provide light during the evening, as the cottages have no electricity. ~ Located 12 miles south of San Ignacio; 82-03002; www.ektunbelize.com, e-mail info@ektunbelize.com. ULTRA-DELUXE.

Easy access makes **Windy Hill Cottages** a good choice for accommodations. It's one of the few country lodges that doesn't require a marathon trek down a rocky road, and it's the only one with a swimming pool, a little above-ground pool set along the hillside. Flowering trees and soft grass fill the grounds, which are sprinkled with red-roofed cottages paneled in wormy cypress— rustic, but quite roomy. Every room has a splendid hillside view. Six rooms are especially good for wheelchair visitors. There's an informal dining room, a bar, and even a thatched-roof game room with a pool table. Perhaps best of all, the Windy Hill staff could not be more congenial. ~ Western Highway, about one mile west of San Ignacio; 82-42017, fax 82-43080; www.windy hillresort.com, e-mail windyhill@btl.net. DELUXE.

Across from Windy Hill and equally as convenient to Cayo sites are the nine log cabins of **Log Cab-inns**. Fashioned of peeled mahogany poles, they sit on a hill amid a grove of orange and custard apple trees next to a swimming pool. The floors are concrete but impeccably clean, the private baths are outfitted with hot showers and the TVs tune into a couple of fuzzy stations (but then, who needs TV when you have the ruins and the rainforest?). ~ Western Highway, about one mile west of San Ignacio; 82-43367, fax 82-42289; www.logcabinns-belize.com, e-mail logcabins@ btl.net. BUDGET TO MODERATE.

Backpackers or anyone on a spare budget should consider **The Trek Stop**. You can rent a rustic cabin with a cot and outdoor, solar-heated shower, or rent a tent and pitch it beneath the mango and sandpaper trees. The 22-acre hillside spread is lush, filled with flamboyant flowers and ancient trees and also beautiful butterflies, thanks to a butterfly hatchery here. There's a medicine plant garden, a nature center and a tiny, tin-roofed restaurant with three tables, although guests are welcome to cook their own meals in the concrete-floored kitchen. There are mountain bike and kayak rentals. ~ Western Highway, six miles west of San Ignacio; 82-32265; www.thetrekstop.com, e-mail susa@btl.net. BUDGET.

HIDDEN ▶ A road offers access to the **Black Rock River Lodge**, but the going may be rough and in rainy season access may require a 20-minute hike or horseback ride through damp, deep woods atwitter with birdsong. At the trek's end is a sheer limestone cliff with a swirling river and black boulders at its feet, and nine fancy slate-

and-thatch cabins (some with private baths) perched near its edge. Banana plants engulf the cabins and 250 acres of private forest surround it. Water from the river is pumped up for drinking, bathing and cooking, and rays from the sun are used to make all the lodge's electricity. Tasty meals (extra charge) are prepared on an open hearth by a friendly staff. Among the many activities here: horseback riding, hiking, exploring nearby Flour Camp caves and birding, as well as swimming, canoeing and tubing on the Macal River. They recently completed a new mountain bike trail along the canyon rim overlooking the water, and they rent top-of-the-line mountain bikes. A great spot, for sure. ~ On the Macal River, upstream from San Ignacio; for reservations, call 82-42341, fax 82-43449; www.blackrocklodge.com, e-mail blackrock@btl.net. MODERATE.

DINING

A combination supermarket, gas station and restaurant, **Three Flags** offers a respite from Western Highway driving. The fare is basic but filling: burgers, sandwiches, hot dogs and rice and beans for lunch; pork chops, fish filets, seafood and chicken platters for dinner. ~ Mile Post 59, Western Highway, Unitedville; 82-43456. BUDGET.

Some people claim you haven't been to Cayo if you haven't been to Eva's. The central nerve of jungle happenings, Eva's is where you go to book tours, meet fellow Americans, buy postcards and hear various tales that get taller as the night—and the beer—wear on. The food is strictly a side attraction, but it's cheap and not half bad. Among the choices are chicken curry, stew chicken, rice and beans, tamales and hamburgers. ~ 22 Burns Avenue, San Ignacio; 80-42267. BUDGET.

Perhaps the best restaurant in the Cayo District, the **Running W Steak House** in the San Ignacio Resort Hotel prides itself on having served Queen Elizabeth II. This colorful indoor-outdoor restaurant with vases of tropical flowers on the tables overlooks the pool and luxuriant surrounding gardens. While it is one of the few restaurants in Belize specializing in steaks, the menu also offers Belizean, Mexican and Caribbean dishes such as conch ceviche, Lebanese kibi and Belizean beans and rice with stewed chicken

THE MANY FACES OF MARTHA

Martha's Kitchen & Pizza House, clean, airy and colorful, serves three meals a day at a few tables outside. Or you can order takeout (recommended: pizza, spaghetti and, if you're famished, the seared steak). Don't mind all the activity here: Martha's is also an arts-and-crafts store, a laundromat and a guesthouse. ~ 10 West Street, San Ignacio; 82-43647. BUDGET.

and plantains. The prices are surprisingly reasonable; even the priciest dishes, such as Creole lobster, is only about US$12. ~ 18 Buena Vista Road, San Ignacio; 82-42034. BUDGET TO MODERATE.

Pollito Dorado easily has the best Belizean food in town. For a few bucks you get liberal portions of stew chicken, pork or beef, beans and rice and tortillas, a tall, cool cocktail (recommended: vodka and Squirt) and little white fans humming overhead. Street noise seeps through jalousie windows and the corner TV is tuned to some talk show, like Maury Povich interviewing a man so gigantic he had to be cut from his house. ~ 8 Hudson Street, San Ignacio; 82-22019. BUDGET.

In San Ignacio, there are two possibilities for Far Eastern fare. You'll easily spot **Serandib** by its yellow clapboard storefront. Inside are wood-paneled walls and whirring ceiling fans and a menu of fried rice, chow mein, Sri Lankan curries and shrimp, as well as burgers and salads. ~ 27 Burns Avenue, San Ignacio; 82-42302. BUDGET TO MODERATE.

More run-down, but still praised around town, is **Maxim's Chinese Restaurant**. In a tiny, dark cinderblock building decorated with wildlife murals, it serves sweet and sour dishes, chop suey, curries, fresh fish and burgers. ~ 23 Far West Street, San Ignacio; 82-42283. BUDGET.

SHOPPING Prices are kind of high but the selection is good at **Caesar's Place Gift Shop**, a boutique of local artwork, jungle healing potions, T-shirts and other high-quality Belizean gifts. ~ Mile Post 60, Western Highway; 82-42341.

San Ignacio has a handful of interesting shops. **Belize Gifts** features a wide selection of local handicrafts and a friendly staff to help you choose among them. ~ Burns Avenue; 82-44159.

The gift shop at **The Trek Stop** is tiny, but it focuses solely on locally made items like clay and bronze whistles and colorful towels dyed with jungle plants. ~ Western Highway, six miles west of San Ignacio; 82-32265.

NIGHTLIFE The live-music jams at **Caesar's Place** garden bar are big local events. The schedule and talent depends on who's passing through Belize, so call ahead for the lowdown. ~ Mile Post 60, Western Highway; 82-42341.

A giant longhouse offering fantastic views across Cayo, **Cahal Pech Disco** is named for the nearby Maya ruins. Easily the most popular nightspot in Western Belize, on weekends it pulses to reggae and punta rock, compliments of top-notch local bands. Cover. ~ 18 Buena Vista Road, San Ignacio; 82-43380.

The **Princess Entertainment Center** in the San Ignacio Resort Hotel has more than 2000 slot and video poker machines, plus a handful of casino gaming tables. ~ 18 Buena Vista Road, San Ignacio; 82-42034.

Were it not for the pockets of cohune jungle and broadleaf forest, you'd think the Mountain Pine Ridge something straight from the Great Smoky Mountains. Chilly streams swirl

around polished black boulders that glint in the sunshine, then disappear into networks of caves that have no end. Hardwood trees drip with ferns and giant bromeliads and orchids, perfuming the cool breeze that trickles through the leaves. Mountains are marbled with every shade of green and creased with rivers as clear as air. Gone is the oppressive jungle humidity one has come to expect in Belize; here in Pine Ridge, as it's called locally, bonfires and fireplaces are the companions of evening.

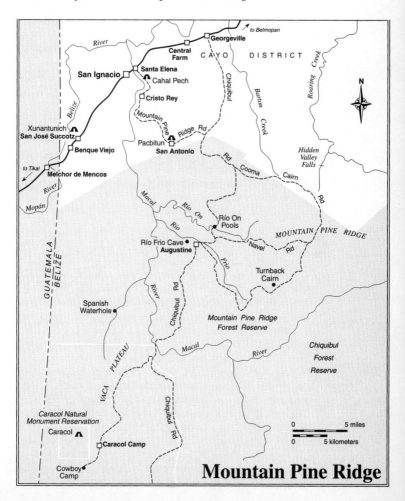

Mountain Pine Ridge

DRIVING TOUR
Caracol Road

The rugged, unpaved road that leads to ancient Caracol is among the most rewarding drives in Belize. It has been improved some in recent years, and a standard passenger car can usually make it with no problem during the winter dry season. A high-clearance four-wheel-drive vehicle, which can be rented in San Ignacio, makes the trip easier and is absolutely necessary if the road is muddy or rivers are high. If you're traveling solo, you'll find that the cost of taking a tour to Caracol is considerably more affordable than renting a four-wheel-drive. Three or four people, though, can split the cost and save money driving the Caracol Road on their own and enjoy the adventure of a lifetime. The road distance from San Ignacio to Caracol is 47 miles; driving time is two to two and a half hours each way. Driving yourself also gives you the option of taking more than one day and exploring magnificent caves, waterfalls and jungle pools along the way. Though there's no lodging along this route, there's a campground midway to Caracol.

BE PREPARED Before starting this trip, inquire about current road conditions at **Eva's** restaurant (page 191), the unofficial backcountry tourist information source in town. Check that your vehicle has a good spare tire, a jack, a lug wrench and a full tank of gas. Take along plenty of water and, if possible, an emergency cellular phone (they'll work almost anywhere in Belize, though the cost per minute can be astronomical). Tour

Deep down south in the Pine Ridge, set atop the Vaca Plateau in the foothills of the Maya Mountains, lies the ancient place everyone is talking about. Caracol, it seems, was a supreme Maya city, surpassing even the mighty Tikal. It says as much on a marker, discovered on a Caracol ball court, that proclaims the victory of the Lord Water of Caracol over the warlords of Tikal. The year was A.D. 562, and Caracol reigned sovereign for the next century.

Caracol slept, consumed by jungle, until 1937, when it was discovered by a mahogany logger named Rosa Mai. Mai reported his find to the Belizean government, which dispatched then–Archaeology Commissioner A. H. Anderson. During a two-week visit in 1938, Anderson recorded the existence of numerous structures, altars and massive intricate stelae. He also bestowed the name Caracol, meaning "snail," for a road that coils through the hilly terrain, though the name could just as well have been for the mounds of snail shells found here.

SIGHTS Two roads lead from the Western Highway to Mountain Pine Ridge: the Chiquibul Highway at Georgeville and the Mountain

groups travel this road regularly during peak winter season, but at other times of the year yours could be the only vehicle to use the route all day.

SAN ANTONIO   Heading south on the road that starts at the traffic round-about west of Hawksworth Bridge in San Ignacio, it's a rockin'-and-rollin' 13-mile ride to the village of San Antonio, where the simple little **Tanah Mayan Art Museum** (page 180) contains ancient and modern pieces that would make big-city museums jealous. Just past San Antonio, the road joins another one from Georgeville. Keep right and continue southward.

MOUNTAIN PINE RIDGE   The road enters the **Mountain Pine Ridge Forest Reserve** (page 181) about a mile south of the San Antonio in-tersection. A couple of miles farther on, a narrow dirt track turns off to the left (east) and goes about nine miles to the start of the short trail to **Hidden Valley Falls** (page 181), the highest waterfall in Belize. Continuing south on the main Caracol Road, in a few miles you'll find the **Río On Pools** (page 181) on your left. In a couple more miles you'll reach the tiny village of Augustine, site of the forest reserve headquar-ters and official campground, as well as the spectacular 65-foot archways and subterranean beach of **Río Frío Cave** (page 181).

CARACOL   Past Augustine, the road takes you out of the pine woods and into tropical rainforest. It's 21 miles from Augustine to Caracol (page 182). Allow plenty of time to explore this huge site. Not only is it the largest known ruin in Belize and one of the largest in the ancient Maya world, but even today the 139-foot central pyramid is the tallest man-made structure in the entire country.

Pine Ridge Road at San Ignacio. Both are wide, graded dirt roads that eventually merge into a single clay trail that plunges into an enchanted forest. Smaller trails of grassy dirt and limestone head toward abandoned logging outposts with names like Turnback Cairn, Cowboy Camp, and Spanish Waterhole.

Despite recent improvements, the roads are often muddy and flooded in the summer rainy season, so it's best to travel them any other time. In some places along the trails, leaves, vines and trees suck up every inch of space, though even here one can spot the toucans that decorate the treetops and the blue and orange butterflies that dance in and out of shadows. Ocellated turkeys dash in and out of the forest and a brocket deer, frozen in the bush, aims his charcoal saucer eyes at a visitor. Green parrots poke their heads out of holes in a cohune palm, their nests con-veniently carved by a woodpecker. Allspice trees provide show-ers of pungent leaves; pluck one and smell it, and find yourself reminded of pumpkin pie and end-of-the-year holidays. Belizeans, however, are reminded of the spicy coconut milk their mothers gave them.

About 13 miles southeast of San Ignacio, at the crook of where Mountain Pine Ridge and Chiquibul roads meet, you'll find the picturesque farm village called **San Antonio**. Here are farmhouses freshly painted, horses grazing on velvet green knolls, a teeny clapboard barber shop with a line of customers, and a one-room schoolhouse that throws its door and windows open to the warmth of day.

HIDDEN ▶

Not far from the school, at the **Tanah Mayan Art Museum**, you will be met by one or more of the five smiling, engaging Garcia Sisters. Sylvia, Carmelita, Aurora, Piedad and Maria will greet you in their *huipiles*, beautiful embroidered dresses traditional of their Yucatecan Maya heritage. They will take you through the many artifacts and artworks of their warmly arranged museum, from the welk shell jewelry, cedar violin and slate carvings to the 100-year-old butak chair handcarved from local Santa Maria wood by their great-great-grandfather. They will show you the cedar baby tub, carved from a single log with a machete and an axe, that their great-grandparents were bathed in, and that their grandparents bathed *them* in. And they will tell you the story of how their museum came to be. Admission. ~ For information, call 82-42023 in San Ignacio.

"In the early 1980s, their father, a village farmer, met a little piece of black stone while working in the field," explains Piedad. It was so smooth and glossy he brought it home, and Aurora instinctively started carving it. When she was done, she had lured from the stone the image of a whale she had seen in a dream. Local villagers pronounced it a grand omen, saying that God had given them the stone to bring back the Maya art and culture that is so quickly disappearing today. Soon Aurora was carving more slate and needed a place to display and sell it. In 1985, in a loosely thrown up wood building, the sisters opened the Tanah Museum.

Since then, the museum has more than tripled in size, and carries many local artworks and handicrafts. Among the exhibits is Aurora's original whale, and though it reveals obvious talent, it is neither as detailed nor as compelling as the images she has gone on to resurrect from local slate. Younger sister Maria has also

ANCIENT AQUATICS
To irrigate the fields and provide drinking water for residents, Maya engineers created a complex reservoir system that indirectly funneled water to crops and homes. It was a necessary system, since, strangely, the Maya had chosen to build their city far from a good water source. Now, nearly 2000 years later, that same reservoir provides bathing water for Caracol's current residents—the excavation team led by the Chases.

proven to have a knack for the ancient Maya art. The talent, Piedad says, is no doubt traceable to their *padre*, who, before he met that little black stone, used to carve limestone bowls and trade them to the neighbors for chickens.

On the way to Mountain Pine Ridge, **Green Hills Butterfly Ranch and Botanic Garden** teems with thousands of bright-colored Belizean butterfly species, as well as a wide variety of orchids, bromeliads and rainforest wildflowers. Besides hosting visitors, the "ranch" supplies exotic breeds to other free-flying butterfly showplaces in the United States and Europe. Admission includes a guided tour, and there's a picnic area. ~ Mile 8, Mountain Pine Ridge Road; phone/fax 82-04017.

Just southeast of San Antonio, you'll pass through a gate that lets you know you've entered **Mountain Pine Ridge Forest Reserve**. The "reserve" designation means logging is legal but regulated to allow the felling of only certain trees. In recent centuries, widespread logging stole plenty of the primary forest, though abandoned logging camps and sawmills are slowly being swallowed by the vegetation they tried to destroy. Headquarters for the reserve are in the village of **Douglas D'Silva**, where tiny white tin-roofed houses gather beneath cathedrals of slash pine trees. For information call the **San Ignacio Forest Office**, which can direct you to the various sites in the area. ~ 82-43280.

One you won't want to miss is **Río Frio Cave**, reached by a pebbled path that ambles down from the road into a dark den of trees. It is not a cave in the normal sense, but an overwhelming tunnel of stone that arches to the heavens, with a mouth that shelters a white sand beach dotted with boulders the size of houses. Water rushes in one end of the cave and out the other, coursing the half-mile length of this stone vault. Dim light filters through the cave, illuminating razor-sharp stalactites and walls smoothed by eons of water. One-hundred-foot-long vines dangle, confetti-like, from the ceiling. As you leave Belize's largest known river cave, notice the steps angling into the cave's mouth: they are stone keepsakes from the nearby ancient city of Caracol. ~ About a mile west of Augustine.

There is nothing dark or mysterious about **Río On Pools**, just a sense of not being able to get enough of the view. Like a great basin of Alka Seltzer, it is a hillside panorama of marbled brown rocks washed by fizzing water traveling in every direction and framed in giant slash pine trees. Where the rocks corral the water are mini-swimming pools, with water that's invitingly cool and clean. The best swimming is reached at the very top; the best views are toward the bottom. ~ About two miles north of Augustine.

Farther north and east lies Belize's most famous waterfall, **Hidden Valley Falls**, also called the Thousand Foot Falls because it thunders down 1000 feet from a granite ledge, disappearing into the misty jungle below. The falls are not viewed from close up, but from an overlook across a great ravine enveloped in a panorama of delicious green mountains and mystic haze that heightens as the sun takes leave. Here, on a platform that begins to jut into the ravine, with the wind whispering through pine needles, you can fixate on the scenery: mistletoe curled atop a slash pine tree, an orange-breasted falcon perched on a dead limb, visual lines between the broadleaf jungle and pine forest etched across the mountains. To make the views last, have a picnic on the nearby covered tables.

HIDDEN ▶ Not far from the overlook is a small tin-roofed frame building with a sign that says **Hidden Valley Institute for Environmental Studies**. Inside, it has the beginnings of a forest lab, the shelves lined with specimen bottles. The institute is the hopeful creation of a Floridian named J. C. "Bull" Headley, who owns the 18,500-acre Hidden Valley Reserve, located within the Pine Ridge Reserve. The Hidden Valley property includes the Thousand Foot Falls as well as the Hidden Valley Inn, which publishes a map to the myriad of lesser known overlooks and sites in the area, most open only to guests of the inn.

HIDDEN ▶ South of here, the cool Pine Ridge slowly slips into a deep, dense forest called the **Chiquibul Wilderness**. This was the mystical terrain epigrapher Linton Satterthwaite encountered in the early 1950s, when he went in search of the great stone stelae of **Caracol**. He found them, and carted some back to the University of Pennsylvania. During the next 30 years, various recovery teams visited Caracol, but they only stayed long enough to extract more of the beautiful stelae. Finally, in 1985, two archaeologists from the University of Central Florida launched a full-scale excavation. What Drs. Diane and Arlen Chase found—and are still finding today—is a glorious city and culture that is reshaping current thinking about ancient Maya existence. ~ www.caracol.org.

Caracol, it seems, had a big middle class. In fact, most of its 150,000-plus residents—three-quarters the number of Belize's entire current population—were probably middle class, enjoying all the wealth and perks historians had thought were reserved for nobility. Throughout the metropolis are elite neighborhoods whose homes are spacious and elegantly arranged, with bedrooms boasting large plaster benches—in effect, king-size beds. The extraordinary causeways that run out from the city center would have afforded scenic views of Caracol's splendorous buildings—not something city planners would have designed for a population of peasants.

Indeed, Caracol's myriad tombs tell much about the city, and perhaps about Maya life. As of mid-2001, about 125 tombs had been discovered—a staggering number, considerably more than have been found at any other Maya site. Caracol's "tomb culture" suggests that ordinary citizens buried their dead in specially made chambers in their homes, not in outlying cemeteries as previously believed. The Chases speculate that the dead may have even played a role in rituals conducted by their living descendants.

Two of the most exciting tomb finds, however, did not reveal middle-class members. Rather, the chambers uncovered by the Chases in 1992 held a king and a woman, likely his wife, and a royal family of four. The king's tomb, which dates to around A.D. 480, was embellished with 17 elaborately painted vessels, obsidian earflares and jade and shell necklaces (though only fragments of these remain). In the second tomb, the floor was dusted with jade flakes. Here there were two men (including one wearing a necklace of human teeth), a woman and a fourth person of unknown sex.

Arriving in the jungle mantle of Caracol today, it is difficult to appreciate the true scope of this Classic city. But as the Chases and their excavation team continue to peel back thousands of years of nature's shroud, they are discovering a place of staggering size, brilliant design and stylish architecture. At least 36,000 structures are spread across about 70 square miles, making Caracol 865 percent denser than the great Tikal. Work here could well continue for many decades; the Chases say that "by the year 2003, we don't even see ourselves out of the major plazas."

Much of their work, which includes "stabilizing" or securing the structures, is concentrated in the city's nucleus, where they

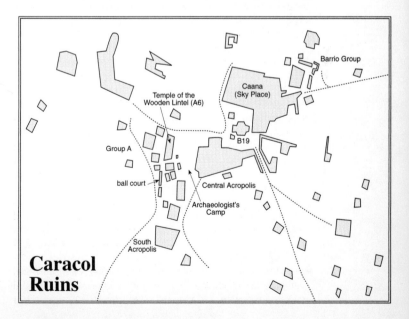

Caracol Ruins

have discovered stucco and plaster palaces, pyramids and temples that were painted dazzling shades of red and blue, and even with red and white stripes. Those that weren't painted were silvery white, their marbleized limestone catching sunrays by day and moonlight by night. Among the grand buildings are several low-lying structures that were perhaps ancient fastfood stands.

From the administrative hub, causeways from 9 to 30 feet wide fan out like the spokes of a wheel, reaching up to six miles all around into Caracol's sprawling suburbia. These were not only footpaths but crucial routes for transporting food and water throughout the region. Where some of the causeways culminate are large plazas with designs that suggest markets and way stations for crops and merchandise. The crops likely came from Caracol's vast agricultural fields, evidenced by thousands of terraces found by the Chases. The terraces indicate not subsistence farming but cash crops—further proof of a sophisticated middle class.

The entire excavation team—the Chases, University of Central Florida undergraduates, postgraduate supervisors and about 45 Belizean bushmen, some of whom are descendants of those ancient Maya—is only in residence from the end of January through the beginning of April each year, and this is absolutely the best time to visit Caracol. Not only can you see how archaeologists live (in meager huts next to banana groves) and work (in musty, dusty excavation pits), but you can tour an ancient city in the throes of modern discovery. Hire a guide in town (on-site caretakers may also act as guides if they're available); visitors are not allowed to wander the site alone—a necessary rule, considering the extent of ongoing excavation and preservation. Admission.

The road sometimes floods in the rainy season and may be closed for up to 24 hours. This is a minor inconvenience, considering Caracol only became accessible year-round in early 1993. Before that, most of Caracol's few visitors came on horseback. Since the road opened, between five and ten thousand people have visited each year.

An on-site **museum**, containing a selection of artifacts and two dozen wall panels with integrated text and pictures, opened in 1999. The Caracol tour begins in the epicenter. Here looms the lofty **Caana**, Belize's tallest manmade structure, emerging 139 feet from the floor of **Plaza B** and crowned by three temples, several pyramids and a courtyard. It is also known as **Sky Place** and **Sky Palace**, the latter name bestowed by students, who love to sleep atop its summit on full moon nights. Caana is so stupendous that its temples are not fully visible from the plaza floor. But ascend its steep steps and you will discover many quadrants and

Though the Maya supposedly entombed only rulers and priests, many of Caracol's tombs held middle-class families and their painted vessels, gems and other valuables.

rooms and sleeping benches. One of the chambers, nicknamed the "dwarf room," has inexplicable two-foot-high doorways and teeny benches.

At the top of Caana is a massive plaza and Caana's highest point, **Structure B19**. Here is where you should take time to look down on the jungle, whose ten-story trees are dwarfed by this proud view. Then stroll next door to **Temple B20**, where looters tunneled into three tombs, taking whatever valuables were there and destroying a painted text on a plastered wall. The Chases spent most of their first season, in 1985, cleaning up the damage and salvaging broken vessels and bones. One of Caana's pyramids, **Structure B18**, reveals a well-preserved staircase flanked by a stone mask. Between structures B18 and B19 are remnants of a decorative baseboard, painted such a deep red that the color remains almost as vivid today.

Situated conveniently near the great Caana is the elite **Barrio Group**. Like a Maya uptown Manhattan, the posh residential area enjoyed easy access to Caracol's epicenter, or downtown. Likewise, the **South Acropolis**, across the city center, was an upscale area right next to the reservoir. Several tombs were uncovered among these homes, including a vertical vault harboring a woman and a man. The capstone, or tomb lid, was not painted red as was traditional for Caracol nobility, indicating the couple may have been buried in their own house.

The South Acropolis residents no doubt watched a lot of *pok-ta-pok*, or Maya ballgames, in the neighboring **ball court**. They also likely witnessed the recording of their ruler's victory over the lords of Tikal. The triumphant battle between Caracol's Lord Water and his former Tikal overlord is recorded on a **ball court marker** that today is sheltered by a piece of aluminum. Several years ago, the marker was, incredibly, crushed by logging trucks. Thus, its 1400-year-old features are, unfortunately, very vague. The best way to admire its hieroglyphs is with a flashlight at night.

Across the epicenter, in **Group A**, some of Caracol's most influential figures lived, conducted business, and were eventually buried. Nine stelae and six altars were found here, as well as numerous burials that belonged to the elite. In **Structure A3**, the Chases discovered an important tomb containing eight pottery vessels, 13 quail skeletons and the badly decomposed body of an adult. Glyphs on the tomb's capstones record a date of approximately A.D. 695 and describe a person of royal lineage.

Presiding over Group A is the **Temple of the Wooden Lintel**, or **Structure A6**, which, amazingly, has its original sapote wood door lintels preserved in a side room. Steep short steps run down the temple's face, but a determined person will want to scale them to explore the temple's myriad floors and rooms. In the core of this building, researchers found an incredible 9000 pieces of jadeite and a spectacular jadeite mask in a stone box. The box held more: 684 grams of liquid mercury—nearly half of all the mercury recovered by researchers throughout the Maya Kingdom. In this area, too, was an urn filled with a cache of mysteries: stingray spines, sharks' teeth, fish vertebrae, pumpkin seeds, pine needles, seaweed and even a beehive that has survived, virtually intact, all these centuries.

There is much more to see and learn at Caracol, even as researchers make new discoveries every day. And now that the roads are open year-round, researchers expect this extraordinary place to become Belize's premier inland destination. With that in mind, the Belize government took out a loan from the World Bank in early 2001 to improve the road into Caracol, stabilize the epicentral architecture (especially the face of the great Caana), and build new visitors facilities.

There is no food, water or gasoline at Caracol, so be sure you're well stocked before you start your journey.

LODGING   In the past decade, several lodges have opened in Mountain Pine Ridge Forest Reserve, offering travelers easier access to this vast wilderness and to the exciting Maya city of Caracol.

Eight miles from the Western Highway on Mountain Pine Ridge Road, you'll find the picturesque 152-acre spread of **Mountain Equestrian Trails**. American expatriates Marguerite and Jim Bevis welcome travelers to their quarterhorse ranch set amid pine forest. Four pleasant stucco-and-wood cabañas with private baths and hot water (but no electricity) offer a comfortable way to sleep in the woods. The two-bedroom villa, "La Casa Vista," with mahogany detailing, verandas, a refrigerator, stove and 24-hour electricity, perches on a hill with a 360-degree view of the forest, mountain range and lush gardens. There's also a cantina serving meals and drinks. Families love it here; kids enjoy the trail rides through the jungle, with visits to beautiful rivers and falls and secret limestone caves. Babysitting and day tours to area ruins, including Caracol, are also available. ~ Mile Post 8, Mountain Pine Ridge Road, Central Farm; 82-04041, or 941-488-0522, 800-838-3918 in the U.S.; www.metbelize.com, e-mail aw2trav2bz@aol.com. DELUXE TO ULTRA-DELUXE.

HIDDEN ►   If you want to feel as if you've retreated to some secret mountain hideaway, stay at **Hidden Valley Inn**. Here, a cluster of lovely stucco cabañas huddle under sky-reaching pine trees surrounded by cushiony trails of pine needles and brilliant impatiens that grow like weeds. Inside, Mexican tile floors, dhurrie rugs and high angled ceilings create visual warmth, while wood-burning fireplaces provide physical warmth on nippy winter nights. Cocktails and tasty meals are served in a big elegant ranch house that feels like something out of the American Southwest. But you'll know it's not when you hear what sounds like a chihuahua yapping— only to learn it's a barred forest falcon calling to its mate. The inn's property spans 18,500 acres and includes the scenic **Lake Lolly-folly** and **Bull's Point**, which looks across a shimmering green valley, and **Butterfly Falls**, a forested haunt where butterflies float across a creek and travel up a waterfall. There's also **King Vulture Falls**, where a mountain is etched with trenches of waterfalls ruled by king vultures. To see the throngs of eerie black creatures, you'll need strong binoculars (preferably 80 power) or a telescope. Rates include breakfast and dinner. ~ An hour from the Western Highway, take the turnoff at Georgeville; for reservations, call 82-23320, fax 82-23334 in Belmopan, or 866-333-4464 in the U.S.; www.hiddenvalleyinn.com, e-mail reservations@hiddenvalley inn.com. ULTRA-DELUXE.

Around the corner, the less fancy **Pine Ridge Lodge** offers ◀ HIDDEN seven wooded cottages ranging from basic to quite comfortable. The "Forest" and "Mayan" cottages are simply decorated, open and airy—but opt for the secluded, spacious "Riverview" cottage with a screened porch along a scenic creek. There's no electricity (kerosene lamps provide light), but there is hot water and the cook manages to turn out good food with a gas stove and generator-powered refrigerator. ~ 60-64557 in Belize, or 216-781-6888, 800-316-0706 in the U.S.; www.pineridgelodge.com, e-mail prlodge@mindspring.com. DELUXE.

Upon arriving at **Blancaneaux Lodge**, one senses the place is ◀ HIDDEN vastly different from any other in Belize, having tremendous warmth and flair in its design, and yet set so far up here in the jungle mountain wilderness. Planters gush with exquisite flowers and frilly ivy masks a stone fireplace. A river churns down below

AUTHOR FAVORITE

A perennial sucker for Italian food, I couldn't resist the menu at **Blancaneaux Lodge**. Especially considering the author was Hollywood director and California winemaker Francis Ford Coppola, whose love of Italian food and wine is well-established. For lunch there are calzones and specialty pizzas; for dinner, the five-course menu focuses on pasta, smoked meats and local seafood. Dishes to try: spaghetti carbonara, gnocchi with real ragout, and Mrs. Scorcese's Chicken—"intense lemon chicken taught to me by Marty's mother," Coppola writes on the menu. The food is superb. The only thing not up to standard on my last visit was the service—slow, snobby and Hollywoodesque. Reservations required. ~ Mountain Pine Ridge, about one hour from the Western Highway; 82-33914. DELUXE.

a hillside decorated with flamboyant foliage—red spikes of ginger, purple sprays of orchids. A curved dining room is suspended above the forest, and the lodge's cabañas, villas and rooms are adorned in a sensual Mayan style. It all reflects the tastes of Francis Ford Coppola and his wife Eleanor, who own the lodge. In 1981, the movie producer and director fell in love with Belize and bought the lodge—the oldest jungle lodge in Belize—and made this exquisite piece of secluded forest his private retreat. Belize, being Belize, didn't pay much attention back then, nor when Coppola opened the lodge to travelers in early 1993.

Coppola's special touches don't end in the kitchen or in the lodge surroundings. He installed his own hydroelectric plant using water from the river that flows just beneath the lodge. He has a private airstrip that eliminates the four-hour drive from Belize City (though chartered flights are expensive—about US$360 roundtrip, minimum three passengers). And he opened seven cabañas, five villas, and two large rooms (the last share a bath). The all-wood cabañas seem built into the trees, their roomy screened porches places to relax and take in the surrounding forest (and while you're at it, uncork a bottle of Niebaum-Coppola Rubicon from Coppola's own winery). ~ Mountain Pine Ridge, an hour from the Western Highway; 82-43878, fax 82-44913, or 800-746-3743 in the U.S.; www.blancaneauxlodge.com, e-mail info@blancaneaux.com. ULTRA-DELUXE.

HIDDEN ► A little past Blancaneaux you'll find the desirable **Five Sisters Lodge**, named for the five waterfalls that gush through the property. Hospitable Belizean owner Carlos Popper, formerly a training officer for the Belize Customs Department for 18 years, will ride with you in his made-in-Minnesota tram, down 30 stories to the five falls, three natural pools and a palapa bar that sits on an island in the Privassion River. Popper and local craftsmen built the 15 thatch-roof cabañas sprinkled among the grounds, along with the main building, which has four shared-bath rooms (two with decks hung over the falls). The cabañas are hand-hewn of ironwood, mahogany, hobillo and granadillo woods, and are a bit more expensive. But you get the extra privacy, a screened deck and a hammock where you can relax and listen to the falls. There's an excellent restaurant here, too. ~ Mountain Pine Ridge, an hour from the Western Highway; 82-04005, fax 82-04024, or 800-447-2931 in the U.S.; www.fivesisterslodge.com, e-mail five sisterslodge@direcway.com. DELUXE.

DINING

HIDDEN ► The gracious service at **Five Sisters Lodge** restaurant is just one reason to call ahead for a table here. Another is the fantastic setting: a clifftop perch that looks 300 feet straight down to the Privassion River and five thundering waterfalls (which the lodge is named for). The building is coated in shaggy pimento bark and lined with mahogany louvered windows, the tables are laid with linen and the menu focuses on local cuisine such as Maya steak with flour tortillas, refried beans and plantains; baked lobster with yellow rice; and pork chops in orange sauce. Reservations required. ~ Mountain Pine Ridge, an hour from the Western Highway; 82-04005. MODERATE.

Chan Chich

If you drive to Chan Chich, you will think you've accidentally exited the earth into some planetary jungle, like when *Star Trek*'s Captain Kirk gets unexpectedly beamed to a strange Eden. The extraordinary lodge and Maya ruin is flung way out in Belize's northwestern hinterlands, almost to Guatemala, nowhere near civilization, and at least a four-hour drive from Belize City in the dry season. Just be careful if you choose to drive during the rainy season.

SIGHTS

◀ *HIDDEN*

Most people who visit Chan Chich do it in a small charter plane, flying low over a wheat-colored plateau that explodes into emerald jungle, then nosing down into a pinpoint clearing called **Gallon Jug**. An old logging camp turned farm center, the Jug is owned by Belizean entrepreneur Barry Bowen, whose beverage company makes Belize's own Belikin Beer, and who in 1984 bought 125,000 surrounding acres and made them a nature reserve.

What Bowen and his crew found when they first arrived were lots of marijuana fields, numerous Maya temples that had been looted, and leftovers from poachers who were hunting with abandon. Indeed, under a single tree, in a bloody, feathery heap, were the bodies of 24 ocellated turkeys. Bowen's solution: build a lodge that would break even, but whose primary goal was to protect the forest by having year-round visitors. In 1988, he opened 12 hardwood cabañas, constructed entirely from local materials and set in the plaza of an unexcavated Maya ruin. The ocellated turkeys found today at Chan Chich preen around the grounds, fearing only rejection by a mate.

CHECKING OUT CHAN CHICH

Guests at Chan Chich Lodge are provided maps of the many trails that radiate out from the lodge, or they can purchase the invaluable *Exploring the Rainforest, Chan Chich Lodge* guide by Carolyn M. Miller and Bruce W. Miller. Local guides, who are not only knowledgeable but really love the jungle, conduct tours of the trails and ruins, including burial chambers painted with friezes, several times daily and on some nights. Horseback riding, canoeing and local sightseeing excursions are available as well.

With virgin rainforest running for miles in every direction, the lodge offers visitors a window on the wildlife of Belize. Howler and spider monkeys navigate the trees overhead, while toucans nest near your room. Nighttime brings the chilling roars of howler monkeys; come dawn, you will think you awoke in nature's own amphitheater, flooded with a symphony of purrs, screeches, whishes, rattles and even pop-pop-pops. After a day or so, you learn the rhythms of the jungle, and they become your own.

In fact, because it is cushioned by protected lands—to the west lies the 1.7-million-acre Maya Biosphere Reserve, to the south are 200,000 acres owned by Programme for Belize—Chan Chich enjoys a spectacular abundance of wildlife. Birders, naturalists and lovers of archaeology are among the lodge's most devoted clientele, though its secrets are lately being divulged among mainstream travelers.

Lest you think building a lodge on a Maya ruin is sacrilege, Bowen points out that since he opened, problems with looting and marijuana growing have ceased. He has his opponents, but Bowen is proving himself an ecotourism advocate, taking care to protect the ruins while guests enjoy them and refusing to interfere with wildlife (even bird feeders are not allowed).

LODGING

HIDDEN ▶

For the ultimate Belize jungle experience, spend the night in a 1700-year-old Maya city. It's possible at **Chan Chich Lodge**, whose lovely thatched cabañas rest atop a Classic plaza encased in ancient temples and tombs. But living in this jungle doesn't mean roughing it. Chan Chich's 12 cabañas are attractive and entirely comfortable with their hot showers, downy linens and spacious quarters. Fashioned from gleaming local woods and crowned with soaring thatched roofs, the cabañas feature ceiling fans, louvered shutters and big screens parked near the ceiling for maximum coolness. Spacious wraparound verandas are ideal for wildlife watching and for admiring the lodge's luxuriant landscaping. A swimming pool and spa beckon for relaxation. Guests frequently report jaguar sightings along the 14-kilometer jungle trail system. There's a restaurant where everyone meets for outstanding meals, as well as a bar where nightly stories sound like something out of Africa in the early 1900s. Here's where you'll get to know Chan Chich caretakers Tom and Josie Harding, former Californians who are responsible for this extremely well-run facility.

During holidays and peak seasons (December through April), book at least several months in advance. ~ phone/fax 22-34419, or 800-343-8009, fax 508-693-6311 in the U.S.; www.chanchich. com, e-mail info@chanchich.com. ULTRA-DELUXE.

There's more to do outdoors in Western Belize than anywhere else in the country. You can pick your level of adventure, from an easy-going

Outdoor Adventures

walk in the rainforest or a leisurely sunset canoe paddle to a hair-raising climb through dim, wormy caves loaded with ancient artifacts. Most lodges will arrange your tours; ask when booking your room or at check-in time. You can also stop by **Eva's** restaurant in San Ignacio, where guides post their phone numbers on the big bulletin board. ~ 22 Burns Avenue, San Ignacio; 80-42267.

The best place for canoeing is in the Cayo District, where the Macal and Mopan rivers provide splendorous scenery and splendid sightseeing stops. Several outfits offer canoe rentals or tours, check the tour outfitters' bulletin board at **Eva's**. ~ 22 Burns Avenue, San Ignacio; 80-42267. **Casa Maya Eco Resort** offers several guided canoe trips. ~ Mile Post 68½, Western Highway; 82-04020; e-mail casa-info@awrem.com. You can also rent canoes from **Windy Hill Cottages**, or sign up for their half- or full-day guided trips. ~ Western Highway, just west of San Ignacio; 82-42017.

CANOEING

David Simson, one of the first guides to take travelers into Barton Creek Cave, promises "unforgettable, intense cave canoeing" through his **David's Adventure Tours**. Among the many canoeing options are a 6-mile upriver trip from San Ignacio to Ix Chel Farm; a 14-mile downriver cruise; and, of course, cave canoeing in Barton Creek. Overnight camping trips are available as well. ~ 82-43674; e-mail rudyjuan@btl.net.

Just east of San Ignacio, **Caesar's Place** will arrange various canoe outings. ~ Mile Post 60, Western Highway; 82-42341; e-mail blackrock@btl.net. Near Belmopan, you can canoe along the scenic Belize River from **Warrie Head Ranch**. ~ Western

AUTHOR FAVORITE

My favorite Cayo canoe is the guided sunset paddle offered at **Chaa Creek Inland Expeditions**. The Macal River is warm and foamy, green as fluorescent moss, as you make your way between high walls of limestone and jungle. Iguanas lie dead-calm on fallen logs, and little blue herons glide overhead. Everyone gets a flashlight to use on the way back, when it's so dark you can shine your beam on rocky grottos and spot sleeping fruit bats. If you can't make it at sunset, you're welcome to rent a canoe and explore on your own. ~ On the Macal River, about eight miles outside San Ignacio; 82-42037; www.chaacreek.com.

Highway, six miles west of Belmopan; 22-72185, fax 22-72513; www.warriehead.com, e-mail bzeadventur@btl.net.

CAVING   There are more caves in **Caves Branch River Valley**, off the Hummingbird Highway, than anywhere in Belize. Among the spiraling network of tunnels and limestone rooms are 36 "crystal" caves with enormous vaults of crystallized columns and statuary. Ian Anderson, a Vancouver native and rugged adventurer, combines caving, hiking and innertubing through five underground river systems on the 50,000-acre Caves Branch Estate. Sign up for one of his **Caves Branch Adventure Company** tours and you'll wear a headlamp, crawl through skinny passages and comb through Maya artifacts and mountains of shimmering crystals. At some point, you'll turn off your lamp and listen to the brittle, echoey sounds of the dark. Anderson's adventure company was also the first to offer cave tubing, now one of the country's most popular guided-tour sports. Depending on the time of year—some caves are completely flooded in the rainy season, others are empty in the dry season—guides can take you on anything from a two-hour excursion to an all-day, seven-mile subterranean float. ~ Off the Hummingbird Highway, 14 miles south of Belmopan; phone/fax 82-22800; www.cavesbranch.com. You can also explore Caves Branch at **Jaguar Paw Jungle Resort**. ~ Mile Post 37, Western Highway, then seven miles west; 82-02023, fax 82-02024.

Farther west, in the Vaca Falls area, Chechem Ha Cave is famous for fantastic pottery and a huge ceremonial chamber set deep in limestone recesses. It's also famously tough to get to (about one-and-a-half-hour's drive from San Ignacio), and once you're there requires a half-hour uphill climb. Tours can be arranged through your lodge, or check with **Eva's**. ~ 22 Burns Avenue, San Ignacio; 80-42267.

A shorter, tamer trip is tubing or canoeing through Barton Creek Cave close to San Ignacio. **Windy Hill Tours** can make the arrangements here. ~ Western Highway, one mile west of San Ignacio; 82-42017, fax 82-43080; e-mail windyhill@btl.net.

Mountain Equestrian Trails offers a full-day trip that combines horseback riding with a swim inside an underground river

AUTHOR FAVORITE

I could hike all day at **El Pilar**, one of Belize's newer Maya sites. Five excellent trail systems take you through areas that are deeply shaded, and there are well-placed tree trunk benches for resting and taking in fantastic mountain views across to Guatemala. ~ Seven miles north of the village of Bullet Tree Falls; 82-43612; e-mail elpilar@btl.net.

cave. The "River Cave Ride" passes through open farmland (with a primitive farming demonstration) and along rivers banked in giant avocado and mango trees. Lunch is served at the mouth of the cave. ~ Mile Post 8, Mountain Pine Ridge Road; 82-04041, fax 82-23361, or 800-838-3918 in the U.S.; www.metbelize.com.

From **Blancaneaux Lodge** you can explore nearby St. Herman's Cave, whose stone steps were carved by the Maya a millennium ago. The cave trip includes a 45-minute hike to Blue Hole National Park, and a swim in the cool, clear natural pool. Another option is a canoe trip through Barton Creek Cave, about an hour away. Bring a flashlight and swimsuit and get wet while checking out stalactites and stalagmites, Maya pottery and skeletons. ~ Mountain Pine Ridge, about an hour from the Western Highway; 82-44914; www.blancaneauxlodge.com, e-mail blodge@btl.net.

Tour guide Zeb Samuel offers half- and full-day trips to most area caves; visit his **Sam's Adventure Tours** at Mile Post 4 on the Chiquibul Road, or e-mail iatours@btl.net.

What could be more enjoyable that a scenic ride through the countryside? Out in western Belize, **Mountain Equestrian Trails** is a popular, well-run facility offering rides across 60 miles of trails, including former logging trails. Along the way you'll dismount and walk next to beautiful rivers and waterfalls and explore secret limestone caves. ~ Mile Post 8, Mountain Pine Ridge Road; 82-04041, or 800-838-3918 in the U.S., fax 82-23361. **Easy Rider**, based in San Ignacio, offers half- and full-day rides through howler monkey habitat and the Mountain Pine Ridge. The full-day trip includes lunch along the Macal River. ~ 82-43734; www.metbelize.com.

RIDING STABLES

"Our hardy Belizean horses are remarkably tolerant of non-riders," say the equestrian experts at **duPlooy's**. "For more experienced riders, there are great gallops through orange groves and over pasture, even swimming the horses in the river." The Cayo lodge offers guided rides through the jungle, stopping at Maya sites and a slate carvers workshop. You can also ride to remote, little-known Flour Camp Cave, where stalactites drip from enormous arching ceilings. ~ On the Macal River, about ten miles outside San Ignacio; 82-43101; www.duplooys.com.

Saddle up one of the 22 horses at the **Chaa Creek** stables and join a guided trail ride through cool forest reserve thick with cohune palms and sapodilla and ceiba trees. Keep a lookout for the shimmery flashes of blue morpho butterflies, raised at Chaa Creek's butterfly breeding center. ~ On the Macal River, about eight miles outside of San Ignacio; 82-42037; www.chaacreek.com, e-mail reservations@chaacreek.com.

The three-hour "Sunrise in the Rainforest" ride at **Blancaneaux Lodge** is a fabulous way to witness the orange wafer ascend among the high, bristly pines of Mountain Pine Ridge. Birds emerge from the night's sleep in a noisy chorus, butterflies dot the air and whitetail deer and grey fox start the day's search for food. If you prefer a shorter ride later in the day, the two-hour "Big Rock Falls" is a leisurely amble through pine forest. When you reach Hidden Falls, you can dismount and duck under the falls for a hydro-massage. There's also an all-day ride that takes you all the way to the rainforest, with terrific views across a valley; and a sunset ride against a backdrop of Maya Mountains. ~ Mountain Pine Ridge, about one hour from the Western Highway; 82-44914; www.blancaneauxlodge.com, e-mail blodge@btl.net.

BIKING

For detailed information on bike trails, mountain bike rentals and tour guides, check the website www.belizex.com/biking.htm.

Crystal Paradise Resort offers guided mountain bike tours around Cayo, including one to the large pottery-filled Chechem Ha Cave, a challenging eight-mile cycle from Benque Viejo. Crystal Paradise will also rent you a bike so you can strike out on your own. ~ Cristo Rey; 92-2772; e-mail cparadise@btl.net. Or you can pick up a mountain bike at **The Trek Stop**. ~ Western Highway, six miles west of San Ignacio; 93-2265.

If you rent from **Chaa Creek Inland Expeditions** you can mountain bike through Maya villages and broadleaf forest, and alongside the Macal River. Chaa Creek has a fleet of Trek 950 bikes with front suspension for taking the bumpy jungle trails. Guided bike tours are also offered. ~ On the Macal River, about eight miles from San Ignacio; 9-22037; www.chaacreek.com, e-mail reservations@chaacreek.com.

HIKING

Online hiking information is available at www.belizex.com/hiking.htm.

The hiking is excellent at **Mountain Equestrian Trails**. Choose from an easy half-hour walk through sunlit woods or a half-day or full-day hike through Slate Creek Preserve. It's probable you'll encounter at least one rare bird or butterfly (the elusive white morpho butterfly has been spotted here). More than 240 species of birds live in the preserve, including toucans and tanagers, oropendolas and raptors. ~ Mile Post 8, Mountain Pine Ridge Road; 82-04041, or 800-838-3918 in the U.S., fax 82-23361; www.metbelize.com.

Chaa Creek's 330-acre forest reserve is crisscrossed with well-marked trails leading to a butterfly breeding center, a natural history center, remnants of Maya houses and promontories that look across to the temples at Xunantunich. There's also a trail down to the Macal River, where you'll be tempted to take a swim. Before setting out, pick up a copy of the *Chaa Creek Trail Map and Bird List*, which enumerates 189 birds spotted within five miles of the lodge. ~ On the Macal River, about eight miles from San Ignacio; 82-42037; www.chaacreek.com, e-mail reservations @chaacreek.com.

I highly recommend that you drive a car here, preferably a four-wheel-drive. The **Western Highway** runs 82 smoothly paved miles between Belize City and Benque Viejo del Carmen on the Guatemala border. It's not a highway in the true sense, but it is wonderfully devoid of cars (the average "other car" encounter is about one every five minutes) and it's filled with scenes of farm and village life. Belmopan, Belize's capital, is off the Western Highway 50 miles west of Belize City. Near Belmopan the newly paved, scenic **Hummingbird Highway** heads southeast and joins the **Southern Highway** 43 miles later at Dangriga.

After Belmopan, the Western Highway runs 22 miles to San Ignacio, the unofficial capital of the Cayo District, with a grid of hilly, skinny streets that are easy to navigate after an initial drive around town. From the Western Highway, dozens of dirt roads spider out through lush rainforest; many are well-maintained and a few are in questionable condition, so inquire at your lodge before setting out. Some of the best lodges, in fact, are secreted down rocky roads, and you may drive for miles at a time before you see a sign, causing you to wonder if you're on the right track (most times you are). If there's any question, don't hesitate to stop and ask a villager. He or she will be happy to confirm your location.

Fanning out south of San Ignacio is Mountain Pine Ridge, where cool slash pine forest is dotted with jungle lodges, waterfalls and the great Maya city of Caracol. There are two ways to the Pine Ridge from the Western Highway: the dirt **Chiquibul Road**, which intersects at Georgeville, six miles east of San Ignacio; and the dirt **Mountain Pine Ridge Road** (sometimes called the road to Cristo Rey) angling southeast from San Ignacio. Near Pacbitun ruins, the two dirt roads merge into **Cooma Cairn Road**, which zigzags for about 40 miles through the Mountain Pine Ridge Forest Reserve and Chiquibul National Park. In dry season the road is flat, hard-packed, and a snap to drive (though expect two to three hours of travel time). In wet season, mud and standing water can keep even the most formidable four-wheel-drives out. Check conditions before you go.

While it's certainly possible to drive all the way to Caracol, I recommend hiring a driver to take you the first time, mainly because the roads are unmarked and the ancient city is extremely remote. There's no need to hire a tour guide, since guides are provided at the ruins. All area lodges, including those in San Ignacio, will arrange a driver.

From San Ignacio you can easily drive to Xunantunich and to Benque Viejo, though you can't take a rental car across the Guatemala border.

AIR

If you're headed to Chan Chich, it's best to fly. The jungle lodge is extremely remote, and so provides charter flights in small planes from Belize City to the nearby outpost of Gallon Jug—a fantastic way to see the wilds of northwestern Belize.

CAR RENTALS

For information on car rentals from Belize City, please see Chapter Five.

BUS

If you're short on cash and long on time, take a bus. Most are along the lines of a fumey, battered school bus and carry everything from farmers toting fertilizer and chickens to European backpackers making their way across Central America.

The **Z-Line** runs express buses from Belize City to Belmopan, where you can change buses for destinations in western Belize. ~ 2371 Magazine Road, Belize City; 22-73937. Sharing the same bus station, **Batty Brothers Bus Line** operates express buses to Belmopan as well as slower local buses that will let you off at intermediate destinations such as the Belize Zoo and the Monkey Bay Wildlife Preserve; another bus comes by every hour or two and will pick you up if you wait by the roadside. ~ 2371 Magazine Road, Belize City; 22-72025. **Novelo's Bus Company** services western Belize all the way to the Guatemalan border and has connections into Guatemala. ~ 19 West Canal Street, Belize City; 22-77372 in Belize City or 82-42508 in San Ignacio. **Andres and Joyce Shaw's Bus Service** makes regular runs across Cayo and offers charters into Guatemala. ~ 82-43458 in San Ignacio.

Addresses & Phone Numbers

Emergency for Police, Fire and Ambulance ~ 911
Belmopan Police Station ~ 82-22220
San Ignacio Police Station ~ 82-42022
Benque Viejo Police Station ~ 82-42038
La Loma Luz Hospital (private, 24-hour facility) ~ 82-42087
San Ignacio Public Hospital ~ 82-42066
E-mail and Internet Services ~ Eva's Restaurant, 22 Burns Avenue, San Ignacio; 80-42267

EIGHT

Southern Belize

The least populated, least visited and most rainy region of the country, southern Belize takes in the chunk of land south of Belize City to the Guatemala border. There are only three real towns—Dangriga, Placencia and Punta Gorda—all nestling against the Caribbean Sea, with primitive coastal villages scattered in between.

Inland is a different story. Here are the Maya lowlands and their foothills, looming as a deep, dark, forbidding chasm of rainforest punctured by jagged peaks of limestone and drop-off granite walls. Rising above all other peaks is Victoria Peak, Belize's highest at 3675 feet, whose "great cone of solid rock [shoots] perpendicularly skyward, seeming to float on the very roof of the forest," or so it was described by a member of the 1927 Grant Expedition, which, like many other teams over the years, failed to reach the summit. Thirty-nine years earlier, a team organized by British Honduras Governor Roger T. Goldsworthy did scale the peak and named it Victoria. Team member J. Bellamy, in a report to the Royal Geographical Society, said the whole area was "enveloped in a cloud of mystery."

"Karstic" is what geologists call the porous rock jungle of southern Belize, where bottomless fissures have been chiseled by eons of incessant rain. In the deepest recesses, the landscape is so dense and threatening it is thought to be unexplored by humans, at least in modern times. Maya ruins are still being discovered, some of which have not seen humans in more than a thousand years. Those areas that have been explored exact respect from their explorers, for here are more poisonous snakes than anywhere else in Belize, and more drug runners. Abandoned logging camps dot inland rivers, their names—"Go to Hell" and *Sale Si Puedes* (Leave While You Can)—reminding one of the tenuous thread of life in these jungles.

Visitors to southern Belize shouldn't venture into these risky wilds, even with a bush guide. During more than ten years of research in southern Belize, one American archaeologist has dodged bandits' bullets and worked in areas that were "loaded with poisonous snakes." Chances are good you, too, would cross paths with a deadly snake, drug runner or looter, or with military patrols who would ask for your government permits (several are needed to travel these jungle reserves) and purpose for being there ("simply having a look around" is *not* good enough).

However, there is much to see in less remote areas (which, incidentally, will seem *very* remote to many people), and you can take forays to several forested Maya ruins and a dense wildlife sanctuary. The Southern Highway provides access to these sights, though relatively few travelers venture all 202 miles from Belize City to Punta Gorda, the end of the line in southern Belize. Although the road has (mostly) been paved over the past few years, the trip is still considered a measure of prowess, and if you want to earn a bit of Belizean admiration, wait until a night when the group rum bottle is near empty and announce that you drove "all the way to P.G.," the nickname for Punta Gorda.

Of course, *not* going all the way to Punta Gorda is a perfectly respectable way to experience the Southern Highway. Dangriga, the first major town, is only about a three-hour drive in the dry season, four to five hours in the rainy season. The next big stop, Placencia, a resort area that is currently experiencing a real estate boom, is another hour and a half. It's a great adventure, and the tight web of jungle that clutches much of the road makes for a thrilling backdrop.

If you're pressed for time and energy, the best way to visit this region is to fly. Local airlines offer service to airstrips in Dangriga, Placencia and Punta Gorda. (Note the emphasis on *airstrips*. The closest thing to an airport is grass worn down by passengers waiting with their luggage. In Placencia, a traffic sign on the highway reads: "STOP—GIVE WAY TO LANDING AND DEPARTING AIRCRAFT.") Flying is not only much faster and also quite scenic, it costs the same as renting a car. Plus, you get to ride in a small tinny plane that feels like an old jalopy with wheels, usually piloted by a polite, clean-cut fellow fresh out of flying school (beverage service is *not* available, in case you had any doubts).

▼▼▼▼▼▼▼▼▼
Dangriga

The largest town in southern Belize, Dangriga, with its downtown hubbub and harborfront vistas, feels like a miniature Belize City. It's not particularly scenic, just smaller and therefore less crowded and dirty. A walkable grid of paved and dirt streets is lined with clapboard hovels and businesses, highlighted by the King Burger restaurant; the Sunrise and Starlight Chinese restaurants (just two of many); and Pepito's Store, which sells breadfruit on Breadfruit Road.

But beneath the drab, simple facade is a strong people with a rich, mysterious, tightly protected culture. More than three-quarters of Dangriga's 7500 residents are Garifunas (pronounced Ga-RIF-unas), whose ancestors came to Belize in the 1800s from the Caribbean island of St. Vincent. Two hundred years earlier, a ship carrying West African slaves ran aground in St. Vincent. No one's sure whether the survivors became slaves or citizens on the island, but what is certain is that they eventually intermarried

Three-Day Getaway

Beaches & Baboons

Day 1 • Fly from Belize City to Placencia. Check into **The Inn at Robert's Grove** (page 216), order a Belizean rum punch at the poolside bar, then snooze out on the plush white beach. When you come to, walk a few steps over to **Robert's Grove** (page 220) for the finest cuisine in Placencia.

Day 2 • Rise early for breakfast, then join a full-day tour of **Cockscomb Basin Wildlife Sanctuary** (page 208) with **Toadal Adventures** (page 230). You'll prowl deep-woods trails lit by butterflies, then hike back to the visitors center for a tropical fruit-and-deli-sandwich picnic. Afterward, hop into an innertube (hint: wear your swimsuit) and float down the Little Sittee River, watching baboons (howler monkeys) play in the treetops overhead.

• Back at the lodge, have a shower before strolling down the beach for a splendid Italian dinner at **Franco's** (page 219).

Day 3 • In the morning, borrow Robert's bicycles for the two-mile ride into **Placencia** (page 215). Roam this funky seaside enclave and have lunch at **The Galley** (page 220), set right off the sand. Alternately, you could opt for a spa morning at **Soulshine Resort and Spa** (page 217). Then return to Robert's to catch a ride to Placencia's airstrip for a late afternoon flight back to Belize City.

with the native Caribs and created the Garifuna. Freedom was the foundation of their culture, and it caused them to rebel against British colonization of St. Vincent in the 19th century and flee to Central America.

SIGHTS

South of Belmopan, the **Hummingbird Highway** is a newly paved road that coils through colorful jungle scenes. Feverish forest air pours in through your car windows, hillsides are masked in tangled greenery, and barefoot children clutch cups of corn kernels, so freshly cut that the sweet juice smell fills the air. If you ask where they are going, they will tell you, "to *madre*," so she can make her tortillas.

Even if you don't see the children, you will eventually spot the tiny signs for **St. Herman's Cave** and the **Blue Hole** (not to be confused with the offshore Blue Hole, which is a favorite destination for divers). Here you will find a pool of sapphire water as clear as air, with schools of fish scooting in every direction, buried deep in the rainforest. Sunlight filters through the treetops, changing the water into greens and blues and every shade in between. Swimming is excellent here. From this cool, enchanted spot, fern-lined trails lead off into a honeycomb of caves that last for miles. The cave, with a creek flowing through it, is pitch-black, so bring a couple of flashlights, good walking shoes and a companion. The cave entrance is a quarter-mile walk through the jungle. You can walk down a stone stairway originally built by the Maya to the low point of the cave, turn around and leave the way you came (as most visitors do), or you can follow the passageway for nearly two miles to the other entrance. Admission. ~ On the Hummingbird Highway, 11 miles south of Belmopan.

At **Ian Anderson's Caves Branch Adventure Co. & Jungle Lodge** you can river cave all day with a guide through terrain that ranges from easy to strenuous. Then you can spend the night riverside, choosing from barebones bunkhouses that lack plumbing to cozy cabañas with living rooms, private baths and elevated king-size beds. There are outdoor hot-water showers for the bunkhouses and the six rustic cabañas, and for anyone who decides to pitch a tent here alongside Caves Branch River. In the morning and evening everyone gathers for Belizean-style buffet meals, and in between they're off river caving on one of Ian Anderson's adventures. ~ Off the Hummingbird Highway, 14 miles south of Belmopan; phone/fax 82-22800; www.cavesbranch.com. BUDGET TO DELUXE.

Twenty miles farther south, take the turnoff for Saint Martins Village. After about two miles on a gravel road, you will land at the crest of a vivid lake that glows phosphorescent blue and green. The lake is the reason **Five Blues Lake National Park** was chris-

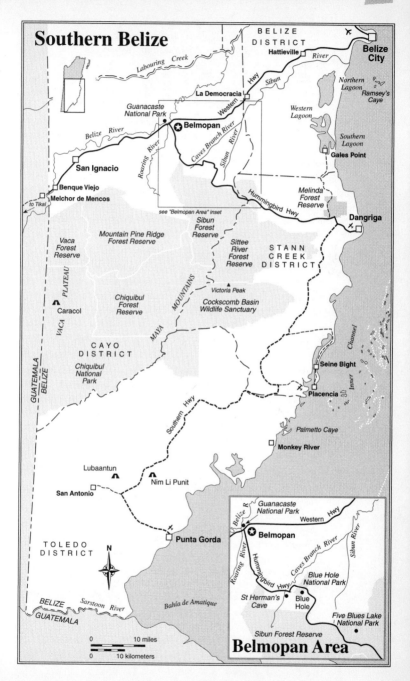

Southern Belize

BELIZE DISTRICT

Labouring Creek

Hattieville

Belize River

Belize City

Northern Lagoon

Ramsey's Caye

La Democracia

Western Hwy

Sibun

Western Lagoon

Guanacaste National Park

⊛ Belmopan

Belize River

Roaring River

Caves Branch River

Sibun River

Southern Lagoon

Gales Point

San Ignacio

Benque Viejo

Melchor de Mencos

to Tikal

see "Belmopan Area" inset

Hummingbird Hwy

Melinda Forest Reserve

Dangriga

Vaca Forest Reserve

Mountain Pine Ridge Forest Reserve

Sibun Forest Reserve

Sittee River Forest Reserve

STANN CREEK DISTRICT

VACA PLATEAU

Chiquibul Forest Reserve

Victoria Peak

Cockscomb Basin Wildlife Sanctuary

Caracol

MAYA MOUNTAINS

CAYO DISTRICT

Chiquibul National Park

Seine Bight

Inner Channel

Southern Hwy

Placencia

GUATEMALA | BELIZE

Palmetto Caye

Lubaantun

Nim Li Punit

Monkey River

San Antonio

TOLEDO DISTRICT

N

Punta Gorda

BELIZE

Sarstoon River

GUATEMALA

Bahía de Amatique

0   10 miles

0   10 kilometers

Belmopan Area

Guanacaste National Park

Belize R.

⊛ Belmopan

Western Hwy

Roaring River

Caves Branch River

Sibun River

Hummingbird Hwy

Blue Hole National Park

St Herman's Cave

Blue Hole

Five Blues Lake National Park

Sibun Forest Reserve

BUS TOUR
The Hummingbird Highway

You can ride buses along every highway in the country for less than the cost of a single day's compact car rental. Saving money is just one of several good reasons to consider seeing Belize by bus rather than rental car. Some destinations are unreachable by passenger car, and it's both costly and risky to leave a rental unattended for days at a time. The best reason to ride the buses, though, is that it offers a perfect way to hurdle the culture barriers that too often separate tourists from locals. On a bus you'll find yourself elbow to elbow with Belizeans of many cultures and walks of life. The newly paved Hummingbird Highway, the most scenic highway in Belize, is a perfect candidate for a bus tour.

BUS STATION   **Venus Bus Line** operates buses to Dangriga and Placencia that will stop and let you off at intermediate destinations such as the national parks mentioned below. Buses come by every hour or two and will pick you up if you wait by the roadside. (**Z-Line** also runs a daily bus to Dangriga, but it's an express bus and makes no unscheduled stops.) The Belize City Z-Line and Venus bus station is at 2371 Magazine Road; 2-73354. Check the current schedule a day ahead—departure times change often.

BELMOPAN   All main bus routes in Belize converge at Belmopan (page 160), the nation's capital, about an hour's bus ride inland from Belize City. Bus travelers with plenty of time may want to check out the **Belize Zoo & Tropical Education Center** (page 156) on the way from Belize City to Belmopan. Buses stop in Belmopan in a large,

tened on Earth Day 1992. Spanning 850 forested acres, it features a labyrinth of hiking trails and a small shelter where you can enjoy a picnic.

Another 34 miles of southern driving brings you to **Dangriga** and its historical Garifuna community. Here, amid simple wood homes by the sea, they practice their centuries-old farming and cooking methods, their painting, woodworking and music, and their enigmatic religion. Only in recent years have visitors to Dangriga been invited to observe some of the Garifuna ways. At the same time, a movement has begun among the younger generation of Garifuna to protect their language and folkways from outside civilization.

The first things you'll see upon turning off the main highway onto the road into town are the concrete tower and flagpoles of

crowded dirt parking lot in the middle of town, where vendors sell sandwiches, soft drinks, Belikin beer and assorted snacks.

DANGRIGA   The Hummingbird Highway winds for 50 wild miles from Belmopan over the Maya Mountains to Dangriga (page 198), the largest town in Southern Belize. Most of the route takes you through rainforest, tantalizing with glimpses of intermittent streams that beckon the imagination into the dappled shadows. Here and there, small homes stand at the edge of citrus groves surrounded by raw jungle, and the air is redolent with the scent of oranges.

BLUE HOLE NATIONAL PARK   Twelve miles from Belmopan, Blue Hole National Park (page 200) is easy to reach. Ask the bus driver to let you off at the parking area. From there, a stairway leads among big ferns and vines to a cold-water pool ideal for swimming and snorkeling. The trail system here is great for birdwatching, and you can hike up to St. Herman's Cave with its impressive stalactite and stalagmite formations (bring a flashlight). When you're ready, return to the highway and flag down the next southbound bus.

FIVE BLUES LAKE NATIONAL PARK   I suggest overnighting in Dangriga or relaxing for a day or two in **Placencia** (page 215), then visiting Five Blues Lake National Park (page 200), situated off Mile 32 of the Hummingbird Highway, on your return trip. A big, deep lake surrounded by wetland lagoons, this park has many miles of hiking and biking trails leading past caves, marshes, large rock formations and small archaeological sites. More than 400 species of birds and animals live here, including the curiously named lesser doglike bat. Although the park lies six miles north of the Hummingbird Highway, bicycles are for rent at the highway turnoff. Once you reach the lake, you'll also find kayaks for rent.

the **Chuluhadiwa Garinagu ("Garifuna Culture") Monument**, the centerpiece of a proposed park. Near its base a low, unpretentious white stucco building with a life-size sculpture of a drummer in front houses the **Gulisi Garifuna Museum**. Bilingual (English and Garifuna) interpretive signs beside drawings and artifacts tell the history of the Garifuna people, and there's a reconstruction of a traditional family hut. Recently opened, the place radiates local pride. Donation. ~ Stann Creek Road; no phone.

One place to learn about both Garifuna art and the art of cooking is at the home of **Austin Rodriguez**. Amidst a gathering of clapboard shacks with chickens pecking around the dirt floors, Rodriguez fashions drums from mahogany, cedar and maple woods, stretching deerskin across the tops. The drums are

◄ HIDDEN

usually made in pairs; the "father drum" is carved from the inside of the deeper-pitched "mother drum" with long chisels. The self-taught drum-maker and Dangriga native has been carving traditional Garifuna drums for more than 30 years. His customers span several continents, and his drums have been played in many a *dugu*, the all-important Garifuna ceremony and feast for reconciling with dead ancestors. There are usually finished drums for sale at the shop, though getting one (or a pair) home can pose a challenge.

While Rodriguez makes drums, the women and children of his extended family are usually busy making cassava bread. You can witness various stages of this day-long process, which includes peeling dozens of the white glistening root vegetables, feeding them into an electric masher (they were all mashed by hand until a few years ago), then stuffing the mashed mixture into a *woala*. Named for the big local snake, the woala is a six-foot-long rattan strainer that, when hung from a tree by several sturdy women, causes cassava juice to drain into buckets. After several hours, the juice is taken away to harden overnight (unhardened, it is poisonous), after which it will transform into starch. Meanwhile, the mashed and juiced cassava root is baked into a thin, white flatbread called *ariba*. To unaccustomed taste buds, it has about as much flavor as a paper towel, which is sad considering the amount of work involved. But to locals, a fresh-baked batch of *ariba* is a treasured thing, and those who receive it are very lucky indeed. Call ahead for an appointment. ~ 32 Tubroose Street; 52-23752.

HIDDEN ▶ Nowhere is this cassava tradition better captured than on the canvases of **Benjamin Nicholas**, whose colorful and compelling portrayals of local life have gained national and international attention. "These are the people in my head. I've been painting them every day, nonstop, all my life," Nicholas will explain. He lives and works in a small, green four-room house with a small sign in the window that says simply "ARTIST." In his mid-70s, the artist fills his days and his canvases in a dim, concrete-floored room that looks out to sea through barred windows, sometimes reminiscing about the time Queen Elizabeth II came to visit and bought a painting. His works, many unfinished, surround him with scenes of somber-eyed Garifuna women toiling over their cassava, and of happy children playing by the sea. All of his paintings are done on commission—you pay first, and he'll mail it to you when it's finished. Personal experience confirms that the painting will arrive eventually. Before you visit, call for an appointment. ~ 25 Howard Street; 52-22785.

HIDDEN ▶ From Dangriga, there are numerous possibilities for day trips, including nearby islands such as **Tobacco Caye** and **South Water Caye** for snorkeling and picnicking, and **Man-of-War Caye** for

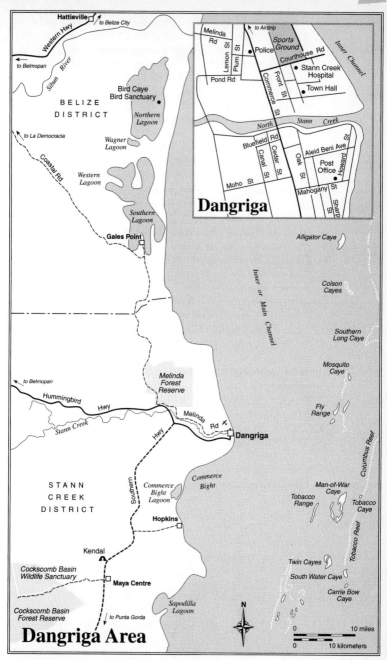

Dangriga

Hattieville
Western Hwy
to Belize City
to Belmopan
Sibun River
to La Democracia
Coastal Rd
BELIZE DISTRICT
Bird Caye Bird Sanctuary
Northern Lagoon
Wagner Lagoon
Western Lagoon
Southern Lagoon
Gales Point

Melinda Rd
Lemon St
Plum St
Police
Sports Ground
Courthouse Rd
Inner Channel
to Airstrip
Stann Creek Hospital
Front St
Commerce St
Town Hall
Pond Rd
North
Stann Creek
Bluefield Rd
Canal St
Cedar St
Oak
Aleid Beni Ave
Howard St
Post Office
Moho St
Mahogany St
Sharp St

Alligator Caye
Colson Cayes
Inner or Main Channel
Southern Long Caye
Mosquito Caye
Fly Range
Columbus Reef
to Belmopan
Hummingbird Hwy
Melinda Forest Reserve
Melinda Rd
Dangriga
Stann Creek
Southern Hwy
STANN CREEK DISTRICT
Commerce Bight Lagoon
Commerce Bight
Man-of-War Caye
Tobacco Range
Tobacco Caye
Tobacco Reef
Hopkins
Kendal
Cockscomb Basin Wildlife Sanctuary
Maya Centre
Cockscomb Basin Forest Reserve
to Punta Gorda
Sapodilla Lagoon
Twin Cayes
South Water Caye
Carrie Bow Caye
N

Dangriga Area

0   10 miles
0   10 kilometers

watching the frigate birds and brown boobies that swarm the island. Or you can head inland.

If you head north for six miles down a bumpy clay marl road, past hillsides masked in citrus and banana groves and vultures perched atop spindly trees, you will discover a real out-of-the-way but very important place. Here, from a humble little building surrounded by weeds come millions of bottles of Marie Sharp's Hot Sauce. *The* hot pepper sauce of Belize, gracing the top of nearly every restaurant and home cook's table, it is made with habañero peppers, the world's hottest chile peppers, measuring between 200,000 and 300,000 on the Scoville Chart, the Richter scale of chile peppers (jalapeños measure 5000). This tiny "factory" and the surrounding 400 acres are called **Melinda Farm**—the birthplace of Marie Sharp's Hot Sauce, formerly called Melinda's Hot Pepper Sauce.

HIDDEN ▶

Melinda Farm is owned by Marie and Jerry Sharp, who called their sauce Melinda's until they had a falling out with their United States bottlers and distributors (distant relatives in New Orleans), who purportedly put the Melinda label on inferior sauces made in other countries. Now the only bonafide Melinda sauce is that labeled Marie Sharp's (bottles in the U.S. still say Melinda's, but owning one in Belize is tantamount to treason).

Depending on the time of day and year, you can walk around the factory and watch the Belizean women giggling in their baker's hats while they stir up a batch of the tasty sauce. Amazingly, every batch goes into a 60-gallon trough with only three spigots, which fill 1536 bottles in just 90 minutes. During an average eight-hour day, close to 8000 bottles are filled. And that's just the hot pepper sauce. This tiny factory turns out many other unusual, delicious concoctions, including mango chutney spiked with ginger and brown sugar; guava, papaya and banana jams; and a hot pickle relish called *curtido*. If you're wondering what all those good smells are in each vat, Marie Sharp can tell you the *basic* ingredients—detailed recipes are, of course, top-secret.

THE TRUTH ABOUT MELINDA

There are many stories surrounding Melinda Farm's pepper sauce, one being that it was named for a woman called Melinda, which it is not. Rather, it is named after the Melinda Forest Reserve within which it lies. Another incorrect belief is that the sauce is made from peppers grown on Melinda Farm, when, in fact, the soil here is not suited for habañeros but for citrus. Farms in the surrounding Stann Creek Valley provide all those peppers for Marie Sharp's Hot Sauce.

Marie will take you outside the factory and show you an habañero plant (there is a small experimental field here), its satiny orange lanterns dangling from a leafy bush. She will also take you through groves of citrus and papaya, and the tiny cemetery wherein resides the Burns Family, who originally owned the farm. Call for directions and an appointment. ~ 52-22370.

North from the farm about 12 miles, at the tip of a skinny peninsula that pokes into the wide Southern Lagoon, is a locked-in-time fishing village called Gales Point. You'll find only one lodge and about 300 people here but many more manatees, who are drawn to the warmth and safety of the lagoon. You can hire a boat (just ask around the village) to take you "manatee watching" through the picturesque Southern Lagoon and up into the Northern Lagoon, with a stop at the **Bird Caye Bird Sanctuary**   ◄ HIDDEN
for glimpses of ibis, herons and egrets.

After exploring the area north of Dangriga, head south, preferably on a different day, since the roads are rough and by now will seem endless. The first southern stop is **Mayflower Bocawina National Park**. Created in 1991, the park provides access to small, partially excavated Maya sites and three impressive jungle waterfalls, and it's one of the few rainforest areas with trails where you can safely hike without a guide. Expect to see exotic birds and perhaps a coatimundi or anteater along the trail. The park is up a well-marked four-and-a-half-mile dirt road that turns off the Southern Highway six miles south of the Dangriga turnoff. The trail to **Mayflower Ruin** starts directly across from the visitors center near the end of the road, where you can get a trail map or directions from one of the caretakers. A one-and-a-half-mile trail leads to **Three Sisters Falls** (the water plunges down a sheer cliff into a pool) and nearby **Bocawina Falls** (the water rushes down a slanted rock slab). Another trail that is twice as long takes you over some fairly steep rock faces to 100-foot-high **Antelope Falls**, as well as the Maya site built at its base, and other, even smaller sites a little farther on. Admission. ~ Southern Highway mile 6.

Hopkins, a Garifuna fishing village where 20th-century life   ◄ HIDDEN
has just begun to trickle in. It's best to arrive by boat: it's not only faster and less stressful on the body but it affords a striking view of the village as you approach the gathering of seaside stilt huts framed by the luscious green Maya Mountains.

Though electricity reached Hopkins in 1994, Garifuna families still cling to the traditions of their ancestors, shunning the trappings of modern life. In fact, before villagers opened several very primitive lodges, the only visitors were infrequent drifters who themselves knew little of the outside world. No matter who seems to wander into their sheltered outpost, the villagers are more than friendly, inviting you to dine in their homes (for a small fee, of course) and learn about their way of life. That might include accompanying a fisherman in a dugout canoe or joining a punta rock party with its feverish beat and fast, sexy dancing. Or, you can explore local waters on your own with a kayak, available for rent at the village docks.

HIDDEN ▶   South of Hopkins, the newly improved Southern Highway will bring you to **Maya Centre**. This is the gateway to the Cockscomb Basin Wildlife Sanctuary and home to an ever-expanding group of Mopan Maya, many of whom gave up their homes and *milpa* farms to make way for the sanctuary. If you patronize the village's one-room **crafts center**, which carries attractive slate carvings and woven baskets, you will be fueling the local economy with tourist dollars and therefore reducing the need for poaching and looting.

HIDDEN ▶   From Maya Centre, it's six miles into the jungle before you reach the **Cockscomb Basin Wildlife Sanctuary**'s visitors center, where there are picnic tables, primitive camping huts and trailheads that disappear into surrounding forest. There's also brief information on Cockscomb and its beginnings, though if you really want the big picture, read Alan Rabinowitz's book *Jaguar*. The fast-moving adventure recounts Rabinowitz's field research in Cockscomb during 1983–84, trapping, tagging and tracking jaguars, living with Maya villagers, surviving a plane crash, battling poachers and arrogant, wealthy American hunters flying down for a quick kill, enduring various jungle parasites and ailments and dodging drug dealers and snakes (though one of his Maya assistants, while chasing a jaguar, was bitten by a fer-de-lance and subsequently died).

Most of the jaguars Rabinowitz tracked died as well, either because of poachers, injuries obtained during capture, or reasons unknown. But the New York zoologist did prove one thing: that despite considerable poaching and wrecking of the forests for farmland, the jaguar still has a chance in Cockscomb, and indeed in Belize itself. Compared to Belize, most other Central and South

AUTHOR FAVORITE

Jaguars prowl at night, so I doubt you'll see one during a daytrip to **Cockscomb Basin Wildlife Sanctuary**, the world's first jaguar preserve. That's why I highly suggest you spend at least one night camping in the sanctuary and joining a guided "flashlight" hike through jaguar forest. Even if you don't see a jaguar, you're bound to glimpse other forest creatures, including scarlet macaws, red-eye tree frogs, boa constrictors and peccaries. For more information on the sanctuary, see above.

American habitats are rapidly dwindling. Even in Costa Rica, Rabinowitz found "only a few places where jaguars might still roam in their natural state."

In late 1984, after much work and support by the Belize Audubon Society, the Forestry Department and local Maya families, Cockscomb was declared a National Forest Reserve where hunting was banned. In subsequent years, it was upgraded to a sanctuary to protect all animal and plant life, and now logging is banned. Today, it is the world's only jaguar preserve, boasting the densest population of jaguars ever recorded. It lies in a 100,000-acre bowl of forest, ringed on three sides by ridges and mountains, including Victoria Peak, which appears as a shard of rock looming in the distance.

A honeycomb of trails coils through portions of the sanctuary, offering hikes ranging from one hour to several days. Many of the trails are former logging roads carved as recently as the early 1980s. The jaguars and other cats of Cockscomb, including pumas, ocelots, jaguarundis and margays, use these roads to travel and stalk their prey. It's doubtful you'll see a jaguar unless it's dark, since this nocturnal beast, despite its ferocious reputation, avoids prey larger than itself, specifically people. The other cats are just as elusive, preferring to watch *you* from their safe hiding place in the bush. It *is* likely that you'll encounter the jaguar's telltale signs—feces and scratch marks—and then you will know he or she is not far away. For a better chance of seeing animals, local tour guides have started offering nighttime trips into the reserve, using night-vision equipment. These tours can be arranged through any area hotel.

Many other Cockscomb inhabitants are less shy about showing themselves. More than 290 species of birds light up the trees with song and color, including keel-billed toucans, scarlet macaws, great curassows and king vultures. You may also encounter a boa constrictor or red-eyed tree frog, or even a tapir (mountain cow), a creature who loves the dense, dewy foliage kept cool by triple canopies of trees.

Along the **Curassow Trail**, phosphorescent butterflies float across footpaths carpeted with silky ferns, and vines seem to drop out of the sky. Palm fronds stretch three stories high and fungi grow as big and brilliant as lacquered seashells. A trail of pebbles beckons down to a swimming hole with water so clear you can drop a coin 25 feet to the bottom and tell if it lands heads or tails. Overhead, waterfalls plunge down from the boulders.

Scattered throughout the basin are the ruins of ceremonial centers and house mounds that belonged to the ancient Maya, perhaps the first humans to call Cockscomb home. But far greater than these small reminders are **four Maya sites**—discovered in 1993—entombed deep in the perilous rocky rainforests southwest of Cockscomb. After ten years of research in southern Belize, including excavations at Lubaantun and Nim Li Punit near Punta Gorda, archaeologist Peter S. Dunham found the sites in terrain so dense and precipitous it was thought no humans could have survived there. But the Maya not only survived, they created thriving communities more than a thousand years ago on what Dunham believes may be "the only volcanic and metamorphic deposits of their kind in the Maya area." For this land of 1000-foot limestone cliffs and hammocks seething with fer-de-lance snakes is also super-rich in minerals, which likely drew the Maya. Dunham suspects the Maya were mining hematite for red ochre, pyrite for mirrors, granite for grinding stone and other minerals that "underwrote the Maya economy."

Although each of these ancient communities had a "downtown" area with pyramids, there are no grand buildings to indicate a "New York" or an "L.A." "This is like finding a Colorado mining town or a Texas oil town," explains Dunham, assistant professor of anthropology at Cleveland State University. The archaeologist and his team of five students, a biologist and a geologist located the sites on tips from hunters. After setting up camp, the Royal Highland Fusileers who patrolled the jungles at the time brought the team supplies, and hence they named one of the communities RHF. They call the other three Tiampiha, the Yucatec Maya word for "between two waters"; Tzimin Che, which is Mopan Maya for tapir; and Ekxux, Mopan Maya for the rare red extremely poisonous fer-de-lances who live at the site.

Dunham's research here will continue for years, though it is unlikely that the sites will ever by accessible to the public. He cautions anyone who even thinks of visiting: "Don't do it. The area is very rugged and very dangerous, full of looters and drug runners. I've been shot at."

Tours to the Cockscomb sanctuary, however, are highly recommended and can be arranged in Dangriga through **Pelican Beach Resort**. ~ North end of town, near the airstrip; 52-22044; www.pelicanbeachbelize.com. Cockscomb is about half-way between Dangriga and Placentia. For information on camping in Cockscomb, contact the Belize Audubon Society at 22-35004 in Belize City or write to the sanctuary at P.O. Box 90, Dangriga, Belize.

HIDDEN ▶   Ecotourism happens on the most grassroots level imaginable at the **Red Bank Scarlet Macaw Conservation Area**, adjoining tiny Red Bank Village, four miles up a side road turning off the Southern Highway 32 miles south of Dangriga. Among the village's 25 Maya families are both indigenous Mopan people and Kekchi refugees from Guatemala. Encouraged by the Nature Conservancy and small grants from the Belize Audubon Society and the Programme for Belize, the villagers banded together as the Red

Bank Conservation and Tourism Association and set aside 20 acres of forest where the endangered macaws gather each year from January through March. They are currently petitioning to expand the protected area and gain official government recognition for it. Meanwhile, villagers are receiving training in tour guiding, research and small business management, with an eye toward supplementing or replacing present slash-and-burn subsistence farming with ecotourist dollars. Visitor facilities operated by the villagers association include a campground, a single four-room cabaña with running water (a creek flows through it), and a small kitchen operated by the village women's group. Guided tours of the macaw habitat are surprisingly inexpensive. ~ Red Bank Village; 62-22233.

LODGING

As befitting a last frontier, the lodging in southern Belize is low on comfort, high on funkiness—and character, if you're lucky. Elegance exists only in the seaside sense, and only in Placencia at a place called Rum Point Inn (see "Placencia Lodging" section later in this chapter).

◀ HIDDEN

You can drive to **Manatee Lodge**, 25 miles south of Belize City along solid dirt roads through plantations and foothills of the Maya Mountains. Or, you can board a small boat and glide through silent mangrove canals and jungly lagoons to an underwater spring, which attracts the manatees. The two-story, white clapboard lodge sits on the Southern Lagoon, on a peninsula that elbows out into the breezes. Fishers are the most frequent guests, using their days to stalk tarpon and snook, though naturalists and other solitude lovers will enjoy the deep seclusion. Each of the eight roomy rooms has ceiling fans and a private bath with hot water and comes with a canoe. Meals are included in the rate. ~ Coastal Road, Gales Point; phone/fax 22-08040; www.manateelodge.com, e-mail manatee lodge@starband.net. DELUXE.

◆◆◆◆◆ ◆◆◆

AUTHOR FAVORITE

My favorite place to stay in the Dangriga area, **Mama Noot's Backabush Resort** is several miles out of town. Most of the drive is on an unpaved road that winds through rainforest lush with orchids and lianas. What makes Mama Noot's unique is its location, surrounded on all sides by Mayflower-Bocawina National Park. As one of the few humans spending the night in the midst of this vast expanse of jungle, I've heard the nearby roar of howler monkeys, seen swarms of butterflies dancing, watched toucans preening and even heard the distant call of a jaguar in the night. See page 212 for detailed information.

In Dangriga, the best place on the sea is the **Pelican Beach Resort**, where several old houses are strung together beneath the palm trees. Checking into one of the spacious, timeworn rooms (some have phones and cable TV) is like climbing into an old bathrobe: vinyl-covered floors creak beneath your feet, a stuffed vinyl chair invites you to rest your body, and a rare-in-Belize bathtub lets you soak off the film of the jungle. Constant sea breezes and strong ceiling fans keep things cool, so you only miss the air conditioning on hot summer nights. Resort owners Therese and Tony Rath are members of the Belize Audubon Society and are well-known conservation pioneers around Belize. Tony's wildlife photos grace the walls of the lobby and dining room, the latter being the best restaurant in town. ~ North end of Dangriga; 52-22044, fax 52-22570; www.pelicanbeachbelize.com. MODERATE TO ULTRA-DELUXE.

Dangriga's most modern digs are at the **Bonefish Hotel**, a two-story cinderblock building washed in seafoam green and situated across from the sea. The rooms are brightly painted and spacious, and while the views aren't great, there are fans and cool air conditioners (go for it—it's *hot* in Dangriga!). The lobby is small and fashioned like a comfortable living room, and there's a cozy bar. The hotel is now owned by the ultra-deluxe Blue Marlin Lodge on South Water Caye (see Chapter Four), and the facilities may soon be upgraded. ~ 15 Mahogany Street, Dangriga; 52-22243, fax 52-22296, or 800-798-1558 in the U.S.; www.bluemarlin lodge.com, e-mail marlin@direcway.com. MODERATE.

HIDDEN ▶ The rolling lawn around **Mama Noot's Backabush Resort** was near-impenetrable rainforest in 1995, when the government granted Kevin and Nanette Denny's request to homestead about 50 acres and build a self-sufficient jungle lodge using renewable energy and organic farming. They built the four-and-a-half-mile road through the dense jungle and erected six rustic cabañas with queen-sized beds draped in mosquito netting, as well as a family cabaña with four beds. What might at first have seemed like an idealistic folly became a popular lodge a few years later, when 7000 acres of rainforest surrounding them on all sides was declared a national park, and theirs was the only human habitation in it. Mama Noot's is as close as you can get to spending a night alone deep in the jungle. Birders flock to the place. ~ P.O. Box 165, Dangriga, Stann Creek District; phone/fax 60-64353; www.mamanoots.com, e-mail info@mamanoots.com. MODERATE.

HIDDEN ▶ About 20 miles south of Dangriga in a secluded jungle setting along the Sittee River, **Bocatura Bank** offers accommodations ranging from simple, minimally furnished treehouses to riverside cottages with queen-size beds, screened porches, private baths and separate living rooms. The owner, Alan Stewart, a veteran photographer, divemaster and marine biologist, enjoys sharing the insights he has gained over two decades living in Belize. His local staff keeps the cabañas and grounds spotless and prepares wonderful homemade meals using local produce and Belizean favorite recipes such as conch fritters, Creole bread and fryjacks. ~ 60-64590, fax 52-37021, or 207-288-3400 in the U.S.; www.bocaturabank.con, e-mail bocatura@aol.com. BUDGET TO DELUXE.

In the primitive village of Hopkins, several ultra-basic spots open their doors, the best being **Sandy Beach Lodge**. It's run by the   ◄ *HIDDEN* Hopkins Women's Cooperative, the only women's cooperative in Belize, and it features 22 rooms, some with shared baths, but all basically clean. Best of all, the gregarious women who run this place are great cooks. ~ Seaside on the south end of Hopkins; 5-37006; e-mail vals@btl.net. BUDGET.

Beaches and Dreams is the only resort indicated by name on the definitive map of Belize. When I drove out to see why, I found a small bed and breakfast for anglers. It had the feel of a fixer-upper. Co-owner Rick Strassburg, who has operated fishing resorts in Alaska and Hawaii, explained that a previous owner had helped the map company get the spellings of place names right, and by way of thanks they put his lodge on the map. After he passed away, Beaches and Dreams deteriorated for several years before the Strassburgs and their partners took it over. Now they have spruced up the central restaurant area and the four spacious guest rooms, which are in two beachfront duplex cabañas with rattan furnishings, dark hardwood paneling and king-sized beds, to create a home-like and relatively affordable base for exploring Coxcomb, Mayflower-Bocawina and other nearby attractions. As Rick talks about their plans for next year, which include building new cabaña units and improvements to the landscaping, it's clear that the place is being reshaped with care. It already has a great beach—one of the widest expanses of golden sand in the area. ~ Sittee Point, one mile south of Hopkins; 38-89073; www.beachesanddreams.com, e-mail vacation@beachesand dreams.com. DELUXE.

A mile south of Hopkins, on one of the prettiest patches of white sand in all of Belize, rest the seven thatch-roof cabañas of

HOPKINS AFTER DARK

In Hopkins on Friday nights, men from the village get together to drum and sometimes dance or sing Garifuna songs at the local outdoor hangout by the crossroads in the middle of town. Caught up in their rhythms, they seem oblivious to the local women and occasional tourists seated at picnic tables sipping beer from the nearby refreshment stand.

HIDDEN ▶　**Jaguar Reef Lodge.** Opened in late 1994, the warm and stylish retreat is no backwoods lodge: rich tile floors, native Belizean hardwood, big cathedral ceilings (with fans) and spacious decks adorn the duplex suites, a total of 14 rooms. Owners Bruce Foerster, Neil Rogers and others spent US$1.2 million on this eco-traveler's haven. A portion of the profits goes to conservation organizations. Ideally situated, the lodge is only 15 minutes from reef or rainforest. Seven-day trips are offered ranging from hikes to Mayan ruins in the jungle to kayaking down freshwater creeks (the price of a day trip is extra). If you would rather relax at the lodge you could always play volleyball or enjoy a full-body massage. The Cockscomb Basin Wildlife Sanctuary, home to many jaguars, is only 30 minutes away by car. The minimum stay is three nights. ~ Sittee Point, one mile south of Hopkins, send mail to P.O. Box 297, Dangriga, Stann Creek District; 52-07040, fax 52-07091, or 800-289-5756 in the U.S.; www.jaguarreef.com. ULTRA-DELUXE.

HIDDEN ▶　Hidden away down eight miles of roads across the tall-grass savannah, **Kanantik** (loosely translated, the name means "pampered" in Maya) has the beach all to itself. The 25 spacious thatch-roofed cabañas are among the most luxurious in Belize, with hardwood floors, large sitting areas and four-poster king-sized beds. All are air-conditioned—a rarity in this part of Belize. There's a freshwater swimming pool with a sea view, as well as a good restaurant and separate bar. While there are no in-room phones, a computer in the lobby offers free Internet access for guests. The management can be overbearing, but the location and accommodations can't be beat. Prince Charles of Great Britain stayed here on his most recent visit to Belize. ~ On a marked road 18 miles south of Dangriga; P.O. Box 150, Dangriga; 52-08048, fax 52-08089, or 877-759-8834 in the U.S.; www.kanantik.com, e-mail guests@kanantik.com. ULTRA-DELUXE.

HIDDEN ▶　**Red Bank Village**, at the edge of the scarlet macaw preserve, has a guest cabaña—a four-room Belizean-style wood house on stilts—with more in the planning stages. Tucked among tall trees near a stream, the cabaña is ideally located for birdwatching from the front porch. There are bath facilities but no electricity. Members of the Red Bank Women's Group run the dining hall for guests staying in the cabaña and the nearby campground. Expect culinary simplicity: you eat the same food as the locals—beans, rice and stacks of corn tortillas. Meat is rarely available. ~ Red Bank Village; 52-22233. BUDGET.

DINING　Listen to the waves roll ashore at the **Pelican Beach Resort**, where an entirely pleasant dining room is decorated with wavy Belizean tiles, louvered windows and pink linens. There are usually three choices for dinner, including some type of steak, chicken and grilled catch of the day. Side dishes of baked plantains and tomato pasta are just as delicious, though some readers don't agree. ~ North end of Dangriga; 52-22044. MODERATE.

There are only three tables and a television that blares all day in Creole and Spanish, but the food is tasty and plentiful at **Ritchie's Dinette**. The blackboard menu is short and simple: saucy stew chicken, beef or fish, with a side of rice and beans. ~ 84 Commerce Street, Dangriga; 52-22112. BUDGET.

Burgers rule at **King Burger** but you might also find corn soup, rice and beans, stew beans (different from rice and beans) and stew chicken. For breakfast there are eggs and bacon, and sausage and cheese omelettes. Closed Sunday. ~ 135 Commerce Street, Dangriga; no phone. BUDGET.

In Dangriga, **The Malibu** is a thatched-roof building that sits along the sea, offering rum drinks and the best punta rock concerts around. ~ 696 Scotchman Town, north end of Dangriga, across from the Pelican Beach Resort; 52-23703. **NIGHTLIFE**

For a quiet evening head to the bar at the **Bonefish Hotel**, which features a water view and slow music. ~ 15 Mahogany Street, Dangriga; 52-22243.

Placencia

Many travelers find Placencia the most desirable place in southern Belize. Its sands are whiter and deeper than most cayes' sand and its seaside resorts are instantly captivating. The area forms a peninsula where a lagoon meets the Caribbean Sea. The peninsula's northern end is a wild and windswept coast with occasional resorts. The southern end is a jumble of weathered stilt buildings perched in the sand and edged by a concrete sidewalk. There are many palm trees, but no road. Placencia's "main street" is called "The Sidewalk"—because that's what it is. In fact, locals claim it's the longest sidewalk in Belize, because there are no side streets to break it up into segments. Could this be the town? Remembering you are in Belize, you realize that, of course, it is.

Spend a few hours in Placencia Village and you'll meet half the town (the other half comes out at night, when seaside watering holes are alive with music and rum).

The face of Placencia changed in October 1991, when Hurricane Iris struck the peninsula and all but destroyed the town. The Sidewalk has been rebuilt wider than before, and most local restaurants, lodges and shops are back in business. Insurance settlements have rebuilt many of the resorts better than before, and Placencia has emerged as Belize's hottest real estate market, with big new custom homes springing up on every available patch of beachfront property.

SIGHTS

Young Anglos adore it in Placencia, and give the sleepy village a bohemian edge. Though still remote and primitive, Placencia has gained a reputation as a savvy ecotourism destination. Surrounding jungles welcome exploration and dazzling, little-explored offshore reefs beckon to divers.

Only about 650 people reside in **Seine Bight,** about two miles north of Placencia Village. This was a traditional Garifuna village until lodges, resorts and eateries, most owned and run by Americans, started fastening themselves to the seaside. Now visitors often outnumber the locals here.

Yet daily Seine Bight activities follow the old-time Garifuna culture. The women gather to wash clothes, tend to the children, make cassava bread and catch up on village gossip, while the men fish, play dominoes and do their own socializing, usually with the help of some cold Belikins. And because the women have their own Garifuna dialect, the gap between the sexes seems even wider—though most everyone is receptive to visitors, especially those interested in their intriguing way of life.

LODGING

In the residential area of Placencia Village, **Lydia's Guest House** offers down-home accommodations in eight guest rooms, most with views of the sea. Rooms are clean and comfortable, with stand-up fans and a shared bath. The wide porch and verandah have hammocks for guests' enjoyment. The beach is a short walk away. ~ North Placencia Village; 52-33117, fax 52-33354; e-mail lydias@btl.net. BUDGET.

AUTHOR FAVORITE

After rustic camping at Cockscomb, nothing feels better than the cool, high-style confines of **The Inn at Robert's Grove.** The languorous little spot was concocted by Robert and Lisa Frackman, two Manhattanites who fashioned 12 one- and two-bedroom suites with mahogany beds, Indonesian armoires, Sri Lankan lounges and beautifully tiled baths, in three haciendas. Part of the pull here is you get everything—louvered doors and windows that open to winter seabreeze or shut tight for air conditioning when summer delivers its blistering blow. Down near the beach are miles of wood deck, a blue pool centerpiece, a safari-style library and exceptional cuisine in two casual restaurants on the water—the Seaside, a steakhouse, and Habanero's, an upscale Mexican eatery. There's even a full Internet center for guests' use. Absolutely one of Belize's top lodges. ~ About two and a half miles north of Placencia Village; 52-33565, fax 52-33567, or 800-565-9757 in the U.S.; www.robertsgrove.com. ULTRA-DELUXE.

Along the sea in Placencia Village, five charming cabañas rest right in the sand at **Ranguana Lodge**. Whitewashed on the outside, the plain interiors each feature plain green walls, two full-size beds, ceiling fans, bathtubs, refrigerators and coffeemakers. Three of the five are air-conditioned, and two have kitchenettes. Ask for a cabaña facing the sea. ~ Phone/fax 52-33112; e-mail ranguana@btl.net. MODERATE.

The name **Serenade Guest House** brings soft, supple images to mind, but this new-in-1998 three-story lodge is starkly minimalist and overwhelmingly concrete. The ornate white porch and verandah have a vaguely Spanish Colonial look. The guest rooms are large and clean as a whistle, the bedspreads pink and ruffle-edged, and the doors formed of dense mahogany to drown out town noise. The same owners run the Serenade Island Resort 28 miles south of Placencia on Frank's Caye. ~ Placencia Village; 52-33380, fax 52-33338; www.belizecayes.com, e-mail hotelserenade@btl.net. ULTRA-DELUXE.

Set at the point of the Placencia Peninsula, **Soulshine Resort and Spa** is the ultimate southern Belize escape. The aqua-and-purple lodge is only accessible by boat; press the buzzer at the end of the road and a staff member will come to ferry you across a channel alive with manatees, dolphins and an occasional crocodile. The five spacious luxury cabañas have air conditioning, private baths and comfortable furniture handmade from bamboo and rough-hewn planks. A swimming pool invites among grounds beautifully landscaped with flowering tropical plants, and there's a sandy sunbathing area and open-air dining palapa with excellent seafood and vegan fare. But what really sets this place apart from other Belizean jungle lodges is the small, full-service spa, where you can soak in a European-style spa tub, then enjoy an aromatherapy massage, a traditional Thai massage, reflexology, a facial or a seaweed body wrap—an unforgettable experience. ~ 1 Placencia Point; 52-33347, or 800-863-5580 in the U.S.; www.soulshine.com, e-mail bookings@soulshine.com. ULTRA-DELUXE.

Deb and Dave's Last Resort isn't exactly a resort, but it's definitely one of the best deals in town. The four bright guest rooms have wooden floors, fans, front doors that open onto a deck and garden, and either one double bed or two singles. All share a large modern bathroom. From Deb and Dave's, it's an easy, breezy walk into town and to the beach. ~ Placencia Village; 52-33207, fax 52-33344; www.toadaladventure.com, e-mail debanddave@btl.net. BUDGET.

A trio of chocolate-brown buildings along the sea signify you've reached **Saks at Placencia**. Formerly Kitty's Place, a longtime Placencia landmark and drinking hangout, it's a comfortably worn spot with warmth and character. Choose from apartment-style rooms with private baths and kitchens or smaller quarters with a shared bath; all have ceiling fans and table fans. Out front, hammocks hang invitingly between palm trees on the picture-perfect beach. There's also a good restaurant, a little bar, and spa services such as massage, reflexology and yoga. ~ One and a half miles north of Placencia Village; 52-33227, fax 52-33226, or 800-866-4265 in the U.S.; www.kittysplace.com, e-mail info@kittysplace.com. MODERATE TO DELUXE.

The dirt road flowing north from Placencia Town has always been hot, holey, treacherously dusty, and home to a string of seaside lodges with more kitsch than class—which is why no one expected the pair of luxurious lodges that have sprung up recently. The first, **Luba Hati** (which means "House of the Moon" in Garifuna but is very much Italian in feel and design), has bright white stucco walls, tree pole staircases, and deep terraces edged in tropical trees. That's because owners Franco Gentile and Mariuccia Levoni are natives of Italy—she's from the north, he's from the south—and bring a passion for the soft pleasures of the Italian countryside. Stone paths wind through flower and herb gardens and seabreeze flows through eight spacious guest rooms, which have clay tile floors and beautiful beams running along soaring ceilings. There are many spaces for retreating—loggias, balconies, the beach, the bar—and there is the superb Franco's restaurant serving vigorous Italian cuisine. ~ About two and a quarter miles north of Placencia Village; 52-33402, fax 52-33403; e-mail lubahati@btl.net. ULTRA-DELUXE.

The 12 rooms (with phones and air conditioning) at the **Nautical Inn** occupy five octagonal buildings, which are painted gray and arranged around a small palm-studded beach. It's an easygoing place with congenial owners and lots of daytime possibilities: beach volleyball, bicycling, motor scootering, canoeing, sailing, and diving or snorkeling from the inn's motor boat. The "Oar House" is the venue for meals and cocktails, and the beach is the place for regular evening barbecues, attended by local Garifuna drummers and dancers. ~ Seine Bight Village; 52-33595, fax 52-33594, or 800-688-0377 in the U.S.; www.nauticalinnbelize.com, e-mail nautical@btl.net. DELUXE TO ULTRA-DELUXE.

At the **Blue Crab** you can choose between two rustic thatch cabañas with fans and screens and three air-conditioned rooms with Guatemalan bedspreads and mahogany doors and floors. There's also a camper hookup and prime spots for pitching a tent. The five-acre spread is a sandy venue facing the sea, with Rosie the resident dog, a tiny restaurant serving American and Chinese food, and owners Kerry Goss and Linn Wilson eager to help arrange tours of reef and jungle. ~ Seine Bight Village; 52-33544, fax 52-33543; www.bluecrabbeach.com, e-mail sales@blue crabbeach.com. MODERATE TO DELUXE.

Toward the north end of the peninsula, **Singing Sands Inn** is as pretty as can be. Landscaped with luxuriant flowers, the inn features a tropical restaurant and a thatched-roof bar that's popular with the locals. Six cabañas line the beach, each with attractive wood furniture, Guatemalan spreads and a porch overlooking the sea. Coral heads right off the beach offer good, easy snorkeling. This is a quiet, relaxing place. ~ Four miles north of Placencia Village; phone/fax 52-08022; www.singingsands.com, e-mail singingsands@direcway.com. MODERATE TO DELUXE.

North of Seine Bight in the blossoming village of Maya Beach, you'll find six simple, peak-roofed beach houses and two larger thatch-roofed cabañas at **Green Parrot**. They're tucked into the coconut palms a few sandy feet from the Caribbean, crafted of local wood and designed with little living rooms, kitchens, downstairs hide-a-beds and sleeping lofts—perfect for a family of four. Travelers like the Green Parrot not only for its sweet seaside spot but because the staff is exceedingly friendly and the food—a changing menu offering such fare as tropical greens, lobster fritters and snapper with papaya relish—is fresh and first-rate. ~ Maya Beach Village; phone/fax 52-32488; www.greenparrot-belize.com, e-mail greenparrot@mail.com. ULTRA-DELUXE.

DINING

Daisy's has traditionally been Placencia's diner, hot and humid, a little rumpled around the edges, with seven vinyl booths for enjoying everything from stew chicken and steamed fish with mashed potatoes to M&M ice cream. The owners have rebuilt the shell of the diner in the wake of Hurricane Iris and plan to reopen soon. ~ Placencia Village; 52-33353. BUDGET TO MODERATE.

AUTHOR FAVORITE

I knew that things were changing in Southern Belize when I encountered gnocchi with sage butter, tofu ragout, and *torta verde* (vegetables and rice wrapped in thin pasta crust). At **Franco's** you get all these plus other superb Italian dishes, many of which are childhood favorites of owner Franco Gentile. The dining room is vast and airy, walled in glass doors beneath arches and set with tile-topped wood tables. If you can't go for dinner, go for lunch and have a wood-oven pizza. ~ At Luba Hati lodge, about two and a quarter miles north of Placencia Village; 52-33402. ULTRA-DELUXE.

The cook and bartender of **The Galley** have been around nearly 30 years, and they know quality. Culinary prospects range from conch stew, fried chicken and steamed fish to stir-fried vegetables and the ever-popular Creole shrimp and lobster. Musical accompaniment is top-notch jazz, compliments of a CD player. Be sure to try one of the smoothies (they call them milkshakes here); choices include soursop, mango, banana, pineapple and seaweed. ~ Placencia Village; 52-33133. MODERATE TO DELUXE.

The **Pickled Parrot Bar and Grill** is perfectly Placencian: a thatched-roof hut set close to the beach, in the path of perpetual sea breezes. The focus is fresh seafood, seconded by homemade pasta, pizza and fresh garden salads. ~ Placencia Village; 60-40278. BUDGET TO MODERATE.

You can enjoy some of the best food in Belize along the rambling wood Seaside Restaurant at **Robert's Grove**, where candles lick at the black island night and waves grumble toward shore. The Canadian chef designs each night's menu that morning, so you never know what's for dinner, but expect such richly textured dishes as sautéed snapper bernaise with seared shrimp; tournedos of tenderloin on garlic crouton with paté; or pasta "rags" with tomato ragout. Steaks, imported from the U.S., are the house specialty. Reservations required. Robert's Grove also has a second dining establishment at the resort's marina—Habanero's, a gourmet Mexican restaurant. ~ At The Inn at Robert's Grove, about two and a half miles north of Placencia Village; 52-33565. ULTRA-DELUXE.

A popular open-air eatery on the beach, the **Cozy Corner** serves breakfast, lunch, dinner and drinks, with a varied menu of American, Mexican and seafood selections. Chicken-fried steak is a specialty. ~ Placencia Beach; 52-33280. MODERATE.

On weekends the **Kulcha Shak** does a beachfront Belizean buffet with live drumming and dancing. The fare is a blend of Creole, Mestizo and Garifuna—seaweed shakes, escabeche, chicken stewed in coconut milk—and draws as many Placencians as travelers. Reservations required. ~ Seine Bight Village; 52-34006; e-mail kulchashak@btl.net. ULTRA-DELUXE.

SHOPPING The best of the few funky shops in Placencia Village are worth a stop. **One World Gifts** has woven bags, hammocks, popular paperbacks and decent sunglasses. ~ Center of Placencia Village; 52-33113. You'll also find handcrafted Belizean gift items at gift shops in several of the resorts, including the **Green Parrot, Saks at Placencia** and the **Inn at Robert's Grove**.

In Seine Bight, you should look for Lola, Placencia's best-known and best-loved artist, working in the front room of her house. The colorfully painted sign out front simply proclaims,

Lola's Art. Here you can buy one of the self-taught artist's vibrant paintings, crafts made of coconuts and wood, dolls or notecards.

Everyone's talking about **Cozy Corner Bar & Disco**, a shuttered white house where you can dance and meet fellow travelers. ~ Placencia Village; 52-33280.

NIGHTLIFE

One of the more popular tourist-oriented drinking establishments in the area is the beachfront **Tipsy Tuna Sports Bar**, which has a big-screen TV, pool tables, a dance floor and karaoke. ~ Placencia Beach; no phone.

Seine Bight is the place for punta rock. **Wamasa Beyabu** leads the punta pack with nightly Garifuna drumming. The venue—concrete and sand floors, banana yellow and mint green striped walls on a palmy beach—is perfectly Placencian. ~ Seine Bight Village; no phone. **Kulcha Shak** combines punta rock with Garifuna drumming on weekends and includes a Belizean buffet on the beach. Reservations are required. ~ Seine Bight Village; 52-34006.

> Wednesday night at the Cozy Corner Bar & Disco features the famous "chicken drop" (guess what the chickens drop).

PLACENCIA VILLAGE BEACH 🏊 A mile of fine, pale sand long spearmint sea, the village beach has the most excitement around—but don't expect Las Vegas. Mostly you'll find Euro bohemians, Belizean families and pencil-thin dogs lazing beneath palm trees. If you're lucky, a drifter will be strumming something soulful on his guitar. Swimming is a good idea here—the water is shallow, fairly clear and calm. And when you get ready for a fish burger, Placencia's snack shacks are but a few sandy steps away. ~ Located along Placencia Village.

BEACHES & PARKS

SEINE BIGHT BEACH 🏊 The central stretch of the Placencia peninsula, this beach runs behind the painted stilt shacks and sea-breezy lodges of Seine Bight village. It ranges from skinny to medium wide, has hard-packed sand, and coconut palms that are a bit wiry. Best spots for beaching it: behind Kulcha Shak Inn or Wamasa Beyabu bar. ~ Located two to four miles north of Placencia Village.

MAYA BEACH 🏊 For those who prefer a beach all to themselves, this northern stretch of wilderness is the place to park your towel. Except for the occasional hut, there's not much here besides sand and sea oats and coastal forest that one can only hope will never be bulldozed. The water is warm, the color of sweet limeade, and nearly see-through. If you're not staying close by, you'll have to arrange for a taxi. ~ Located at the northern tip of the Placencia peninsula, about ten miles north of Placencia Village.

◀ HIDDEN

▼▼▼▼▼▼▼▼▼▼▼▼▼▼
Punta Gorda Area

Perhaps no town in Belize is quite so edge-of-the-world as Punta Gorda (or "P.G.," as it's known in Belize). Just before the Guatemala border, it's about as south as you can get on the Southern Highway. Indeed, there's a certain mystique about this place where Garifunas still practice sacred ceremonies, pounding on drums, shuffling their feet and calling to dead ancestors. But only rarely are outsiders permitted to witness these impassioned rituals.

What brings most travelers all the way to P.G. isn't the town itself—little more than a ramshackle fishing village consisting of five streets paralleling the sea—but what lies inland: remote ruins, rivers and villages amid craggy mountains, thickly coated in rainforest and tipped with clouds. Lubaantun, a Late Classic Maya city, simmers in stony heaps atop a sunny ridge not far from a secret swimming hole called Blue Creek. Primitive Maya villages dot the surrounding jungle and invite travelers to spend the night in rustic style, sleeping in a hammock beneath a palm-thatch roof.

SIGHTS

HIDDEN ▶

On the Southern Highway, about 25 miles north of Punta Gorda, Golden Stream Village marks the turnoff to **Golden Stream Falls and Pool**. A trail through the pasture from the road's end leads to the first of several large, idyllic pools fed by waterfalls on the crystalline stream perfect for a cool dip and a picnic. Villagers use the pools to wash clothing and bathe, especially in the mornings, but much of the time you'll have the spot all to yourself.

Just past Golden Stream Village on the Southern Highway, you'll see a sign for **Nim Li Punit**. This Late Classic site lacks the scope and architectural intrigue of Lubaantun, but boasts at least 25 intricately sculpted stelae. One measures more than 30 feet, making it one of the tallest along the Maya Route. Nim Li Punit means "Big Hat," likely referring to its location along a ridge overlooking coastal plains.

South of Nim Li Punit near the turnnoff to Lubaantun, the **Toledo Botanical Arboretum** is actually a self-sufficient, energy-independent experimental farm developing methods for using the area's renewable resources. There are 55 varieties of fruit trees, including starfruit, Malay apples and flying potatoes, which are used to make jams and preserves for home use and sale. Excess fruit is used to feed the farm's pigs. In turn, the pigs' waste is used to produce methane gas for cooking, refrigeration and electricity. There are also an orchid grove and gardens of frangipani and ylang-ylang flowers, which are used to make perfume, and the arboretum's nursery sells bedding plants and seeds to other farms in the area. Admission includes a guided tour.

From there, you'll find nothing much along the Southern Highway until you reach **Punta Gorda**—and some would argue

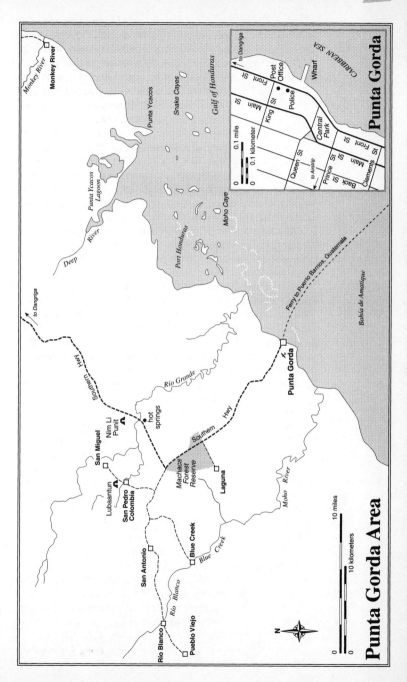

Punta Gorda

to Dangriga

CARIBBEAN SEA

Post Office

Police

Wharf

Front St

King St

Main St

Central Park

Front St

Back St

Main St

Clements St

Prince St

Queen St

to Airstrip

0   0.1 mile

0   0.1 kilometer

Monkey River

Monkey River

Punta Ycacos

Snake Cayes

Gulf of Honduras

Punta Ycacos Lagoon

Deep River

Port Honduras

Moho Caye

Ferry to Puerto Barrios, Guatemala

Bahía de Amatique

to Dangriga

Southern Hwy

Río Grande

hot springs

Nim Li Punit

San Miguel

Lubaantun

San Pedro Columbia

Southern Hwy

Punta Gorda

Machaca Forest Reserve

Laguna

Moho River

San Antonio

Blue Creek

Blue Creek

Río Blanco

Río Blanco

Pueblo Viejo

N

10 miles

10 kilometers

0

0

Punta Gorda Area

there's not much there either, it being a thoroughly quirky outpost where chickens sprint across the roads and filmy store windows advertise five-gallon buckets of pigs' tails. There are Americans here who will tell you that life in this banana republic is a big adventure, fraught with occasional bouts of malaria or dengue fever, cars breaking down and not being fixed (getting a simple part can take weeks), and pesky plane crashes. To really "get away from it all," they take a skiff to nearby deserted Moho Caye, sit on the beach and drink a beer.

Punta Gorda itself is pretty much "away from it all," and there's not much to do in town. However, the lush jungles outside town harbor several sightseeing treasures. Tours to these areas can be arranged through the **Toledo Visitors Information Center** (Front Street at the wharf; 72-22531) or **Requena's Charter Service** (12 Front Street; no phone).

Heading west from Punta Gorda, a dirt road climbs through dense rainforest, skirting Maya villages where cacao beans are

HIDDEN ▶

drying next to thatched huts. In the village of **San Antonio**, the **San Luis Rey Church** was built in 1954 with stones from surround-

HIDDEN ▶

ing Maya ruins. A mile from the village, **San Antonio Falls** is a wide, beautiful, shallow pool surrounded by shady forest. Beyond the falls lie the ruins of **Uxbenka**, a small Mayan ceremonial center adjacent to tiny Santa Cruz village. Though it doesn't rival other ancient sites in the region such as Lubaantun, archaeology buffs will find it interesting because it is built on stepped terraces up the hillside, it contains an open royal tomb, and best of all, the uppermost plaza commands a spectacular view of the surrounding hills and valleys as well as the distant

THE CRYSTAL SKULL CAPER

The most astonishing find at Lubaantun—allegedly—was a crystal skull, perfectly carved from a single cube of rock crystal. Void of tool marks, its construction seems impossible. In 1927, British adventurer Mike Mitchell-Hedges and his daughter Anna supposedly discovered the skull in a temple vault. Mitchell-Hedges claimed the skull was proof of a link between residents of Atlantis and the ancient Maya. After Mitchell-Hedges described the discovery of the skull and the curse that supposedly went with it, in his 1954 autobiography, critics noted that he had never mentioned the "find" until 1943, when records show he bought it at a Sotheby's auction; he removed the account from later editions of the book. Nonetheless, after his death Anna toured the world exhibiting the skull. The story has spawned dozens of other crystal skull "discoveries" around the world and a brisk business in reproductions sold in New Age stores.

Maya Mountains. Although Uxbenka is not yet officially open to the public, the villagers keep the ruins cleared of vegetation and are eager to escort you there for a small fee. Continuing south, **Rio Blanco Waterfall** is the centerpiece of a 500-acre "Indigenous Peoples Park"; the waterfall plunges 20 feet from a limestone overhang into a big pool deep enough to allow local kids to cannonball from the top of the cliff into the water. Still farther along the road, you'll come to the village of Pueblo Viejo ("Old Town") and, nearby, **Pueblo Viejo Falls**, a series of waterfalls spilling down limestone cliffs like stairsteps into one jungle pool after another.

West of the Southern Highway near the turnoff to San Antonio, **Lubaantun**, a major Late Classic ceremonial center, stands cleared ◀ HIDDEN
and partly reconstructed. This isolated ruin sees few visitors, but those lucky enough to come will find Santiago Coc, the Maya caretaker who gives enthusiastic tours. Coc should know the area: in 1970, he assisted archaeologist Norman Hammond, then a doctoral student at Cambridge, with excavations. ~ Five miles west of San Antonio, just past the village of San Pedro Colombia.

Lubaantun means "Place of Fallen Stones," and that's just what it looks like. Within a mile of cleared jungle are mound upon mound of stones, some masked in fungi and others sprouting big trees. Eleven major buildings are set in five plazas, built atop a ridge similar to western Belize's Xunantunich. But unlike any other Maya site, the structures here were built without any mortar. Instead, each stone was painstakingly cut to fit another—yet the only tools found were pieces of flint. Archaeologists also found grinding stones for corn and an open chamber with a human jawbone and 1000 mollusk shells, though their purpose is unknown.

A little farther down the dirt road, a path winds through cool jungle to **Blue Creek**. There's no sign for this marvelous swimming ◀ HIDDEN
hole and local secret. A tangle of vines sway overhead, and schools of fish dart through the lucid water. Water gushes down from the jungle hills, creating many small falls. A quarter-mile farther on the trail are several caves and a wood shed for camping.

Back on the dirt road, and heading east, a sign on an abandoned, weed-choked clunker advertises **Dem Dats Doin**. It's owned ◀ HIDDEN
by a Hawaiian couple who call their spread a "Self-Sufficient Integrated Farm System." A guided tour introduces you to their "biogas digester," which uses pig manure to create methane gas to run their lights and refrigerator. The manure also fertilizes their gardens, which provide food (the pigs are for sale, by the way). You'll see a "solar oven," a foil-lined box that even bakes cakes, and vials where jungle plants are being converted to perfumes, rums and oils. If this weren't Belize, it would seem a very strange place! Admission. ~ For information, call 72-22470.

Once you've seen the jungle side of Punta Gorda, you can head out to sea. Day trips to the **Snake Cayes** and **Moho Caye** offer snorkeling and fly-fishing in pristine, remote waters. Try to connect with a guide who will take you to **Temash/Sarstoon National Park**, a little-known wildlife sanctuary on the river that marks the border between Belize and Guatemala. Orchids and bromeliads festoon the thick root systems of red mangrove trees that grow to an astonishing 100 feet in height, providing secluded habitat for tapirs, jaguars, macaws, rare white-faced capuchin monkeys and many manatees. ~ Information: Toledo Visitors Information Center, Front Street at the wharf; 72-22531.

HIDDEN ▶ Another exciting excursion from Punta Gorda is a three-day trip down the **Río Dulce** to **Livingston, Guatemala** (also arranged through the visitors center). **Requena's Charter Service** offers scheduled trips to Puerto Barrios, Guatemala, on Monday, Wednesday and Saturday, and charters on other days. ~ 12 Front Street. For more information on visiting Guatemala, see Chapter Nine.

LODGING Punta Gorda has many older, sad-looking lodges whose rooms are sporadically occupied—which means if you don't mind slumming it, you can stay here for low budget prices, especially if the hotel is empty and you wrangle a good deal (perhaps US$15 or $20).

Sea Front Inn is in fact across from the sea but has nice water views, along with some of the most comfortable rooms in Punta Gorda. Florida natives and former medical missionaries Larry and Carol Smith opened Sea Front in 1998, offering 11 extra-large accommodations finished in rosewood and mahogany by local craftsmen. All rooms have air conditioning and cable TV—luxuries for Punta Gorda. A third-floor seaview restaurant serves daily breakfast; lunch and dinner are available to groups who reserve in advance. ~ Northern end of Punta Gorda; 72-22300, fax 72-22682; www.seafrontinn.com, e-mail office@seafrontinn.com. MODERATE.

Nature's Way Guest House gives the impression it's been here a very long time. Engulfed in flowering plants and vines, the funky seaside building has concrete floors of varying colors and a number of stoops and terraces. The rooms are one step up from a youth hostel, and have shared baths. The owners are an American-Belizean couple who also offer local tours. ~ 65 Front Street, Punta Gorda; 72-22119; e-mail thfece@hotmail.com. BUDGET.

The 12 rooms at the cinderblock **Hotel Mira Mar** seem respectable enough, with their newish vinyl floors, tidy bathrooms and eccentric decor of paneled walls, butterfly-patterned shower curtains and terrycloth bedspreads. The concrete porches have views ranging from good to forget-it; some rooms have air conditioning and some even have televisions, which you'll need to

Sleeping in a Jungle Village

No doubt the best deal for an ecotourist is to stay outside Punta Gorda in a remote Maya village. As part of a successful eco-tourism program, several Maya and Garifuna villages are welcoming visitors. In one of the best programs, called the **Toledo Ecotourism Association Guest House Ecotrail Program**, travelers spend one or more days with the residents of Laguna, San Miguel, San Antonio, San Pedro Columbia or Pueblo Viejo. During a stay, guests can help village women grind corn for tortillas, watch basket weaving and pottery making and explore a local cave that has 1000-year-old Maya paintings. At night, there's barefoot dancing around a bonfire.

Accommodations are in guest houses with concrete floors and eight beds covered with mosquito nets, a slight step up from the villagers' own mud-floored huts strung with hammocks. There are also separate bath houses for men and women. Guests get a basket with their eating utensils, which they carry to various homes for meals, as local families share the responsibility for feeding visitors.

In case you're wondering about a language barrier, many villagers speak English, including giggling children who become elated at the sight of a visitor. Profits from the program help fund village schools, waste disposal and homestead farming, an alternative to slash-and-burn methods. All meals and two tours are included in the rates. Transportation to the village is arranged but not included.

No more than eight visitors can stay in the same village at the same time, so if you're planning a trip during the winter months, make reservations at least a month in advance. ~ P.O. Box 157, Punta Gorda Town; 72-22096, fax 72-22199; www.plenty.org/mayan-ecotours/index.html, e-mail tea@btl.net. MODERATE TO DELUXE.

drown out the noise from the Chinese restaurant downstairs. ~ 95 Front Street, Punta Gorda; 72-22033. BUDGET TO DELUXE.

The **Saint Charles Inn** has rooms that are less run-down than most in its price range. There are 13 units in all, spread between two buildings facing a grassy courtyard. All have private baths with hot water, ceiling and wall fans, satellite TV, pretty linoleum floors and walls painted a soothing cream. ~ 23 King Street, Punta Gorda; 72-22149, fax 72-22199. BUDGET.

HIDDEN ► Eighteen miles inland from Punta Gorda, near Lubaantun, the Río Grande loops almost completely around the **Lodge at Big Falls** to create almost a mile of river frontage for the lodge. Accommodations are in attractive thatched-roof huts with Mexican tile floors, handmade hardwood furnishings and Guatemalan fabric decor. Each has a private bath and a wraparound porch from which to watch the myriad colorful birds and butterflies that frequent the landscaped grounds or to admire the views of the Maya Mountains and the nearby village of Big Falls. ~ P.O. Box 103, Punta Gorda; no local phone, reservations 888-865-3369; www.thelodgeatbigfalls.com, e-mail info@thelodgeat bigfalls.com. ULTRA-DELUXE.

DINING   If someone listed a couple of restaurants in Punta Gorda—say, the Sea Front Inn and the Mira Mar—you might begin to think you have culinary prospects, that this is what you have been waiting for in Belize. But these thoughts should be put to rest, since P.G. is not a culinary kind of place but a town of stifling, bare-bones eateries serving strangely cooked food.

One bright spot on the restaurant horizon can be found at **Traveller's Inn**, a small, airy motel near the bus station. Crisp linens and fresh flowers top the tables, and an air conditioner chases away the sweltering heat. Tender grilled steaks, saucy chicken and fresh seafood are the bill of fare, and the accompanying vegetables and salads are crisp and flavorful. ~ José Maria Nunez Street, Punta Gorda; 72-22568. MODERATE.

The area around San Antonio boasts a number of hidden swimming holes and waterfalls that are virtually undiscovered by tourists.

For breakfast, stop by **Sea Front Inn**. The third-floor restaurant has handcrafted cedar and rosewood tables and glass windows that let you see the sea. The menu focuses on in-season tropical fruit, though feel free to order the usual bacon and eggs or pancakes. Dinner and lunch are buffet-style and are available only to groups staying as guests. ~ Northern end of Punta Gorda; 72-22716. MODERATE.

Punta Caliente is a sure bet for Belizean food, fast, cheap, available at all hours of the day. Not to mention it's well-prepared and tastes good. Choose from Garifuna and Creole specialties such as cassava bread, stew chicken and stew beans, fish filet in coconut milk, fried whole snapper with lime, or—for the diehard

American in the crowd—hamburgers and ham sandwiches. ~ 108 Jose Maria Nunez Street, Punta Gorda; 72-22561. BUDGET.

The menu's not limited at the **Mira Mar**, where you can order anything from beefsteak, pork chops and sweet-and-sour pork to baked pigeon, fried rice and seashell soup. P.G.'s best-known Asian restaurant comes with air conditioning and a vagabond motif of colored beads, tourist photos of China and folding metal chairs. ~ 95 Front Street, Punta Gorda; 72-22033. MODERATE.

Your only real shopping possibility is the Guatemalan market in downtown Punta Gorda. However, the clothing, radios and beach towels sold in the market are better purchased across the border (see Chapter Nine for more information).

SHOPPING

Placencia has great diving and snorkeling, and no lack of guides waiting to take you out. One attraction for divers is that the sheltered waters off the protected inner side of Placencia's sandy spit are frequented by whale sharks, which are completely harmless but up to 30 feet long.

Outdoor Adventures

DIVING & SNORKELING

Don't be surprised if the crew aboard **Kevin Modera Guide Services** stops to catch lunch after leaving the Placencia docks. Once you reach the cayes, they'll cook the catch on the beach while you snorkel surrounding waters. The full-day trips takes up to six snorkelers to various cayes, including Ranguana, Laughing Bird and Tarpun cayes and the Silk Cayes. ~ Placencia Village; 52-23243, or 314-776-3496 in the U.S.

Advanced Diving Dive Shop offers a full lineup of half- and full-day dive and snorkel trips, as well as manatee-watching excursions and beach barbecues. ~ Placencia; 52-34037.

For snorkeling trips from Punta Gorda out to the Snake Cayes and Moho Caye, stop by the **Toledo Visitors Information Center**, which can recommend a guide. ~ Front Street at the wharf, Punta Gorda; 7-22470.

In Southern Belize, you can river fish, flats fish, reef fish and even billfish, if you want some high seas action. The best way to focus on fishing is to stay at a fishing lodge, and there are a couple of possibilities. **Lillpat Sittee River Resort**, 20 miles south of Dangriga, is "dedicated to adventurous explorers and fishermen/women." It rightfully claims its spot as the only full-service resort on the Sittee River, though "resort" is a loose term for simple wood cottages set among riverine forests. Tarpon and snook fishing are superb in the river and in nearby Anderson and Boom Creek lagoons. Permit and bonefish can be caught in the flats and around the cayes, about a half-hour by boat from the lodge. Farther out, on the reef, you can troll for kingfish, wahoo and barracuda. ~

FISHING

◀ HIDDEN

P.O. Box 136, Dangriga; phone/fax 52-07019; www.lillpat.com, e-mail lillpat@btl.net.

Among the angling options at **Kevin Modera Saltwater Fishing** are fly-fishing for tarpon and snook in Placencia Lagoon and the Monkey River; fly-fishing for permit in the Punta Ycacos Lagoon; and rod-and-reel fishing for grouper, king mackerel and barracuda in open water. Modera will also arrange custom tours with overnight camping on area cayes. ~ Placencia; 52-23243, or 314-776-3496 in the U.S.

For a list of reputable fishing guides in Seine Bight, call the **Seine Bight Tour Guide Association**. ~ 52-33583 or 52-33515.

In Punta Gorda, the **Toledo Visitors Information Center** can recommend local guides with boats. ~ Front Street at the wharf, Punta Gorda; 72-22531.

KAYAKING & No one does Belize sea kayaking like **Slickrock Adventures**. The
CANOEING Utah-based outfitter runs multiday trips from its private camp on Long Caye, 35 miles offshore from Dangriga, and incorporates kayaking with diving, snorkeling and windsurfing. If the waves are high enough, you'll even have a chance to "kayak surf." ~ Long Caye; P.O. Box 1400, Moab, UT 84532, 800-390-5715, fax 435-259-6996 in the U.S.; www.slickrock.com, e-mail slick rock@slickrock.com.

▼▼▼▼▼▼▼▼▼▼ If what you seek in Southern Belize is sheer adventure
Transportation and the flexibility to reach remote villages and ruins on your own, consider driving a car. The **Southern High-**
CAR way is in fairly good shape except for 12 miles of dirt road along the way from Placencia to Punta Gorda—just enough to give you an idea of what the whole Southern Highway was like a few years ago. Travel off the main highway is another matter entirely and, in the rainy season, can be too much for even the toughest four-wheel-drive vehicle.

AUTHOR FAVORITE

Dave Vernon, co-owner of **Toadal Adventures**, told me he chose the name "because it was something that would get people's attention." What's really getting local attention, though, are Dave's superbly run tours of Southern Belize, including a "Mangrove Ecology Paddle" through Placencia waters, with a good chance to see manatees and dolphins. Or, if you want something a little more strenuous, sign up for the sea kayaking and snorkeling tour to the inner cayes off Placencia. Overnight camping is an option. ~ Located at Deb & Dave's Last Resort, Placencia; 52-33207, fax 52-33334; www.toadaladventure.com, e-mail debanddave@btl.net.

The time of year will actually determine your route south. From Belize City to Dangriga, for instance, you can take the shorter, 77-mile drive in dry season, angling west from Belize City on the **Western Highway** to Mile Post 31, then south on the dirt **Coastal Highway** to Gales Point and then Dangriga. This "highway" is unpaved, however, so in the rainy season, you'll have to make the 107-mile trip, following the paved Western Highway all the way to the paved **Hummingbird Highway** near Belmopan, then heading south among steep, rainforest-clad hills for about three hours. The Hummingbird is probably an hour or more faster than the Coastal Highway. From Dangriga, it's another hour and a half on the Southern Highway to Placencia, and about the same distance farther on to Punta Gorda.

AIR

Maya Island Airways has the most frequent air service to the airstrips at **Dangriga**, **Placencia** and **Punta Gorda**. Otherwise, check with Tropic Airways, which also flies puddle hoppers around Southern Belize. Be aware that the farther south you're traveling, the more stops you're likely to make (in other words, planes bound for Punta Gorda will stop in Dangriga and Placencia).

CAR RENTALS

In Placencia, pick up a set of wheels from **Westwind Auto Rentals**. ~ Located in the Westwind Hotel; 52-23255.
For car rentals from Belize City, see Chapter Five.

BUS

The **Z-Line** has the best and most frequent service from Belize City to Southern Belize. You'll spend much of the eight- to ten-hour trip crowded among Garifunas and Mexican orange pickers while punta rock honks and clangs over a loudspeaker. Still, the bus trip only costs one-fourth as much as flying. ~ Magazine Road, Belize City; 22-73937.
James Bus Service travels the Punta Gorda area, and has service to Belize City. ~ Punta Gorda; 72-22049.

Addresses & Phone Numbers

Emergency for Police, Fire and Ambulance ~ 911
Dangriga Police Station ~ 52-22022
Placencia Police Station ~ 52-23129
   Seine Bight Police Station ~ 52-24022
   Punta Gorda Police Station ~ 72-22022
   Placencia Medical Center ~ 52-24004
Toledo Visitors Information Center ~ Front Street at the wharf,
   Punta Gorda; 72-22531
Belize Tourism Board ~ 22-31913 in Belize City

NINE

Side Trips from Belize

Belize is part of a much larger area, known these days as the Mundo Maya, unified by the remnants of the most advanced civilization in pre-Columbian America. The Mundo Maya also takes in all of Guatemala and the Mexican states of Yucatán, Quintana Roo, Campeche and Chiapas, as well as parts of northern Honduras and El Salvador. Accidents of history and arbitrary borders through trackless jungle have enabled remarkably different cultures to evolve in the Maya lands beyond the boundaries of Belize. If you find yourself enchanted by Belize's tropical wilderness, ancient ruins and present-day indigenous Maya people—and assuming you have plenty of time—you may wish to explore beyond Belize. This chapter looks at the areas that lie a short distance over the Mexican and Guatemalan borders. For complete information on other areas of the Mundo Maya, consult *Hidden Cancún and the Yucatán* and *Hidden Guatemala*, both published by Ulysses Press, from which the material in this chapter is excerpted.

If you proceed beyond Corozal, Belize's northern border town, you'll cross the bridge over the Río Hondo and enter Mexico near Chetumal. Although the small city is the capital of the state of Quintana Roo, which also includes Cancún, the biggest tourist destination in Mexico, Chetumal sees almost no tourist trade. Instead, its economy focuses on the business of government and the flow of Belizeans who cross the border to shop. (You know why they do if you've looked for any kind of manufactured goods other than T-shirts in Belize.) Yet inland from Chetumal the rainforest shrouds a series of extraordinary archaeological sites that few travelers ever see.

If you choose to venture beyond the west of Belize, you'll find a badly beaten dirt road that punches into the ever-darkening well of Guatemala's vast northern jungle known as El Petén, past great guanacaste trees filled with the chatter of monkeys and sapodilla trees scarred by the machetes of *chicleros*, to Tikal, the most splendid of all cities in the Maya world. The lofty kingdom of Tikal rears up from the depths of North America's largest rainforest like some ferocious giant, its proud pyramids appearing to float above the dark green ceiling of the jungle. Anyone seeing Tikal for the first, or even the fifth, time will realize it is one of the true wonders of the world. No other Maya ruin boasts such majestic architecture and a setting that captures the imagination and won't let go. And if you want to experience primeval rainforest up close, Tikal is one of the best places on earth to do it.

On the southern fringes of Belize lies the threshold to a vastly different Guatemala, a paradox of paradisiac rivers and rainforests and villages virtually unchanged for 200 years, backing up to vast banana plantations, hot and dirty ports and squatters shacks—the fruits of 20th-century enterprise. From the locked-in-time Río Dulce and village of Livingston, not far from the Belize coast, through the magical Río Dulce National Park and mammoth Lake Izabal to the tough-and-tumble town of Puerto Barrios, this is a land of contrasts, and of extremely rewarding adventures.

Whether you choose to take the southern side trip from Belize, the western foray to Tikal or the northern expedition into Mexico, you should allow several days in each region.

There is so much to see and absorb and ponder—and distances are deceptively long—that travelers to these areas agree unanimously that they are well worth the effort.

Chetumal Area

Chetumal, the capital of Quintana Roo at the edge of Belize, is probably Mexico's nicest border town. The bus trip there from the northern Belize town of Corozal is inexpensive and short in distance, though it can take a while to clear Mexican immigration. You'll need your passport and will receive a tourist card upon entering Mexico, which you'll surrender when you leave. Belizean car rental agencies won't authorize you to drive their vehicles into Mexico, but there are numerous car rental agencies at the Chetumal airport, where rates are considerably lower than in Belize, and many hotels have travel desks where you can arrange to have a rental delivered to you.

On the north shore of the mouth of the Río Hondo, which defines the border between Quintana Roo and Belize, Chetumal is slowly casting off its former isolation and its shady past as a smugglers' haven by developing into a modern free port where imports of all sorts of foreign goods and exports of hardwoods from the nearby jungle pass through. Chetumal's 100,000 inhabitants include many white-collar government workers and other educated professionals who give the city a corporate edge and create a daily hustle and bustle downtown. The city has a large Lebanese ethnic minority but few Maya residents.

SIGHTS

Opened in 1998, Chetumal's **Museo de la Cultura Maya** features fewer stone sculptures but lots more high-tech multimedia gimmickry than other archaeological museums in the region. One highlight is a flight simulation featuring bird's-eye views of major Maya sites across the Yucatán, Belize, Guatemala and Honduras. Other exhibits vividly demonstrate the complexities of Classic Maya society and religion. Admission. ~ Avenida de los Héroes between Avenidas Colón and Gandhi; 983-832-6383.

Across Avenida de los Héroes from the Mercado Nuevo stands the Centro Cultural de las Bellas Artes, housing the **Museo de la Ciudad**. This tiny museum would be utterly unimpressive except for the marvelous model of Chetumal as it appeared in the 1920s. The wooden storefronts and many old-fashioned houses are exact miniature reproductions copied from old photographs. The model was built entirely by a local artisan named (no kidding) Luís Reinhardt McLiberty. Admission. ~ Avenida de las Héroes 68; no phone.

Take an eight-block walk south along **Avenida de los Héroes**, the city's original main street. There's low-budget shopping galore, but very little of the old-time Caribbean architecture McLiberty memorialized in his model. Chetumal seems as newly built as downtown Cancún. Most of the downtown area was destroyed by Hurricane Juanita in 1955 and quickly rebuilt in concrete. Keep an eye out and you'll spot a few older historic buildings here and there.

Avenida de los Héroes passes the **Palacio del Gobierno**, or State Capitol, the largest building in the city that isn't a hotel. Then you arrive at the waterfront, where a pleasant *malecón* curves along Boulevard Bahía, following the contours of the bay. A *balneario,* or bathing resort, northeast of the square provides swimming facilities but no beach. In a town full of statues, the most arresting is the **Alegoría de Mestizaje**, a sculpted Indian woman, Spanish man and their children, representing the first *mestizos*. ~ Avenida de los Héroes near Avenida Mahatma Gandhi.

The city of Chetumal forms a largely imaginary dividing line between the Bahía de Chetumal, which curves south through Belize to the point of Ambergris Cay, and the Bahía de San José, which reaches north into the jungle heartland parallel to Laguna de Bacalar. The northern half of Bahía de San José has been set aside by the government as the **Chetumal Manatee Refuge**. Travel agencies in the city's better hotels can arrange boat excursions to the refuge, where endangered West Indian manatees gather in the bay to take advantage of its thick underwater vegetation and mix of freshwater and saltwater.

Newly opened to the public after a 1997 restoration project, the archaeological zone of **Oxtankah** served as a major Maya seaport for at least 12 centuries. Archaeologists believe it was the seat of a kingdom once governed by Gonzalo Guerrero, one of the two castaways who were the first Spaniards to set foot on the Mexican mainland in 1511, who became a Maya military leader and led the resistance against the conquistadores. Impressive

Three-Day Getaway

Tantalizing Tikal

Day 1 • From Belize City, fly to **Flores, Guatemala** (page 253). From the airport, it's about an hour's drive by shuttle van to the **Tikal Inn** (page 263). Note: The inn is the best lodging in Tikal National Park but still somewhat rustic. If comfort and air conditioning are important to you, stay in El Remate at the **Westin Camino Real Tikal** (page 264).

• From the Tikal Inn, you can easily take an afternoon tour into the park for an introduction to the marvels of Tikal.

Day 2 • Rise early and be at **Tikal National Park** (page 251) by sunrise to enjoy a surreal jungle moment. Spend the day exploring the central city as well as venturing to outlying ruins.

• Return to your lodge for dinner before being lulled to sleep by the sounds of the Tikal jungle.

Day 3 • Take a shuttle to Flores and fly back to Belize City, or return home. If you have a late afternoon flight, consider stopping in Flores for lunch and a stroll around the historic island.

stairways surround a central plaza and cenote at this medium-sized site. There are also ruins of a Spanish church believed to have been the oldest church in the Maya region. Admission. ~ 16 kilometers north of Chetumal. Take the Carretera Calderitas, which turns off Route 307/186 just west of Chetumal, through the village of Calderitas, and continue about five more kilometers on the paved road that follows the shore of Chetumal Bay.

Pretty and peaceful **Laguna Milagros**, little sister of Bacalar, lies about 12 kilometers west of Chetumal off Route 186. Little restaurants fringe its grassy, palm-shaded shores.

Few visitors stay long in Chetumal, preferring to see the real wonder of southern Quintana Roo: **Kohunlich**. The ruins are reached via Route 186, the nearly deserted highway that crosses the southern limits of the Yucatán from Chetumal to the big highway junction at Escárcega, Campeche, 270 kilometers away. Outside of Chetumal, farms hug the highway but soon become smaller and more scattered as the forest closes in. The turnoff to the marvelously obscure ancient Maya site of Kohunlich lies 61 kilometers west of Chetumal, and from there it is a ten-kilometer trip down a side road to the ruins. Admission.

Kohunlich was built over a long timespan, with older temples dating back to the Early Classic period (A.D. 300–600) buried beneath larger, later structures built in Late Classic times (A.D. 600–900). The rough stone structures of Kohunlich were stuccoed over with layers of the thick, sticky clay that underlies most of southern Quintana Roo. The temples were almost certainly covered with stucco sculptures that have been washed away by centuries of tropical storms. Not only the buildings were covered with clay; the central **Great Plaza** and a series of reservoirs downhill were also paved to form a giant water catchment that channeled runoff from summer rains into an artificial lake to sustain the community through the dry season.

Deep in the palm forest stands Kohunlich's crowning glory, the Early Classic **Pyramid of the Masks**, where six huge, impeccably detailed and remarkably humanized sculptures of Kinich Ahau, the "Sun-eyed Lord," line both sides of the pyramid stairway. The masks were part of the highly ornamented stucco facade of an early temple that was buried within a larger, round-cornered pyramid similar to the one at Uxmal, protecting them from the elements for more than 1400 years. A thrill for any Mayaphile, the masks stand about six feet high, their bulging tongues, handlebar mustaches and saucer eyes forming a haunting image in the dim light filtered through protective thatch roofs. The eyes of the masks contain the hieroglyph *kin,* meaning sun, day or time.

Exploration of the Kohunlich archaeological site is still in its early stages. A 1991 dig found royal burials at the foot of another temple platform here, and a satellite survey has disclosed about

Side Trips from Belize

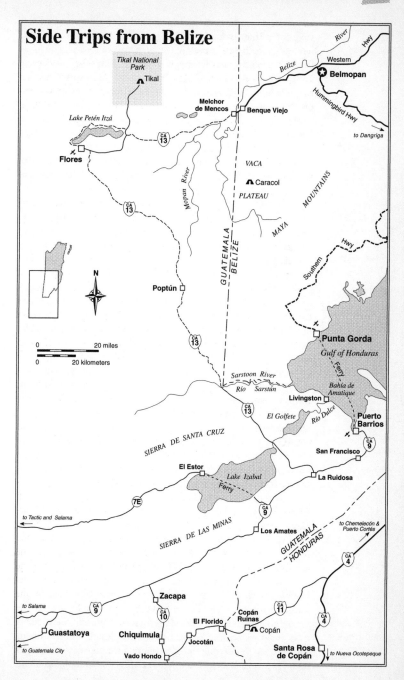

Tikal National Park

▲ Tikal

Lake Petén Itzá

✕ Flores

Melchor de Mencos

Benque Viejo

Belize River

Western Hwy

★ Belmopan

Hummingbird Hwy

to Dangriga

VACA PLATEAU

▲ Caracol

Mopan River

MAYA MOUNTAINS

GUATEMALA BELIZE

Southern Hwy

CA 13

CA 13

Poptún

CA 13

N

0   20 miles

0   20 kilometers

✕ Punta Gorda

Gulf of Honduras

Sarstoon River

Río Sarstún

CA 13

El Golfete

Livingston

Río Dulce

Bahía de Amatique

Ferry

Puerto Barrios

CA 9

SIERRA DE SANTA CRUZ

San Francisco

El Estor

Lake Izabal

Ferry

La Ruidosa

CA 9

7E

to Tactic and Salama

SIERRA DE LAS MINAS

Los Amates

GUATEMALA HONDURAS

to Chemelecón & Puerto Cortés

CA 4

to Salama

CA 9

Zacapa

CA 10

El Florido

Copán Ruinas

▲ Copán

CA 11

CA 4

Guastatoya

Chiquimula

Jocotán

to Nueva Ocotepeque

to Guatemala City

Vado Hondo

Santa Rosa de Copán

200 mounds similar to the Pyramid of the Masks hidden by the surrounding jungle. Today we can only speculate as to what additional wonders they may contain.

HIDDEN ▶ If Kohunlich gets your imagination racing, there's an even more undiscovered Maya site nearby. To reach the ruins of **Dzibanché**, follow a paved road marked to Morocoy, which turns northward off Route 307 less than a kilometer east of the road to Kohunlich. The pavement deteriorates before the road reaches the village of Morocoy, 30 kilometers from the highway. Not far beyond the village, a potholed hard-surface road to the right is marked to Dzibanché. The Classic-era city was inhabited from about A.D. 300 to 900 and covered 26 square miles. There are two main pyramids, at least one of which contains two mysterious royal tombs. One of the tombs has been excavated but is not open to visitors. Several smaller temples are also of special interest. The Temple of the Lintels still contains the original carved wood lintels (the horizontal beams across the tops of doorways) some of which date back almost 1300 years—a rare discovery in the Maya world. Another structure, the Building of the Captives, is festooned with hieroglyphs and has a big monster mask beside its staircase. Though archaeologists only began studying this site in 1993, restoration is in full swing, and by the time you visit you may find it cleaned up to join the ranks of "new" ancient ruins.

A marked side road that branches off the Dzibanché road takes you to the site of **Kinichná**, which has been partly excavated but not restored. This unique site consists of a single acropolis that was among the most massive structures in the southern Yucatán. It was built over a span of more than 600 years, and the differences in stonework between levels are striking. The ground-level platform, dating to around A.D. 100, is not tall but covers a vast area. On top of it is a tall, classic-style pyramid flanked by smaller temples. From the top of this pyramid, a very steep stairway takes you up to another pyramid, on top of which is a temple that contained two royal tombs. Admission.

Returning to the main highway and continuing westward on narrow, two-lane Route 307 for 35 miles will bring you to a series of other archaeological sites including Xpujil, Chicanná and Becán near the highway, and Río Bec, Hormiguero and Calakmul deeper in the forest. The truck-stop village of Xpujil, across the road from the ancient ruin of the same name, is the only town along the otherwise unpopulated route. Its population has grown to about a thousand and continues growing rapidly, since the government is actively encouraging homesteaders. Most of the people living here are Chol Maya who have recently moved here from the lowlands of Chiapas, where overpopulation has joined forces with traditional slash-and-burn farming methods to destroy vast areas of the Lacandón rainforest. Unlike other Maya people of the Yucatán Peninsula, most are evangelical Christians. A raw, frontier excitement pervades the area—as well as a nagging sense of impending environmental disaster. Given the government's decision to bring population into the area, whether the largest remaining rainforest in Mexico will be cleared by family farmers or preserved depends on whether the villagers can develop other sources of income—particularly ecotourism.

Certainly the most "undiscovered" destination in the Yucatán today, Xpujil is in the midst of a concentration of large, little-known Maya ruins from the Río Bec culture. These elaborately decorated ruins hold great interest for archaeologists, but until quite recently they were too far away from modern civilization for many travelers to visit. In 1993, the local roadside restaurant built half a dozen wooden cabañas out back, so for the first time visitors can spend a few days exploring the ruins and the surrounding rainforest.

Several of the largest Río Bec ruins are just off Route 186. Approaching the Xpujil area from the west, the first ruin is **Chicanná**. The name *Chicanná* means House of the Serpent Mouth, which is also the name of the most completely restored structure at the site. The facade of this temple is a Chenes-style monster mask almost exactly like the one at Hochob, which was

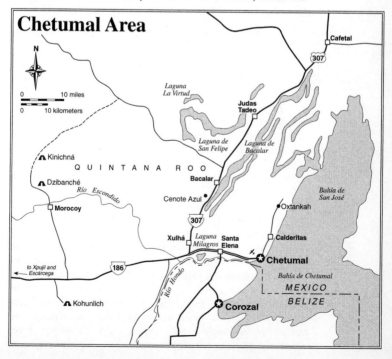

INTERNET TOUR
El Mundo Maya

The Internet offers a wealth of information on other destinations just beyond Belize's borders. Lacking the objectivity, selectivity and portability of a printed guidebook, it nonetheless offers dazzling color photos and so many sites—thousands, in fact—that you can spend countless hours getting in the mood for your trip while daydreaming your way through cyberspace. The following sites were kindly contributed by Richard Harris, author of this book's companion volumes, *Hidden Guatemala* and *Hidden Cancún and the Yucatán*, as good starting points.

EL MUNDO MAYA Soon after the governments of Belize, Mexico, Guatemala and Honduras mounted their joint effort to promote tourism throughout El Mundo Maya (the Maya world), *Mundo Maya Magazine* began as a slick, colorful publication about the region's archaeology, nature, history, handicrafts and people. The online version, with a rich archive of articles on the region, is now on the web at www.mayadiscovery.com/ing. Planeta.com, another online magazine with more articles, many links to other sites, and an emphasis on ecotourism in the region, is located at www.planeta.com/ecotravel/maya/maya.html.

THE YUCATÁN Websites in Mexico tend to be more commercial than informative, and there's little solid information available on the southern part of the Yucatan Peninsula near the Belizean border. Search for archaeological articles using the names of specific Maya ruins such as Kohunlich and Calakmul. The best information available on the border city

separated from these southern sites by more than 39 kilometers of uninhabited jungle. Most archaeologists believe the mask represents Itzamná, the Maya sun god. Admission. ~ Off Route 186, 500 meters south of the highway.

Although Chicanná was not discovered until 1966, it has been the focus of three major excavation and restoration projects, the latest begun in 1991. Today, four temple groups can be seen. They are connected by trails that lead through dark forests under a dense canopy of leaves. Several temples have monster-mask fronts as well as tall decorative roof combs.

Becán, two and a half kilometers east of Chicanná, was inhabited from A.D. 550 to 1200. Temples at Becán once stood as much as 115 feet tall. Long stairways reach the tops of two pyramids and command a view of the forest for miles around. The ruins of ancient Xpujil thrust above the treetops about four miles

of Chetumal is found on the website of Belize's Corozal Community College, www.corozal.com.

GUATEMALA   Thanks to governmental support for its rapidly growing tourist industry, Guatemala rivals Belize when it comes to web savvy. One reasonable starting place is the official site of INGUAT (the Guatemalan Institute of Tourism), which is full of general tourist information but has few links to other sites; it's at www.tradepoint.org.gt/travelguate.html. A website created by the University of Georgia contains more information than you'll ever want to know, from business and economic news to poetry and recipes, including links to all Guatemalan newspapers, at mars.cropsoil.uga.edu/trop-ag/guatem.htm. For an American expatriate's perspective on Guatemala, check out www.go2guatemala.com or subscribe to their online e-mail newsletter, Guatemala Lifestyles, by e-mailing gtlnu-subscribe@topica.com. Tikal is the subject of many websites, most of them photographic showcases. The coolest of all is at www.destination360.com/tikal.htm, where you'll find a tour of the site complete with QuickTime mini-movies and sound effects. Also impressive is the large-format helicopter view of Tikal at www.maya-art-books.org/html/tikalaerial.html.

HONDURAS   The worldwide web scene is a hodgepodge. The place to start is www.honduras.net, a commercial site that features a photo tour of Copán and links to more than 100 sites that range from amateurish to academic. The coolest is the virtual reality view that lets you "walk around" in the Copán Museum with a mouse click, found at www.maya-archaeology.org/html/copanm.html.

to the east. The most unusual feature of Becán is the mile-and-a-quarter-long moat that once surrounded the city and is still visible today. All the Río Bec cities were built with defensive features much like those of medieval European castles, suggesting that wars plagued the region during the early part of the Classic period. The political situation seems to have stabilized eventually; around the end of the 7th century A.D., the people of Becán started using their moat as a trash pit. Most of the buildings that stand here today date from the 8th and 9th centuries, when the region was at peace. A dozen temples surrounding three large ceremonial plazas have been excavated and stabilized or restored since the mid-1970s, and the work is still going on. Admission.

The ancient city of **Xpujil**, believed by many archaeologists to have been the capital of the region in the Late Classic period, is on the outskirts of the present-day village. Maya people have continuously inhabited Xpujil since around A.D. 400. Although an archaeological survey conducted in the 1970s shows that the city of Xpujil covered an area of several square miles and had at least four large building groups, so far only the structures of **Group I** have been excavated and consolidated. They are one of the best examples of the architectural feature that is unique to the Río Bec zone: massive towers disguised as pyramids with as many as 12 tiers. Stairways too steep to climb lead to false temples adorned with stucco masks and lofty roof combs. The ancient Maya used a technique known to modern movie-set designers as "forced perspective" to make Xpujil's towers look much taller than they actually were. Admission.

Between Becán and Xpujil, the highway crosses a narrow strip of protected rainforest that connects the two vast expanses of the **Calakmul Biosphere Reserve** that lie a few miles north and south of the highway. The reserve is intended to save a portion of the Petén rainforest on the Mexican side of the border, where so much of it has already been burned off for farming. Established under UNESCO's Man and the Biosphere program, the reserve adjoins Guatemala's Maya Biosphere Reserve north of Tikal National Park and Belize's smaller, hard-to-reach Río Bravo Conservation Area on the northwest border. Supporters of the Mundo Maya concept, hoping to improve the region's economy by developing ecotourism, envision the three reserves as a single international park, which they refer to as the Maya Peace Park.

At the reserve's northern boundary is the tiny village of X-Kanhá. Several sites at least as impressive as Chicanná, Becán and Xpujil are found in the southern part of the reserve. Chol Maya homesteaders who live along the reserve's boundary have been recruited to serve as caretakers, accompanying anybody who goes to the ruins. Travel is limited on the roads south of Xpujil, which run all the way to Guatemala and are regularly patrolled by the Mexican army. In good weather, a passenger car can usually manage the roads to Hormiguero and the Río Bec sites, though few signs mark the way through the maze of little back roads along the edge of the reserve. You can save wear and tear on your rental car and your nerves by taking a **guided tour** with one of the guides who offer ruins trips from the local hotels and from Rancho Encantado on Laguna Bacalar, about 70 miles to the east.

HIDDEN ▶ Among the best adventures going in the Yucatán today is a guided all-day trip to **Río Bec**, which is only about 15 kilometers south of Xpujil but takes more than two hours to reach on a narrow four-wheel-drive road through the jungle. The archaeological zone sprawls nearly 20 square miles, completely overgrown by jungle, and the ruined structures are difficult to find without a knowledgeable guide. Río Bec is not a single site but a series of at least 20—some a single building, others a group of temples around a central plaza—five of which are worth the formidable effort required to see them. Trying to see all five sites on the same trip is not realistic, however, because it takes about eight hours to hike the forest trails that link the main sites. Any daytrip to Río Bec should include **Río Bec B**, which has a temple with a tall roof comb flanked by two nearly 55-foot-tall towers disguised as pyramids. It is the only structure at Río Bec that has been completely cleared and stabilized. Of the other possible side trips, the best in my opinion is **Rio Bec N**, where the central temple looks almost exactly like the one at Rio Bec B did when archaeologists found it in 1973.

A shorter daytrip into the biosphere reserve, involving almost as much rough road driving but less hiking, is to **Hormiguero**, ◀ HIDDEN

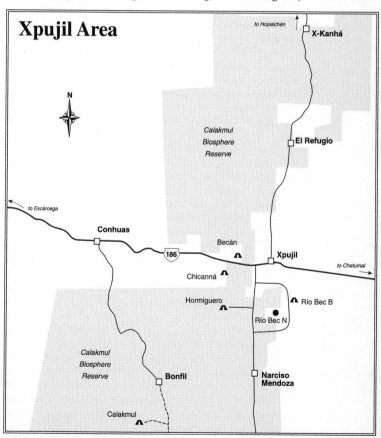

Xpujil Area

where there are two temples. **Structure II**, nearest to the road, is a favorite among archaeologists because it combines Río Bec–style fake pyramids and Chenes-style monster-mouth facades more completely than any other ruin in the region. A short trail through the forest brings you to **Structure V**, a small but elaborately decorated temple on top of a mound that was once a small pyramid. The tunnels in the base of the mound, from which Hormiguero (Ant Hill) got its name, were dug by looters before Carnegie Institute archaeologists located the site in 1933.

HIDDEN ▶ A small palace and steam baths known as the **Bird Mask Temple** illustrates just how much must still await discovery in this dense forest. It was first seen in 1967 by an archaeologist who, unfortunately, was himself lost. He photographed the temple with its ornate facade and tall roof comb and published the photograph along with an account of his discovery, estimating the location to be about 25 miles southwest of Xpujil.

Twenty-four years later, a local woodcutter told archaeologists that his nine-year-old son had found an old stone house in the woods. When the archaeologists saw it, they realized they had rediscovered the missing Bird Mask Temple. It is within walking distance north of the village of Xpujil—and only about 750 yards from the main highway. But you still need a guide to find it.

HIDDEN ▶ The Calakmul Biosphere Reserve is named for the ancient Maya city of **Calakmul**, located about 33 miles southwest of Río Bec in the heart of the reserve and reached via a paved but badly potholed one-lane road that leaves Route 186 at the tiny settlement of Conhuas, 35 miles west of Xpujil. You pay a fee at the turnoff for the use of the road into the reserve, and another fee to enter the archaeological site itself. Driving to Calakmul is half the adventure. From the turnoff at the main highway, expect the drive to take between two and three hours. It's unlikely that you'll see another vehicle—more likely that you'll see a coatimundi or forest fox dash across the road, or a tree full of oropéndolas or toucans. Leave your car in the small parking lot at the end of the road and walk for a kilometer along an ancient Maya *sacbé* through the forest. Suddenly you reach a clearing and find yourself surrounded by the pyramids and palace of Calakmul.

Although Calakmul was discovered in the 1930s, excavations did not begin until 1984. Only then did archaeologists begin to realize how vast the site really was. It covers 27 square miles, and more than 7000 structures have been identified there so far. Experts now believe that Calakmul was the largest city in the Classic Maya world; population estimates range from 60,000 to as many as 200,000 inhabitants at its peak between A.D. 600 and 800. Hints about Calakmul's history are only now beginning to surface, and archaeologists now believe that it was the "capital"

Pepsin and Poisonwood

In the Maya language, *bec* means "elm"—one of the nearly 700 tree species that make up the forest around Río Bec and Hormiguero. In both areas, the diversity of tree and plant life in the practically primeval jungle is as fascinating as the ruins themselves. While some of the region's flora is the same as that found in old woodlands of the southeastern United States, much is tropical and as exotic as anything you could hope for in a rainforest experience. One tree that is encountered frequently—trails are laid out to lead to them—is the sapodilla, an economic mainstay for villagers in the region, who tap it for chicle; its fruit, which has a sweet taste similar to *flan* (custard), is a regional delicacy as well as a favorite food of spider monkeys and coatimundis. Another cash product harvested in the local forests is pepsin, which is used as a digestive aid in remedies such as Pepto-Bismol. In earlier times, the most lucrative tree in the region was the lofty *caoba*, or mahogany. Hundreds of thousands of these rainforest giants were cut in the southern Yucatán Peninsula and Central America, shipped to Europe and sold there for as much as $30,000 per tree. Today, though they are rarely found in parts of the forest that can be reached by road, great stands of mahogany still exist deep in the biosphere reserve, where they are protected by law.

Besides its *cohune* palm trees, palmettos and myriad climbing and hanging vines, much of the exotic look of Campeche forests can be attributed to their colorful orchids, bromeliads and other epiphytes, which grow in the branches of trees and never touch the soil. But not only small plants grow in the high branches. The tiny seeds of the strangler fig tree are deposited by birds in the high branches of other trees, and by dropping fine tendrils to the forest floor, they take root. The tendrils thicken to become a whitish trunk that wraps around the host tree, engulfs it and, over a period of about 20 years, kills it.

The Maya people who make their homes in this forest believe that the lush environment provides a natural solution for every problem encountered there. The *chechén*, or poisonwood tree, and the *chacah*, or gumbo limbo tree, are a commonly cited example. The poisonwood tree can be spotted by the black sap that oozes from its trunk and exposed portions of its roots; the poison, which causes instant, painful burns to the skin and can be fatal if it touches an open cut, is in the sap. Fortunately, the peeling, copper-colored bark of the gumbo limbo contains an antidote for the poison. Local people believe—and it appears to be true—that a gumbo limbo tree grows within a few feet of every poisonwood tree. The gumbo limbo also provides the Maya with a powerful natural antibiotic used to prevent infections and cure certain fevers.

of an alliance of cities that also included El Mirador on the Guatemalan border and Uaxatún just north of Guatemala's Tikal National Park. Together, the allied cities vied with Tikal for political, military and economic control of the Petén rainforest. At least 118 stelae have been found here so far—more than at any other Maya site. Many have been defaced, and centuries of erosion plus decades of acid rain have obliterated the faces of many of them; but the hieroglyphs along the outside edges of the monuments remain legible and may one day provide the most detailed historical record of the Classic era in the rainforest that lies at the center of ancient Maya civilization.

References to Calakmul have been identified in hieroglyphs at many other sites, including Palenque and Yaxchilán in Chiapas, and Naranjo, Caracol, Piedras Negras, El Peru and Dos Pilas in Guatemala. In 1994, scientists discovered a 10th-century royal tomb containing a body mummified using a method previously unknown in the Maya world and similar to the technique used in classical Egypt. In 1985 the vaulted crypt of a 7th-century noble was found beneath one of the many temples. It contained 2000 pieces of jade, the most precious of Mayan treasures, in the form of jewelry and an elaborate mosaic burial mask.

At other deep forest cities like Tikal, the central plaza is cleared and sometimes planted with grass. But at Calakmul, a minimum-impact approach keeps the central plaza covered with tall trees and thick vegetation. The forest has been cleared for only a few feet away from the partially restored pyramids and palaces, making them hard to photograph. From the ground, a wide-angle lens can't take in the immensity of the largest pyramid—at 175-feet, one of the tallest in the Maya world. To find great photo possibilities, you have to climb to the top, where you get a sense of the ancient city's size and layout as you look across the sea of greenery at many more unrestored pyramid mounds, each a temptation to hike farther into the tall forest festooned with orchids and teeming with wildlife. Don't lose sight of the fact that the long drive back to Xpujil is much longer in the dark, so watching the sunset from one of those amazing temples three or four kilometers up a jungle trail is a temptation you may want to pass up.

LODGING   Unless you're a fan of hot, bustling cities, you probably won't want to stay long in Chetumal. For those who do need a bed for the night, there are several low-cost, no-frills hotels. No matter what time of year you visit, Chetumal is steamy, so go for a room with air conditioning.

The best place to hang your hat is the somewhat classy **Hotel Los Cocos**, where visiting politicians stay. The peaceful interior garden, with its swimming pool and gardens dotted with white furniture, gives respite from the city. Good-sized, the 80 guest rooms have been redone with tirol (textured) walls, contemporary decor, televisions, phones, small terraces and seating areas. It's not what you'd call fancy, but maids do leave candies on your pillow when they turn down the bed in the evening, and a full complement of bath amenities is provided, including tiny bottles of imported French cologne. Air conditioning. ~ Avenida Héroes 134, Chetumal; 983-832-0544, fax 983-832-0920. MODERATE.

A pleasant alternative is the reasonably priced **Hotel Caribe Princess**, a few blocks off the main drag. Its ugly concrete-molded exterior belies a comfortable, friendly interior of plain rooms with carpets, phones and balconies. Air conditioning. ~ Avenida Alvaro Obregón 168, Chetumal; 983-832-0520. BUDGET.

The **Hotel Holiday Inn Puerta Maya** looks strangely out of place with its stark modern facade wedged between chaotic storefronts. Inside, things brighten up in the lush atrium decorated with fountains and a swimming pool. The 61 rooms are sterile but thankfully clean, with servibars and televisions. Air conditioning. ~ Avenida de los Héroes 171, Chetumal; 983-835-0401, fax 983-832-0429. DELUXE.

If all you desire is a simple room with small private bath, air-conditioning, TV and a double bed, you'll find it at the 20-room **Hotel Nachancán**, located within walking distance of the public market and the Museo de la Cultura Maya. ~ Calzada Veracruz 379, Chetumal; 983-832-3232. BUDGET.

The most unusual lodging in the area is **Campamento La Pirámide**, a single large, screened camping cabin with a palapa roof located several miles from the village of Tres Garantías in the heart of primary rainforest, part of a Maya chicle-tapping *ejido* owned by the people of Tres Garantías. The daily rate, $100 a night for up to four guests, includes transportation from Chetumal

AUTHOR FAVORITE

A massage on the shore of a still lake, a jacuzzi soak under the stars, a hammock in front of a comfortable cabaña—these are a few of the things I look forward to at **Rancho Encantado**, on the shore of idyllic Laguna de Bacalar. As if that weren't enough, the resort also has a special permit to guide tours to magnificent, little-known Maya ruins (such as nearby El Resbalón, where archaeologists are uncovering and restoring three spectacular hieroglyphic staircases) that are off-limits to the general public. See page 248 for more information.

and meals prepared and served by local Maya women. There's no furniture except a large table, so you need to bring your own sleeping bag or hammock. The people of the *ejido* are looking for outside investors to help expand this humble beginning into an ecotourism resort. Their success or failure may well determine the future of the region: a dozen other *ejidos* in the region are facing imminent decisions about whether to preserve their forest lands in hopes of attracting visitors or to cut them down for timber and so are closely watching the progress of this pilot project. ~ Tres Garantías; for reservations, Avenida Carmen Ochoa de Merino 143, Chetumal; 983-832-9802. BUDGET TO MODERATE.

In an entirely different price range from La Pirámide, the **Explorean Kohunlich** is owned and operated by the Fiesta Americana chain, which runs megaresorts all over Mexico and Latin America. Secluded in the rain forest near the Maya ruins of Kohunlich, the Explorean resembles the luxury jungle lodges found in many parts of Belize but rarely in Mexico. Its 20 palm-thatch luxury cabañas are patterned after traditional Maya homes, build using local construction methods and materials, and decorated with regional furniture and handcrafts. Far less rustic than they appear at first glance, these "huts" come complete with air conditioning and satellite telephones. There's a colorful garden terrace, a swimming pool and a dining room where gourmet meals are served. Nature and archaeology tours, as well as all meals, are included in the room rate. Three-night minimum stay. ~ Carretera Kohunlich; 214-891-3157, 800-950-1363. ULTRA-DELUXE.

On the shore of Laguna de Bacalar, about 25 miles north of Chetumal, **Rancho Encantado** pioneered the concept of ecotourism in southern Quintana Roo when it opened in the early 1980s. The owners have a long-term vision for this place and keep improving it year by year, making it the kind of secret Caribbean hideaway dreams are made of. **Laguna de Bacalar,** a 36-mile-long lake, is also known as Lago de Siete Colores (Lake of Seven Colors) because of the contrasting bands of brilliant green and blue that shimmer like strips of satin in the crystal-clear, placid water. This is the second-largest lake in Mexico (only Lago de Chapala, in Jalisco, is larger). Wild orchids and coconut palms, along with a few private vacation homes and a couple of lodges, dot the lakeshore. The constant breeze across the lake has given Laguna de Bacalar a reputation as one of the most exotic places on earth to go windsurfing. Accommodations at Rancho Encantado are in eight individual casitas with tile floors, hardwood ceilings and furniture handcrafted of mahogany and rattan. Each one has a separate living room and bedroom, a kitchenette, and a patio porch facing onto a carefully groomed lawn and gardens. Fresh fruit can be picked from the orchards. Continental breakfast, lunch and a four-course dinner of freshly caught seafood are included in the rates. The owners also organize environmental and archaeological tours throughout the region, including trips to several Maya ruins that are closed to the public except by permit, such as nearby El Resbalón, where archaeologists are uncovering and restoring three spectacular hieroglyphic staircases. They have also added new spa facilities that include massages next to the water and an open-air jacuzzi surrounded by night-blooming jasmine. ~ Laguna de Bacalar; reservations, P.O. Box 1256, Taos, NM 87571; 505-894-7074 or 800-505-6292; www.encantado. com, e-mail bookings@encantado.com. DELUXE TO ULTRA-DELUXE.

The original Maya name of Laguna de Bacalar meant "Where the Rainbow Is Born."

In the Xpujil region, the **Restaurante y Cabañas El Mirador Maya**, on the west edge of the village, has 14 guest units including thatch-roofed huts with shared baths, rustic tin-roofed cabins and a few motel-style rooms with varnished hardwood trim and modern plumbing. There are no TVs or telephones, but a swimming pool is under construction. ~ Route 186 Km. 159, Xpujil; phone/fax 9-832-3304. BUDGET.

Nearby, the newer, equally basic **Hotel Calak Mul** offers 14 plain rooms situated on a hillside, but not high enough to isolate it from the noise of the truck traffic on the highway. ~ Route 186, Km. 153, Xpujil; 9-832-3304. BUDGET.

The classiest base for exploring the ruins and rainforest of the Calakmul Biosphere Reserve is the **Chicanná Eco Village**. Set well away from the highway and village on a gated side road, this jungle lodge has 28 guest rooms in two-story stucco buildings with palapa roofs. Each unit has a living area and a separate bedroom with a king-size bed or two double beds, and a patio or balcony with a view of the Xpujil ruins. There are no TVs or phones, but the lodge does have a pool and jacuzzi surrounded by lush flower gardens, as well as a full restaurant, coffee shop and bar. Make reservations through the Ramada Inn in Campeche city, which owns and manages the resort. Ceiling fans. ~ Off Route 186, Km. 144 at Zona Arqueológico Chicanná; reservations: 9-816-2233 in Campeche city, fax 9-871-1608; e-mail diro_62@uol.com.mx. DELUXE.

DINING

Chetumal offers a myriad of dining choices at reasonable prices. Start with **Restaurant La Ostra**, off Avenida Héroes near the "Agua Potable" tower. Air conditioned and clean, it serves typical Mexican dishes and a hearty breakfast. ~ Calle Efraím Aguilar 162, Chetumal; 983-832-0452. BUDGET.

A pleasant spot for breakfast or evening coffee, **Café Pérez Quintal**, located adjacent to the Government Palace, is an open-air café facing the tree-filled Parque Central. Here you'll find delicious omelettes, seafood, sandwiches, fruit salads and meat entrées. ~ Edificio 7 de Deciembre 4 at Calle 22 de Enero, Chetumal. BUDGET.

For pizza you cannot go wrong at popular, attractive **Sergio's Pizza**, where the excellent service is second only to the crisp crust. Air conditioned and as sparkling as an English bistro, it is adorned with beautiful stained glass, wood-paneled walls and bottles of pricey liquor lining the bar. Sergio's also features a salad bar, cheese fondue, barbecued ribs and a respectable wine list. ~ Avenida Alvaro Obregón 182, Chetumal; 983-832-2355. BUDGET TO MODERATE.

Next door, under the same ownership, is the modern and elegant **María Restaurante**, a splendid room with an open kitchen, polished tile floors, beamed ceilings and wooden tables and chairs. It serves the best pasta in Chetumal, as well as delightful bean soup, churros, tacos, seafood, steaks and giant goblets of fruity sangria. ~ Avenida Alvaro Obregón, Chetumal; 983-832-0491. BUDGET TO MODERATE.

You can watch your chicken baking through the window of **Pollo Brujo**, where variations on the bird include baked, roasted or barbecued chicken wrapped in a steamy tortilla. ~ Avenida Alvaro Obregón 208, Chetumal; 9-832-2713. BUDGET.

A traveler's friend is the **Super & Restaurant Arcadas**. Open 24 hours, it attracts a local crowd and feels like a sidewalk café with its open walls, ceiling fans and breezy ambience. A large selection of Mexican-style sandwiches is on hand; menus are available in English. ~ Corner of Avenida Héroes and Calle Zaragoza, Chetumal. BUDGET.

Outside of Chetumal, almost all the hotels and lodges have their own dining rooms, and there are few, if any, other restaurant options.

AUTHOR FAVORITE

While **Restaurante Cenote Azul**, with its daily-special seafood menu, is one of the few dining options along the hundred-mile stretch of highway north of Chetumal, the real reason I look forward to chowing down here is the setting—overlooking the Yucatán Peninsula's largest cenote. The restaurant's menagerie of exotic birds makes it worth a stop even if you're not hungry. ~ Route 307; no phone. MODERATE.

Tikal was one of the other great capitals of the
ancient Maya world. Founded as early as 600
B.C., it reached a peak population of about
50,000 a thousand years later and was one of
the largest cities in the Western Hemisphere during the Classic
Period, along with Calukmal and Teotíhuacan in central Mexico.
Tikal was situated in the exact center of the Maya land, and had
close cultural ties to all parts of the region. Many experts believe
the knowledge and ideas that shaped the classic Maya civilization originated in Tikal around A.D. 250, and the abandonment
of Tikal around A.D. 900 coincided with the collapse of high
Maya civilization everywhere.

▼▼▼▼▼▼▼▼▼▼▼▼▼
Tikal National Park
and El Petén

One aspect of Tikal's magic is that it is so hard to reach. What
was once the wealthy and populous centerpiece of the ancient
Maya world is now a remote frontier backwater surrounded by
millions of acres of almost impenetrable rainforest called El Petén.
There is no easy way to get there overland. But it is much faster
to go there from Belize than from southern Guatemala. One reason is that in the early 1980s, Guatemala's government at the
time received international aid to widen and pave the road from
southern Guatemala to El Petén, but the funds were diverted by
corrupt leaders and the road never got built. More recently, in
connection with the present Guatemalan government's agreement to set aside a large part of the Petén rainforest as a UNESCO
Man and Biosphere Reserve, the World Bank pledged new funding to improve the road and stimulate tourism in El Petén—but
the money will not be released until Guatemala convinces the
bank it will take all necessary measures to protect the Petén rainforest from pioneers flocking there to build new settlements and
destroy the forest.

The border crossing between Belize and Guatemala has become much easier in recent years. If you're a U.S. or Canadian
citizen, you will need only your passport, and the formalities are
perfunctory. Although official paperwork and customs procedures may make you wish you'd taken a tour, these problems disappear with a modest cash payment. (The border guards don't really care what's in your baggage; they'd prefer that you pay an
unofficial per-bag fee for a customs sticker.) Citizens of some other
countries—particularly "troubled" countries such as Ireland and
Israel, even though the troubles have nothing to do with
Guatemala—are required to obtain visas in advance from a
Guatemalan embassy or consulate. Check current requirements
by contacting the Embassy of Guatemala in Belize City. ~ 64-A
St. Matthew Street, Belize City; 20-33150.

The road from the Guatemalan border to Tikal is only about
40 miles. Though unpaved, it has recently been widened and is

well graded during the dry season. The occasional banditry that plagued this route a decade ago is no longer a problem. One option is to travel overland to Tikal with a tour arranged from one of the many lodges in Belize's Cayo District (see Chapter Seven). A package tour eliminates potential problems of going it on your own—changing buses at the border, being denied entry if you're in a rental car (which are rarely allowed across the border), being denied a tourist card (or having to pay a generous "tip" for one), trusting taxi drivers to take you all the way to Tikal on the agreed fee, or dealing with Guatemala military officials who may stop you en route to Tikal to check your passport. If you do decide to cross the border on your own, make sure you obtain a visa in advance, either in the United States or Belize.

The easiest way to get to Tikal is by plane, a surprisingly short hop—about 45 minutes—from Belize City. Once you're in the place, you'll be rewarded with a rich tapestry of smooth plateaux and dense rainforest. Notice the difference between the forests in Belize and Guatemala: in Belize, there are but a few tiny pockets of *milpa* farming, but flying over the Petén, you can see vividly the deforestation that is taking place in this environmentally delicate region. Thick rainforest still blankets the ridgelines and hilltops, but each valley is cleared for crops and livestock as fast as a narrow dirt jeep road can penetrate it.

Passenger planes land in Santa Elena on the south shore of Lake Petén Itzá, about an hour's trip by shuttle bus from Tikal National Park. Adjacent to Santa Elena, on an island in Petén Itzá, is the tiny, atmospheric town of Flores. Here you'll find cafés and nightspots where expatriates, backpackers and travelers excitedly engage in "Tikal talk" (as in, what temple they climbed or rare bird they saw that day). You'll also likely hear about the Maya Biosphere Reserve, a 5400-square-mile protected piece of the Petén, home to the Maya city of Uaxactún, once a rival to Tikal and now a remote ruin—but not as remote as Yaxha, a Preclassic to Postclassic Maya city about two and a half hours from Santa Elena on rock-and-washboard roads. Secreted along the shores of deep blue Lake Yaxha, the city has had only minuscule excavations (you can, for instance, climb the great ceremonial center) and remains beautifully entombed in emerald rainforest.

SIGHTS   Most of the Petén's 40,000 residents live in **Santa Elena** and the contiguous town of **San Benito**. Together, the two towns form a frontier boomtown sprawl laced with open sewers and rattling with gas-powered electrical generators. While a modest tourist trade provides income for some area residents, more of them harvest renewable forest products such as chicle gum and pepsin leaves or join crews for oil exploration, the newest threat to the rainforest.

The capital of El Petén, **Flores**, is an island town with just 1500 residents. It's reached by an earthen causeway from Santa Elena, and is a quintessentially quaint little town with an Old World feel to its tangled, claustrophobic streets. Flores is built on the site of Tayasal, the last ancient Maya stronghold to fall to the Spanish empire. Tayasal was visited by Hernán Cortés, conqueror of Mexico, in 1525, but endured unmolested for nearly two centuries before a military expedition captured and razed it in 1697. You can walk all over town in less than an hour. La Ruta Maya Conservation Foundation and George Washington University's Institute of Urban Development Research have developed plans that would encourage the cultivation of Flores as a tourist center complete with houseboat tourist accommodations on Lake Petén Itzá, a regional museum in the abandoned prison building facing the hilltop town square, and even a sewage treatment plant. All this is years in the future, though. For now, Flores is one of Central America's more low-key and isolated frontier towns.

Ask at any restaurant or hotel in the Flores–Santa Elena area and they can probably put you in touch with a guide who will take you on an inexpensive three-hour boat tour of the islands near Flores. Stops on the tour include a group of small temple mounds—all that remains of the old Maya fortress city of **Taya-**

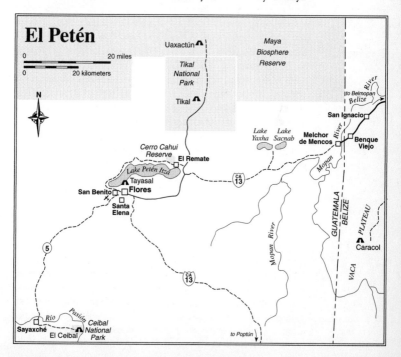

sal—as well as a spot called **La Garrucha**, where you can climb a tall tower, hang from a cable and zip above the water to land on another island nearby, then climb another tower there and zip back. The final stop on most boat tours is **Petencito** (admission), a zoo occupied exclusively by animals native to the Petén rainforest, including many rare or elusive species—jaguars, cougars, marmosets, tepezcuintles—that visitors are unlikely to spot in the wild. If you thought the cable slide at La Garrucha was fun, give the very scary 300-foot concrete water slide at Petencito a try!

The 38-mile stretch of wide blacktop highway that runs between Santa Elena and Tikal National Park is, incredibly, the only pavement in the northern half of Guatemala. For much of the distance, the road runs past a huge but not very active army base left over from Guatemala's long civil war, during which rebel guerrillas are said to have operated within the national park and throughout El Petén. Midway along the highway, at the eastern tip of Lake Petén Itzá near the intersection with the road from Belize, a dirt road turns off and follows the north shore of the lake all the way back to San Benito. A few miles from the main highway on the north shore road brings you to the **Cerro Cahui Reserve**, a 1600-acre sanctuary set aside to protect a last fragment of natural habitat for several endangered wetland species—the Petén turkey, the Petén crocodile and the tapir. Explore the network of trails through the luxuriant forest of the reserve. You'll spot bright tropical birds and maybe javelinas, armadillos and spider monkeys.

Tikal National Park is a different kind of experience from other major Maya ruins, in part because the archaeological site is so big. Most visitors find that trying to see everything at Tikal in a single day is too exhausting and that three days is just about right to fully appreciate the park. Admission.

Guides-for-hire await visitors outside and inside the entrance, with the going rate anywhere from US$25 to US$40 a day. Make sure your guide has a government permit and (unless you're fluent in Spanish) can elaborate on Tikal in English. One excellent guide not only for Tikal but all of Petén is Noe Hernández. Ask for him outside the main entrance.

There are two museums near the entrance to the ruins area. The **Tikal Museum**, located near the Jungle Lodge, contains many of the best small artifacts that have been found among the ruins, including pottery painted with elaborate scenes of ancient Maya life and polished bones etched with pictures of gods, demons and warriors. The highlight of the museum is a replica of the tomb of Lord Ah Cacau, the greatest ruler of Tikal, containing his bones, eight pounds of jade jewelry, incense pots and other treasures positioned as archaeologists originally discovered them in a vault below the Temple of the Great Jaguar. On the other side of the parking lot, a fairly new building houses the **visitors center and Stelae Museum**. Although the Petén rainforest seems far removed from the industrial world, within the past few decades acid rain has seriously damaged many stelae, making it necessary to move the best ones indoors for protection. Outside the visitors center is a huge model, about one thousand square feet, showing what Tikal looked like 1100 years ago.

From the parking lot near the hotels and museums, a rocky causeway, or pedestrians-only road, built by the ancient Maya and restored by modern archaeologists, cuts through the dense forest for nearly a mile to the central Plaza Mayor, the heart of ancient Tikal. From there, a triangular loop trail takes you through the Mundo Perdido complex, to lofty Templo IV, then to clusters of nondescript structures, called simply Complex M, Complex P, Group H and Complex Q, before returning to the Plaza Mayor. A separate trail leads to the solitary Temple of the Inscriptions. Park rangers have placed small concrete water basins beside the causeways at several points to attract monkeys and birds. A full circuit of the main ruins involves a hot, fairly strenuous hike of some six miles through the rainforest.

At the center of the Tikal ruins area is the meticulously restored group of buildings flanking the four sides of the two-acre **Plaza Mayor** (Great Plaza). Now covered with neatly mown grass, the whole square was paved with stucco in ancient times and resur-

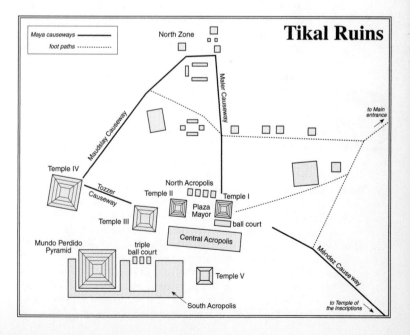

Tikal Ruins

Maya causeways ———
foot paths ············

North Zone

Maler Causeway

Maudslay Causeway

to Main entrance

Temple IV

Tozzer Causeway

North Acropolis

Temple II

Temple I

Plaza Mayor

Temple III

ball court

Central Acropolis

Mundo Perdido Pyramid

triple ball court

Méndez Causeway

Temple V

South Acropolis

to Temple of the Inscriptions

faced about once every century-and-a-half. The plaza was in use as early as 150 B.C. The first layer of pavement has been dated to about A.D. 100 and the final layer to A.D. 700—a generation before any of the temples that now surround the plaza were completed. All of the structures at Tikal were painted bright red, with colorful bas-relief murals on the roof combs.

Along the north side of the plaza stand two rows of tombstone-shaped **stelae** with round altars in front of them. Other, similar stelae are set near the stairways of the various structures around the plaza. Most of the stelae are carved with the images of Tikal's noblemen in ceremonial garb with elaborate plumed headdresses, and many have hieroglyphs carved along the sides. As you explore outlying parts of the ruins, you will see dozens of massive stone stelae like these scattered throughout the forest. On some, the relief carving has been obliterated by time; others were quarried but never carved or erected, or smashed on purpose as the leaders they glorified fell into disrepute; and the best-preserved still invite us to wonder about the meanings of the messages so painstakingly inscribed and dispatched across the centuries to us, the people of the future. The oldest dated stele at Tikal was erected in A.D. 292, and the most recent in A.D. 771.

At the east and west ends of the plaza stand two of the extremely tall, stepped pyramids unique to Tikal. On the east end, **Temple I,** sometimes called the Temple of the Great Jaguar, is the taller. Towering 170 feet high with its lofty, crumbling roof comb, it is one of the few pyramids in the Maya world that the public is not allowed to climb. A sign on a chain across the narrow stairway says it is closed temporarily for restoration, but tour guides claim that it has been closed indefinitely since a tourist fell down the steep stairs to his death in the early 1980s. The tomb of Ah Cacau, the most important of ancient Tikal's leaders, was dis-

sights

AUTHOR FAVORITE

Of all the Maya pyramids I've climbed, none was as spectacular—and challenging—as Tikal's **Temple of the Masks.** Also called Temple II, it's located directly across from the plaza from Temple I. Squat and wider than Temple I, it has but three levels to Temple I's nine. Yet the stairway is steep, narrow and well-worn, and stretches to the height of a 20-story building. At the top, a magnificent view spreads the center of the ancient Maya world at your feet like a map, sets you above a forest canopy festooned with orchids and teeming with tropical birds, and lets you view the vast Petén jungle, unbroken from horizon to horizon. See page 257 for more information.

covered at the foot of this pyramid. He reigned during the early part of the 8th century A.D., and his name translates as "Lord Chocolate." His remains, along with artifacts from his tomb including priceless jade jewelry, can be seen in a replica of the burial vault at the Tikal Museum. Just to the south of Temple I is the main **ball court**, surprisingly small for such an important ceremonial center as Tikal.

Directly across the plaza, on the west side, is the **Temple of the Masks**, also known as **Temple II**. It is squat and wider than Temple I, with three levels to Temple I's nine. The top level's broad walkway around all sides of the temple offers good views of the Plaza Mayor, the acropolises and the surrounding forest canopy. Temples I and II were built at the same time and are thought to represent the male and female principles. Carvings on the lintels and walls of the temple chambers on top suggest to some archaeologists that Temple II was a burial pyramid for the wife of Ah Cacau, who was buried under Temple I. This is mere theory, however, as her tomb has not been found.

While the **North Acropolis** may lack the dramatic architecture of the pyramids, it is by far the more interesting structure to explore. It is a broad mound with a number of separate temples, apparently dedicated to different gods, and a tricky labyrinth of stairways and passages to reach them. Eight temples made up the acropolis in the 8th century, when Tikal's great pyramids were built. Archaeological digs have revealed that the mound on which the temples stand contains older temples built upon the ruins of yet older ones, dating back to 400 B.C. One excavation of the facade of a buried temple contains a stucco mask, taller than a person, of a fierce-eyed rain god with a bulbous, warty nose, perfectly preserved by earth and rubble while the stucco sculptures on the exposed buildings of Tikal were being obliterated by the rainforest climate. To the right of the giant mask, a dark vaulted passageway leads into the pyramid. Feel your way through the darkness to the end, then strike a match and you'll find yourself face-to-face with another gargantuan god mask. The first new stele to be discovered in 40 years, Stele 40 was unearthed within the North Acropolis in 1997. Dating back to A.D. 468, it is now on display in Tikal's Stelae Museum.

The **Central Acropolis** sprawls across four acres. It is believed to have been the royal palace of Tikal, a complex of spacious multistory residences built around six separate courtyards. Only the front part of the palace, facing the plaza, has been completely excavated; the back part blends gracefully into the forest. The stupendous roof comb that breaks the skyline behind the Central Acropolis is the top of **Temple V**, the second-tallest pyramid at Tikal at 185 feet in height. Still unexcavated and shrouded by trees, it shows what all five of the great temple pyramids at Tikal must have looked like when early archaeologists came to explore and photograph the site at the end of the 19th century. A narrow foot trail from the east end of the Central Acropolis leads into the rainforest to Temple V, then returns to the main trail near Mundo Perdido.

The **Mundo Perdido** ("Lost World") complex, which lies southwest of the Plaza Mayor, presents a sharp contrast to the central ruins area. The massive **Main Pyramid** at the center of a group of 38 structures was built at least 500 years before the pyramids of the Plaza Mayor, suggesting that this area may have been the main ceremonial center for much of Tikal's history. Unlike the main plaza with its formal, landscaped feel, the Mundo Perdido complex has been excavated with an eye toward minimizing the impact on the surrounding forest, so the lower structures are nestled among the roots and trunks of forest giants. From the top of the great pyramid, you can see the summits of Temples I and II on the Plaza Mayor, just the roof combs rising face-to-face, sun-and-moon, he-and-she through the canopy of a rainforest that rolls unbroken, astonishing in its vastness, all the way to the distant horizon. East of the pyramid and north of a small plaza with seven temples is a **triple ball court** thought to be the only one of its kind in the Maya world.

At the westernmost end of the ruins area, **Temple IV**, known as the Temple of the Double-Headed Serpent, is the tallest man-made structure at Tikal. At 228 feet high, this pyramid was also the second-tallest structure in the ancient Maya world. It was believed to be the tallest until one pyramid at El Mirador, 42 miles straight-line distance to the north across the roadless depths of the Petén rainforest and presently inaccessible to sightseers, was measured at about a yard taller. Temple IV has been cleared but not excavated, so instead of a very steep stairway to the top, there's a very steep foot trail. As you reach the summit, a metal ladder affixed to the temple wall lets you climb all the way up to the roof comb. Near Temple IV are a parking lot, reached by a road that circles around the archaeological zone, and a group picnic area, so it is common to find busloads of school children swarming up and down the pyramid.

On the other side of the main ruins area, the Méndez Causeway branches away from the main trail and leads in a straight line through the forest for half a mile to the **Temple of the Inscriptions**, a large, solitary temple on Tikal's outskirts. Covering the entire surface of the roof comb, you can still make out the only major hieroglyphic inscription found at Tikal. The temple is so far removed from the main ruins of Tikal that it was not discovered until 1951. Why this unusual and impressive temple should be set apart by both distance and architecture from the rest of the city is unknown. The stele that stands in front of the temple was intentionally smashed, probably by the people of ancient Tikal.

Visitors are not allowed to spend the night in the ruins area. Park rangers check to see that everybody is out before dark. They explain that jaguars and other dangerous beasts roam the forest at night, and if pressed ("But I thought jaguars were almost extinct. . .") admit that it is other, supernatural beings that make the ruins a place to be avoided at night. Outsiders doubt it, they say, but everybody around there knows it is true.

So many visitors used to sneak in after midnight to experience the ruins by moonlight that the entrance is now guarded all night. However, the opening hour in the morning has been moved back to 6 a.m. Dawn as experienced from the ruins at Tikal is an ultimate travel experience, absolutely worth the inconvenience of rising before first light. Early-to-bed, early-to-rise is less of a hardship here than it would be most places because the electricity shuts off at 9:30 p.m. in the national park hotels.

A mist as thick as ocean fog shrouds Tikal in the pre-dawn hours. As the sun rises, the mist glows first pink, then golden. For a moment, you can glimpse the glory of Tikal in ancient times. Then the temples, shadows at first, turn to stone as the mist burns away. The forest comes alive suddenly with the cries of monkeys and birds and the throbbing drone of insects, and the heat of the day begins. A dawn tour led by freelancing off-duty park rangers is well worth the small fee. The rangers, many of whom were born and raised on the edge of the Petén rainforest, are amazingly knowledgeable about the plant and animal species found in the park.

At any time of day you choose to walk among the various outlying ruins of Tikal, they quickly become a mere excuse for venturing deeper into the rainforest. At every turn, a smaller trail beckons you off into the deep jungle for a spontaneous visit to some half-buried temple or hidden forest glade. Monkeys create

TIKAL TRANSIT AUTHORITY

The biggest problem facing visitors who would like to explore more remote areas of El Petén is lack of transportation. Very few travelers come to Tikal in their own vehicles, and public transportation is quite limited. A few enterprising guides, who don't advertise but can be found by word of mouth through any hotel or restaurant owner or shuttle van driver, run tours from Flores and Tikal to other Maya ruins in the Petén—especially **El Ceibal**, which can also be reached by public transportation.

a din of excitement as you enter their territory. Colorful toucans scatter from the trees in front of you. The diversity of plant and animal life in the Petén jungle means that around every bend in the trail you discover something new—a tree full of orchids, a strange fruit, a kaleidoscopic butterfly swarm, a line of leaf cutter ants marching in single file for as far as you can see.

Mammals that live in the Petén forest include several species of predatory cats—margays, jaguarundis, ocelots, cougars and jaguars—as well as other uncommon species such as anteaters, kinkajous and tapirs. Visitors are unlikely to see any of these rare, elusive animals in the wild, but there are other jungle creatures you can expect to see. Foremost among them are spider monkeys, easy to spot because of the rattling, crashing noises they make as they leap from branch to branch. Black howler monkeys, common in Belize and reportedly common throughout the Petén just a few years ago, are still spotted once in a while. Armadillos, tepezcuintles and coatimundis may be seen in the underbrush toward dusk, as are javelinas (called peccaries in Belize), a small piglike beast. Visitors often catch glimpses of silver foxes, known to the locals as "gatos de la selva" ("forest cats"), gliding through the ruins of Tikal. Other forest denizens include weasels, opossums, porcupines and deer.

The Petén rainforest supports the richest array of wildlife to be found anywhere on the North American continent.

Anywhere you go in the backcountry of Tikal National Park, you will find low mounds and tumbled-down stone walls that remain from those ancient homesteads—even in places that are almost inaccessible today. Archaeologists will probably never excavate all of the sites in the jungle of Tikal National Park, and visitors will always be able to wonder what undiscovered treasures may lie hidden there. Whenever you explore and wherever you wander, use good judgment. Jungle trails have a way of tempting people onward. Remember that there is a risk of getting lost in this terrain.

MAYA BIOSPHERE RESERVE   Despite its size, the 222-acre Tikal National Park protects less than two percent of El Petén, the largest contiguous expanse of rainforest on the North American continent. The northern third of the Petén rainforest—all the land north of Tikal to the northern, eastern and western borders of Guatemala, has been designated as the **Maya Biosphere Reserve**, a unit of the UNESCO Man and Biosphere program that protects inhabited wilderness areas, allowing some economic use of the forest in a buffer zone around a protected core area. The Maya Biosphere Reserve, encompassing an area of 5400 square miles, is one of the most ambitious efforts to save the rainforest anywhere in the world. La Ruta Maya Conservation Foundation, armed with

Beyond Tikal

One Maya ruin site you may want to visit is **El Ceibal**, noted by archaeologists as having the only circular temple in the entire Maya world. It also has 31 carved stone stelae, including one that certainly seems to depict a Maya warrior talking on the telephone! The stelae, altars and stone walls at El Ceibal are covered with a bright orange lichen, creating a dramatic contrast to the amazingly lush rainforest that constantly threatens to swallow the ancient city once more.

The trip to El Ceibal involves traveling 36 miles by car or bus on a good dirt road to the jungle village of Sayaxché and hiring a boat there to take you 11 miles down the Río Pasión to the ruins. The ruins can also be reached by a four-wheel-drive track, but the jungle boat trip is more fun.

Several trails lead from the ruins into the surrounding protected rainforest of Ceibal National Park, the most likely place for visitors to the Petén to see rare howler monkeys. The forest here is also known for its abundant bird life, including parrots, macaws and toucans. One bird unique to the forest along the Río Pasión is the snail hawk, a small raptor that preys on tree snails.

Heading toward Belize from El Remate on Lake Petén Itzá, it's about 30 miles to beautiful, remote **Yaxha National Park**. The drive takes nearly two hours, since part of the way is on a road that looks and feels like a rocky creek bed (in other words, don't attempt this in a rental car—hire a driver!). Eagles cruise overhead, so keep a lookout. At the park "headquarters"—a scattering of hillside huts with laundry strung on lines—you can walk down to the calm blueness of Lake Yaxha, watch whitefish and alligators, and stare across to a curvy coast of emerald hills. Yaxha was a Maya city from Preclassic to Postclassic times, and most of the hundreds of structures here are shrouded in rainforest. However, the Guatemalan government is working on the Grupo Maler ceremonial center—a fantastic chance for visitors to witness various stages of pick-and-trowel excavation as workers carve troughs up pyramid sides to unlock their shapes and contents. Yaxha's main ceremonial temple has been excavated, and you should climb the steep wooden steps and root banks up to the top. From here the lake is a shroud of blue mist and bumpy islands that harbor ancient Maya houses and burial grounds. ~ About 30 miles northeast of El Remate, off the dirt road to Belize.

a large grant from the MacArthur Foundation, hopes to go one step further, merging Guatemala's Maya Biosphere Reserve with Belize's Río Bravo Conservation Area and Mexico's Calakmul Biosphere Reserve to form the Maya Peace Park, a huge international park that would span the three nations' often-troubled borders and allow cooperative ecotourism development in the region.

At least 25 other major ceremonial centers have been found in the Maya Biosphere Reserve and another dozen along the Río Pasión in the southwestern part of the department of Petén. Of those in the biosphere reserve, most are accessible only by very primitive four-wheel-drive tracks that can only be used during the dry season, and several are in terrain so impassable that archaeologists can only reach them by helicopter. None are currently open to the public, though proponents of the Maya Peace Park plan hope that El Mirador, site of a large ceremonial center whose temples include the tallest known Maya pyramid, will someday be opened to tourists by shuttle bus or even monorail.

HIDDEN ▶ At present, the only ruin in the Maya Biosphere Reserve that casual visitors can get to from Tikal is **Uaxactún**, located 12 miles north of the Tikal ruins and just a short distance outside the north boundary of the national park. A newly improved road is passable by car during the dry season. For centuries, Uaxactún was a rival city to Tikal. Nothing about these partially excavated but unrestored ruins suggests that this ceremonial site even came close to achieving the grandeur of Tikal, but inscriptions on Tikal's temples and stelae reveal that the two cities fought bloody wars and that, at least once, the army of Uaxactún conquered Tikal. Backpackers may choose to hike from Tikal to Uaxactún. Camping equipment is a must, since even strong hikers find it impossible to walk there and back the same day.

LODGING Many travelers prefer to stay at Tikal National Park because there is too much in the park to experience in a single day, and the shuttle trip between Flores–Santa Elena and Tikal, an hour each way, costs nearly what a hotel room does. Staying in the park also lets you spend the night surrounded by the sounds of the jungle and visit the ruins in the eerie dawn mist. However, several lodges outside the park offer lovely lagoon and lakeside settings and more comforts of home, if that's important to you.

There are three hotels in Tikal National Park, totaling 49 rooms between them. Because of development restrictions imposed by the Guatemalan government when the Maya Biosphere Reserve was created, no new hotels can be built. Sometimes tour groups fill the rooms to capacity and other times they are almost empty. You don't know until you go there, because it's not easy to make advance reservations and none of the hotels has a telephone. The men who drive shuttle vans between the airport at Santa Elena and the national park may know about room availability. Otherwise, the best plan for travelers arriving on the morning plane is just to go to the park by noon and see whether you can find lodging. If you can't get a room, you'll have time to return to Flores by mid-afternoon and find one there.

The most comfortable, and most interesting, place to stay inside the national park is the 17-room **Tikal Inn**, a classic jungle lodge that consists of an attractively rustic main building, where you'll find the dining room, lobby and four rather elegantly decorated guest rooms with four-poster beds, as well as a row of thatched-roof cabañas along one side of a broad expanse of lawn with a swimming pool in the center and dense rainforest around the perimeter of the grounds. The cabañas have complete modern conveniences, including electric light from 6 p.m. to 10 or 11 p.m. and private bathrooms with running water that is warm late in the day. Reservations can only be made by sending a letter to "Tikal Inn, Tikal, Petén, Guatemala" telling what dates you want, then sending payment in full after you receive confirmation. A modified American plan is available. ~ For reservations, call 502-9-261-917 or fax 502-9-262-413. MODERATE.

The largest hotel at Tikal is the 48-room **Jungle Lodge**. It was originally built in the 1930s to house archaeological teams working at Tikal. A recent remodeling has converted the rustic old cabins into spacious, pleasant cabañas with tin roofs that are noisy in the rain and private baths with reliable hot water. There are white ceramic tile floors and attractive armoires. The rates are higher than at the Tikal Inn. ~ 502-9-260-519, fax 502-4-760-294; www.junglelodge.guate.com. DELUXE.

The third option, the **Jaguar Inn**, next door to the Tikal Museum, has nine guest rooms in simple thatched-roof cottages with

AUTHOR FAVORITE

What most impressed me about **Villa Maya** was the peaceful setting: a lagoon edged by rainforest and filled with birdsong. Situated between El Remate and Santa Elena, the villa has 38 rooms spread among stucco and wood bungalows, immaculate, fan-cooled spaces with mahogany floors, beam ceilings and brilliant weavings on white walls. The 67 grassy acres are thick with ceiba trees and spider monkeys, and there's a swimming pool, open-air restaurant and reception area with immense pole architecture. ~ Seven miles east of Santa Elena; 502-9-260-086, or call 502-3-348-136 in Guatemala City. ULTRA-DELUXE.

private baths. During the dry season, several large furnished tents are also rented out as guest accommodations. The food here is not very good, so it is better to opt for a room only, without meals, and eat across the road at the campground. ~ 502-9-260-002, fax 502-9-262-413; www.jaguartikal.com. MODERATE.

At the ruins of Uaxactún, you can spend the night at the **Posada y Restaurante El Chiclero**. The seven hut-like guest accommodations are as simple as can be, but they're the only lodging for many miles. ~ Uaxactún; no phone. BUDGET.

The most luxurious accommodations in El Petén are at the **Westin Camino Real Tikal**, outside the national park near the intersection where the road from Belize intersects the highway between Santa Elena and Tikal. All 120 rooms have private baths, air conditioning and satellite television complete with remote control—and there are a swimming pool, a lakefront beach, tennis courts, restaurants, a bar and a disco. ~ El Remate; 502-3-312-020, fax 502-3-374-313, or 800-278-3000 in the U.S.; e-mail camino-realtikal@quetzalnet.com. ULTRA-DELUXE.

Near Cerro Cahui, **El Gringo Perdido** is a primitive jungle lodge with 12 four-bed cabins that share a restroom and shower facilities with eight low-budget camping *palapas* designed for hammocks. There is also an open-air dining *palapa* where budget-priced meals are served. ~ El Remate; 502-9-267-683. BUDGET.

The former location of El Gringo Perdido in El Remate, located a block or so from the present location, now goes by the name **La Casa de Don David**. It has been upgraded a little, and although the rooms are basic, they're completely enclosed (unlike many accommodations around El Remate). ~ El Remate; cell

◆◆

TIKAL TRIVIA

The abundance of wildlife in Tikal is particularly astonishing considering much of its habitat is almost certainly less than a thousand years old. Using satellite mapping to reveal the outlines of ancient farmers' fields, archaeologists have determined that virtually all the land within a 60-mile radius of Tikal had been cleared for cultivation 1100 years ago. Here, peasants grew maize, beans and tomatoes on small suburban farms, supplying food for themselves as well as the priests and rulers who lived in the great city center. After the abandonment of the city began, around A.D. 900, it is difficult to estimate how long it took for the lofty ceiba, mahogany and sapodilla trees to take root among the ruins. The jungle existed in something like its present form when Spanish conquistador Hernán Cortés visited the region in 1525.

phone 502-3-062-190; www.lacasadedondavid.com, e-mail info@lacasadedondavid.com. BUDGET.

In Santa Elena, one of the better hotels is the **Hotel Maya Internacional**. This compound of 20 rustic rooms in duplex bungalows on stilts over Lake Petén Itzá used to be the top of the line in the Petén region, but has lost most of its formerly landscaped grounds to the rising water level of the lake over the past few years. Nature lovers can watch from the bungalow porch as multitudes of egrets, herons and other wading birds fish among the water lilies just a few feet away. Rooms have private baths. Be careful of the electric water-heating shower heads, common in hotels around Santa Elena and Flores, but said to be dangerous because of the possibility of electrocution. ~ 502-9-261-276. MODERATE TO DELUXE.

One of the most pleasant hotels in the Santa Elena and Flores area, the **Hotel del Patio Tikal** offers 22 air conditioned rooms with satellite TV, private baths around a parklike courtyard with a fountain. ~ 2 Calle at 8 Avenida, Santa Elena; 502-9-261-229, or 800-327-3573 from the U.S., fax 502-9-261-229. DELUXE.

At the other end of the lodging spectrum is the venerable **Hotel San Juan**. The hotel doubles as a bus terminal, where second-class buses from Río Dulce, Poptún, Sayaxché and Cobán come and go day and night, making the rooms on the hotel's street side very noisy. This is a long-established gathering place for adventurous travelers, and most local guides organize their tours from the lobby. The 55 rooms (some with satellite TV, 37 with private baths, but only a very limited supply of solar-heated water) are as plain as can be. ~ Santa Elena; 502-9-260-042. BUDGET.

La Casona de la Isla has small, plain rooms with ceiling fans, private baths and central hot water. The best thing about this hotel is its swimming pool, where you can cool off in a pretty garden setting. ~ Flores; 502-9-260-523; www.corpetur.com, e-mail reservaciones@corpetur.com. MODERATE.

DINING

At Tikal, each of the hotels has its own small restaurant serving a set menu at set hours, with the price of breakfast and dinner included in the "modified American plan" room rate. The only alternatives are a series of *comedores* situated down the road from the campground, serving basic food at budget prices. The restaurant at the campground itself is the largest in the area and serves a low-priced selection of soups, sandwiches and spaghetti.

Flores has a number of rustic-but-nice restaurants that offer entrées of local game from the Petén rainforest, typically including alligator, venison, tepezcuintle, armadillo, wild turkey, pheasant and rabbit. This is the traditional food of the region, and travelers who feel queasy about dining on freshly killed jungle animals may have to subsist on fruit salads. More conventional meats such as chicken and pork are only found in the dining rooms of better hotels. The town's best restaurants are in a cluster along Calle Centroamérica, the main street one block north of the island end of the causeway.

The tastiest meals in Flores are found at **La Mesa de los Maya**. The servings are generous and the cuisine is out of this world. Handwoven tablecloths and wall hangings brighten the two cozy plain-but-honest little dining rooms, as does the friendly pet toucan. There is a full bar on the premises, though a drink costs much more than a dinner does. ~ Calle Centroamérica; phone/fax 502-9-261-240. BUDGET.

Around the block, facing the waterfront about a block west of the causeway, **El Faisan** is another small restaurant and bar serving a similar selection of grilled wild animal meats. Rough wood paneling decorated from floor to ceiling with photos, drawings and maps of Tikal create an archaeology ambience that sets it apart from the other restaurants nearby. It is open later in the evening than most of the others, too. ~ Flores; 502-9-261-322. BUDGET.

SHOPPING The souvenir industry in Flores and Tikal is in its infancy. A cluster of shops near the Tikal Museum and the entrance to the ruins area has a high-priced selection of native *típica* clothing from other parts of Guatemala that is worth looking at only if you are not planning to visit the highlands on your trip. It also has lots and lots of Tikal T-shirts. Other makeshift shops along the narrow streets of Flores also stock limited selections of *típica*. The best souvenirs of Tikal are the videotapes with aerial footage of the rainforest and the ruins and an audio tape of jungle sounds recorded at Tikal.

▼ ▼ ▼ ▼ ▼ ▼ ▼ ▼ ▼ ▼ ▼ ▼
Río Dulce Area

From Punta Gorda in southern Belize, it's a short, scenic ride across the Gulf of Honduras to the Guatemala coast, stopping first at Puerto Barrios and then Livingston.

Perched at the mouth of the Río Dulce, where the gorge spills into the gulf, Livingston is an outcropping of a village in the southwestern corner of the Caribbean Sea. Isolated by unbridged river, roadless forest and the Belizean border just up the coast, it is a small place, with about 3000 people who make their livings fishing the Río Dulce or ferrying travelers in their dinghies.

The Río Dulce, or "Sweet River," flows up from Livingston, winding 18 hill-studded miles into a gorge and to the crossroads of Castillo San Felipe. You can hire a boat in Livingston to take you up river, or conversely, you can cruise *down*river from Puerto

Barrios to Livingston, after disembarking in Puerto Barrios from
Punta Gorda, Belize.

SIGHTS

◀ *HIDDEN*

Livingston's brightly painted wooden houses and storefronts run
uphill from the docks along a single main street, which is paved,
although there is not a single motor vehicle in town—a fact to
which the town owes its timeless charm.

Once you feel rejuvenated, you won't want to miss a trip up
the **Río Dulce**. This truly rewarding excursion up the "Sweet
River" will undoubtedly be one of the highlights
of your southern side trip from Belize. As you
paddle down the Río Dulce, spectacular scenery
presents itself at virtually every turn—sheer silver
cliffs soar above the riverbanks behind the colossal
trees upholstered in emerald greenery. The remote
tropical paradise feel of the Río Dulce is in part illusory,
for just beyond the top rim of the gorge are endless banana fields and the shacks and villages of some of the
poorest country people in Guatemala. Yet the river still allows glimpses of one of the last fragments of primeval America,
much of it practically unchanged since the days of Columbus.

> Livingston is Guatemala's
> only Garifuna community,
> though most villagers are
> multilingual, speaking
> Spanish and English as
> well as their native,
> African-based
> Garifuna patois.

The river narrows abruptly into a steep canyon whose walls,
dripping with lush vegetation, reach hundreds of feet above the
water. Egrets peer from every tree, pelicans glide by just inches
above the water, turtles sun themselves along the riverbank. Here
and there a cluster of thatched-roof huts nestles between the cliffs
and the water. People who live along the Río Dulce—mothers
with infants and bundles of groceries from Livingston, even unaccompanied young children—paddle their hand-hewn dugout
canoes called *cayucas* up and down the river in a kind of uncom-
plicated purity that daydreams are made of.

After the steep canyon, the Río Dulce opens into a broad expanse of open water called **El Golfete**, where local fishermen cast
their nests. Much of the north shore of El Golfete is protected as
the **Chacón Machaca Reserve**, a wildlife sanctuary for the endan-   ◀ *HIDDEN*
gered West Indian Manatee. Guides claim that jaguars and tapirs
also still roam the deep forest along the north shore.

Upriver from El Golfete is a scattering of expensive vacation
homes and several marinas mostly full of American yachts and
sailboats. Then there is **Lake Izabal**, the largest lake in Guatemala,
stretching some 12 miles wide and 27 miles long. Its waters reach
a depth of 60 feet. The lake's shoreline, dotted with more than a
dozen fishing villages, is virtually inaccessible by land. The largest
village, El Estor, can be reached by a grueling 84-mile unpaved
road that leaves the highway midway between the Mario Dary
Quetzal Reserve and Cobán, and takes all day to drive. The other

villages can only be reached by boat. Fishing is the main pastime on the lake, and motor launches with pilot can be hired at the Castillo San Felipe bridge or any of the resort hotels nearby.

Presiding over the lake is **Castillo San Felipe**, a small stone fort complete with lookout towers, a drawbridge and cannons on the ramparts. It was built in 1686 to guard the mouth of Lake Izabal from British privateers like Sir Francis Drake. The fort has a shady picnic area and a swimming beach. Admission.

LODGING   An anomalous 45-room resort hotel tucked off the main street about a block above the docks in Livingston, the **Hotel Villa Caribe** (formerly the Tucán Dugú) offers bright, modern rooms and suites in a large thatched-roof building with a swimming pool. Prices are moderate for regular rooms in the main building and deluxe for the more private bungalows along the walkway that leads down to the hotel's private beach. ~ 502-3-341-818, fax 502-3-348-134; www.hoteltucan.com. MODERATE TO DELUXE.

Practically across the street from the Tucán Dugú, you'll find a completely different kind of Caribbean charm at the **Hotel Río Dulce**, a plain but picture-perfect little blue two-story inn with a white picket fence, flower gardens, a big front porch perfectly situated for main-street people-watching, and basic rooms (shared bath) at a very low budget price. Youthful backpackers find their way here from all over the world. ~ 502-4-481-059. BUDGET.

The waterfront **Hotel La Casa Rosada** has ten thatched-roof bungalows with handpainted Guatemalan furniture, and shared baths. Canoes are available to guests. The hotel serves a hearty breakfast, including the only freshly ground coffee in town. ~ Livingston; for reservations, call 510-525-4470, fax 510-525-5427 in the U.S. BUDGET.

At the upper end of the Río Dulce near the Castillo San Felipe Bridge, you'll find the **Hotel Catamaran**, a 30-unit complex of bungalows on an island downriver from the bridge. There is an inexpensive guarded parking lot under the bridge, and motor launches—often the same ones that go downriver to Livingston in the morning—wait nearby to take you across to the hotel. Guest accommodations, set along the shore and around grounds bursting with colorful flowers with a cage of parrots and a swimming pool in the middle, are rustic and simply furnished but quite large and airy, with private baths, screens to keep the mosquitoes out and balconies overlooking the water. The river gently lapping outside the window assures guests a sound night's sleep. ~ 502-9-478-361, fax 502-038-860. MODERATE.

Another resort complex in the best sense of the word, the **Hotel Izabal Tropical** is situated on the shore of Lake Izabal about two and a half miles down a dirt road from Castillo San Felipe. Fourteen thatched-roof bamboo-and-stucco guest cabañas are

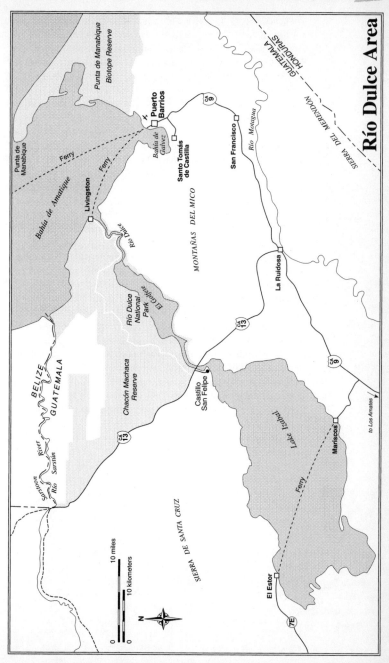

Río Dulce Area

scattered across a hillside along the lake. Each has ceiling fans and a private bathroom with a shower. The hotel has both a children's and an adult's swimming pool and luxuriant gardens that blossom year-round. It also has its own dock, and you can usually find boats for hire there with or without a captain. ~ 502-9-478-401. MODERATE.

HIDDEN ▶ Campers will find their dream spot at **El Tortugal Resort,** a backpackers' retreat in a jungle setting a half-mile upriver from the San Felipe bridge. It offers swimming, windsurfing, and kayak and canoe rentals. Sites for tent and hammock camping are in the low-budget price range. A boat takes passengers there for a nominal fee, leaving on request between 8 a.m. and 5 p.m. from the Cafetería Emy near the bridge. ~ Phone/fax 502-9-478-352. BUDGET.

DINING Livingston has several modest restaurants that cater to the low-key lunchtime tourist trade, since the locals generally catch their own meals. The **Restaurante Tiburongato,** a clean place with checkered plastic tablecloths and an open-air latticework facade that looks out on the town's main street, is typical. Menu items include ceviche and a local seafood stew called *tapado*, made with coconuts and plantains. ~ No phone. BUDGET.

In the Río Dulce resort area around the bridge at Castillo San Felipe, the best meals are served in restaurants at the various hotels along the river. The **Hotel Catamaran** has a thatched-roof open-air restaurant built out over the water. The menu includes most of the standard Guatemalan restaurant items—fruit salads, *desayuno chapín*, roast chicken, spaghetti, local fish—and you can watch the big luxury sailboats with American names glide past as you eat. Hours of service are limited. ~ 502-9-478-361. MODERATE.

Accessible by a dirt road instead of by boat, the **Hotel Izabal Tropical** also has a restaurant built over the water, with a range of menu choices and prices similar to those at the Catamaran. ~ 502-9-478-401. MODERATE.

AUTHOR FAVORITE

I'm constantly amazed at the cultural kaleidoscope of the Caribbean coast. At the amazing **African Place** restaurant, for instance, you can dine on fresh fish and shrimp caught by Garifuna fishermen, prepared with an international flair, and served in a mini-Moorish-style "castle" built by an expatriate Spaniard. Order the curried fish or shrimp in garlic sauce, dining among archways, ornate tilework and wrought iron–framed windows that peer out into jungle. ~ No phone. MODERATE.

Budget-priced food stands clustered around the Castillo San Felipe bridge sell fish—most likely perch or tarpon—freshly caught from the lake, grilled with spices and served with tortillas and rice on the side. Try **Mary's**, a tiny place at the end of a dock just east of the bridge. ~ No phone. BUDGET.

SHOPPING

Many of the storefronts that line the main street of Livingston offer various handcrafted goods. Prices are high for clothing brought in from other parts of Guatemala, but locally made gift items such as coconut carvings and Afro-Caribbean paintings may bring a smile to your face as they tug at your billfold.

A few roadside stalls near the Castillo San Felipe bridge offer limited selections of native *típica* clothing. A hut near the pool at the **Hotel Catamaran** houses a small gallery where members of a cooperative network of American artists—who live on boats nearby—show their work.

Outdoor Adventures

FISHING

RÍO DULCE AREA   Resort hotels on Lago de Izabal and Río Dulce, as well as innkeepers in Livingston on the Caribbean coast, can usually arrange a fishing trip with a guide in an open motor launch. There is no fishing tackle for rent, though. Local people here fish with nets. The catch in the Caribbean off Livingston includes snook, tarpon and barracuda.

BIRD & WILDLIFE WATCHING

CHETUMAL AREA   Birders often take guided kayak trips to **Ibis Island Bird Rookery** in Chetumal Bay. The island is a nesting area for thousands of ibis, storks, pelicans and roseate spoonbills. All-day trips often include paddling through the **Chetumal Manatee Refuge**, home to more than 100 of the large, endangered aquatic mammals. Other tours by kayak or skiff take visitors up the **Río Hondo**, the river that forms the border between Mexico and Belize, through dense jungle teeming with tropical birds, deer and wild boar, to remote Cenote del Cocodrilo Dorado (Cenote of the Golden Crocodile). For tours, contact **Luis I. Téllez**. ~ Chetumal; 9-832-3496. Wildlife-viewing tours of the Chetumal region can also be arranged in advance through **Ecoturismo Yucatán**. ~ Calle 3 No. 235, Colonia Pensiones CP 97219, Mérida, Yucatán; 999-920-2772, fax 999-925-9047; www.eco yuc.com.

TIKAL & EL PETÉN   Tikal National Park is an outstanding area for birding not only because the protected status of wildlife there attracts birds in abundance but also because a good field guide, *Birds of Tikal*, is available in most Guatemalan bookstores and an audiotape identifying various bird calls, *Sounds of Tikal*, is sold at the park. Bird life, as well as wild animals such as monkeys and coatimundis, is becoming noticeably more abundant, or at least less shy of people, each year in Tikal National Park.

Eagle-Eye Tours, a company that organizes birding expeditions throughout the world, offers trips from Belize City to Tikal. ~ 800-373-5678 in North America, fax 250-342-8644; www.eagle-eye.com, e-mail travel@eagle-eye.com.

Elsewhere in the Maya Biosphere Reserve, a major hiking trail for rainforest birdwatching called the Guacamaya Trail has recently been opened. Use is presently limited to organized groups. To make arrangements, contact **U and I Tours**. ~ Hostel de Acuña, Cobán; 502-9-521-547.

RIDING STABLES

TIKAL & EL PETÉN   Horseback rides in the Petén rainforest, including pack trips to the newly discovered Maya ruins at Yaxha, are organized by **Campamento El Sombrero**. ~ 502-2-050-5229 in Guatemala City.

DIVING & SNORKEL-ING

CHETUMAL AREA   Cenote Azul, about 12 miles north of Chetumal, attracts scuba divers, though you'll have to bring your own equipment. The largest cenote in the Yucatán, it is more than 300 feet deep and bell-shaped—broader in its depths than at the surface—with a wide ledge at 130 feet. Snorkelers enjoy the placid waters of **Chetumal Bay**, which is known for its big, nonstinging jellyfish.

SAILING & WIND-SURFING

CHETUMAL AREA   Rancho Encantado has sailboards available for guests who wish to windsurf on Laguna de Bacalar. ~ 505-758-9790 or 800-505-6292, fax 505-716-2102 in the U.S.; www.encantado.com.

RÍO DULCE AREA   Three-day yacht tours around Lago de Izabal and down the Río Dulce to Livingston on a 46-foot catamaran, for a price in the same range as a river raft trip, visit waterfalls, hot springs, steam caves and the Chacón Machaca Preserve along the way. **Aventuras Vacacionales, S.A.** organizes these tours and also arranges private Río Dulce charters on 33-foot to 55-foot yachts. ~ 1a Avenida Sur No. 11-B, Antigua; 502-8-323-352; in the U.S., fax 502-255-3641.

HIKING

TIKAL & EL PETÉN   Tikal National Park is a great place for rainforest hiking, with an extensive network of well-worn trails. The ultimate hike is to the ruins of **Uaxactún**, located 20 kilometers north of the Tikal ruins and just beyond the north boundary of the national park. It is a full-day (one-way) hike along a rough jeep trail through the jungle.

Now considered the ultimate rainforest trek in the Petén, the hike to the Maya ruins at El Mirador (15 kilometers one way) starts at the village of Carmelita. You can (and should) arrange guide services in either Flores or Carmelita.

Chetumal Airport has no direct flights to or from Belize City at this time. It is possible to fly from Belize to Chetumal by changing planes (and carriers) in Cancún, but the bus is quicker and much cheaper. ~ 983-832-0898.

▼▼▼▼▼▼▼▼▼▼
Transportation
AIR

The simplest way to get to Tikal is by plane—flying time from Belize City is only about 45 minutes. **Tropic Air** offers two flights daily; the fare is about US$160 roundtrip. Be aware that flights are often delayed or canceled altogether, especially if there aren't enough passengers, so stay flexible. ~ 2-245-671 in Belize City, or 800-422-3435 in the U.S.; www.tropicair.com.

CAR

If you're driving from Belize into Mexico in your own vehicle (no Belizean car rental agency will let you take their vehicle into Mexico), you'll come to a four-lane divided highway immediately after crossing the bridge over the Río Hondo and clearing Mexican immigration. Follow the highway eastbound for six miles to reach Chetumal. If you turn west instead, a six-mile drive will bring you to a fork in the highway where Route 307 heads north to Laguna Bacalar and continues north for another 231 tedious miles to Cancún, while Route 186 goes west toward such archaeological Maya sites as Kohunlich, Xpujil and Calakmul.

If you prefer the land route from Belize to Tikal and the Petén, it's best to take a package tour. Many lodges in Belize's Cayo District offer tours lasting from one to several days, though I recommend staying at least two nights because the ride is rugged and lengthy (about two and a half hours one-way down a dirt road), and because you can't possibly begin to experience Tikal in a few hours. **Chaa Creek**, out in Cayo, has excellent trips to Tikal. ~ 82-42037 in Belize. You can also get to Tikal with **duPlooy's** (82-43101 in Belize), **Windy Hill Cottages** (82-42017 in Belize) and **Blancaneaux Lodge** (82-43878).

To arrange an excursion from Punta Gorda, Belize, to Guatemala, stop by the **Toledo Visitors Information Center**, which has trips lasting from one to several days. ~ Next to the Punta Gorda Wharf, Punta Gorda; 72-22531.

CAR
RENTALS

Car rentals are available in Chetumal from **Continental Rent-a-Car** (Holiday Inn; 9-832-1100 ext. 191) and **Aventura Maya** (Hotel Los Cocos, 9-832-0920. Both agencies will provide complimentary airport pickup and dropoff service.

Though most car rental agencies won't let you take their vehicles out of the country, you can rent a car to drive to Tikal in

Guatemala from **Crystal Auto Rental Ltd.** ~ Belize International Airport; 22-31600, fax 22-31900, or 800-777-7777 in the U.S.; www.crystal-belize.com, e-mail reservations@crystal-belize.com.

BOAT
You can easily catch a boat ride from Punta Gorda, in southern Belize, to Puerto Barrios, Guatemala, and then on to Livingston. Stop by the Punta Gorda Wharf, where there is scheduled daily ferry service, with boats leaving Punta Gorda at 9 a.m. and returning from Puerto Barrios at 2 p.m. For reservations, contact **Requena's Charter Service.** ~ 12 Front Street, Punta Gorda; 7- 22070; e-mail watertaxi@btl.net.

BUS
Batty Brothers (22-72025) and **Venus** (22-77390) bus lines operate more than 20 buses a day between Corozal and Chetumal. Fares are minuscule, ranging from US75¢ on battered second-class buses to US $1.50 for *primera clase* ones.

▼▼▼▼▼▼▼▼▼▼▼▼▼▼▼▼▼▼▼▼▼▼▼

Addresses & Phone Numbers

Cruz Roja (Chetumal) ~ Avenidas Héroes de Chapúltepec and Independencia; 9-832-0571

Hospital General (Chetumal) ~ Avenida Andres Quintana Roo 399; 9-832-1932

Policia (Chetumal) ~ 9-832-1500

State Tourism Office (Chetumal) ~ Prolongación Avenida de los Héroes; 9-835-0860

INGUAT (tourist information) ~ Santa Elena Airport; 502-9-260-533

INGUAT (tourist information) ~ Parque Central, Flores; 502-9-260-022

Police ~ 6 Avenida and 5 Calle, Puerto Barrios; dial 120

Police ~ main street, near the dock, Livingston; no phone

Fire Department and Ambulance (Puerto Barrios) ~ 5 Avenida between 5 and 6 Calles; dial 122

Internet access (Chetumal) ~ Webcenter Internet Satilital, Calle Efraín Aguilar 1–D; 832-2581

Recommended Reading

Atkins, Louann. *Here Our Culture Is Hard.* Austin: University of Texas Press, 1997. Stories of domestic violence from a Maya community in Belize.

Baudez, Claude and Sydney Picasso. *Lost Cities of the Maya.* New York, Harry Abrams, 1992. An excellent account of recent discoveries and revelations in the Maya World.

Chaplin, Gordon. *The Fever Coast Log.* New York, Simon & Schuster, 1992. A telling sailboat journey through the ports of Belize and Central America, related with biting wit and an eye for the offbeat.

Coe, Michael D. *The Maya.* New York and London: Thames and Hudson, 5th edition, 1993. The definitive book about the Maya culture, by the author of the bestselling *Breaking the Maya Code.*

Conforti, Anthony. *Acalan.* Albuquerque: Putun Press, 2001. An epic historical novel juxtaposing the stories of an ancient Maya shaman and 1920s adventurer Mike Mitchell-Hedges' purported discovery of a mysterious crystal skull at Labaantun. Fascinating!

Conroy, Richard T. *Our Man in Belize.* New York: St. Martin's Press, 1997. A fascinating historical memoir of Belize in the 1960s.

Ellis, Zoila. *On Heroes, Lizards and Passion.* Benque Viejo del Carmen, Belize, Cubola Productions, 1988. A collection of seven short, warmly told stories by young Belizean writer Zoila Ellis.

Foster, Byron. *The Baymen's Legacy.* Benque Viejo del Carmen, Belize, 1992. A history of Belize City, spanning the 18th to the 20th centuries, it's packed with interesting anecdotes.

Horwich, Robert H. and Jonathan Lyon. *A Belizean Rain Forest: The Community Baboon Sanctuary.* Gay Mills, Wisconsin, Orangutan Press, 1990. How a group of Belize farmers joined together to create one of the world's most unusual sanctuaries.

Kelly, Joyce. *An Archaeological Guide to Northern Central America: Belize, Guatemala, Honduras, and El Salvador.* Norman, University of Oklahoma Press, 1996. Provides structure-by-structure descriptions of the major Belizean Maya sites as well as their modern-day discovery and excavation.

Kricher, John C. *A Neotropical Companion.* Princeton University Press, 1999. A fascinating and comprehensive handbook to the plants and animals of the rainforest.

Miller, Carlos L. *Belize: A Novel.* Xlibris Corporation, 2000. An informative and exciting story about Belizean independence by a former resident.

Rabinowitz, Alan. *Jaguar: Struggle and Triumph in the Jungles of Belize.* New York, Doubleday, 1986. The highly entertaining story of a New York zoologist who befriended the local Maya and survived plane crashes, drug dealers and ruthless poachers in his quest to establish the world's only jaguar preserve. An excellent insight into Belize's Maya culture.

Rauscher, Freya. *Cruising Guide to Belize and Mexico's Caribbean Coast.* Westcott Cove Publishing Company, 1996. The most comprehensive guide to Belize's offshore, weaving navigation and description with local color and anecdotal history. Sailors will find it indispensable.

Sabaloff, Jeremy A. *The New Archaeology and the Ancient Maya.* New York: Scientific American Library, 1994. How modern archaeological techniques have transformed our understanding of the Ancient Maya.

Schele, Linda and David Freidel. *A Forest of Kings: The Untold Story of the Ancient Maya.* William Morrow, 1990. The authors decode Maya hieroglyphs to unlock an astonishingly complex world of rulers and kingdoms. With detailed diagrams and splendid color photos.

Stephens, John L. *Incidents of Travel in Central America, Chiapas and Yucatan.* New York, Dover Publications, 1969 (two volumes). Originally published in 1841, this book covers Stephens' groundbreaking discoveries of the Maya world in Belize, Copán and Quiriguá.

Stephens, Katie. *Jungle Walk: Birds and Beasts of Belize.* Belize, Angelus Press, 1989. An amusing, informative guide to Belize's wild animals.

Thomson, P.A.B. *Belize: A Concise History.* Oxford, Macmillan Caribbean, 2004. This rather dry book tells you everything you might ever want to know about Belize from a British Colonial viewpoint.

Wright, Ronald. *Time Among the Maya.* Grove Press, 2000. Told with passion, wit and cynicism, this follows the author's eventful journey through the Maya world.

Snakes of Belize. Belize City, Belize Audubon Society. A handy guide for anyone headed into the jungle.

Glossary

CUISINE

ariba—Garifuna flatbread made with cassava

bamboo chicken—iguana

Belikin—Belize's ubiquitous national beer

boil up—a stew, usually made with fish

Caribbean Rum—Belize's best rum

cassava—ruddy white tuber and a staple of the Garifuna diet

ceviche—raw white fish cured in lime juice with diced onions, chilies, seasonings and tomatoes

fryjacks—ribbons of dough that are crisp-fried and showered with confectioners sugar

gibnut—a large, nocturnal rodent whose white meat is considered a delicacy (also called paca)

habañero—an extremely hot pepper, and the primary ingredient in Marie Sharp's Hot Pepper Sauce

heart of palm—tender, snow white core of the cohune palm, considered a delicacy since the time of the Maya

Marie Sharp's Hot Pepper Sauce—addictive habañero pepper sauce, brewed in southern Belize and found on most Belizean tables

stew—stewed as in stew chicken or stew beef

MISCELLANEOUS DEFINITIONS

baboon—black howler monkey

Belize breeze—marijuana

biosphere reserve—a nature preserve where human activity is controlled but not prohibited

biotope—a protected habitat for an endangered species

breeze—marijuana

brukdown—rhythmic island music, originating in 19th-century Belizean logging camps

cayo—Spanish for caye, or island. San Ignacio was named Cayo because from the air it appears as an island surrounded by rivers

chicle—the sap from the sapodilla tree, used during the early 1900s to make chewing gum

chiclero—Maya bush man who gathered *chicle*, mainly for the Wrigley's chewing gum and Life Savers companies

coatimundi—also called a quash; a forest dweller, similar in appearance to a raccoon, that is easily spotted around Maya ruins and on back roads

dory—dugout canoe

garifuna—also *garinagu*; person of African and West Indian blood who immigrated from the island of St. Vincent

glyph—hieroglyph, as in those found in Maya cities

high bush—thick jungle

Kekchi—a distinct Belizean Maya group with its own Maya dialect

kinkajou—also called honey bear; a member of the raccoon family, with soft fur and a gregarious, endearing personality

Kukulcán—Maya sun god

Mestizo—person of mixed Spanish and Indian blood

milpa—corn field; often a slash-and-burn field

Mopan—a distinct Belizean Maya group with its own Maya dialect

peccary—a bristle-haired, snouted mammal that looks like a cross between a porcupine and a pig

pit-pan—wooden boat that plies the Belize rivers. Just 50 years ago, pit-pans were a primary transportation in Belize

pok-ta-pok—a basketball-style Maya sport using a small rubber ball

punta rock—Caribbean-style music that sounds part reggae, part disco and part rock-and-roll

sacbé—a Maya causeway that was paved with limestone in ancient times

sleeping policeman—speed bump

tapir—also called mountain cow, the shy, portly, long-snouted forest dweller is Belize's national animal

tayra—also called bushdog, it is a weasel-like animal that's extremely territorial

tiger—local term for jaguar

tiger cat—local word for ocelot; a "small tiger cat" is a margay

Yucatec—a distinct Belizean Maya group with its own Maya dialect

wee-wees—leaf-cutter ants

wowla or *woala*—boa constrictor

Index

Lodging Index

Dining Index

HIDDEN GUIDES

Adventure travel or a relaxing vacation?—"Hidden" guidebooks are the only travel books in the business to provide detailed information on both. Aimed at environmentally aware travelers, our motto is "Where Vacations Meet Adventures." These books combine details on unique hotels, restaurants and sightseeing with information on camping, sports and hiking for the outdoor enthusiast.

PARADISE FAMILY GUIDES

Ideal for families traveling with kids of any age—toddlers to teenagers—Paradise Family Guides offer a blend of travel information unlike any other guides to the Hawaiian islands. With vacation ideas and tropical adventures that are sure to satisfy both action-hungry youngsters and relaxation-seeking parents, these guides meet the specific needs of each and every family member.

Ulysses Press books are available at bookstores everywhere. If any of the following titles are unavailable at your local bookstore, ask the bookseller to order them.

You can also order books directly from Ulysses Press
P.O. Box 3440, Berkeley, CA 94703
800-377-2542 or 510-601-8301
fax: 510-601-8307
www.ulyssespress.com
e-mail: ulysses@ulyssespress.com